Library of
Davidson College

POLITICAL MARKETING

General Editor
Steven E. Permut
Yale University

Praeger Series in Public and Nonprofit Sector Marketing

POLITICAL MARKETING

An Approach to Campaign Strategy

Gary A. Mauser

PRAEGER SPECIAL STUDIES • PRAEGER SCIENTIFIC

Library of Congress Cataloging in Publication Data

Mauser, Gary A.
　　Political marketing.

　　(Praeger series in public and nonprofit sector marketing)
　　Bibliography: p.
　　Includes index.
　　1. Campaign management.　2. Electioneering.
3. Marketing.　I. Title.　II. Series.
JF2112.C3M38　1983　　　324.7　　82-25973
ISBN 0-03-052591-8

Published in 1983 by Praeger Publishers
CBS Educational and Professional Publishing
a Division of CBS Inc.
521 Fifth Avenue, New York, New York 10175 U.S.A.

©1983 by Praeger Publishers

All rights reserved

3456789 052 987654321

Printed in the United States of America
on acid-free paper

To the next generation,
Mathieu Xavier and Aaron Kendrick

FOREWORD
By Philip Kotler

The field of political campaigning is undergoing a basic transformation. For centuries, political aspirants and their supporters constructed campaigns from their experience and commonsense. They knew the voters through years of living in the community and meeting with them. Candidates simply had to know how to "get around," "say the right things," and "out-appeal the opponent." These talents were arrived at intuitively.

The "new politics" differs from the old in two ways. First, politics has changed from an art into a partial science. Today's candidates are turning to powerful modern marketing research tools—those used by large corporations to understand a market's needs, develop the right products, and communicate and distribute them in the most effective ways. Candidates do not have to guess what voters think and want; they can get a very accurate picture by running focus groups, telephone surveys, and applying sophisticated methods of data analysis.

The other major change is the growing importance of electronic media, especially television, for communicating with voters. Thanks to television, more voters than ever can view the candidates, follow their actions, and see how they respond. Today's candidate must master the medium of television, with its own rules, which has made or broken many candidates.

Candidates and their consultants who examine the marketing discipline will find much gold to mine. While political marketing and commercial marketing have some differences, their similarities are strong enough to warrant their interest in the tools of marketing. Marketers have been evolving scientific methods for effectively positioning their products in the buyer marketplace, and these tools can be used by the candidate seeking to develop his position in the voter marketplace.

Political marketing is a relatively new field in terms of academic treatment. Political scientists such as Glick and Nimmo hinted at the marketing metaphor in the mid-1960s but did not fully understand the scientific character and tools available to the political candidate. Marketing scholars, on the other hand, did not see the applicability of their concepts and tools to the political arena until the early 1970s with the "broadening of marketing" movement. Marketing began to be broadened beyond just commercial products to include marketing the services of nonprofit organizations and to marketing ideas, but little work was done on the marketing of persons, especially political candidates. In *Marketing for Nonprofit Organizations* (1975), I devote a whole chapter to political candidate marketing, arguing for the development of this field and outlining the major concepts. A trickle of articles by marketers followed in the subsequent years, with the most important current development being the launching of the journal *Campaigns and Elections*, which has published a number of important articles on the marketing aspects of political campaigning.

Professor Gary Mauser's book is especially welcome at this point. It promises to be a milestone in promoting the idea of scientific marketing in the development of political campaigns. Professor Mauser lucidly explains how marketing tools and concepts can be used to position political candidates for strategic purposes. He illustrates how these tools have been used in several campaigns, and evaluates their results. Candidates and campaign consultants will find this book a *must* in developing campaign strategies, and it is hoped that the research will inspire further scientific studies by marketers of electoral politics.

The question is often raised as to whether a marketing approach to campaign strategy will ultimately lead to better elected officials. We know that every new tool has its good and bad consequences. In principle, a marketing orientation should lead candidates to better understand what voters want and to give voters what they want. Otherwise they won't "stay in business." The question will have to be answered by observing how the character of political campaigning changes and the consequences of these changes. Marketing will be used by candidates regardless, and a book such as this, by making the knowledge more available to more candidates, hopefully contributes to a better understanding of the nature of modern political representation by the electorate as well as the candidates.

SERIES EDITOR'S FOREWORD

Political Marketing: An Approach to Campaign Strategy marks the fourth volume in the Praeger Series in Public and Nonprofit Sector Marketing. This book also provides the first substantial application of contemporary marketing to the domain of electoral politics. As such, this volume along with others in the Series reflects a strong scholarly commitment to explore the limits of marketing thinking far beyond its traditional boundaries within the private, for-profit world of industry. At the same time, these volumes also recognize the need for "managerial relevance," and thus strive to relate theory to practice without losing the rigor of richness of either.

The Praeger Series was created to foster in-depth scholarly research and pragmatism in a wide variety of areas of pressing contemporary concern. Volumes currently in progress focus, for example, on marketing of urban mass transportation, higher education, health care, and professional services. In each volume, the authors have attempted to expand marketing thinking and, at the same time, "map" those unexplored domains that have just begun to engage the imaginations of marketing professionals.

Although marketing has well served the for-profit sector for many years, there are those who feel that its greatest and most meaningful contributions are likely to be found in the public and nonprofit arenas. This is not to suggest that concepts, theories, and marketing practice can simply be transferred wholesale to these other sectors. Rather, it is to recognize explicitly that we are only beginning to sense the benefits of applying a marketing orientation in new and unusual ways to the problems and challenges that affect our public institutions, social systems, and the very way of living in the modern world.

The Series will continue to publish scholarly work that contributes in a meaningful way to either the theory or practice of marketing in nonbusiness sectors. It will not offer textbooks, case books, or books of readings, but instead will foster integrated, leading-edge contributions that will find their way into the classroom and onto the desks of practicing managers in many diverse fields of interest.

Steven E. Permut, General Editor
Yale University

PREFACE

Political marketing is a vigorous but somewhat neglected stepchild of political science and marketing. While the study of elections is central to political science, few political scientists have concerned themselves with the problems that face candidates (or potential candidates) in their efforts to mount winning campaigns. By and large, political scientists are more interested in the problems of formulating government policy or in developing scientific explanations for political phenomena. Marketing, on the other hand, a more pragmatic discipline, is oriented toward developing problem-solving procedures for assisting decision makers. But few marketers have ventured beyond the private sector to explore the uses of marketing in other domains, such as electoral politics.

This book shows how sophisticated marketing research methods can be adapted for use in political campaigning and identifies some of the pitfalls in their use. In contrast with most books on political campaigning, this book focuses on questions of strategic analysis rather than on the minutiae of campaign tactics. It presents an empirical procedure that can help candidates (or parties) position themselves strategically in electoral contests. This procedure is designed to work in any electoral system in any country in the world—as long as the votes are honestly counted. Case studies illustrate how this "strategic positioning" procedure has been used. A wide variety of political contests are included: presidential and parliamentary elections, French as well as American contests, and both low-involvement and high-involvement races. The concluding section of the book pulls together these studies to empirically evaluate the overall success of the procedure.

This book takes a managerial perspective and has been written primarily for political campaigners. I approach problems from the point of view of campaigners struggling with practical decisions and I introduce procedures for dealing with those problems. Advanced analytical techniques are presented, but my emphasis throughout is on how to use these techniques rather than on their technical nature. In writing this book, I have drawn on more than a decade of experience in political campaigns in several countries, as well as on a broad academic background in behavioral science, marketing, and quantitative methods.

Academics may also be interested in this book since it describes how state-of-the-art methods in marketing research, originally designed to aid management screen concepts for new products, can be adapted to position candidates strategically in political campaigns. Political scientists particularly may be interested in the implications for democratic politics of the adoption of increasingly sophisticated marketing methods in electoral campaigning. Can candidates simply buy elections? Will political leadership be forfeited to pollsters? Marketing academics may be interested in examining how well these procedures perform in the political arena. This book represents one of the most thorough evaluations ever published of a concept evaluation procedure.

ACKNOWLEDGEMENTS

I owe a large debt to many people who have helped me in writing this book. Perhaps the most important person to thank is Volney Stefflre, who first encouraged me to attempt this task. Moreover, he also provided the intellectual framework without which I could not have begun. I would like to thank my colleagues who have read various drafts of portions of the manuscript as it slowly, painfully took shape: Martin De Waele, Roger Heeler, Richard Johnston, Jim Myers, Larry Pinfield, John Richards, Bert Schoner, Benny Rigaux-Bricmont, Michael Saykaly, Bent Stidsen, Volney Stefflre, and Mark Wexler. All of these people served as sounding boards at important points and made significant contributions to the development of the book. I would particularly like to thank Mark Wexler for his unflagging willingness to read and criticize unending drafts of the manuscript. He taught me much about how to organize my thoughts and how to write a book. I am not sure I would have persevered if it had not been for his encouragement and supportive criticism. John Richards provided very valuable help with the chapters on French politics. Despite this help, I have been able to make all of the mistakes by myself.

Most of the work on the book was done at Simon Fraser University in Burnaby, British Columbia. The Department of Business Administration and the Dean of Arts Office have generously provided numerous resources, including computer time, photocopying, typing, and the preparation of the artwork. I deeply appreciate the devotion of Anita Mahoney in typing and retyping the manuscript on the Wang.

The first draft of the book was written in Quebec City where I spent a fascinating year at *Université Laval*. I owe special thanks to the *Laboratoire de recherche des sciences de l'administration* and to the Marketing Department for their extremely generous support for my single-minded devotion to this book. I am particularly grateful for the cheerful abilities of Céline Pouliot in typing and retyping the first draft. Every week she had to struggle with 30-50 handwritten pages as well as retyping, after my extensive modifications, what we had done the previous week. I'll always remember her enthusiastic greeting Monday mornings when I'd arrive with another sheaf of pages to be typed ("*Monsieur Mauser, vous travaillez dans le bain!*"). Her excellent typing skills—in English as well as in French—were of immense help.

Permission to extensively paraphrase material from "Elections and Social Choice: The State of the Evidence," *American Journal of Political*

Science, 21 (Aug. 1977): 639–68, is gratefully acknowledged here from Benjamin Page. Figures 3.2, 3.3, and 9.1 are adapted from Volney Stefflre, Figs. 2 and 5 in "New Products: Organizational and Technical Problems and Opportunities," in *Analytic Approaches to Product and Market Planning* A. Shocker (ed.), MSI Report No. 79-104 (April 1979) © by Marketing Science Institute, 1979. Table 3.1 is reproduced from Management of New Products, © 1968 by Booz, Allen and Hamilton, Inc. Table 3.2 is adapted from Table 1 in "Multiattribute Approaches For Product Concept Evaluation and Generation: A Critical Review," by A. Shocker and V. Srinavasan, *Journal of Marketing Research*, 16 (May 1979), © 1979 American Marketing Association. Permission to extensively paraphrase material from "An Introduction to Nonmetric Multidimensional Scaling," by George Rabinowitz, *American Journal of Political Science*, 19 (May 1975): 343–90, published at that time by Wayne State University Press, now published by the University of Texas Press, has been granted. Figures 5.2, 5.3, 11.1, tables 5.3, 5.4, 5.6, 5.10, 9.3, 11.3, and paraphrased material in Chapters 5 and 10 from my article, "A Structural Approach to Predicting Patterns of Electoral Substitution," in *Multidimensional Scaling, Theory and Applications in the Behavioral Sciences*, Vol. II/Applications, (eds.) A. K. Romney, R. N. Shepard, and S. B Nerlove (1972) pp. 249–87, are reproduced here with permission of Seminar Press.

Tables 5.11, 9.3, 9.5, 10.1, 10.2, 10.3, 10.9, 11.1, 11.2, 11.3, and 11.5, Figures 6.2, 8.2, and 8.3, and extensive paraphrased material in Chapters 5 and 10 are reproduced here from my article "A Technology For Marketing Political Candidates," in *Analytic Approaches to Product and Marketing Planning*, (ed.) Allan Shocker, MSI Report No. 79-104 (April 1979), © 1979 Marketing Science Institute. Extensive paraphrasing and excerpted material in Chapter 6, Figure 6.2, and Table 6.9 are reproduced from the *Journal of the Market Research Society* 22(3):181-91 (July 1980). Extensive paraphrasing, excerpted material in Chapter 8, Figures 8.1, 8.2, and Table 8.5 are reproduced with permission from Jacqueline Freyssinet as they appeared in my article "Exploring Political Space: A Study of French Voters' Preferences," in I. Budge, I. Crewe, and D. Farlie (eds.), *Party Identification and Beyond*, pp. 203-24, © London: Wiley, 1976.

Tables 7.4, 7.5, 7.11, and 8.1 are reproduced from *Le Monde* (1973) where they appeared as tables in *Les forces politiques et les élections de mars 1973*, supplement to "Dossiers et Documents du Monde." Figure 7.1 and Table 11.5 are reproduced from my article in the *Revue Française du Marketing*, Vol. 50 (1974), pp. 19–38, © ANDTM, 1974. Table 9.2 is adapted from Tables 9.5 and 9.6 in *The Measurement and Prediction of Judgement and Choice* by R. Darrell Bock and Lyle V. Jones, © Holden-Day, 1968.

CONTENTS

FOREWORD by Philip Kotler		*vi*
SERIES EDITOR'S FOREWORD		*viii*
PREFACE		*ix*
ACKNOWLEDGEMENTS		*xi*
1	INTRODUCTION: MARKETING AND CAMPAIGN STRATEGY	1
	What is Marketing?	2
	A Marketing Approach to Campaign Strategy	11
	Organization of the Book	20
	Notes	23

PART I: CAMPAIGN ANALYSIS AND STRATEGY

2	FRAMEWORKS FOR CAMPAIGN ANALYSIS	29
	The Academic Perspective	31
	The Pragmatic Framework	48
	Summary and Conclusions	53
	Notes	54
3	STRATEGIC ANALYSIS FOR NEW PRODUCTS	57
	New Product Development	58
	The Strategic Positioning Approach	65
	Summary and Conclusions	81
	Notes	82
4	AN APPROACH TO POSITIONING CANDIDATES	85
	The Framework for an Approach	89
	Multidimensional Scaling	94
	Summary and Conclusions	102
	Notes	103

PART II: POSITIONING POLITICAL CANDIDATES

5	THE ART OF STRATEGIC POSITIONING	109
	Vote-Splitting	110
	Third-Party Candidates	112
	The Setting of the Election	114
	Methods	116
	Results	118
	Conclusions	138
	Notes	139

6	PRAGMATISTS vs. PURISTS IN CALIFORNIA	143
	The Political Situation	144
	Identifying the Problem	147
	The Study	149
	Conclusions	162
	Notes	164
7	STRATEGIC ANALYSIS IN FRANCE	167
	A Brief Introduction to French Politics	169
	The Study	175
	Conclusions	185
	Notes	187
8	IDEOLOGY, IMAGE, AND POLITICAL STRATEGY	189
	The Constituency	190
	The Study	192
	Strategic Analysis	195
	Conclusions	209
	Notes	210

PART III: EVALUATION

9	ESTIMATING THE SHARE-OF-VOTE	217
	The Estimation Procedures	218
	The Election Studies	227
	Conclusions	235
	Notes	239
10	SIMILARITY AND COMPETITION	241
	A Common Underlying Structure	244
	Predicting Patterns of Draw	246
	Key Features and Positioning	250
	Conclusions	253
	Notes	255
11	STABILITY OF PERCEPTIONS AND PREFERENCES	257
	Homogeneity	258
	Temporal Stability	264
	Conclusions	265
	Notes	267
12	A CONCLUDING NOTE	269
	Review	269
	Evaluation	275
	Notes	280
BIBLIOGRAPHY		281
INDEX		298
ABOUT THE AUTHOR		305

1

INTRODUCTION: MARKETING AND CAMPAIGN STRATEGY

To understand is hard. Once one understands, action is easy.
Sun Yat-sen

No man is good enough to govern another man without that other's consent.
Abraham Lincoln

Thus it is well to seem merciful, faithful, humane, sincere, religious and also to be so; but you must have the mind so disposed that when it is needful to be otherwise, you may be able to change to the opposite qualities.
Niccolo Machiavelli, *The Prince*

In the pages that follow, practical procedures for identifying effective campaign strategies based upon modern marketing principles and techniques are presented. It is argued that these procedures, originally developed to aid management, generate and screen new product concepts, can be adapted for "strategically positioning" political candidates. These procedures map political contests so that strategic opportunities may be identified for candidates or parties. In addition to simply describing a new approach, this book illustrates how the approach has been used by political candidates in both the United States and in France. Moreover, a section of the book empirically evaluates these techniques and procedures.

Marketing offers political campaigners a variety of benefits.[1] First, marketing offers a framework for thinking about political campaigning that is both pragmatic and realistic. The problems facing political candidates parallel those facing marketing managers, and candidates, like marketing managers, need a framework to assess their position and to determine campaign strategy. By taking the point of view of the political campaigner, marketing is oriented to helping real-world actors make effective decisions. The pragmatic nature of marketing contrasts with the explanatory and scientific intent of the traditional academic approach to analyzing political campaigns.

In addition, marketing offers a professional approach to analyzing and managing political campaigns. Marketers routinely must deal with problems of strategic analysis and campaign management. Consequently, marketing has developed a body of knowledge and expertise pertaining to methods of analyzing and persuading large groups of people. Marketers are responsible for launching a continual stream of new products for large corporations. In the past few years, powerful new procedures have been developed to generate and to screen new products. These procedures involve fashioning spatial models of customer perceptions and preferences and have proved successful in "positioning" new products in the marketplace where management desired. With appropriate adaptation, these procedures may be extended to political campaigns and used to identify and evaluate alternative positions that political candidates may be considering.

To introduce the reader to the marketing approach to political campaigning, the first section of this chapter will discuss the nature of marketing and examine the similarity between marketing commercial products and campaigning for political office. The second part will outline a marketing framework for strategically analyzing political campaigns as well as introducing an empirical procedure for generating and screening alternative strategic positions for political candidates or parties.

WHAT IS MARKETING?

To some, the term "marketing" conjures up images of cynical salesmen, interested only in pushing their products, forcing unnecessary, or even dangerous products, upon a gullible public. Whether feared or admired, marketing is commonly seen as an all-powerful tool for manipulating people by creating artificial desires for products with claims that promise far more than they can possibly deliver. From such a perspective, the extension of marketing to politics, as urged in this book, could only be seen as an evil, Machiavellian proposition. At the very least, "political marketing" would be opposed by such critics because it would be seen as leading to an over-concern with superficial trivia, such as a candidate's "image," his smile or his TV manner, and so divert attention from the matters that really count, such as taking stands on important public issues.

Such critique is both too flattering and too severe. Marketing is hardly an all-powerful method for manipulating people. Certainly, the aim of marketing is to influence and persuade people, and unabashedly so, but it is not as powerful as is often imagined. Marketing is helpless if individuals are not already favorably predisposed to the basic idea that the marketer is trying to push. In Western society, individuals possess a considerable degree of freedom to accept or reject the alternatives presented to them; all marketing can do is to attempt to persuade. That marketing is not all-powerful can be seen in the high failure rate in the launching of new products (striking examples leap forward readily: the Edsel, the "midi" skirt, and the Susan B. Anthony one-dollar coin) as well as in the lack of success of government information campaigns, such as recent efforts to encourage people to use seatbelts or to conserve energy.

The use of marketing in politics may be Machiavellian, but it is not evil. Marketing, like Machiavelli, is reviled, not because it is evil, but because it dares to analyze publicly what many political leaders prefer to discuss in private. Almost all politicians *use* marketing techniques and ideas, but very few wish to admit it openly. The tactical usefulness of hypocrisy, however, should not blind us to the value of a pragmatic analysis of political campaigning. Politicians must, at least in private, recognize the legitimacy of acting in their own self-interest.

Marketing offers more than just campaign tricks and gimmicks; it offers a professional approach to assessing and managing political campaigns. Despite such a promise, the use of marketing in the past has all too often earned a reputation of relying on superficial gimmicks. Some commercial marketers have tried to market politicians using exactly the same techniques that they had used for their other accounts, such as beer, deodorant, or soap. However, such an approach fails to take account of the profound differences between politics and consumer products. One cannot market politicians or political parties as one markets soap. Indeed, one cannot market banking services, symphony orchestras, or even industrial products like one markets soap. Every market (or, more generally, "competitive domain") is unique and requires marketing techniques that reflect its special character.

Nevertheless, the same basic marketing *principles* apply in all of these domains. Specific techniques may be context bound, but the true value of marketing lies in its pragmatic framework for analyzing political campaigns and in its professional approach to campaign management. This point will be picked up again and discussed more fully later in the next chapter. First, it is necessary to look more closely at what marketing actually entails; this will involve considering its origins and discussing the various attempts to define marketing.

Some Definitions of Marketing

Marketing originally grew out of the need of business firms to communicate with their customers and to deliver goods to them. All the firms in a competitive marketplace must let potential customers know about the existence of their products, and they must try to persuade customers of the *comparative advantages* of their products over those of their competitors. Closely tied in with the selling function is the necessity of firms to deliver their products to customers. Firms cannot sell what they do not have, so they are vitally interested in ensuring that they have the correct number and sizes of product available for their customers to buy. Both of these business functions came to be called *marketing*, distinguishing them from other business functions such as accounting, personnel, or management.

As the profession grew, it began to develop an interest in defining "marketing." One early attempt that had a powerful impact on the profession was that of Wroe Alderson (1958), who said "The marketing process matches materials found in nature or goods fabricated from those materials against the needs of households or individuals. . . . Marketing brings about the necessary transformations in heterogeneous supplies through a multiphase process of sorting." In the same vein, the American Marketing Association took the official position that marketing was "the performance of business activities that direct the flow of goods and services from producer to consumer or user" (AMA 1960). However, this definition has not gained universal acceptance. Marketing educators, particularly, were dissatisfied and sought more suitable alternatives. A tempestuous debate continues in marketing over just what marketing really is. There are several alternative definitions that have each attracted a following.

One widely accepted definition focuses on marketing's managerial responsibilities. In the "4 Ps" model (McCarthy 1960), marketing is seen as being charged with determining the "marketing mix" for a firm, that is, as being responsible for formulating the "price," the "place," the "promotion," and the "product." Traditionally, these four variables are said to determine the firm's offering: product—what is offered for sale; price—how much to charge; place—where it is available; and promotion—what is claimed for it. This definition does not differ much in scope from that of the AMA, since both view marketing as restricted to business functions, but by emphasizing the variables that marketers control, it adopts the perspective of the marketing manager. But such a managerial approach has left many dissatisfied.

In the 1970s, attempts were made to broaden the scope of marketing to include nonbusiness activities. Kotler and Levy (1969) pointed out that churches, public schools, and police departments, for example, could be considered as having "products," "customers," and as using the standard tools of the marketing mix. They argued that:

> the choice facing those who manage non-business organizations is not whether to market or not to market, for no organization can avoid marketing. The choice is whether to do it well or poorly, and on this necessity the case for organizational marketing is basically founded. (Kotler and Levy 1969, p. 15)

Kotler later formulated a "generic" concept of marketing by proposing that "marketing is specifically concerned with how transactions are created, stimulated, facilitated and valued" (Kotler 1972, p. 49). Transactions are seen here as exchanges of value between two parties. The domain of marketing thus encompasses not only public and not-for-profit organizations, in addition to business firms, but also the marketing of ideas, people, and places. In Kotler's view, the goal of marketing is to satisfy the needs and wants of the exchange partner. The equation of marketing with any and all exchanges of value has been criticized as overextending the proper domain of marketing (Luck 1969; Carman 1973), and as ignoring activities that one would like to classify as marketing, but that do not seem to fit easily into the notion of exchange (Rados 1981). For example, what is being exchanged when a family planning agency persuades pharmacists to display condoms publicly rather than keep them in a drawer behind the counter?

An alternative approach is to define marketing as a managerial technology for influencing mass behavior in competitive situations (Capon and Mauser, 1982). In this perspective, marketing includes two basic types of methods of influence: (a) "persuasive communications, notably advertising and personal selling," and (b) "adaptations to existing patterns of behavior, by designing products and services that are easy to use and by distributing them so that they are easy to find" (Rados 1981). Such an approach is less inclusive than Kotler's "transactional" approach, but it clearly would not limit marketing to commercial markets. According to this approach, any nonbusiness organization adopting either of the two methods of influencing behavior, persuasive communications or adaptative offerings, would fall into marketing's purview.

It is not possible to settle this dispute here; but we can adopt the definition that will be the most convenient for our purposes. In this book marketing will be considered as a technology for influencing mass behavior. During the past 30 years, marketing has developed an impressive set of methods for studying large populations and for communicating effectively with them. Much of this technology is useful in politics. Political campaigners would be well-advised to consider marketing's accumulated knowledge as a potential resource. However, before arguing that marketing techniques are applicable to electoral campaigns, it is necessary to consider just how similar commercial marketing and political campaigning actually are.

Electoral Politics and Marketing

The claim that marketing concepts and techniques are applicable to political campaigning depends upon the extent to which commercial marketing resembles electoral campaigning. If we adopt a managerial perspective, we find that the problem situation confronting the political campaigner is strikingly similar to that facing the marketing manager.

First, there are a set of organizations (e.g., companies, political parties, or organized factions) in both domains that are competing with each other for the loyalty of the members of a target audience (e.g., consumers or citizens) by fielding various alternatives (e.g., products or political candidates). In order to command a significant share of the market (vote), each company (political party) must develop a *differential advantage* over all of its competitors.[2]

Second, both consumers and citizens have virtually the same role to play in the two domains, that of decision maker. Both are called on to select among the alternatives presented to them on the basis of the available information in the light of their personal goals. In each case, choice implies some degree of commitment. Moreover, the same basic psychological and sociological processes (perception, decision making, diffusion, or socialization) may be seen as occurring in both citizens and consumers.

Third, the channels of communication and persuasion that are available to candidates in most Western democracies are basically identical to those used in modern marketing: personal contact (door-to-door selling or canvassing precincts) and mass communications (radio, television, newspapers, magazines).

These similarities are perhaps obvious to any casual observer of politics, but they have rather far-reaching implications for how political campaigns may be conducted. To the extent that the situation facing political candidates resembles that facing marketing managers, marketing analyses and strategies will be appropriate in politics. Similar problems suggest similar solutions. But the two domains are not so identical that techniques can be blindly transposed from one domain to the other. That would be folly. Every marketing concept or technique adapted for use in politics must prove its usefulness anew.

Each of these parallels, the competitive situation, the citizen's role, and the channels of communications, will now be considered in greater depth.

Competitive Situation

Many observers have remarked on the strong similarity between electoral politics and commercial markets. This idea is not new. What might be somewhat novel is that the emphasis will be placed here on the pragmatic implications of the similarity. The competitive nature of both elections and markets means that the strategic problems facing political candidates are essentially the same as those facing product managers.

Candidates, and marketers, have the same basic problems and the same goals. Both are competing for the support of a target group. Moreover, both attempt to achieve their goals under the same kinds of constraints: limited resources of time, money, and skilled personnel. This point follows the arguments of Schumpeter (1950) and Chamberlin (1962) in economics, which have been developed in political science by Downs (1957) and Riker and Ordeshook (1973). Practically speaking, the competitors in both domains need to develop a differential advantage in order to survive. Parties, like business firms, are not homogeneous. Each political party (or business firm) must differentiate itself from all others by the characteristics of its offering—its candidates, its policies, its leadership style. Support for political parties, like business firms, is drawn from a core of strong supporters that is supplemented by a fringe of occasional supporters.

The goal of this competition is growth and survival of the organization, not simply victory in the next election. Business firms, like political parties, should be constantly searching for "a favorable place to stand" rather than immediate profits (or votes). In dynamic markets (elections), differential advantage is subject to change; competitors need to be continually alert for new developments in the situation in order to preserve or enhance their differential advantage.

Success is determined in much the same way: by "share of vote" or "market share." Both political parties and business firms must elicit a certain percentage of support in any given constituency to maintain their viability.[3]

Beyond this basic similarity, however, lurk some crucial differences, which have clear strategic implications. First, commercial markets typically support a large number of business firms, while most political systems tolerate only a small number of political parties. The United States has only two major parties; the United Kingdom and Canada have three national parties; France only four. Moreover, the number of candidates elected in any given contest is typically much fewer. For example, only one victor emerges in "first-past-the-post" electoral systems, such as is used by the United States and the French Fifth Republic. A second difference lies in the periodicity of elections. Elections are held at definite intervals, while markets typically run more or less continuously. The principal implication of these differences is that the risks are greater in politics so the players may be more ruthless.

A third major difference in the nature of political and business competition lies in the precise nature of the immediate goal. In politics, the goal is getting elected, while in business it is to make a profit. Candiates are typically elected by winning a majority of the vote, that is, at least one more vote than 50 percent of the total votes cast. Only the relative percentage counts; the absolute number of votes obtained is irrelevant. However, in business, the absolute size of the profit is important. This implies that all businesses are motivated by a desire to continually increase the absolute number of their customers since absolute number bears directly on increased profits. Not so with political parties or candidates. Depending upon their strategic position, some candidates will find it to their advantage to discourage turnout rather than to encourage it. Such will be the case whenever a candidate estimates that he will be able to command a higher share of the vote in the lower-turnout situation. Typically, the more conservative or elitist parties, such as the Republicans, the Conservative Party in the United Kingdom, or the Gaullists in France, have more to gain from restricting the franchise than do more broadly based parties—the Democrats, the Labour Party in the United Kingdom, or the French Socialists. A number of strategies are classically employed by parties to discourage turnout, and tend to be adopted more often by elitist parties: supporting complex and strict regulations for registration and voting, running "boring" campaigns, restricting the financial support for nonpartisan voter education or registration campaigns, and eschewing "get-out-the-vote" drives.

Still other important differences between marketing and electoral campaigning have important consequences for strategy. A few of the more readily apparent will be mentioned in passing. Campaign organizations tend to be much more ad hoc than business firms and they may even have to be created from scratch prior to each and every election. Moreover, political organizations must often rely upon volunteers rather than paid employees for many routine tasks. Fund raising activities play a much more central role in campaigning than they do in business, since attracting votes and raising money are two distinct, if not separate, functions for political candidates. While business firms and candidates must both deal with multiple publics (e.g., creditors, government regulators, key supporters, or the general public), these publics tend to be more closely interrelated in politics than they are in business. This means that there is a greater demand upon candidates to be consistent than there is on business people, in dealing with their various publics. It is quite reasonable for business people to approach their bankers and partners in a manner totally different from how they approach their customers. This is less possible for political candidates.

Citizen's Role

The second major parallel between marketing and electoral campaigning is that both citizens and consumers adopt the same role, that of decision maker. An overwhelmingly number of citizens are only peripherally involved in politics, so that they have only a limited knowledge about the alternatives on the ballot. Nevertheless when election day arrives, they select one of the alternatives available to them, or they refuse to make a selection at all. This is not unlike many consumers. Some elections, like some product classes, elicit a high degree of involvement on the part of citizens (or consumers), but many others do not. The psychological processes that determine a consumer's decision in situations of high interest or high involvement should parallel those of a voter in a similar situation; and likewise for low-interest or low involvement situations.[4] Thus, one would suppose that the same psychological models and theories would be equally applicable to both citizens and consumers. This opens up a valuable avenue for cross-fertilization between political science and business, with both fields the richer for the exchange.

Citizens, like consumers, do not exist in a vacuum but rather live in a social context. Both are subject to influence from their families, friends, and workmates. The culture, social class, and reference groups of an individual play important roles in understanding mass behavior in both domains. For example, in business as in politics, there are stable patterns in the social choices that consumers and citizens make. Just as certain social groups historically have tended to vote Democratic, while others have voted Republican, social patterns exist in people's commercial purchases. For example, blacks often vote Democratic, while German and Japanese Americans frequently support Republicans. Parallel patterns may be found in the commercial arena: Jews tend to buy matzo; older people purchase more bran products; western Americans have a greater preference for black coffee than do easterners; while beer is more a "working class" drink.

The similarity of the psychological and sociological processes in both domains allows students of politics to study not only the literature on voting behavior, but also the research in marketing bearing on consumer behavior, advertising, and new product development. This parallel is valuable to political campaigners in primarily two ways. First, campaigners may develop a richer understanding of citizens reactions to political campaigns by comparing their behavior with consumers' reactions to commercial advertising campaigns. New possibilities may be seen this way, as well as an increased sensitivity to the limits of the changes that may be introduced. Second, political campaigners gain access to marketing technology, which is oriented more to solving managerial problems than are voting research methods.

There are two basic kinds of technologies in marketing: persuasion technologies and consumer research technologies. Most political campaigners are familiar with the standard marketing techniques that have been available for some years: voter surveys and computer analytical methods, which have been borrowed from marketing research; and television and radio advertising methods as well as computerized procedures for targeting "personalized" appeals, which were developed by marketers for persuasive purposes. Fewer campaigners are aware of the powerful new techniques recently developed in marketing for introducing new products. Sophisticated methods have been devised for evaluating customers' reactions to new products and for testing alternative advertising appeals. Techniques such as concept testing, multidimensional scaling, audience measurement, and computer simulation are routinely used in new product development. As yet, these techniques are not widely used in campaign politics. Only the most sophisticated campaigners feel comfortable with such advanced techniques. Due to the increasing size and complexity of modern election campaigns, the 1980s will see a much wider diffusion of this technology so that candidates other than the presidential frontrunners will be using these techniques.

Channels of Communication

The third major parallel between electioneering and marketing lies in the channels of communications that are available to political campaigners and marketers. Not only are the problems facing political candidates and marketers essentially the same, that of competing for popular support, but the tools available to both candidates and marketers for reaching their potential supporters are virtually identical in most large modern nations. Communications channels can be thought of as falling into five basic types:

- electronic media (television, radio)
- print media (newspapers, magazines)
- display media (billboards, signs, posters)
- personal contact (canvassing precincts, rallys)
- other media (direct mail, telephone)

Candidates, like marketers, must decide on the most suitable combination of media to use in attempting to reach their potential supporters. The extent to which they rely on each of the alternatives is called their *communications mix*. Some candidates may prefer to rely more on television than on canvassing precincts, while others will tend to trust direct mail campaigns. No campaigner can rely exclusively upon any single medium, since to do so would unduly restrict the number of people that are exposed to his message as well as squandering his scarce resources. However, the precise mix of media adopted by any given campaigner depends upon his or her specific situation.

The second major communications decision facing political campaigners and marketers alike is that of *media scheduling*. Scheduling involves both timing and distribution. Campaigners need to decide whether they will concentrate their communications efforts at key times or whether they prefer to spread out their efforts. This decision is related to the issues of "pulsing" and "peaking"; two perennial issues in political campaigning. Distribution refers to the frequency with which alternative media vehicles are employed. That is, if a candidate has decided to use radio, how frequently will he run ads on one station or another? To determine the most appropriate distribution, campaigners must know which target groups they wish to reach with which messages, as well as which media vehicles are most effective in reaching each target group.

Despite the similarities between political and marketing communications, the two domains are by no means identical. A few of the most important differences are readily apparent:

1. Political campaigners must attempt to reach their target audiences while operating under much more severe constraints in both time and money.
2. Political campaigners have much less control over their communications than do marketers, being more dependent upon the news media and independent organiza-

tions to reach their target audiences.
3. The public nature of electoral politics means that candidates must operate much more publicly than marketers. Thus, there is a greater vulnerability to attack from various groups for real or imagined grievances.

A MARKETING APPROACH TO CAMPAIGN STRATEGY

Marketing offers political candidates a professional approach to analyzing and managing political campaigns.[5] As mentioned earlier, this book presents a method for determining campaign strategy and for strategically positioning political candidates where desired in electoral contests. Before describing this method in detail, it is necessary to place it in context and explain briefly what marketing can and cannot do for political campaigners.

Much of "the marketing approach" to political campaigning is just commonsense and, as such, is not new to savvy political candidates. What is noteworthy, perhaps, is that this approach, developed in commercial marketing, fits political campaigning so well.

A Framework for Strategy

The first step in determining campaign strategy is to assess the political situation. An ordered conceptual framework can aid immensely in this task. A framework is a list of variables to consider and a set of questions to ask. To be useful, a framework should include all essential elements of the situation and show how they fit together. Conceptual frameworks permit a systematic assessment of problems and opportunities, allowing decision makers to assign priorities confidently to their many tasks. Without such an apparatus, it is all too easy to miss a critical element in the environment and make a poor decision.

Marketing cannot give formulas for success, for there are none. There are no "proven" techniques for brainwashing the public to be found in marketing. There are only *heuristics*. A heuristic is a procedure that can help solve problems but that does not guarantee a solution. Nothing else is possible given that every political campaign is unique and different from all others. An approach that worked in one election, or market, may not work in another.

The key to developing a winning strategy remains the intuition of the individual asking the questions and analyzing the answers. Only a gifted person with a sense of "how it all fits" can put the elements together to form a strategy. Frameworks may certainly help a candidate, but they offer no guarantee of success. A framework is only a guide for asking the right questions. Campaign managers, or the candidates themselves, must put it all together to create an effective tool. Mechanically following the framework will not generate a viable strategy.

The only way to gain a sense of how it all fits is through experience. Analysis cannot substitute for experience. However, if campaigners do not attempt to analyze their experiences or submit their ideas to rigorous questioning, they will not learn from their experiences. A suitable analytical framework is an important aid to experience in that it can help campaigners learn from their experience.

Viewed pragmatically, there are three tasks in campaign movement that confront all political candidates. They must analyze their political situation, determine their strategy, and run the campaign. Figure 1.1 shows how these three tasks are interrelated.

A political candidate must first analyze the situation that he or she faces.[6] Both internal and external factors must be considered. Internal factors refer to the nature of the candidate himself and his organization. Every candidate must identify his goals before entering a political campaign. This is crucial but very difficult to do. A candidate must also honestly assess his resources—his personal strengths and weaknesses and those of his campaign organization.

External factors include the candidate's competitors, the electorate and all other elements in the political situation, such as the national and world situation. Before determining strategy, it is necessary to have a full understanding of who his competition is (or is likely to be), what their campaigns are likely to look like, and how the electorate will probably respond. Voter surveys are crucial in this regard.

The goal of analysis in a marketing perspective is to determine strategy. For our purposes, a campaign strategy will be seen as a master plan for directing and integrating all of a candidate's campaign activities. The key to effective campaign strategy lies in a candidate identifying his competitive advantage. As discussed earlier, competitive advantage refers to the unique characteristics that differentiate a candidate from his competitors, which give his supporters reason to prefer him over the competition. Shrewd analysis should be able to discover those issues or postures that put any candidate in a favorable light and give him an edge over his competitors.

To determine strategy, the candidate must identify the problems and opportunities that he faces in the campaign. It is all too easy to skip over this step, leaping to solutions before the problems have been adequately considered. Next, a candidate should consider as wide a variety of options as possible and begin to identify those that appear to be the most suitable for him.

Analysis and strategy formulation are not as distinct and separate as implied here. They are intimately intertwined; strategists must continually switch back and forth between collecting and assessing information. Typically, several iterations (that is, cycles of switching back and forth) between these two steps are necessary before strategic plans can be adequately formulated.

FIGURE 1.1. A General Framework for Political Campaigning

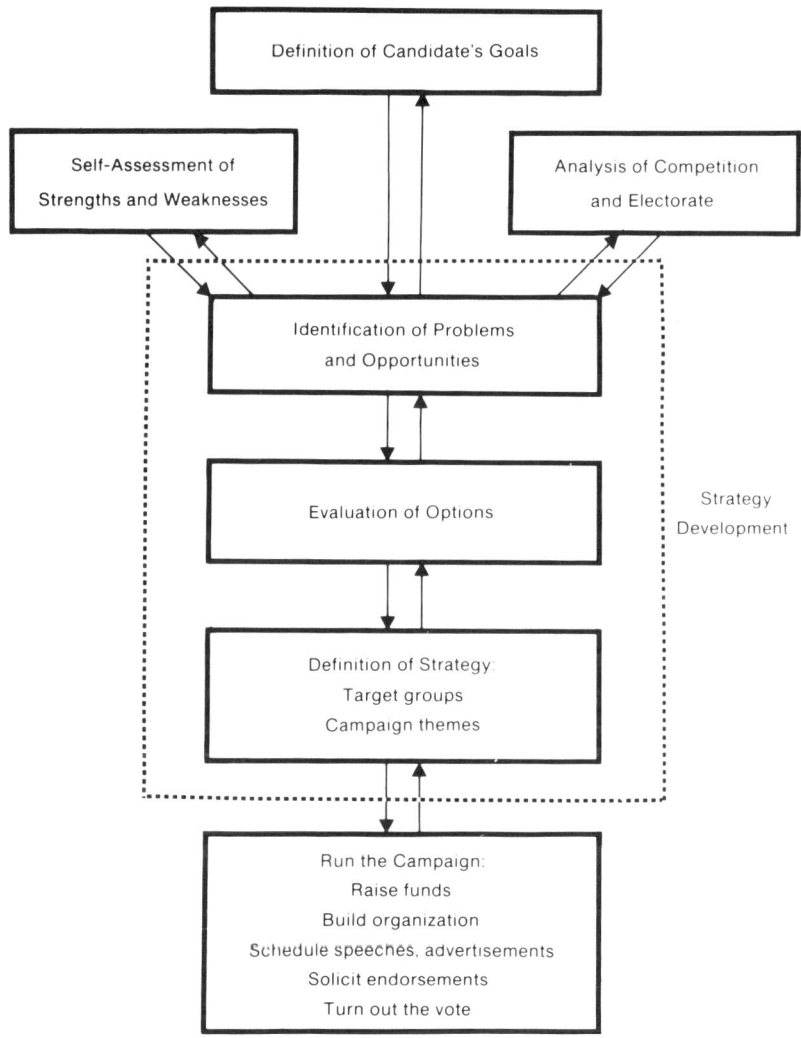

The third and last step in political campaigns is the most obvious one, that of actually conducting the campaign. The major tasks in political campaigning include: fund raising, organization development, monitoring events—particularly the activities of the competition, and scheduling appearances and other campaign activities. Given limited resources, candidates must be concerned with campaigning both effectively and efficiently. Efficiency refers to accomplishing set tasks with a minimum of time and effort, while effectiveness means the tasks that are completed actually have the effect intended, presumably, that of electing the candidate.

How can strategies be implemented? Candidates, like product managers, are able to directly control only a few aspects of their situation. Everything else lies outside their immediate control. In marketing, the tools available to the product manager are called the "marketing mix": price, product, promotion, and place. In order to increase sales, marketers can modify the nature of the product itself, its price, the way in which the product is promoted, or the place where it is offered for sale to potential customers.

Similarly, in campaigning for elective office, a political candidate has only a few variables that he can control. They could be called the "campaigning mix." In politics, the tools for implementing campaign strategy consist of the candidate himself, the communications program, the fund-raising methods, the campaign organization, and the get-out-the-vote drive. When a candidate has made decisions about how to handle each of these elements, so that they fit together in a harmonious way and take best advantage of the situation, he has a viable campaign strategy.

Consider each of these elements in turn. In this discussion special attention will be paid to the treatment of the candidate and to the communication program. The remaining elements of the campaigning strategy mix will be treated very briefly, not because they are less important, but because these two domains lay the groundwork for the remainder of the book.[7]

The Candidate

Voters decide whom to support on the basis of what they know about the candidates and what they stand for, that is, their "images" of the candidates. Consequently, candidates must be vitally concerned with their images. To be successful, a candidate must think about himself as if he were a new product, formulating his image to meet his target populations' needs and expectations and taking into account his competition.

The key to political image planning is the candidate concept. The candidate concept is the candidate's unique selling proposition that encapsulizes the reasons that voters should support him over the opposition. The political candidate may choose the concept to express his personal leadership style, his ideological position, or his partisan affiliation. For maximum effectiveness in campaigning, the candidate concept should be used as the central orienting theme in building voter interest and used as the basis for planning the entire campaign.[8]

The candidate concept is not just a slogan. It reflects the candidate's thinking about why voters should support him, and as such it should shape the positions on issues he takes, the coalitions he enters, the voter groups he appeals to, among other decisions he makes. His choice of candidate concept is the single most important decision in formulating the campaign. If a candidate is confused or indecisive concerning this decision, it could severely cripple his campaign.

Candidates should not base their choice of candidate concept simply on expediency, or on the immediate demands of the political contest. Their concept should be based on their long-range career goals. This follows from two arguments principally. First, voters are not fools. Voters can often remember what candidates stand for from one election to the next. Candidates who cynically shift their positions and images too grossly can lose their credibility. Second, a candidate should choose a concept that he feels comfortable with, one that is compatible with his background and political philosophy. Since he has to live with the role he selects, he should avoid any role that is unnatural for him regardless of how useful it is in the particular campaign.

How may a candidate practically choose a particular concept from the range of possible alternatives? The methods developed by marketing for launching new products may be adapted for this purpose. Chapter 3 surveys the recent developments in new product development methodologies and Chapter 4 presents a procedure for generating and evaluating alternative candidate concepts.

Communications Program

There are three principal concerns in determining communications strategy: identifying the target audience, defining the message content, and fixing the communications mix. These concerns are intertwined with each other so that decisions about one strongly influence decisions about the others.[9] Given its centrality, the candidate concept should be used as the key to decisions about all aspects of the communications program.

As discussed earlier, the communications mix refers to the combination of media used to reach the target audience. It involves decisions to be made at two very distinct levels: the selection of types of media (e.g., television, personal contact, or magazines), and, within each communications medium selected, the choice of specific media vehicles (e.g., which radio station or which magazine). In other words, candidates must decide the relative advantages of relying upon the mass media versus canvassing precincts as well as determine the appropriateness of each radio station for reaching the target audience.

To determine the communications mix, the following must be considered:

1. the need to reach the target audience
2. the need to maintain control of the message versus cost
3. the nature and limitations of resources
4. the conflicting requirements of reach and frequency

The importance of the first criterion is self-evident, but the other criteria may require a few clarifying comments.

Political candidates must continually weigh the advantages of paid advertising against those of free news coverage. While advertisements are expensive, the candidate has much greater control over message content and timing than he does with news coverage. Several studies have shown that voters rely on TV for most of their information about candidates and that much of this information comes from paid advertisements placed by the candidates (Blumler and McQuail 1969; Patterson and McClure 1976; Patterson 1980). Unless TV news coverage changes drastically in the future, candidates will continue to rely heavily on TV ads for reaching their target audiences.

The nature of a candidate's resources has a strong bearing on his choice of communication mix. Some candidates have an abundance of funds, but a scarcity of volunteer workers, while others have more volunteers than money. The candidate with money would, other things being equal, concentrate his efforts on the paid media and minimize campaigning efforts requiring a large amount of volunteer labor. The candidate who attracts large numbers of volunteers, but who is cash-poor, can correspondingly afford to invest heavily in canvassing precincts, since he has resources, but he may wish to play down paid advertising.

Finally, the demands of reach and frequency are both important but conflict due to the existence of fixed budget constraints. *Reach* refers to the total number of people in the target audience that are exposed at least once to a message, while *frequency* means the average number of times a message is presented to the target group. Both reach and frequency are desirable in campaigning, but candidates must decide the optimal balance that they prefer.

The Campaign Organization

The candidate either inherits, or he must invent, a campaign organization that will be responsible for conducting all of the necessary tasks in his campaign. The first question that presents itself is how should the organization be managed? Candidates must decide whether they wish to retain control of the key decisions themselves or whether they should hand over control of the campaign to a trusted campaign manager. Opinions are somewhat divided over this point. Professionals tend to take the position that candidates who attempt to key day-to-day control of the campaign have a fool for a campaign manager (Napolitan 1972). Many nonprofessionals disagree, arguing that candidates should not lose control of their own campaign. If a candidate knows how to properly delegate authority, it is possible, however, to delegate the responsibility for the details of the campaign while reserving control of basic strategy to himself. Of course, the delegation of such responsibilities carries with it heady risks: candidates have to live with the results of the decisions that their staffs make.

A related issue is that of paid professionals. Should professionals be relied upon for filling executive staff positions or should such high level positions be reserved for trusted personal friends of the candidate? During the 1980 presidential campaign, Reagan's campaign leadership was rent by a dispute over this kind of issue. Machiavelli, in *The Prince*, vehemently opposed relying on professionals since they were not loyal to the cause or to the leader. On the other hand, friends may not be competent. It is sometimes a difficult choice to make. See Steinberg (1976a) for an extensive discussion of this point.

Fund Raising

Fund raising is one of the most vital and sensitive tasks facing a political candidate. The past decade has witnessed a tremendous revolution in the rules governing fund raising and in the methods that are the most successful. Still more changes are expected in the near future. The basic questions remain: who should be contacted and how should they be approached? One of the dimensions of concern here is the relative importance of large contributions from a few silent backers ("fat cats") as opposed to many small contributions generated by mass appeals. Computerized mail-order fund raising has recently become popular and will continue to be important in the future (Viguerie 1975). Beyond the hoopla, however, mail-order campaigns are expensive and frequently cost nearly as much as they bring in (sometimes more).

A related question is the extent to which candidates should seek support from specific organizations—national (or local) party structures, single-issue groups (e.g., pro-life, pro-choice, NAACP, or the Citizens for Space Political Action Committee) or community organizations (e.g., churches, newspapers, labor unions)—or should seek support directly from the public. The candidate must carefully weigh the advantages of winning the group's support against the restrictions that are placed on his abilities to take public stands on the issues.

Get-Out-the-Vote

On election day, the candidate's supporters must go to the poll and cast their ballots for him. If not, all of his campaign efforts have been futile. What should be done by a candidate to ensure that his supporters turn out to vote in sufficient numbers? There are primarily two criteria to bear in mind in attempting to maximize the turnout of favorable voters: the nature of the candidate's resources, and who his supporters are.[10] Other things being equal, a candidate should play to his strengths. If he has an effective campaign organization, he may be able to count on walking precincts to identify his potential supporters and then returning on election day to get them to the polls. If he is "mediagenic" and has a large campaign chest, he may prefer instead to emphasize a media campaign, rather build an organization large enough to canvass the precincts in his district.

Turnout tactics are also highly dependent upon who a candidate's supporters are. If they are not likely to turn out to vote, special efforts may be required to discern what keeps them from the polls and to remove the obstacle. Do his supporters need rides to the polls? Do they need babysitters information about the location of the polling places or the nature of the alternatives? This can be provided. Are they disinterested in the election? Perhaps the campaign can be made more exciting.

On the other hand, if his supporters are more likely to turn out to vote than his opponent's, a candidate faces different choices. In such a case, he may wish to identify ways to discourage nonsupporters from voting. Perhaps his campaign should be conducted as quietly as possible, or in a low-key manner, in order to keep interest in the election to a minimum. Door-to-door campaigning and direct mail are "quieter" than television or radio campaigns and may owe their effectiveness, at least in part, to the specificity of their appeal. Another alternative is to run a boring media campaign, refusing to take stands on emotional topics or to debate opponents.

A Procedure for Strategic Positioning

The intent of the strategic positioning is to generate and screen alternative positions or postures for political candidates so that they may position themselves to their best advantage. While it will be described more fully in later chapters, this section simply presents a brief outline of the procedure to be developed in the rest of the book.

This procedure was originally developed to analyze consumer goods markets in order to identify opportunities for new products (Brown et al. 1968; Stefflre 1968, 1972, 1979a). It has been used successfully in a wide range of commercial markets (e.g., scotch whiskey, several brands of coffee, breakfast cereal, analgesics) in several countries (e.g., the United States, Brazil, France, Germany). During the past decade, I have used this approach to analyze a variety of electoral contests: American presidential and gubernatorial contests, both primary and general elections, as well as French parliamentary and presidential contests.

The Stefflre procedure is one of several procedures designed to aid management to generate and to screen concepts of new products (Shocker 1979; Urban and Hauser 1980; Wind 1973). At the heart of each of these procedures lies a mathematical model of consumers' perceptions and preferences. The specific techniques used to empirically construct these consumer models vary from procedure to procedure, but almost all of these procedures rely upon a spatial model of consumers' preferences and perceptions to identify strategic opportunities for management.

Stefflre was one of the first researchers to develop a multidimensional analytical procedure, based on consumer input, expressly to generate and evaluate new product concepts. His approach is based on work that he had done earlier in psycholinguistics on the relationship between language and behavior (Stefflre 1965; Stefflre et al. 1971). In this procedure, multidimensional scaling techniques are used to build aggregate models of consumers' perceptions and preferences. These models are then used by management to develop and to test hypotheses about where alternative new products would be positioned in the structure if introduced. Inspection of the perceptual model gives rise to hypotheses about which features govern positioning and which determine consumer preferences. These hypotheses are then tested by concocting descriptions of hypothetical new products using these features and seeing where they position in the preference model.

Stefflre's procedure is designed to empirically screen a large number of new product concepts. This permits management to evaluate a wide diversity of market strategies rather than focusing on only a few alternative executions of the basic strategy, which is more typical. By increasing the range of alternatives considered by management, as well as the rigor of the testing procedure, this evaluation approach considerably increases management's chances of discovering viable new products that respond to valid consumer needs.

This procedure has an immediate extension to campaign politics. Models of voters' perception and preferences may be constructed empirically just as readily as can models of consumers' perceptions and preferences.[11] As mentioned earlier, there are strategic benefits that a candidate achieves by treating himself as a "new product." This procedure enables a political candidate to measure his image, determine how his image compares with those of other candidates, examine alternative positions and postures, and position himself in the contest so as to take maximum advantage of his strengths or his opponents' weaknesses.

The strategic positioning approach, as presented in this book, stands out from other pragmatic approaches to analyzing political campaigns in that it is not primarily oriented toward exploiting the "floating vote" or the "undecided vote." All too often, the votes of a candidate's "loyal voters" are taken for granted, with disastrous results. If candidates wish to win more than a single election, they should look beyond simply scoring well in the next survey; they must build stable constituencies. The danger of politicians relying upon transitory polling majorities has been vividly described by Blumenthal in his book *The Permanent Campaign*. The strategic positioning approach includes special methods for explicitly evaluating the extent to which a candidate's supporters find his adoption of any new position or posture consistent with their current image of him. This permits candidates to select positions according to their "credibility" with their supporters as well as their general popularity.

A wide variety of elections are amenable to this approach: multiparty as well as two-party contests, partisan and nonpartisan elections, presidential and congressional races, general and primary elections, and high-interest and low-interest contests. This is suggested by the success of the Stefflre approach in a wide range of commercial markets in various countries, as well as by my own work in a variety of electoral contests. It appears to successfully meet reasonable standards for reliability and validity across a range of elections. The reader interested in the details of these tests is urged to refer to Part III of this book where the approach is empirically evaluated. The approach, however, is not without limitations.

Probably the most important limitation is that it relies upon respondents' comments and stated choices. This is a feature that all survey-research approaches share, to be sure, and all researchers must keep in mind the limits of their methods. However, this limitation is particularly important in evaluating alternative positions, since this approach relies so heavily on voters' stated reactions to verbal descriptions of hypothetical positions and postures. Predictions will be unreliable to the extent that voters do not understand the verbal descriptions in the same way as the researcher, or if voters act differently in the privacy of the polling booth than they do in the interview situation. Thus, it is particularly important that great care be taken to ensure that the respondent's frame of reference is the same as the investigator's in order to obtain accurate estimates.

As with all surveys, the results only reflect public opinion at the time it is conducted and cannot be used, strictly speaking, to predict future events. Nevertheless, predictions must be made in planning campaign strategy. While political perceptions of well-known politicians tend to be fairly stable across time, political preferences may be quite volatile, subject to dramatic changes in relatively short time periods. Less familiar candidates, campaign issues or positions are particularly volatile, as public awareness is so low. Thus, support for hypothetical positions and postures is extremely vulnerable to new information or new events that can influence the electorate, particularly early in the political campaign.

Another limitation is that this approach is quite expensive. Most political campaigns are done on a "shoe-string," with only limited funds available for surveys. Relatively few campaigns can afford sophisticated voter studies. As with all surveys, the costs do not vary appreciably with the size of the electorate surveyed. It costs roughly the same to study 25,000,000 people as 25,000. Thus, this procedure is more cost-effective in national or statewide elections rather than local or municipal contests.

ORGANIZATION OF THE BOOK

This book presents an approach to strategically analyzing electoral contests and shows how this approach has been used to help political candidates identify opportunities for positioning themselves to their best advantage. The book is divided into three sections. Part I describes the technical procedures involved in this approach and puts these procedures into perspective by discussing alternative ways to approach electoral analysis. Part II illustrates how this approach has been applied in various political campaigns, and Part III empirically evaluates the technical methods used in the approach. Pragmatically oriented readers may wish to skip ahead to the case studies. The academically oriented readers, however, may be more interested in Part I or Part III.

Figure 1.2 shows a chapter-by-chapter schematic view of the book's organization. Chapter 2 reviews the principal frameworks available in political science for analyzing political campaigns. Each is briefly summarized and assessed in terms of its usefulness to political candidates for formulating campaign strategy. I argue that none of these frameworks offer much help to candidates. Political campaigners are urged to turn to marketing for a pragmatic approach to the problems that face them in mounting a modern campaign for political office.

There are two fundamentally different orientations to campaign analysis: academic and pragmatic. The academic approach is primarily concerned with developing scientific theories to explain electoral phenomena. This emphasis on theory development has led theorists to focus on problems and methods that are somewhat distant from the concerns of political campaigners. The pragmatic approach, on the other hand, addresses the problems that are most important to political campaigners and is concerned with campaign strategy and tactics. Unfortunately, much of what is written in this vein tends to be so superficial that it is virtually useless as a guide to action. Campaigners must turn elsewhere for systematic methods for analyzing political campaigns designed to identify strategic opportunities.

Chapter 3 reviews analytical procedures for assessing market opportunities for new products that have been developed to aid marketing managers. This review focuses on new procedures developed recently for generating and screening concepts for new products that rely upon spatial models of consumer perceptions and preferences. Such procedures promise to greatly improve management's ability to assess market opportunities and are general enough to be used to strategically analyze political campaigns.

Chapter 4 outlines an analytical approach for strategically positioning political candidates in competitive elections. This approach is based on Volney Stefflre's procedure for assessing new product concepts and is designed (a) to evaluate the impact of the introduction of any new candidate to the campaign—or any new strategy by a current candidate, and (b) to position candidates to take advantage of their strengths or their opponents' weaknesses.

The next four chapters (Part II) show how the strategic positioning approach has been applied in a wide variety of elections. Chapter 5 looks at

FIGURE 1.2. The Organization of the Book

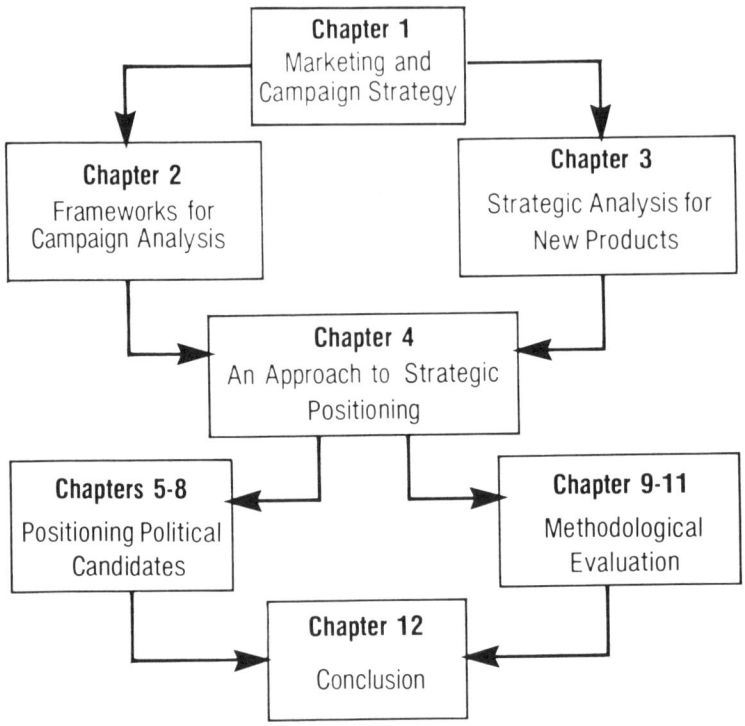

the three-way 1968 U.S. presidential election, showing how this approach can predict patterns of vote-splitting in multicandidate contests. Chapter 6 analyzes the 1970 contest between Ronald Reagan and Jesse Unruh for governor for California. In this contest, the approach is used to evaluate alternative campaign themes and to identify viable campaign strategies for one of the candidates.

The strategic positioning approach is neither limited to two-party political systems nor to U.S. elections. Chapter 7 shows how the approach was used to determine partisan strategy in the 1973 French Assembly elections and Chapter 8 takes a detailed look at a selected Assembly district in this election. The political situation in France is somewhat different from that in the United States in that four or five major parties typically field candidates in French elections, while there are only two principal parties in the United States. The approach is successfully used to evaluate strategic alternatives in multiparty contests and to position selected candidates.

Part III examines the empirical support for the fundamental assumptions that underpin the strategic positioning approach. If these assumptions were found to have little empirical support, the approach would be misleading to say the least. Chapter 9 evaluates the method of estimating share-of-vote for candidates and vote-drawing power of alternative positions and postures. Chapter 10 examines the basic premise underlying this approach that individuals will behave toward new things (e.g., political candidates or parties) in ways that are similar to how they behave toward the familiar things that resemble the new thing. In elections, this implies the existence of a similarity structure. Chapter 11 takes up the issue of the stability of political perceptions and preferences. If perceptions or preferences fluctuate wildly from one moment to the next, structural analysis is useless. This chapter also examines the extent to which, in the elections covered in this book, voters' perceptions are shared across the entire electorate or differ depending upon the backgrounds of the voters.

The last chapter, Chapter 12, summarizes the findings of the preceding chapters and suggests directions for future research. It also briefly discusses the implications for democracy of the introduction of new product development methods into electoral politics.

NOTES

1. Marketing is sometimes confused with public relations, advertising, selling, or merchandising. Each of these terms refer to related but somewhat different business functions. In this book, marketing will be used as the general term that includes the other terms mentioned as specific functions within marketing. See Dunn and Barban (1978), Kotler (1982) for more extensive definitions of business terms.

2. Some other terms that refer to the same notion are "comparative advantage" or "competitive advantage," and "unique selling proposition."

3. This parallel is the most striking for idealized models of pure competition, but, in the real world, a host of legal or traditional constraints on the nature of competition permitted or encouraged can cause markets and electoral contests to deviate widely from the idealized models. The electoral systems that are most similar to markets are those that use proportional representation (Belgium and the Netherlands), and, those systems that select presidents by popular vote in large constituencies (France, Ireland, the United States). Parliamentary systems (e.g., the United Kingdom, Canada, France), where leaders are determined by the winning of a majority of the *seats* in parliament, resemble markets somewhat less.

4. Some recent work has been done in this area by Ray et al. (1973) and Rothschild (1978).

5. This discussion will be oriented toward political candidates rather than political parties for two reasons. First, I wish to include elections that do not explicitly involve political parties, such as intraparty primary contests and nonpartisan elections (e.g., California State Superintendent), and second, it is increasingly true in U.S. politics that political candidates have the initiative, making the key choices of how to raise and use resources and how to wage a political campaign.

6. Obviously, political candidates may be either men or women. For ease of exposition, however, all references will be limited to the masculine gender. This practice should not be taken to imply either the lack of existence or the undesirability of female candidates. I merely wish to avoid a cumbersome repetition of references to "he or she" or neologisms, such as "s/he."

7. I direct the reader to a few excellent books on the nuts-and-bolts of political campaigning: Napolitan (1972), Shadegg (1964, 1972), Lamb and Smith (1968), Levin (1966), and Steinberg (1976, a, b).

8. Under certain circumstances, candidates may find it more advantageous to use two or more central candidate concepts. Care must be taken however, to ensure that the concepts are consistent with each other. For example, a candidate who desires to base his campaign on the concept of "an independent outsider" could also add a companion concept of "fiscal integrity" or "cleaning up the mess in Washington." If the concepts are inconsistent or too disparate, the candidate risks confusing the electorate or not being able to communicate effectively either of his essential messages. Political campaigns must be kept simple in order to be effective. Kotler (1982) discusses the centrality of candidate concepts at some length.

9. Dunn and Barban (1978) give an excellent analysis of the demands of communication strategy.

10. This analysis assumes the legal qualifications for voting have already been fixed. Obviously, the complexity and nature of such laws or customs can be crucial in determining who actually votes (Kelley et al. 1967).

11. Spatial models of voters' perceptions or preferences are not new in political science. Downs (1957) popularized the notion of spatial models of electoral competition, and within ten years political scientists were using multidimensional scaling to empirically describe voters' patterns of preferences (e.g., Converse 1966; Weisberg and Rusk 1970). Another group of political scientists, shunning empirical methods, constructs spatial models axiomatically (e.g., Riker and Ordeshook 1973; Page 1977). The approach taken here differs somewhat from both of these traditions. Chapter 2 takes up the different approaches in political science and discusses their similarities and differences, while Chapter 3 covers the development of multidimensional procedures in marketing.

PART I
CAMPAIGN ANALYSIS AND STRATEGY

The three chapters in Part I introduce the reader to the approach that will be used in the rest of the book to position political candidates strategically in electoral contests. The first concern is to put the approach into perspective before presenting a detailed description of the procedures that the approach entails. Chapter 2 reviews alternative frameworks in political science that have been used to analyze electoral campaigns, and Chapter 3 compares alternative procedures that have been developed to aid marketing managers assess market opportunities for new products. The final chapter in this section of the book, Chapter 4, shows how these analytical procedures may be used to position political candidates in competitive elections.

2

FRAMEWORKS FOR CAMPAIGN ANALYSIS

> The common meaning he [Machiavelli] has for democrats and dictators alike is that, whatever your ends, you must be clear-eyed and unsentimental in pursuit of them and you must rest your power on a cohesive principle.
>
> Max Lerner, introduction to *The Prince and the Discourses*

> There's only one way to hold a district: you must study human nature and act accordin'.
>
> William Riordan, *Plunkitt of Tammany Hall*

This chapter reviews the principal frameworks for analyzing political campaigns available in political science in order to assess their usefulness to political candidates for determining campaign strategy. My net will be cast as widely as possible, including work on elections and voting behavior that does not explicitly address political campaigning, for I wish to discuss the principal analytical frameworks in political science that shape how political scientists, and their students, approach the topic of political campaigning. However, no attempt will be made to cover all of the work that bears on political campaigning. The size and diversity of this area is so enormous that any such effort is ruled out.[1] There is no need to do such a comprehensive review, for my goals are more modest. All I wish to do here is to show how political marketing compares with alternative analytical frameworks in political science.

I argue here that none of the traditional academic approaches in political science is particularly well suited to the needs of political campaigners. This immediately follows, since academic political science is oriented toward the goal of constructing scientific theories and does not concern itself with helping political campaigners come to grips with the practical problems in election campaigns. Such theoretical knowledge is only of limited practical value. Political campaigners require a pragmatic approach for analyzing political campaigns due to the complex problems that face them in such a dynamic situation. Campaigners must identify the important factors, assess their problems and opportunities, and set priorities for achieving their goals. All of this must be done in a complex and dynamic situation, where candidates rarely have direct contact with the electorate and are forced to rely on indirect methods for finding out what voters want (or can accept) as well as for communicating with them. Candidates can no longer just rely on their instincts to tell them what to do. They need an analytical framework to help them deal with the problems of mounting a political campaign.

In the past few decades, political science has been preoccupied with the scientific approach to politics. This has meant that the discipline has moved away from policy-oriented work to emphasize the study of basic political processes and structures. The study of current events has been left to journalists and to the politicians themselves. The scientific orientation has also led mainstream political scientists to virtually ignore the normative aspects of politics—questions concerning what should be done—to focus on descriptive or explanatory studies of political behavior. A second factor that has led political science away from the study of political campaigning has been methodological. Election research has been largely limited to single-shot national surveys. While such surveys can provide an excellent description of attitudes and behaviors at a particular point, this approach is not sensitive to the measurement of short-term changes. The upshot has been that political science, by and large, has not addressed the questions that are most important to political campaigners.

An alternative approach is to take a pragmatic orientation, focusing on the day-to-day decisions made by political candidates during campaigns and assessing the effects of those decisions on the outcome of the campaign. In contrast with the academic perspective, the pragmatic approach has evolved primarily outside of the university. Writers in this genre are typically journalists or political campaigners, who despite their diverse objectives (e.g., muckraking, problem solving, or "objective" news reporting) share an interest in current events and are normative in their orientation. There are two basic types of writing styles available: journalistic exposés, which purport to show how campaigns "really" work, and how-to manuals, which focus on the nuts-and-bolts of political campaigning. While a pragmatic perspective may be more appropriate for the needs of political campaigners than an academic one, much of the work in this vein is too shallow to offer much guidance. It tends to be superficial, anecdotal, and to focus on tactics and techniques to the exclusion of campaign strategy.

This chapter first reviews selected academic approaches to elections and voting behavior, and then discusses the pragmatic approaches to campaigning that can be found implicit in the pragmatic authors. I conclude by arguing that, while the pragmatic perspective is the more appropriate, there is a pressing need for an explicit analytical framework within the pragmatic tradition. Such a framework could help candidates assess their political opportunities and problems in order to develop effective campaign strategy. As discussed in the previous chapter, such a framework is available in marketing.

Despite the inappropriateness of the scientific orientation for political campaigners, the various academic approaches are not without practical value. For example, the spatial model of party competition, originally developed by the positivists, offers a powerful analytical framework that could be quite useful in practical politics. Later chapters in this book show how empirically constructed spatial models can be used to help political candidates develop campaign strategies.

THE ACADEMIC PERSPECTIVE

Three principal academic approaches will be reviewed here: behavioralism, communications, and positive or rational-choice. Behavioralism draws primarily upon sociological and social psychological theories in its efforts to understand the processes involved in elections. The communications approach views elections as one form of persuasive communications and focuses on understanding persuasion and influence in political campaigns. The positive approach grew out of the attempt to apply the rational choice model of economics to the explanation of political decision making.

Behavioralism

The behavioralist approach got its start in political science with the early refinements in sample survey techniques made during the 1940s and has dominated the discipline ever since. From the beginning, the central goal of this research stream has been to understand individual voting behavior. There are primarily two alternative approaches to studying voting behavior within the behavioralist perspective: the sociological approach—which got its start from the early work by Paul Lazarsfeld at the University of Columbia, and the social-psychological approach—which developed at the Survey Research Center (now the Institute for Social Research) at the University of Michigan under the direction of Angus Campbell. Each of these perspectives will be considered in turn.

Sociological Approach.

Two landmark studies by Lazarsfeld's group, the Bureau of Applied Social Research (BASR), at Columbia University, have had a powerful influence on the way in which political scientists study political campaigning (Lazarsfeld et al. 1944; Berelson et al. 1954). In both of these studies, the goal of the researchers was to identify the major factors that influence how people decide to vote. In their first study, this group focused on a small sample of registered voters in Eire County, Ohio, during the 1940 presidential contest between Franklin Delano Roosevelt and Wendell Wilkie. A panel of 600 respondents was interviewed regularly at monthly intervals throughout the campaign from May through November. During the 1948 presidential election, the BASR used the same approach to follow a somewhat larger sample of voters, about 1,000 in all, through the campaign period. As in the first study, respondents were selected from a single small community. This time, Elmira, New York, was selected. The researcher's conclusions were basically the same in both studies.

In these studies Paul Lazarsfeld pioneered the use of large-scale panel surveys to study voters' attitudes and political preferences during an election campaign. Panel designs are widely considered as ideal for studying the effects of political communication, since the same samples are observed over time, and thus changes in voters' beliefs and attitudes may be related to changes in the political environment (Campbell and Stanley 1963). Current research on political communications, to be discussed in the next section, maintains a reliance on the panel survey.

Lazarsfeld's analytical approach was distinctly sociological in character in that voters' social characteristics were relied upon as the major explanatory variables for understanding the voting decision. Depending upon their religious affiliation, social class, and rural or urban residence, voters were considered to be predisposed to voting for either the Democrats or the Republicans. Catholics, working-class, and urban residents had the strongest tendency to vote Democratic, while Protestants, middle-class, and rural residents tended to vote Republican. The major independent variable was the Index of Political Predisposition, which simply summarized the respondents' standing on each of the three demographic variables. A respondent's predisposition to vote Democratic was found to increase the more consistently his social background was Democratic. Voters were found to assimilate their stands on issues to their long standing loyalties to the parties (Lazarsfeld et al. 1944).

Only limited change was found in voting intensions during the campaign period of either election. In 1944, for example, most of the people who cast a ballot that November (69 percent) had already decided in May or June how they would vote. This was somewhat surprising, as this was even before the presidential nominees had been selected by either of the major parties. Only 5 percent changed party preferences during this period. The remaining 26 percent waffled between a preference for one of the parties and being undecided (Lazarsfeld et al. 1944, p. 102). The researchers were much more impressed by the stability that they found inherent in the voting decision than they were with any changes observed during the campaign, although important, if subtle, changes were found (Berelson et al. 1954, pp. 253-73).

The efforts of political campaigners were seen by these researchers as having little to do with the change in voting intention that took place (Klapper 1960; Rossi 1966). First, the level of exposure to campaigning efforts through the mass media was quite low: only half of the people paid any attention to front-page newspaper stories concerning the campaign even during the last week of the campaign (Lazarsfeld et al. 1944). Moreover, the mass media primarily reached the voters who were the most interested in the campaign. Since the people who were interested in the election tended to be already committed partisans, the campaign propaganda did not often reach undecided voters. Thus political campaigning was seen as primarily activating latent predispositions and as reinforcing weakly held partisan preferences, but it was not seen as having a large converting (or persuasive) effect (Sears 1969). This conclusion is widely known as the "limited effects model" and has remained somewhat controversial (Chaffee 1975).

Critique

Despite the use of the panel design, the approach taken by the Columbia group was not well designed to account for the short-term changes that take place during political campaigns. First, by focusing on voters' social characteristics as the major explanatory variables, the role of political campaigning was artificially minimized. Campaigning was treated as merely a mechanism for reactivating latent predispositions. The independent influence of candidates and issues on voters' decisions was heavily discounted. Any influence of campaigning was considered to be nullified by the voters' tendency to distort their perceptions of candidates and issues in accordance with the political predispositions.

Second the Columbia group paid relatively little attention to a consideration of political strategy or campaigning efforts beyond demonstrating that the campaign somehow reactivates latent predispositions and reinforces weakly held partisan preferences. How campaigning might have done this was not thoroughly examined. There was no systematic effort to evaluate the effectiveness of alternative campaigning strategies or techniques. Moreover, the authors did not adequately explain why these particular demographic variables were so important in this particular election. Was this due to the nature of the community selected for study? Was it due to the issues raised in that particular election? Perhaps, these effects were primarily due to the Democrats' decision to stress socioeconomic issues during the campaign. We do not know what would have happened if they had run a different sort of campaign. These questions demand to be answered before anyone may be able to assess the relative importance of campaigning and sociological characteristics for determining the vote. Would a different campaign have reinforced or activated different predispositions? Would another type of campaign fail in reinforcing these predispositions that had been reinforced in this election? The sociological approach is mute.

Third, by overemphasizing on the importance of persuasion (that is, conversion) on voters' partisan preferences, other kinds of campaign effects were downplayed. Campaigns have other effects that are more subtle than changing political opinions, but are not necessarily less important for determining the outcome of the election. For example, campaigns can affect how candidates or parties are perceived by the electorate (their images), or they determine the relative importance that voters accord to particular campaign issues, this has been referred to as "setting the agenda" of the voters' decision (Chaffee 1975). Such effects were amply documented by the Columbia group in their Elmira study, but their importance went unrecognized until the recent work on political communications. Whether or not a particular campaign is successful at reinforcing latent partisan preferences may depend upon the success that a candidate or party has with changing voters' perceptions of the candidates or in changing the relative importance that is perceived for the issues in the campaign.

Social-Psychological Approach

The second major approach within the behavioralist framework has been pursued by the researchers in the Institute for Social Research (ISR) at the University of Michigan (Campbell et al. 1954, 1960, 1966). While this approach has undergone several changes in emphasis since their first study of the 1952 presidential election, there are a few central elements that may be seen as characterizing this approach. As with the Columbia group, they focused on understanding the individual voting decision. However, the Michigan researchers take a social-psychological approach rather than the sociological approach of the Columbia group. This approach is characterized by its concern with measuring attitudes toward political stimuli rather than classifying voters sociologically. Political attitudes serve as the central variable for understanding the voting decision. In their influential book, *The American Voter* (Campbell et al. 1960), three distinct types of attitudes are identified and used to explain the individual voting decision: party identification, support for campaign issues, and candidate appeal. In this formulation, party identification is seen as antecedent to the other attitudes and as partially organizing them. Short-term effects are admitted primarily in terms of the appeal of new candidates and new issues. Importantly, the Michigan group recognizes that elections may be determined almost wholly by short-term effects.

In contrast to the BASR at Columbia, which selected small, relatively isolated communities to study, the ISR conducted nationwide sample surveys. This meant that generalizations were able to be made much more confidently about all U.S. voters than could be made from the small communities that the Columbia researchers chose. This has given the ISR studies an impact on political science that is hard to underestimate.

The American Voter has been the dominant source of portraying the electorate since it was first published. This portrait was drawn largely from the authors' nationwide surveys during the 1956 presidential election, and was supplemented by studies of the 1952 presidential election and the 1958 congressional election. From voters' answers to a unique series of open-ended questions, the ISR attempted to assess both the level of sophistication that voters brought to the task of voting as well as the kind of political cues that people attended to in reaching their decision.

The ISR work reinforced the conclusions reached by the BASR earlier about the basic nature of the individual voting decision. Partisan choice was seen as primarily the result of longstanding loyalties (that is, party identification) and the role of the mass media in influencing the voting decision was minimized. The stability of partisan opinions and behavior was emphasized by the Michigan researchers as it had been by the Columbia group, although they differed somewhat in their explanations for the stability. One of the principal reasons for the stability, both agreed, was that voters were relatively uninterested and uninformed about political issues or events (Sears 1969).

Critique

The cumulative effect of both series of studies was that their basic conclusions were widely accepted in political science (Klapper 1960; Sears 1969). More recently, however, lively debates have sprung up over their conclusions. Debate has been particularly spirited about the level of political sophistication that the typical voter displays and the extent to which voters can be influenced by political issues rather than by party identification (Brown 1970; Budge et al. 1976; Key 1966; Marcus, Tabb, and Sullivan 1974; Page and Brody 1972). These criticisms have been based on a wide variety of conceptual and methodological grounds. Bennett (1977), Chaffee (1975), and Nie et al. (1976) provide comprehensive discussions of these criticisms.

The social-psychological approach of the Michigan researchers falls short of providing a useful framework for understanding the short-term influences on voting behavior. Despite their concern for measuring voters attitudes, their methodology was not designed to evaluate the effects of political campaigning. This follows directly from their concern with the relationships between attitudes and behavior to the exclusion of the link between political events and voters' attitudes or behavior. Their reliance on one-shot, national-level studies, while permitting close study of the dynamics of the individual voting decision, effectively divorced this decision from its political context. Because the ISR group did not attempt to assess political events, beyond anecdotes, independently of voters' perceptions of these events, it is difficult to know to what extent voters' attitudes are influenced by political events or political campaign activities.

The linkage between political events and voters' beliefs and behavior has been dramatically shown in longitudinal studies in which archives of national surveys were analyzed to show how political attitudes systematically reflect the changing political world since the 1950s (Key 1966; Nie et al. 1976). In V. O. Key's words:

> The nature of voter perception of the political world gains import when we recall the earlier discussion of the resemblance of the electoral system to an echo chamber. Voters respond to what they see and hear; the nature of their response depends upon what they see and hear (which, in turn, is conditioned by what is in their heads to begin with). Points of political leadership and of communication of political intelligence, by influencing what people see and hear, fix the range of voter response (within the limits of the situation as shaped by the irrepressible flow of events) as they transmit information to the electorate. (Key 1966, pp. 110-11)

In order to understand how political campaigns work, we need to look elsewhere.

Communications Approach

In addition to behavioralism, the early voting studies (Lazarsfeld et al. 1944; Berelson et al. 1954) gave rise to a second research stream that bears on political campaigning. This stream of research takes the study of political communications as its primary interest. Due in large part to the work of this group, the study of political campaigning is just now emerging from the shadow of behavioralism. The communications approach takes issue with the behavioralists' assumption that political campaigns do not play a major role in determining election outcomes. The importance of political campaigns is based on two arguments, primarily that the early work underestimated the true impact of political communications, in that it has been seen as concluding that few voters change their preferences during political campaigns and that the mass media do not change many votes during a political campaign, and the changes that do take place during a campaign (while often somewhat limited) can be quite critical in determining electoral outcomes. The claim that political campaigning does play a crucial role in elections involves re-interpreting the findings of the early voting studies conducted by the Columbia group. Communications researchers argue that previous work has focused too narrowly on only one kind of effect, that of conversion (Blumler and McQuail 1969; McCombs 1972). Elections can be won (or lost) by campaigning effects such as activating latent predispositions, motivating partisans, or by shifting voters' "frames of reference." All of these effects were well documented in early studies (Berelson et al. 1954). Moreover, even the restricted number of changes in voting intention that has been observed in presidential elections can be critical.

Research on political campaigns and the mass media has been conducted by an extremely diverse group of academics active in the areas of journalism (Chaffee 1975; Kline and Tichenor 1972), political science (Graber 1980; Patterson and McClure 1976; Patterson 1980; Rose 1967), psychology (Bauer 1964; Hovland et al. 1953; Sherif et al. 1965), sociology (Katz and Lazarsfeld 1955; Lang and Lang 1970) and marketing (Ray et al. 1973; Rothschild 1978). Despite their varied perspectives and methodologies, this research stream shares the common assumption that election campaigns are one form of persuasion and they attempt to understand communication processes in that context.

For all of its diversity, most of the communications research on political campaigns has tended to focus on the effects of the mass media (Chaffee 1975; Klapper 1960; Weiss 1969) and to favor the same research tool as that pioneered by Lazarsfeld: the panel survey of intact communities (Kline and Tichenor 1972; Kraus and Davis 1976). Recent research has tended to support the basic empirical findings of the early voting studies. Over the period of the electoral campaign, panel studies have found that between seven and eleven percent change their intention to vote from one party to another (Lazarsfeld et al. 1948; Berelson et al. 1954; Benham 1965). Larger shifts are reported for people moving from a neutral stance (e.g., "no preference," "no opinion," or "don't know") to stating a preference. Shifts between 10 and 28 percent were found for the elections studied. Turnout has been less well studied but some effects have been found, particularly for personal contact (Gosnell 1927; Eldersveld 1956; Katz and Eldersveld 1961).

The traditional approach, the so-called limited effects model, has come under attack for the relative passivity that is assumed for the audience of political communications (Blumler and McQuail 1969; Kline and Tichenor 1972; Patterson 1980). Rather than asking what mass communications do to people, a new approach has developed that asks what people do with mass communications. Because of this orientation, this way of looking at the problem has been labeled the "uses and gratification" approach.

Communications research in political campaigns has tended to focus on the mass media, principally television and newspapers, and to ignore personal contact (Kraus and Davis 1976; Patterson and McClure 1976; Graber 1980). This is particularly surprising given the early findings that personal contact is quite effective in eliciting changes than are the mass media (Berelson et al. 1954; Cutright 1963; Katz and Eldersveld 1961; Katz and Lazarsfeld 1955; Eldersveld 1956). Moreover, few studies compare the effects of different media, but rather treat all media as if they were equivalent and investigate the global effects (or uses) of media. Much more needs to be done in understanding the media's role in political campaigning. How does television differ from radio? from newspapers? from personal contact? The early studies only provided sketchy answers to these questions, and, moreover, political campaigning has changed somewhat since the 1950s. It is not known how dependent the results of the early studies are on the specific political epoch in which they were conducted. Much of what we think is timeless may prove to be limited to specific conditions (Nie et al. 1976).

Political communications research has tended to ignore questions pertaining to the importance of differences in the source of communications or the message itself in preference to studying audience variables.[2] A few recent studies are exceptions in this regard (Patterson and McClure 1976; Rothschild 1978). The first study examined the differential impact of news programs and paid advertising during the 1972 presidential campaign. The authors argue that advertisements provide voters with the bulk of their knowledge about political issues and the candidates' stands on those issues (Patterson and McClure 1973, 1976; McClure and Patterson 1973). The second study also investigated political advertising in political campaigns, but it concentrated specifically on the issue of voter involvement in the election. Rothschild (1978) argues that political advertising has a greater impact on voters' preferences and likelihood to turn out in conditions of low involvement than high involvement. More research needs to be done on the nature of political advertising effects and the conditions under which it will and will not be effective.

Critique

Communications research addresses questions that are ignored by the behavioral approach, offering valuable insights into the workings of political campaigns. To be able to campaign effectively, candidates need an intimate understanding of the communications media, including personal contact as well as the mass media, that they must use to reach their electorate. What kinds of effects can, and cannot, be anticipated? Under which conditions will personal contact be most effective? political advertising? direct mail? How should messages be designed for maximum effectiveness? Recent conceptual and methodological advances have renewed interest in the communications approach.

Despite the promise of the communications approach, several problems should be mentioned that seriously restrict the value of this approach for political campaigners. First, the focus of most research within this framework has been at a very global level, investigating the effects, for example, of *all* mass media together on voters during a political campaign. Typically, no effort is made to distinguish among alternative media, comparing the effects of, say, television with newspapers with personal contact. This global level of analysis corresponds poorly with the interests of political campaigners, who are interested in evaluating alternative communication strategies—that is, in determining the most suitable mix of media and media vehicles to adopt in their campaign. Results for one level of analysis may not hold at another level. Moreover, it is by no means clear that treating a mass medium as an independent variable is a valid research strategy at the level it is usually applied (Blumler and McQuail 1969; O'Keefe 1975). A mass medium may not be homogeneous nor consistent enough to be able to elicit systematic effects. Context or situational effects may be very strong.

Second, the nature of communications effects typically has been too narrowly defined as political conversion. Very little effort has been made to determine other kinds of effects, such as voters' perceptions (images) of political candidates or parties, changes in importance of voters' agendas (problems or issues to be addressed), or changes in values or criteria to be used in evaluating the performances or promises of political candidates or parties.

Third, the bulk of research on mass media in political campaigns has focused on a limited range of political contests, primarily presidential campaigns, which are unique in that they attract a very high level of media attention and voter interest. Some support has been shown for the existence of very different decision-making processes in the electorate depending upon the degree of involvement in the election (Ray et al. 1973; Rothschild 1975). Since voter involvement with a political campaign would be expected to vary with the type of campaign, and with the level of media attention a campaign receives, it would be reasonable to suspect that the effects of political communications would vary depending upon the type of political campaign. Moreover, little is known about how sensitive the effects of political communications are to other situational factors, such as political culture, economic conditions, or even the strategic positions of candidates or parties.

Fourth, much of communications research is based on correlational data. This implies that actual causal sequences might be the reverse of what has been hypothesized. Changes in vote intention might have preceded and led to political discussions or to changes in media habits, for example, rather than discussion or media habits influencing changes in political preferences. Panel community surveys, which are the predominant research method used in media studies, following Lazarsfeld, need to be supplemented by experimental methods, both laboratory and field studies, to clarify tangled patterns of causal influence (Eldersveld 1956; Rothschild 1975).

The Positive Approach

The third academic framework for analyzing elections is that of the positive theorist. This approach attempts to use rational-choice theory, originally developed in economics, to explain how candidates, political parties, or voters make political decisions (Riker and Ordeshook 1973). Rational-choice models view political actors as purposive so that their behavior is seen as an attempt to maximize their individually held goals. This is stark contrast with the behavioralist framework, which reflects a view of man as primarily responsive to his environment rather than purposive (Fiorina 1975).

The positive approach differs quite sharply with the behavioral perspective in another important way. While behavioralism is basically inductive and empirical, sticking quite closely to the empirical richness of natural phenomena, the positive approach is boldly abstract and deductive. Formal, mathematical models are devised in order to characterize underlying processes. The models are based on a minimum of assumptions about the phenomena and make no pretense to capture a full "portrait." Positive theorists have a different goal: to specify as simply as possible the essential processes underlying the observed phenomena.

The use of formal models permits inferences to be deduced from the initial assumptions of the model in a logical clear manner. This means that the consequences of adopting any particular model of a phenomenon can be readily assessed, so that it is then possible to empirically test the model, verify if it is able to predict with sufficient accuracy for our purposes, and if not, modify it in such a way to improve its predictive ability.

The positive approach is potentially quite powerful. Formal models permit the implications of alternative strategies to be systematically compared, and competitive reaction assessed. If formal models can be devised that successfully capture the essence of political processes, the superfluous detail of events may be ignored and the nature of the underlying process will be laid bare.

Models always involve a tradeoff between simplicity and realism. While the principal way to evaluate a model is by the accuracy of its predictions, rather than by the intuitive plausibility of its assumptions, it is important not to get too carried away with this argument. If the assumptions clash violently with our notion of reality, the model may not capture the essential aspects of the situation of interest. Moreover, the model ought to be built on something more solid than accidental production of correct predictions from false assumptions. Developing models requires both an enthusiasm for subjecting the models to empirical tests as well as a serious concern with the realism of the model's assumptions.

A variety of models have been introduced in order to analyze various aspects of elections. For example, a decision-theoretic model of individual voting decision (Buchanan and Tullock 1965); game-theoretic models of political coalition formation (Riker 1962); spatial models of party competition (Downs 1957); resource-allocation models of campaigning decisions (Brams 1978; Kramer 1966). The last two classes of models are particularly useful to political candidates: resource-allocation models, which can help candidates decide how to use their scarce resources of time and money most effectively in a political campaign, and spatial models of party competition. The spatial model is a device to explain how political parties develop distinctive electoral strategies in an effort to win contested elections.

Spatial models of party competition have been developed in the positive tradition. These models offer a potential useful approach to thinking about political competition, particularly when three or more parties or candidates are involved. In the positivists' hands, the spatial model has become an arid mathematical toy, divorced from political reality and devoid of empirical context. Hybrid spatial models, empirically constructed using techniques, such as multidimensional scaling, offer more promise for political campaigners (Converse 1966; Kessel 1980; Mauser 1972, 1979, 1980; Weisberg and Rusk 1970). Marketing uses such models in new product development quite fruitfully. In the following chapters, I show how such an approach can be modified for use in campaign politics.

Spatial Models of Party Competition

In the positive tradition, the spatial model has been used to analyze elections primarily in order to reveal the normative properties of alternative institutional arrangements. Researchers focus on explaining how individual preferences are aggregated in elections to reach social decisions on public policy. While the model is supposed to approximate real world institutions and processes, the central interest of theorists is on determining the conditions under which "populistic" democracy may function (Page 1977). Within this framework political parties are seen as selecting strategic positions in an issue-space in order to attract electoral support. A party's electoral strategy consists of its stands on the issues of concern to voters. Downs (1957) introduced this approach to analyzing party competition by borrowing heavily from earlier economic models of competition.

More than 50 years ago, Harold Hotelling (1929) introduced a one-dimensional spatial model to argue that two businessmen, competing for customers along Main Street (or a railroad line), would tend to locate their stores next to each other. He also claimed that the Democratic and Republican parties, competing for votes, would likewise take stands next to each other on a policy continuum, in the center of the distribution of voters. Smithies (1941) and Downs (1957) elaborated on this unidimensional model by introducing considerations based on the nature of the distribution of voters along the continuum and the possibility that voters may abstain from voting.[3]

Since Downs's early efforts at formulating spatial models, major advancements have been made by a group of researchers at Carnegie-Mellon University following the reformulation of multidimensional spatial models with formal proofs by Davis and Hinich (1966). The models of the Carnegie group typically assume that individual preferences are complete, fixed and transitive for each of the issues in the N-dimensional policy space. Moreover, voters' preferences are represented by continuous cardinal utility frameworks such that utility is a monotonically declining function of distance from the most preferred point (Riker and Ordeshook 1973).

The Carnegie group characteristically assumes that there are only two competing candidates or parties that can freely choose any clear stand in the N-dimensional space. Citizens are assumed to perceive correctly the parties' stands, and to vote (when they vote) for that party whose stand on the issues is more preferred.

Spatial models tend to be preoccupied with two-party contests primarily because there are no general theoretical solutions for equilibrium positions that parties would tend to assume in multiparty contests (Page 1977).

Within the general framework outlined above, the theory encompasses a number of major variations:

1. In some models all citizens vote, while in others citizens may abstain—either due to indifference (when the parties are too close together) or to alienation (where the parties one too far away from the citizen) or both.

2. The precise form of the utility function.

3. Parties are assumed to maximize either the number of votes or the size of their plurality.

For a thorough discussion of these variations see Riker and Ordeshook (1973), Ordeshook (1976), and Page (1977). See Fiorina (1981) for a radically different theory of voting that is also derived from Downs (1957).

The most well known prediction of spatial models is that both parties take the same stand at the center of the electorate's preference distribution—in either one-dimensional or multidimensional models. This outcome is used to argue for "me-too" campaign strategy in two-candidate contests that typify U.S. elections.

If abstentions are permitted, parties still converge toward each other but do not end up adopting exactly the same stand. Unfortunately, the conditions under which there is an equilibrium strategy are very narrow. Only severe restrictions on either the voters' preference distribution, or the parties' strategies, permit the theory to make predictions about parties stands in the most common empirical situation (Riker and Ordeshook 1973, p. 343).

Spatial models of party competition, as they have been developed by the Carnegie group, rest on an integrated set of very specific assumptions about the behavior of citizens, political candidates, and parties. These assumptions have been strongly criticized by political scientists as not conforming to what is known about political behavior (Converse 1964; Stokes 1963; Page 1977).

At the risk of telescoping the discussion beyond recognition, I will attempt in the next few pages to briefly summarize the key assumptions underlying the Carnegie version of spatial models and to indicate the criticisms that have been lodged against each of these assumptions.[4]

Individual Preferences

The model assumes that individual citizens are "rational."
Rationality is defined here as including the following components: that voters act instrumentally in order to achieve politically relevant ends, that the voting decision is based on public policy issues, that voters are able to rank order their preferences for the policy alternatives, and that voters have full and complete information about the positions of political parties on the issues.

Instrumentality. In classical political economics voters are seen as acting in order to obtain individual (typically selfish) goals. This description appears to fit pitifully few voters (Campbell et al. 1960). To the extent that voters act to obtain future goals at all, their goals are often expressive rather than instrumental. Survey studies reveal that voters' decisions are, moreover, frequently linked, because of loyalty, duty, or friendship, to those of others. However, it is possible to use a broader definition of goals to include expressive and affiliative benefits, but this would threaten the validity of elections as democratic social choice processes in the eyes of positive theorists.

Public policy. Elections are assumed to be simply instruments for aggregating individual preferences for alternative public policies in order to reach a group decision. In the Carnegie group's scheme, the voting decision is based exclusively on issues of public policy. The weight of the evidence is in stark contrast with this assumption. While the role that public policy issues play in the individual voting decision has been recently reassessed, there is no support for public policy to be the sole, or even the primary factor in determining how the typical voter decides to cast his ballot (Nie et al. 1976). Other factors, such as party identification and the attractiveness of individual candidates play an important role in voting decisions (Stokes 1963).

Rank-order preference. Spatial models require at the very minimum that individual voters can rank all policy alternatives in the order that they prefer them. Furthermore, these rankings are assumed to be fixed and transitive. There is considerable evidence that voters typically cannot meet such stiff requirements. Voters are neither sufficiently aware nor interested in the policy alternatives facing their governments to be said to have firm preferences on many important issues of public policy. Even the simplest policy questions typically elicit "don't know" or "no opinion" responses from over 20 percent of those polled. (Gallup 1979). Moreover, voters' preferences are not fixed in the sense that they are immune to persuasion. Elections cannot be said to be simple aggregators of voters' preferences as is presumed by positivists.

This is not to say, however, that voters are totally without political preferences, but rather that the criteria for rationality set by the spatial models are too strict. Recent studies of the U.S. electorate have found greater structure to voters' public policy preferences (Nie et al. 1976) than had earlier been found (Campbell et al. 1960; Converse 1964). It is difficult to tell the extent to which this is due to changes in the electorate over time or to differences in the measurement procedures used by the researchers. Other studies suggest that voters have much firmer preferences for political candidates and parties than they do for public policy alternatives (Mauser 1972).

Full information. The assumption that voters have perfect information about political candidates and parties is not supported by what is actually known about the electorate. Most voters have very little information about either the structure of government or about policy alternatives. This has been systematically documented in repeated surveys. Consider, for example, that only half of the adults in the United States could name their congressman, or that, in 1964, fewer than half knew that the Soviet Union was not a NATO member (Erikson and Luttbeg 1973). While survey researchers disagree about how structured or sophisticated voters' political conceptions are, there is no disagreement that their knowledge about politics and government is quite imperfect. This lack of knowledge is most likely due to the high costs of obtaining and understanding political information rather than the laziness and stupidity of the typical voter. It may also be attributed to the individual voter's calculation that the marginal value of his vote is not worth enough for him to expend more than a minimal effort in trying to obtain additional political information (Riker and Ordeshook 1968). Whatever the reason for it, the voters' lack of information has clear implications for their decision processes. If voters cannot base their voting decisions on issues of public policy, they will use what information they have, such as their impressions about past government performance, candidate "character," or their group affiliations as indicators of what parties would do if elected. This puts a high premium on media campaigns to define the situation for the typical voter and to convey favorable images through manipulating the appropriate symbols (Edelman 1964, 1971; McGinniss 1969; Patterson and McClure 1976).

Aggregate Preference Structure

At the heart of spatial models is the assumption that political parties compete with each other in a "space" that is determined by the aggregate political preferences of the voters. The reasonableness of such an assertion has been questioned, most notably by Stokes (1963) and by Converse (1966).

There are three quite different critiques of the appropriateness of the spatial model: continuous rather than discrete dimensions, consistent meaning across the full length of each dimension, and agreement by all blocs of voters on a common framework.

Continuous dimensions. The model assumes that there are one or more ordered dimensions with an indefinitely large number of positions on each dimensions for parties and voters to occupy. Dimensions are interpreted as alternative positions that parties may adopt on particular issues. But what if certain positions along some dimension are impossible or simply ridiculous? This would mean that holes would exist in the spatial model—a situation that is not easy for the Carnegie group's spatial models to deal with. Dimensions may be discrete in that only a limited number of positions are available for parties or voters to occupy. Political partisanship may be like sex, in that only a limited number of categories are possible. Stokes (1963) has pointed out that such a formulation ignores the existence of "valence issues" and is limited to a consideration of "position issues." Stokes defines valence issues as those that the public has simply linked with the parties to some good or bad condition (e.g., corruption versus honesty, withdrawal versus escalation of the war).

Empirical studies have tended to support the existence of discrete dimensions and, indirectly, valence issues (Mauser 1972; Mauser and Freyssinet 1976; Hinich 1978; Weisberg and Rusk 1970). Mauser (1972) has pointed out that there is no necessity to interpret spatial models using continuous dimensions. Discrete dimensions, including "holes," may be embedded in spatial models if it is admitted that holes may exist in the space (Degerman 1972).

Consistent meaning. Spatial models assume that each dimension means the same thing at all locations along its length. Mauser and Freyssinet (1976) have argued that parties at one end of a given dimension may differ from each other in ways that do not correspond with the differences between parties at the other end of the same dimension. This may be true even if the projection of the parties' differences on the given dimension is identical in length and direction. In their study of the 1974 French presidential election they found that consistent interpretation could not be assigned to differences between parties on the left and on the right of the political spectrum. Efforts to force agreement were so general and abstract as to be meaningless.

Blocs of voters. Spatial models typically assume that all voters share the same frame of reference for evaluating political alternatives (Converse 1966). Support exists for the argument that different blocs of voters under some circumstances use different dimensions in evaluating political parties (Mauser and Freyssinet 1976). However, it may be possible to admit individual differences in models of voters' preferences by permitting differential weighting of the dimensions used in the model (e.g., Nygren and Jones 1977). This may not always be a reasonable approach if there are no common dimensions used by distinct subgroups.

Stability of Political Preferences

The spatial model of aggregate preferences is assumed to be stable and not to change with time.

In Hotelling's economic model, Main Street was fixed and only the businessmen could move. However, in electoral politics, the dimensions that are salient to the electorate may change drastically over time. Abundant support can be found that the relative importance of dimensions change between elections with new dimensions arising in response to changing political events and issues (Stokes 1963; Nie et al. 1976; Weisberg and Rusk 1970).

However, spatial models appear to be much more stable *during* a political campaign. For example, little fundamental change was found in the electorate's perceptions of national level politicians during the 15 months preceding the presidential election in 1968 (Mauser 1979; Mauser and Stefflre 1974).

Common Frame of Reference

Political parties are presumed to share the same framework for evaluating public policy issues as that of the electorate.

Given the greater interest in and knowledge about public policy that political leaders would have compared with that of the typical voter, it is hard to accept this assumption. Even Downs (1957) was skeptical about its validity. Nevertheless, two arguments can be made for its reasonableness. First, because of lack of information, political leaders may believe that the voters share the same frame of reference as they do. They would be encouraged in these misperceptions, because the few voters and journalists that political leaders did manage to meet would probably be sufficiently active in politics to share the same basic frame of reference as that of the politicians (Crouse 1973; White 1961).

An alternative argument in support of this assumption is that political leaders would be motivated to adapt the same frame of reference as that used by their constituents in order to successfully compete in electoral contests. The leaders' frame of reference, following this argument, should only differ from that of the voters' to the extent that political leaders cannot get accurate information about voters' preferences.

Neither of these arguments are particularly convincing. The tension between the two distinct frames of reference probably accounts for much of the "slippage" of political communication. However, the second argument may still be practical counsel for political candidates.

Critique

Spatial models in the hands of the Carnegie group correspond very poorly to the needs of political campaigners. There are three reasons for this negative assessment. First, while the problem of identifying affective party strategy is central to spatial models, as it is to political candidates, the way in which this problem is posed by positive theorists strips it of any practical interest. The normative interests of the positivists lead them to view elections as mechanisms for simply aggregating citizens' preferences for public policy rather than as opportunities for persuasion and influence. Since voters' preferences are seen as fixed, that is, not subject to any outside influence, there is no consideration in the model for any political campaign activities. The model is completely static. Moreover, given the positivists' assumption that citizens have full information about the positions taken by each of the political parties, the only strategy that remains for political candidates and parties is to adopt detailed positions on issues of public policy. This way of defining the problem rules out any real world application of spatial models.

Second, the assumptions of spatial models, as we have seen, fail strikingly to capture the essential nature of electoral politics (Page 1977; Stokes 1963). At the very minimum the assumptions of any model should crudely correspond to the empirical situation being modeled. If they are wildly inaccurate it is impossible to know what situation is being modeled and how to put it to test (Fiorina 1975, p. 139). The gross discrepancy between the positivists' models of elections and observed electoral behavior puts in doubt the intent of the Carnegie group to accurately depict electoral competition (Budge et al. 1976, p. 282). However, Ordeshook's (1976) call for a greater integration of positive and behavioral approaches to the study of elections does reflect at least interest in accommodating the behavioralists' criticisms.[5]

Political campaigners need to have as accurate a map as they can get of voters' perceptions and preferences, much as military strategists need a map of the terrain of the battlefield, in order to determine effective campaign strategies. The positivists' use of spatial models cannot offer a map that is accurate enough for campaigners.

Third, spatial models have not been particularly successful in predicting political strategies. It is legitimate to demand that positive theories of elections predict the strategies that parties will adopt under specified conditions, particularly in the light of the argument that positive theories should not be judged by empirically evaluating their assumptions. Nevertheless, the positive approach has dramatically failed to identify general equilibrium strategies. No general solutions have been found for multiparty contests; the only solutions that have been found are for two-party contests and these are very narrow (Page 1977; Riker and Ordeshook 1973). This situation parallels the classic result of social choice theory (Arrow 1963; Plott 1976). Moreover, much of the nature of political competition lies outside the narrow bounds of the problem as stated by the Carnegie group, such as the persistence of party differences, the persuasiveness of ambiguous stands, and the importance of persuasive communications. Shepsle (1972), however, has introduced the notion of a lottery in an effort to account for ambiguity within the positive framework.

This critique of the positivists' version of the spatial model should not be misconstrued to include all spatial models of party competition. Models constructed empirically, rather, than axiomatically as the positivists would do, offer a way to map accurately the interrelationships among political parties, issues, and personalities in an electoral campaign (Kessel 1980; Mauser 1972; Weisberg and Rusk 1970). The next few chapters introduce an approach for developing new products, which uses spatial models, and shows how this approach may be extended to political campaigns.

THE PRAGMATIC FRAMEWORK

Three academic approaches that are available to political campaigners for analyzing elections and campaigns have been reviewed. While each approach offers valuable insights into electoral processes, none of them is considered particularly useful for political campaigners. None of the academic approaches addresses the practical problems facing political campaigners; none adopts the perspective of the campaigner. The principal concern of the academic framework is theory construction, not practical problem solving. The theoretical interests of the academics have led them to ignore problems and concepts of great practical value to political campaigners. The behavioralists prefer to focus on long-term determinants of the vote, such as party identification, rather than short-term forces, such as political campaigning. The positivists, while ostensibly addressing the question of electoral strategy, are committed to normative models of politics that depart radically from political reality. Finally, the communications researchers adopt a very global level of analysis, attempting to evaluate the impact of mass media in general, rather than looking at communications variables that would be of use to political campaigners, such as media type or message content.

Political campaigners must turn elsewhere to find a suitable framework. Campaigners need a framework that helps them assess their problems and opportunities and that can aid them to determine effective campaign strategy. In short, political campaigners require a framework that is pragmatic and managerial.

The second major framework for analyzing political campaigns that will be considered in this chapter is the pragmatic framework. This framework differs from the academic approach in that it takes the point of view of political campaigners and it attempts to come to grips with the practical problems facing someone trying to mount a political campaign. The pragmatic tradition has flourished primarily outside of the university, close to the everyday political world. Writers in this vein tend to be either professional journalists (such as Crouse 1973; Schram 1976; Thompson 1973; or White 1961), or professional campaigners (such as Agranoff 1976; Baus and Ross 1968; Greenfield 1980; Napolitan 1972; or Shadegg 1964, 1972). Unfortunately, since work in the pragmatic tradition is oriented toward a lay audience, the writing tends to be superficial and anecdotal. All too often its focus is on campaign minutiae rather than on strategic analysis. A striking exception is the work by Pool, Abelson, and Popkin (1964).

There is a need for an in-depth systematic analysis of political campaigning from a pragmatic, managerial perspective, but such an analysis has not been done. A few political scientists have attempted to approach campaign analysis from such a perspective but the results have been meager (Hershey 1974; Kingdon 1966; Leuthold 1968). The authors typically limit themselves to presenting a superficial analysis, after interviewing a small number of political candidates. However, there are a few exceptional analyses of campaign decision making (Lamb and Smith 1968; Levin 1962, 1966).

This part of the chapter will classify the alternative ways to approach political campaigning identified in the pragmatic literature. The emphasis here will be on showing how political marketing differs from the alternative approaches. No attempt will be made here to evaluate the effectiveness of each of these approaches, as all of them may be effective under different circumstances. The selection of a campaign approach depends primarily upon the personal taste or style of each individual candidate, as well as the candidates' strategic situation; that is, the nature of his resources, opposition, and potential supporters. As in the first part of the chapter, this section will close with a general critique of the approach.

A review of the books and articles written about campaigning from the pragmatic perspective reveals a few key factors that may be used to classify the basic types of electioneering. The first factor is that of professionalism. Candidates differ considerably in how professionally they approach the decisions that need to be made in campaigning for political office. Some are quite professional, using sophisticated computer techniques, systematically analyzing voters' opinions to identify strategic alternatives, and skillfully managing their resources to effectively present their position.[6] Typically, such campaigns are managed by experienced campaigners who often employ marketing consultants or advertising agencies to handle the more specialized tasks in the campaign, such as voter analysis, fund raising, and media contact. Political marketing necessarily involves a professional approach to electoral campaigning.

Other campaigners simply rely on their instincts or common sense to deal with problems as they arise. Such campaigners may never develop a detailed, explicit campaign strategy, preferring to set only vague guidelines so that they can retain maximum flexibility. Typically, such campaigns rely upon the candidate's close friends or volunteers to manage the campaign, frequently attempting to do all of their own analytical and communications work themselves. This contrast has been drawn somewhat starkly in order to highlight the nature of the professional continuum. Most campaigners fall somewhere between these two extremes.

The second factor that is important in identifying the basic kinds of political campaigns is the principal medium of communications. While almost all campaigns involve both mass media and personal contact to reach the voters, there are important implications for the campaign in how much relative importance is accorded to one over the other.[7] The traditional method of political campaigning has been to rely on a party organization to canvass precincts so that voters may be personally contacted. Ever since the introduction of television in the 1950s, the mass media (e.g., electronic, print, and display media) have played an increasingly important role in political campaigning. This has meant the rise of specialists skilled in the use of the mass media: advertising agencies, television consultants, and survey researchers. Political marketing has been identified with a heavy use of the mass media.[8]

Four basic types of political campaigning approaches may be identified by combining the two key factors—professionalism and the principal medium of communication: (a) political marketing—the professional use of mass media, (b) protest movements—the nonprofessional use of mass media, (c) professional organizers—the professional use of personal contact, and (d) the party machine—the nonprofessional use of personal contact. Each of these orientations to political campaigning will now be discussed, starting with the most traditional approach, that of the party machine, and ending with political marketing. (see Table 2.1.)

The classic party machine is based on patronage and attempts to win elections by getting voters obligated to them and then turning out their supporters on election day (Riordan 1963). Its leaders are experienced politicos who rely on their "horse sense" to run a party organization. At the base of this structure are the precinct captains and ward bosses whose job it is to get the votes of the people in their precinct or ward. Through continuous personal contact with the voters in his precinct or ward, it is possible for the precinct captain, or ward boss, to identify supporters, determine how to get the votes of the noncommitted, and turn out the faithful on election day. This system is rare in the United States today, the victim of modern trends such as the elimination of many patronage jobs, the growth of the civil service, the rise of public welfare agencies, and the increasing size and mobility of the electorate.

TABLE 2.1. Methods of Political Campaigning

	Campaign Management	
	Professional[a]	*Nonprofessional*[b]
Principal means of communication		
Mass media	Political marketing[c]	Protest movements[d]
Personal contact	Professional organizers[e]	Party machines[f]

[a] The use of systematic analytical campaign methods
[b] The exclusive reliance on intuition or common sense
[c] e.g., professional public relations, Whitaker and Baxter, Jos. Napolitan
[d] e.g., the abolitionists, muckrakers, the SCLC, Greenpeace, Clamshell Alliance
[e] e.g., the new right (Shadegg, Viguerie), the moral majority
[f] e.g., Tammany Hall, Mayor Daley's Democratic organization in Chicago, Pendergast

With the decline of traditional party organizations, candidates have turned elsewhere for help with electioneering. One style that has developed in the last 20 years is the use of a professional organizer. This individual recognizes the strength in political organization, as did the traditional party bosses, but he approaches the campaign in a more professional manner. Rather than simply relying on common sense and traditional party patronage, professional organizers, such as Shadegg and Sears, have developed systematic methods for screening voters in order to identify and deliver their supporters. For example, Shadegg (1964, 1972) has developed systematic methods for creating political organizations to canvass precincts and Sears is credited with being the best political operative the Republicans have, organizing both the Nixon and Reagan campaigns (Blumenthal 1980). This approach is credited with a good deal of success in the past, most notably in the Goldwater and McGovern organizations, which both captured their party's presidential nomination.

The professionals differ from the old-style party bosses in another way: typically they work outside of political parties. While they tend to work only for candidates of one major party, or for only one political persuasion (both Shadegg and Viguerie work exclusively for conservative Republicans), the professionals are freelancers, working for hire outside of established political organizations. With the increasing importance of presidential primaries, the professional organizers will become more prominent in the 1980s.

Throughout U.S. history, protest and reform movements have sprung up to challenge the entrenched power of established political parties. During the first quarter of the twentieth century, when political parties were still quite strong, "good government" groups would periodically try to wrest control away from political machines. To do this, the reform groups often relied upon the mass media. For example, the Progressive Republicans, led by Hiram Jonson, set out to destroy political parties in California with the help of the *Los Angeles Times* and the *San Francisco Examiner*. They were so successful that the state is still dominated by the mass media (Bell and Price 1980; Leary 1977).

A more recent example of a reform movement using the mass media to circumvent entrenched political organizations is the civil rights movement of the 1960s and 1970s. While Martin Luther King, Jr. and the other leaders of the Southern Christian Leadership Conference (SCLC) were not experienced public relations experts, they successfully used the media to dramatize their cause, and, eventually, they succeeded in getting some of the laws they desired enacted as well as electing many black officials throughout the South. The environmentalists and antinuclear groups are making similar efforts today; the extent of their success remains to be seen.

The last orientation to campaigning that will be discussed here is political marketing. With the increasing importance of the mass media in political campaigning, the professional use of the mass media has become more and more important. Political candidates, at all levels, turn to specialists in order to use the mass media to reach the voters. Such professionals, drawn for the most part from commercial marketing, offer candidates a wide range of services: for example, help in presenting themselves on television, aid in designing and producing advertisements, as well as buying and scheduling time on the various media during the campaign. Frequently their role is limited to technical advice or technical decisions about how to effectively use the mass media. However, professionals are used to probe the electorate's political views or to help develop campaign strategy. With the increasing sophistication of political candidates, and the increasing competitiveness of political contests, the use of professional marketing concepts and techniques in politics should continue to grow in the 1980s. For example, the use of direct mail to target groups of campaign contributors has been and will continue to be of great importance (Viguerie 1975).

Critique

While the pragmatic approach takes the point of view of political campaigners and addresses important practical problems, much of the analysis in this domain is quite superficial. Typically, very little effort is made to go beyond a simple description of the events that occur in political campaigns.

Pragmatic work in political science is superficial in that very little attempt to explain events is made. Only rarely are observations or conclusions based on solid analyses of electoral phenomena. Few authors make more than a perfunctory attempt to integrate the academic work on mass communications or voting behavior with the concern for political campaigning. The result is that a large gap exists between empirical observations and the strategic recommendations that are drawn, so that the pragmatic literature is of dubious validity.

Another problem with the pragmatic approach is its reportorial style. Most writers in this vein are journalists who tend to concentrate exclusively on reporting ongoing events rather than presenting a practical framework for thinking about political campaigning. This criticism can be made about almost all of the "how-to" books.

A framework is needed that is able to be carried out. Political campaigners need to have a practical framework that can assist them in formulating campaign strategy. Currently, this is not available within political science. Campaigners have to turn to other fields for the kind of framework they are seeking. What is needed is a managerial framework that can help campaigners identify their problems and opportunities, marshall their scarce resources, and aid them in making strategic decisions. As was argued in Chapter 1, such a framework may be found in modern marketing. The next few chapters show what new product development offers political campaigners.

SUMMARY AND CONCLUSIONS

This chapter has reviewed the major frameworks in political science that could be used to analyze political campaigns. Each approach contributed some insight into campaigning, but tended to draw the focus too narrowly, leaving out important considerations, or ignoring vital questions. None of the frameworks offered practical help with the immediate problems facing political strategists.

The academic approaches are overly concerned with the task of providing scientific explanation to offer the political campaigner a useful guide for developing campaign strategy. The behavioralists for the most part focus on explaining individual voting behavior to the exclusion of political campaigning. This work has powerful implications for political campaigners but these implications have, by and large, been left undeveloped. Moreover, the boundary conditions have not been clearly specified, so that it is not clear how generalizable the results of these studies are.

The positivists, to their credit, have addressed the issue of party strategy in competitive elections, which is all but ignored by the behavioralists. Moreover, their use of mathematical models offers a powerful tool for political strategists. The spatial model particularly has tremendous potential. Unfortunately the normative orientation of the positivists leads them to rule out important political elements, such as persuasion, symbolism, and mythology. Spatial models, in the hands of the positivists, fail to capture the essential nature of electoral politics. What is even more debilitating is that modelers do not appear to show much interest in empirically testing their models. Despite its initial promise, the positive approach offers very little to political strategists.

The second framework considered here was that of pragmatism. This approach is basically nonacademic and is rooted in the "real world." Writers in this vein tend to be journalists or experienced campaigners. Unfortunately, many books and articles written from this perspective are superficial and are limited to description of contemporary events. Typically, little effort is made to analyze events or to draw practical implications for other political campaigns.

In order to find a practical framework for generating and evaluating campaign strategy, political campaigners are encouraged to turn to marketing. None of the frameworks discussed in this chapter is particularly well-suited to help political strategists tackle the problems that confront them. Chapter 3 presents an approach, which uses spatial models, that has been developed in marketing for assessing opportunities for new products. This approach should interest political campaigners since they, as well as marketing managers, are vitally involved with the problem of how to introduce something new (or at least somewhat modified) into an uncertain environment. Moreover, these procedures are designed to help managers make better strategic decisions. The following chapters show how this approach can be extended to analyze political campaigns.

NOTES

1. Political campaigns are complex, fascinating events and may be fruitfully approached from a variety of perspectives. The following topics will not be covered here or will only be mentioned in passing: attitude change (Fishbein and Ajzen 1975; Hovland, Janis, and Kelley 1953; Hovland and Rosenberg 1960; McGuire 1969; Rokeach 1968; Sherif, Sherif, and Nebergall 1965); attribution theory and person perception (Bruner and Tagiuri 1954; Harvey, Ickes, and Kidd 1976: Tagiuri 1969; Tagiuri and Petrullo 1958; Wyer and Carlston 1979); diffusion (Rogers 1965; Rogers and Shoemaker 1971); game theory (Goffman 1959, 1970; Luce and Raiffa 1957; Brams 1978); propaganda (Doob 1948; Ellul 1962; Edelman 1964); psycholinguistics (Brown 1958; Deese 1965; Osgood and Sebeok 1965; Lucey and Shweder 1979); socialization (Dennis 1973; Easton and Dennis 1969; Hyman 1959).

2. Early studies by Hovland and his associates at Yale examined source and message variables in a laboratory setting (Hovland et al. 1953), but this focus has been curiously missing from studies in more natural settings.

3. An alternative approach to the use of the spatial metaphor can be seen in Lancaster's (1966, 1971) work where he developed a model of consumer behavior that assumes that utility is derived from the properties or characteristics of goods rather than from the goods themselves as in traditional demand theory in economics.

4. This discussion draws heavily on Page (1977). I recognize my debt to him in this note and will not cite each individual reference. However, I remain responsible for any misinterpretation or embellishment.

5. Fiorina (1981) has made an impressive effort to develop a theory of voting within the positive framework that reflects the behavioralists' objections.

6. The distinction that is being made here is between campaigners who use precise, analytical methods and those who do not. The former are termed "professionals," whether or not they are experienced campaigners or are paid for their services. Many experienced campaigners would be termed "nonprofessionals" in this classification, as would many paid campaigners if they did not use precise, analytical methods of decision making.

7. Recent developments in communications media have blurred the traditional distinction between the mass media (e.g., television, radio, and newspapers) and personal contact (e.g., door-to-door canvassing). Direct mail and telephone soliciting fall between these two categories. On the one hand, they resemble personal contact because of the intimacy of their contact and the specificity of their focus. But they have some of the nature of the mass media, in that they are very flexible and demand a relatively small number of campaign workers.

8. As mentioned in the previous chapter, marketing is not restricted to the mass media; it also includes personal contact as a selling medium and other media, such as direct mail and telephone soliciting. Personal contact is central to commercial marketing, as only a few examples show: the helpfulness of salespeople in small shops, door-to-door selling, and the stocking of a grocer's shelves. While it could be argued that marketing includes *all* ways of reaching the voters, that approach will not be attempted here, for this book focuses on marketing's reputation of expertise in the use of the mass media.

3
STRATEGIC ANALYSIS FOR NEW PRODUCTS

> The topography of the battlefield, too, must be carefully considered, since its extent and conformation condition the ease (or difficulty) with which troops can be moved, the possibility (or impossibility) of employing shock tactics, and the degree to which fire can be brought to bear upon the enemy. It follows therefore, that a skilled analysis of the nature of the terrain plays an important part in the general offensive plan.
>
> Charles de Gaulle, *The Edge of the Sword*

At first glance, it might seem strange to urge aspiring political candidates to familiarize themselves with new product development techniques. However, a little reflection shows the utility of such a request. First, as argued earlier, the strategic problems facing political campaigners parallel those confronting marketing managers. In particular, the problem of evaluating strategic alternatives in political contests resembles the task of assessing market opportunities for new brands or products. Central to both situations is the problem of introducing new objects (e.g., products, candidates) into an uncertain, competitive environment. Moreover, the approach taken in new product development is managerial, that is it is oriented toward helping decision makers deal with the problems that face them.

Recent developments in new product development technologies offer political campaigners powerful new techniques for assessing their strategic opportunities. Analytical procedures have been developed, based on sophisticated measurement techniques, that yield spatial models of the patterns of competition among brands or products. These spatial models are used by management as "market maps" to identify opportunities for new products. Such mapping procedures may be readily extended to electoral politics. In this way, political campaigners can assess alternative positions and postures and determine how to strategically position themselves in any political contest.

This chapter reviews the analytical procedures for assessing market opportunities for new products. Particular attention is given to those procedures based on multidimensional models of consumer perceptions and preferences that are designed to generate and screen new product concepts. Such procedures have only recently emerged in marketing and promise to greatly improve management's chances of launching new products successfully.

The first part of this chapter discusses the problems involved in launching new products and briefly reviews the traditional approaches to dealing with these problems. The second part describes the analytical procedures based on models of consumer perceptions and preferences: the strategic positioning approach. Volney Stefflre's methods for identifying new product opportunities are central to this discussion and are compared with alternative methods. His approach serves as the basis for the "strategic positioning" procedure, presented in Chapter 4, for assessing strategic opportunities in political contests.

NEW PRODUCT DEVELOPMENT

The development of new products or brands is a complex and risky endeavor.[1] It is complex because the process requires coordinating the successful resolution of a host of very different problems. In large firms, this necessarily implies the successful integration of many if not all of the separate and diverse departments in the firm. It is risky because it often involves the very survival of the firm itself. Unfortunately, the success rate for launching new products is not very high. A widely cited estimate is that fewer than one out of 50 new-product projects leads to commercially successful products (Booz, Allen and Hamilton 1968).

Before continuing, it is necessary to clarify what is meant by a "new product." Two definitions are commonly used. Depending on whether one adopts the point of view of the business firm or that of the consumer, a product may be seen as a physical object or a set of potential customer benefits. From the firm's perspective, a new product is any significant change made to the set of physical units that it produces. From the consumer's perspective, however, a new product results from any change in benefits that may be introduced.

Clearly, the two definitions are not always in agreement. The product seen as new by a business firm need not be recognized as such by consumers. For example, a manufacturer may radically change the technical nature of a product without publicizing his efforts. In such a situation, the changes may not be noticed by consumers. Would consumers be able to tell if drastic changes were to be introduced in the internal make-up of, say, television sets or processed food, if such changes were not well publicized? A manufacturer may also simply add products to his product line that are already being sold by other firms. Even if such products were advertised as new products, as they no doubt would be to the manufacturer in question, they need not be seen as new by consumers.

On the other hand, a new product may be created by changing a product's advertising, packaging, pricing, or distribution pattern in such a way as to attract new users or to stimulate new uses, without making any changes at all in the physical product. For example, the physical nature of milk has not changed recently, but the marketing of milk in "bladder bags" or pouches rather than in cardboard or glass containers makes consumers see it as a new product. Another example is the discovery by manufacturers that powdered soup mixes could be promoted as party-dip mixes. No physical change was necessary in the product, but by changing the advertising message, an entirely new market was opened up. From the consumer's perspective, the change in the product's "positioning" creates a new product.

The definition adopted by the analyst should depend upon his objectives. To understand the patterns of competition in the marketplace, it is useful to adopt the consumer's perspective, where products are seen as bundles of benefits, so that any major change in a product's perceived benefits is defined as a new product. Throughout this chapter, in light of its focus on patterns of competition, products will be seen as benefit bundles.

Planning for New Products

Traditionally, the new product development process has been viewed as falling into six stages, although the boundaries are somewhat fuzzy (Booz, Allen and Hamilton 1968). These are shown in Table 3.1.

New product ideas are born in small, informal groups. Typically, a single committee is charged with searching for, and screening, ideas for new products. While ideas might originate in any department of the firm, the search committee collects the ideas and begins the screening process. Out of a very large number of product ideas, only a few are usually selected as worthy of further consideration by the firm. It is important to point out that screening at this early stage is almost completely subjective in that the new product ideas traditionally are assessed without recourse to empirical tests. Managers simply make judgments about the compatibility of the ideas with company resources and objectives, primarily on the basis of their accumulated experience.[2] However, because of the critical importance of preliminary screening steps in the development of new products, improved effectiveness in these early stages could reduce two kinds of possible errors: accepting product ideas that will fail at later stages, and screening out product ideas

TABLE 3.1. The Stages in New Product Development

I. *Exploration*: the search for product ideas to meet company objectives
II. *Screening*: a quick analysis to determine which ideas are pertinent and merit more detailed study.
III. *Business Analysis*: the expansion of the idea, through creative analysis, into a concrete business recommendation including product features and a program for the product.
IV. *Development*: turning the idea-on-paper into a product-in-hand, demonstrable and producible.
V. *Testing*: the commercial experiments necessary to verify earlier business judgments.
VI. *Commercialization*: launching the product in full-scale production and sale, committing the company's reputation and resources.

Source: Booz, Allen and Hamilton (1968).

that would have been successful had they been commercialized. The second type of error is more serious since it cannot be corrected in later stages of the development process. More about this point later.

Ideas for new products originate in one of two ways: a prototype of a new physical product is developed by the research and development staff, or a new product concept is introduced by marketing management or marketing research (Stefflre 1971). Further development by the firm of the new product depends on its origin. The prototype acquires a marketing concept, including a name, package, and advertising campaign; while the concept is mated with a physical product in further development.[3] Ideas that make it past the first few stages receive a larger commitment from the firm. Product prototypes are built and tested—in the laboratory as well as in the market. Marketing plans are developed and may be tested along with the prototypes. It has been estimated that about two-thirds of the money wasted by management on unsuccessful products is spent in the development stage (Booz, Allen and Hamilton 1968). In this context, it should be noted that the later stages in new product development require the close coordination of a wide range of activities, necessarily involving several independent departments in a firm: the research and development department (or an outside firm) builds and tests the prototypes; the marketing department (or often, an advertising agency) designs advertising and packaging programs around new product concepts; and responsibility for testing the market's response to the prototypes, advertising, or packaging may reside with staff, rather than line departments. Still other departments may be charged with the remaining elements of responsibility (e.g., legal and distribution) involved in developing and testing new product concepts.

Primarily two reasons have been put forward to explain the high failure rate in the traditional method of developing new products: difficulties in planning and managing the development process (e.g., Johnson and Jones 1957; Rothberg 1976), and difficulties in estimating market demand effectively (e.g., McDonald 1967; Stefflre 1979a). These problems have attracted considerable attention from management scientists and marketing researchers. Until recently, work bearing on problems in new product development tended to focus exclusively on one or the other of these types of problems. Management scientists attempted to improve management's decision-making abilities by formulating a variety of analytical models, but they typically ignored the problem of estimating consumer response to the firm's actions. Marketing researchers, on the other hand, have focused on obtaining a deeper understanding of consumer behavior, but have largely ignored the problems of how their new knowledge might be applied to practical problems facing management.

In the past few years a new research mode has emerged that attempts to integrate these two previously distinct research traditions (Shocker 1979; Stefflre 1968; Urban and Hauser 1980). To understand these recent efforts in new product development, it will be helpful first to review work in both management science and consumer behavior.

Management Science

The goal management science sets for itself is to improve decision making on the part of management by formulating analytical models for conceptualizing and solving problems. The traditional approach of relying on common sense to solve business problems is rejected in favor of approaches based on scientific methodology (Montgomery and Urban 1969, pp. 7-9, 347-59). At the heart of the scientific approach are mathematical models specifying how managers *should* solve problems in order to optimize some selected value criterion. Such models can aid decision making by providing important frameworks for understanding the problems facing management. By structuring the problem in a systematic and logical fashion these models can help management identify and define their key problems in a more effective fashion than would be possible using simple "rules of thumb." Management science attempts to do more than just help managers conceptualize their problems. The ultimate goal of models in management science is to find optimal solutions to problems.

While management science emerged in the period shortly after World War II, and it has been successfully applied to a wide range of problems, it was only in the late 1960s that significant attempts were made to extend management science to marketing problems (King 1967; Montgomery and Urban 1969; Amstutz 1967). During this period, a variety of attempts were made to formalize the steps in new product development process, for example, DEMON (Charnes 1968) and SPRINTER (Urban 1970).

In order to formulate workable models of the new product development process, the models had to be kept as simple as possible. This meant omitting important problems that could not be immediately dealt with. These early efforts tended to focus exclusively on specifying elegant mathematical models and to ignore the input demands of the models. Unfortunately, the input requirements are crucial.

At each stage of the new product development process, a host of developmental and testing activities take place that shape management's decisions about the nature of the eventual new product. The early models relied on management's estimates of how consumers would react rather than include the results of market or laboratory tests. The models assumed that either historical market data could be used to estimate consumer response, or failing that, managers could be relied upon to provide subjective judgments based on their business experience. Since most firms could not be expected to develop or to maintain the extensive data banks required concerning historical market activities, which were of dubious value. At any rate, this meant that the normative models had to depend upon highly unreliable subjective estimates.

Since very little concern has been shown for obtaining adequate information for management decisions, normative models are open to severe criticisms about their usefulness. First, managers are simply not able to make the judgments required of them by the models. Managers are called on to estimate how new product concepts and prototypes would perform on each of a number of criteria (e.g., marketability, durability, and growth potential). They must make these estimates in the face of considerable uncertainty, not only with respect to the technical and commercial characteristics of the potential new product, but also about the firm's strategic goals and constraints. Moreover, the manager's subjective estimates necessarily reflect their own individual and departmental goals to some unknown degree rather than the firm's corporate objective (Grayson 1973). Predictions based on unreliable estimates can hardly be very accurate, regardless of the sophistication of the predictive model.

Second, the models rely upon weighted checklists of factors to be considered in evaluating new product alternatives. Such checklists typically rely upon unrealistic assumptions that seriously impair their usefulness, such as dimensional invariance and independence of evaluative dimensions (Rothberg 1980). Even if management could make reliable estimates along the required dimensions, considerable work needs to be done in specifying the model for each situation, for example, selecting the most appropriate dimensions and determining the best criterion weights.

A related problem with normative models is that management does not use them (Conference Board 1973; Grayson 1973; Little 1970). Perhaps this should not be too surprising, since management scientists have shown little concern, until recently, for the problem involved in applying their models (Baker and Freeland 1975; von Hippel 1978; Shocker 1979):

It is standard operating procedure for most management science people to strip away so much of a real problem with "simplifying assumptions" that the remaining carcass of the problem and its attendant solution bear little resemblance to the reality with which the manager must deal. . . . They [management scientists] should get themselves some education and direct experience in the power, politics, and change-resistant factors in the real world of management so they can better incorporate the imperfect human variables in their work. (Grayson 1973, p. 44)

Managers persist in refusing to see the models developed by management scientists as useful for solving their problems and in objecting to the unreasonable demands placed on them by the models.

The root of the problem with normative models is that new product development deals with behavioral rather than technological phenomena. Before adequate models can be formulated, a theory is needed of how consumers respond to new products (Montgomery and Urban 1969; Silk 1969). This observation naturally leads to an examination of what research on consumer behavior has to offer management science.

Consumer Behavior

Two areas of research in consumer behavior are of particular importance to understanding consumer reactions to new products: the work on diffusion of innovation in rural sociology and marketing (Robertson 1971; Rogers 1965, 1971; Rogers and Shoemaker 1971), and the work on attitude measurement (Feldman 1966; Festinger 1957; Fishbein 1967; Rokeach 1968; Sherif, Sherif and Nebergall 1965). Research in both of these areas has provided valuable insights into the processes underlying consumer behavior (Howard 1977; Howard and Sheth 1969; Engel, Kollat and Blackwell 1968, 1978).

Diffusion research, for example, has helped marketers to understand the role of opinion leaders in the acceptance of innovations (Robertson 1971; Rogers 1971). This knowledge has helped identify the type of person who would be likely to adopt a particular type of product, as well as the type of characteristics a new product should exhibit for it to be readily adopted (Donnelly and Ivancevich 1974; Robertson and Myers 1969).

Attitude measurement has made tremendous strides in the past ten years in understanding the relationship between attitudes and individual choice (Day 1970; Green and Wind 1973; Ryans 1974). The Fishbein model has proven particularly attractive to researchers in marketing (Ahtola 1975; Fishbein 1963, 1965, 1967; Fishbein and Ajzen 1975; Ryan and Bonfield 1975; Wilkie and Pessemier 1973). Researchers now have the capability to evaluate the effect on purchase intentions of consumers' reactions to any aspect of commercial products.

Despite the importance of recent work in the behavioral area, the practical impact of most consumer behavior research or marketing management has been slight. One of the major reasons for the failure of this work to diffuse beyond academia is that it is not actionable. Research on consumer behavior has been conducted to answer theoretical rather than managerial questions (Engel et al. 1978, pp. 571-74; Kover 1976). Therefore, it should not come as a surprise that the concepts and ideas that are developed in the area are not readily picked up by marketing managers. They were not designed to be.

In the late 1960s, Al Silk called for:

> a workable and valid methodology [for developing new products] based on a theory of how consumers respond to new products. In particular, we need a theory that permits evaluation of consumer response to product possibilities at an early stage in their development—preferable while they are still ideas and before much such cost has been incurred to develop and produce the physical product. (Silk 1969, p. 22)

By calling for a "methodology," Silk wanted to emphasize that what management needed was not only a framework for analysis, but, more important, a set of procedures designed for management to use. At the time these words were written, an approach was emerging that promised to meet this description.

One of the originators of this new approach was Volney Stefflre, who was among the first researchers to offer an analytical procedure, based on user input, explicitly designed to aid management find and evaluate new product concepts (Brown et al. 1968; Stefflre 1965, 1968, 1972, 1979a). In the nearly two decades since Stefflre's early work, a new research mode has emerged in management science that attempts to integrate analytical models of the new product development process, derived from management science, with attitude theory and measurement methods from consumer behavior. These procedures permit management to include information about probable market response to alternative new product possibilities at the earliest stages of development. Because these procedures promise to markedly increase management's effectiveness in identifying successful new products, management can take a more aggressive role in new product development, taking the initiative more often, rather than simply reacting to market events as they occur. Thus, this research mode is sometimes called "proactive" in contrast with the traditional research mode, which is called "reactive" (Shocker 1979; Urban and Hauser 1980). In this book, this mode will be referred to as "the strategic positioning approach."

The next section of this chapter briefly reviews some of the analytical procedures that have been developed recently to help management generate and screen concepts for new products.[4] This review will focus on those procedures that are designed to facilitate management participation, and, in particular, Volney Stefflre's approach. Stefflre is central to this review, not only because of his historical importance but because his work still stands with the best.[5] Indeed, his approach forms the basis of the analytical procedure, described in later chapters, for generating and screening political positions and postures for political campaigners. Stefflre's approach has the most impressive track record of commercial applications. Indeed, most of the others have never been field tested. Moreover, recent studies tend to support the assumptions underlying Stefflre's approach (Lucey and Shweder 1979; Mauser 1972, 1979; Tversky 1972, 1977; Tversky and Sattath 1979).

THE STRATEGIC POSITIONING APPROACH

In the early 1960s a few pioneering researchers had developed procedures for analyzing consumer product preferences that could be used to discover opportunities for new products (Kuehn and Day 1962; Benson 1966). Kuehn and Day, for example, used a probabilistic model to describe consumer preferences in paired comparison testing. Both procedures were illustrated with commercial data, but neither study provided empirical support for the reliability or validity of the methods.

This early work introduced the spatial model to marketing for the description of consumer preferences and provided practical procedures for measuring consumer preferences. The spatial model involves the concept of "ideal point," that is, that preferences for any object are determined by the distance from an individual's "ideal object," which represents his most preferred level on that attribute. These researchers recognized that the spatial model could be used to identify opportunities for new products, as well as ways to modify existing products, by comparing the locations of existing and ideal products in the spatial model.

While these procedures were pioneering, they were quite limited. The preference models were unable to handle consumer tradeoffs among product attributes, since the models were one-dimensional. While their procedures could be replicated for each attribute independently, the models could not incorporate multiple attributes simultaneously. This meant that the models had no way to deal with interactions among attributes. Furthermore, the attributes considered in these models were those judged by the researcher to be the most important. Since the consumer may see the world from a different perspective, the researcher may overlook the most important attributes to consumers. Finally, their early approaches were restricted to aggregate preference data. The use of paired-comparison methods forced the researchers to drastically restrict the consideration that they could accord to individual differences and market segments.

Stefflre's Analytical Procedure

Stefflre was one of the first researchers to develop a multidimensional analytical procedure, based on consumer input, expressly to generate and evaluate new product concepts. While previous work had suggested this possibility, Stefflre put together a methodology that management could use (Brown et al. 1968; Stefflre 1968, 1971). Stefflre's procedures are designed to empirically screen a large number of diverse new product alternatives. To generate new product ideas, Stefflre encouraged broad participation by management. This was done by forming venture groups that typically involved representatives of the marketing research department, the research and development group, product managers, and the advertising agency. Since Stefflre's procedures could empirically evaluate a large number of alternatives, management did not have to rule out as many alternatives, early in the generation and evaluation process, on the basis of intuitive judgment alone. Stefflre recognized the importance in developing new products of testing diverse market strategies rather than limiting testing to alternative executions of the same basic strategy.

Theory

Stefflre's approach is based on the work that he had done in psycholinguistics on the relationshp between language and behavior (Lantz and Stefflre 1964; Stefflre 1965; Stefflre et al. 1966; Stefflre et al. 1971). Stefflre describes his approach as resting on three interlocking assumptions about human behavior:

1. An individual will behave similarly toward things that seem similar to him.
2. If a new item is introduced into an individual's culture, the individual will behave toward it in a manner similar to the way he behaves toward familiar items that he sees as similar to the new item.
3. The close relationship between what is psychologically similar for the individual and those things that are behaved toward similarly by that individual holds across individuals and across cultures despite the wide variation between individuals and cultures as to which objects are seen as similar and in how the objects or situations are behaved toward. (Stefflre 1972, pp. 213-14)

These are simple ideas, but they have quite powerful implications about human behavior; that is, if they can be empirically supported. In developing new products, Stefflre argues that products compete with each other to the extent that consumers see them as being similar to each other, so that the patterns of competition for any new product can be predicted from its pattern of perceived similarity with the other products in the market. Practically speaking, this means that marketers can design products to compete with competitors' products, rather than with their own, simply by analyzing perceived similarity of products. Moreover, Stefflre points out that consumers' verbal reactions to descriptions of new products can be used to predict how the market would respond to an actual product that was seen as matching the description, were it to be produced and introduced to the market.

The assertion that individuals behave similarly toward things that they see as being similar is, of course, tautological unless behavior and perception are measured independently. In marketing, this means developing measures for perceived similarity of products/brands and for competitiveness or substitutibility. Specifically, the following hypotheses follow from Stefflre's basic assumptions:

1. Objects will compete with each other to the extent that they are judged to be similar to each other.
2. New objects will compete with old subjects to the extent that the descriptions of the new objects are seen to resemble to the old objects.
3. The relationships between competitiveness and perceived similarity will remain close across individuals in a market and across product classes despite the wide variation among individuals as to which objects are seen as similar and in how the objects are behaved towards.

Stefflre developed an integrated set of measurement techniques to generate and screen new product concepts. In 1979, he reported on his experiences with this methodology in 33 studies over a 12-year period (1965-77). The studies included a wide range of consumer products (e.g., analgesics, coffee brands, and snack items). In addition to consumer goods, Stefflre's procedures have been applied to a wide variety of other domains: new religions, architectural design (Harding 1979), and fertility regulation methods (Harding and Clement 1974). Stefflre has claimed that his procedures performed satisfactorily: in all but one case he was successful in identifying a concept that met the client's goal (1979a, p. 467).

Procedures

Stefflre's methodology consists of two sets of procedures: Phase I and Phase II. Phase I is designed to find and evaluate concepts of new products that will meet or exceed management specifications. Phase II is designed to build prototypes of the new products (including name, packaging, and advertising theme), that will match the concept found in Phase I and that will perform in the marketplace in the same manner as the concept has performed in the consumer test. Phase II, like Phase I, is based on extensive consumer tests.

Phase I involves an integrated series of consumer interviews designed to generate and test hypotheses about the market demand for new products. Stefflre was among the first to recognize the need to define products and markets from a consumer perspective, rather than from that of the producer. Thus, in his first set of interviews, he asks respondents to name products/brands (and the perceived uses of these products/brands) that were relevant to a broad definition of the market. Once the market boundaries have been identified, another sample is drawn and interviewed concerning their perceptions of these products/brands. Still other samples are asked about their preferences for these items. Figure 3.1 shows a schematic view of the steps in Phase I.

Consumers' perceptions are determined by asking for judgments of similarity of products/brands, and comments about the ways that the products/brands were seen to be similar to each other. Spatial models (typically three-dimensional) of perceptions are found using multidimensional

FIGURE 3.1. The Format for Phase I: Stefflre's Procedure for Identifying New Product Concepts

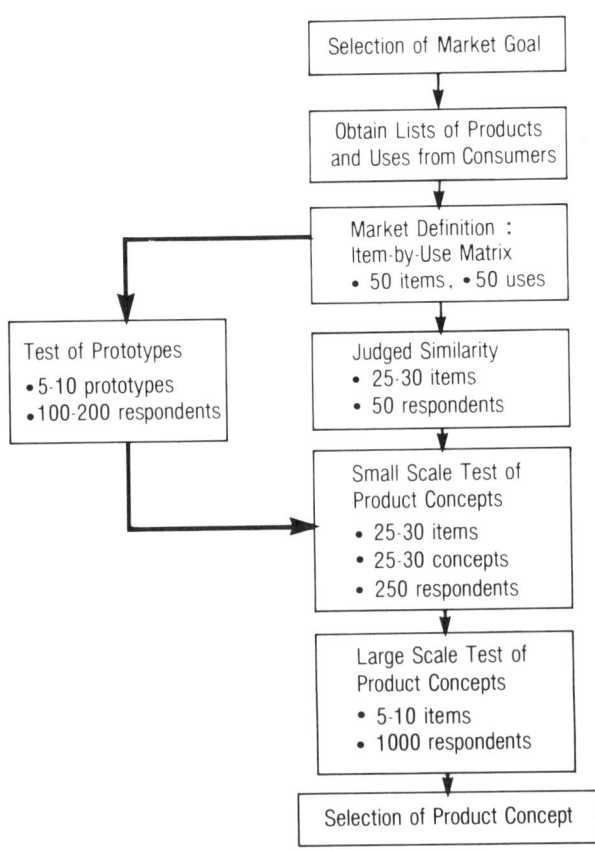

scaling techniques.[6] Stefflre uses the respondents' comments to discover the features that determine where products/brands position in the model. Since a series of interviews are collected in a Phase I study, hypotheses about which features are important in determining positioning, and where specific new products, identified by combinations of features, would position in the model can be tested in subsequent interviews.

At this point, Stefflre employs psycholinguistic rules to generate a wide range of promising new product concepts (Stefflre 1971). Some of the concepts are included merely to increase understanding of the underlying structure; others are new combinations of features that management thinks may be promising.[7] All of these alternatives are then empirically evaluated in subsequent steps. In this way, Stefflre's approach enables management to empirically evaluate a diverse set of alternative market strategies rather than limiting testing to a few alternative executions of the same strategy.

To evaluate the new product concepts, consumers are asked to compare descriptions of new products with existing products/brands. Specifically, consumers are asked to rank order the full set of products and descriptions in terms of their preferences. Multidimensional scaling (MDS) models are then used to analyze the preference data as was done with the similarity data. The resulting model shows where the new product descriptions position in the marketplace with respect to the current products. Typically, at least two waves of preference interviews are conducted. In the first wave, a large number of new products concepts are evaluated by a small sample of respondents. This permits a large number of alternatives to be screened quickly and cheaply. In the second wave, those few concepts that survive the first screening are subjected to a more rigorous test using a larger consumer sample. If no concept is found at this point that meets management's goals for performance, the procedure can be repeated, starting from wherever appears most appropriate, until a concept is identified that performs as desired.

The objective of Phase II is to build a product (including physical prototype, name, packaging, and advertising theme) that matches the concept description found in Phase I and to demonstrate that the product performs in a manner acceptable to the client.[8] Typically, the format involves six rounds of consumer tests at 4 to 10 week intervals. Each round consists of 200 to 300 consumers responding to a variety of tests pertaining to perceptions and preferences for product attributes. The research problem is to analyze how people respond to complex multi-attribute objects and then to synthesize new objects by recombining the components. Each element of the new product (i.e., package, prototype, name, and advertising theme) must elicit the same reaction from consumers as did the original description found in Phase I, and fit harmoniously with other elements. Figures 3.2. and 3.3 show a schematic view of this procedure.

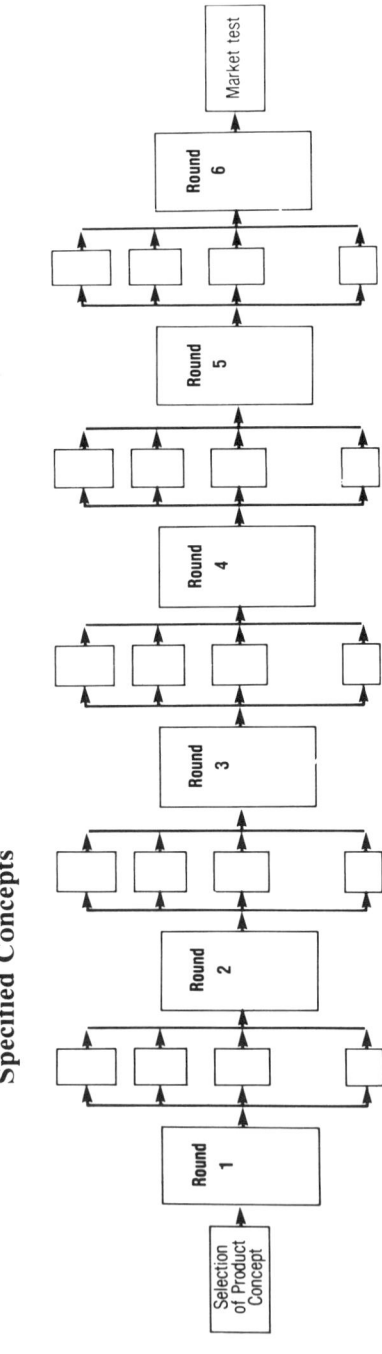

FIGURE 3.2. Overview of Phase II: Steffire's Procedure for Building Product-bundes that Match Specified Concepts

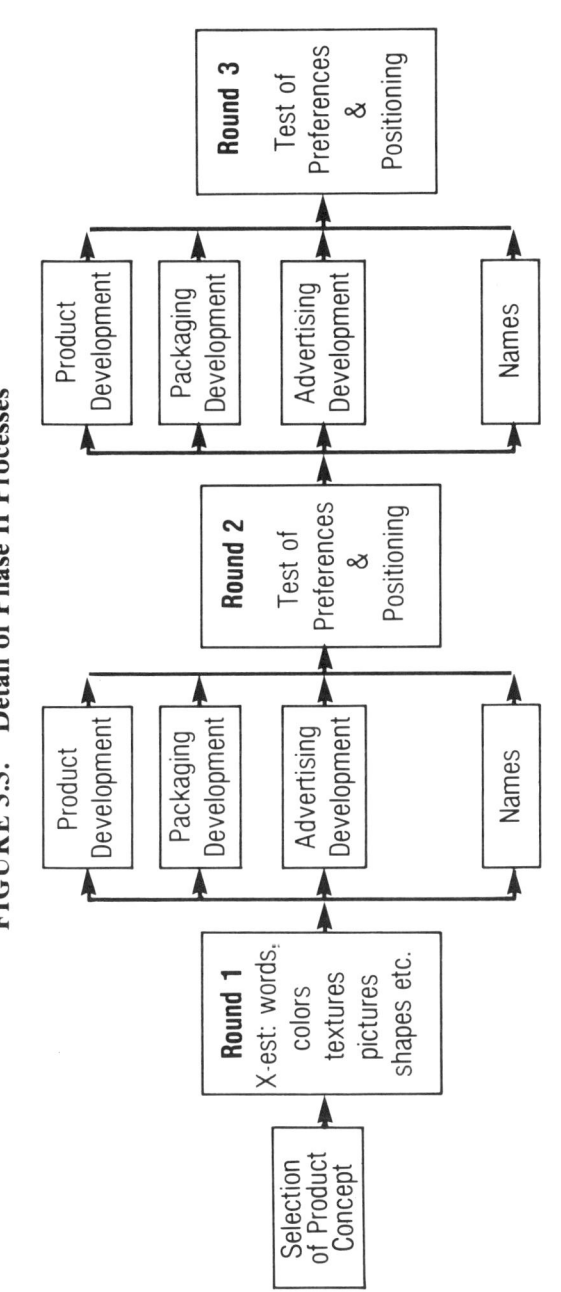

FIGURE 3.3. Detail of Phase II Processes

As in Phase I, Stefflre uses psycholinguistic rules to explore consumers' perceptions and preferences in each round of studies. Component boards are used to display the results in a readily accessible manner, for example, consumers' reactions to a wide variety of alternative colors, shapes, symbols, pictures, tastes, smells, and textures. The goal is to ensure that management does not rule out any new product opportunities on the basis of subjective judgment alone.

The principal criterion for judging the impact of the new product on the market is its preference relative to the current competitive array. Stefflre (1979a) argues that such a criterion is more pertinent than more traditional measures such as average preferences or paired comparisons. His insistence on context-dependent preference measures is a minority view in marketing research.

Evaluation

First, Stefflre designed his procedures primarily to help management solve practical problems. That his procedures are designed to be used can be seen in many aspects of his approach, for example, his use of physical models (rather than mathematical models) of the market structure to generate and to examine new product opportunities. Through this device, management is encouraged to contribute their hypotheses and observations. However, the success of the approach does not depend upon management's ingenuity but rather on the systematic exploration of the product class coupled with strict empirical testing. Stefflre's approach has been criticized for the lack of formalized procedures for identifying "optimal" new product opportunities. He adopted the approach he did because he did not believe that formal models could work as well as systematic empirical testing.

Second, Stefflre's procedures encourage a substantial variety of new product concepts to be generated and screened. This can be seen in his use of a broad definition of the relevant product-market as well as in the use of creative descriptions for product concepts. Since his procedures could easily screen a large number of concepts, Stefflre encourages broad participation by management as a means of eliciting a wide variety of proposals for empirical testing. This means that a wide range of strategic alternatives are empirically evaluated, many of which would have been informally eliminated by management. In contrast, typical new product development procedures limit themselves to considering only a small number of alternative executions of the same basic concept.

Several researchers have pointed out the critical importance of the first stages in new product development, which are devoted to searching and screening preliminary ideas (Rothberg 1980; Shocker et al. 1969; Stefflre 1968, 1979a). Stefflre (1979a) argues strongly that one of the major reasons for new product failures is that the informal screening processes, which are relied upon by the firm to estimate market demand, are subject to strong biases originating in interdepartmental rivalries and individuals' career needs. Such problems are not limited to new product development. Alexander (1979) suggests that the range and quality of the options that are considered by a typical organization are severely limited by informal screening in the early stages of organizational decision-making where problems are first defined and the major options identified. He argues that greater attention should be paid to the early stages of organizational decision processes and that the effort spent on further refining evaluative methods in the later stages are probably misdirected.

Third, Stefflre's approach is one of the few in new product development that shows a serious concern with testing and validation (Shocker and Srinavasan 1979). This can be seen in a variety of aspects. Each step in the procedure is designed to test hypotheses formulated in earlier steps. To test these hypotheses, independent samples are drawn and different measures employed in each step. For example, spatial models are constructed independently to describe consumers' perceptions and preferences. Thus, hypotheses, derived from perceptual data, are tested against preference data about which features determine where products/brands are positioned in the structure, and where specific new products will position if introduced. Hypotheses are tested by introducing precisely tailored descriptions of plausible new products in subsequent rounds of interviews. This cannot be done in the more recently developed procedures since they do not involve independent samples from the same target population (Shocker and Srinavasan 1974; Hauser and Urban 1977; Silk and Urban 1978).

Fourth, Stefflre's approach relies on aggregate level models to estimate consumer perceptions and preferences. This level of analysis reflects the inherently aggregate nature of marketing phenomena. However, Stefflre has been criticized for not building models of individual consumers. It is alleged that aggregate models do not adequately take account of individual or market segment differences (Green and Rao 1971; Shocker and Srinavasan 1979). The first question to consider is whether it is necessary to model individual consumers in developing a model of market response to new products. Recent work has shown a higher degree of interindividual similarity in perception than had been earlier thought to exist by marketing researchers (Mauser 1972, 1979; Stefflre 1972, 1979b). Moreover, Stefflre's aggregate level models appear to have amassed an impressive track record, both in identifying new product opportunities and in positioning new products to exploit those opportunities (Stefflre 1979a). The next section reviews recent attempts to construct market models by first developing models of individual consumer preferences.

Modeling Individual Preferences

The past decade has witnessed a great deal of work on problems related to concept generation and evaluation. The goal of much of this effort has been the formulation of procedures that can analytically identify optimal new product opportunities. Recent developments in this area will be briefly described here and compared with Stefflre's approach. My comments will be limited to a brief characterization of the most important models and procedures. I will not attempt to discuss the full variety of models and procedures that have been formulated, since a comprehensive review of this work has already been published (Shocker and Srivanasan 1979).

The recently developed analytical procedures for generating and evaluating new product concepts have tended to share a common framework for formulating the problem. This framework, closely related to Stefflre's approach, consists of three principal elements: first, brands or products are viewed as bundles of attributes that are potentially relevant to consumer choice, and competition among products or brands in a market is represented by locating the products as points in a "product space" where the axes are determined by the key attributes. Second, consumer preferences for products are modeled as a function of the determinant attributes. Such models are referred to as compensatory multi-attribute models. Third, a common series of analytical stages are followed in analyzing product-markets and in identifying new product concepts. The procedures differ from each other, and from Stefflre's original procedure, in how the various stages are formalized and in the empirical methods used to collect and analyze data.

Analytical Stages

Despite their variety, all procedures rely upon a common series of analytical stages:

Market definition. The market or submarket that is to be analyzed is identified by empirically delimiting the set of products/brands and customer subpopulations that are considered appropriate. Frequently, market definition also includes the specification of the appropriate uses or situations for the products.

Identification of determinant attributes. The characteristics or attributes of the products that are important in explaining consumer preferences and choice are determined, usually using consumer interviews.

Representation of markets. A mathematical model is constructed to represent the product space where all products or brands are situated according to their key attributes and patterns of competition. Typically, the model is geometric and considered continuous without singularities (that is, "holes" in the spatial model).

Modeling individual consumers. A multi-attribute model is developed to characterize the preferences (or choices) of each individual in a representative sample. Parameters are typically permitted to vary across individuals in order to capture individual differences. Some of the procedures are limited to modeling segments and cannot model individual consumers.

Search for new product opportunities. Opportunities for new products are sought by scanning the market model following prespecified criteria in order to achieve desired marketing objectives. Typically, such criteria include estimates of market potential, cost, competitive implications, and the possibility of cannibalizing the other brands or products of the firm.

Evaluation of new product concepts. Each concept to be evaluated is first positioned in the market model and then evaluated in terms of its appeal to individual consumers, market segments, and the total market.

Products as Attribute Bundles

One of the distinguishing features of these analytical procedures is that brands or products are conceptualized as bundles of attributes that determine consumer perceptions and preferences. Once the attributes have been identified, models of individual consumer preferences are formulated and then, aggregating across consumers, models of market segments as well as the entire market are constructed. Following Stefflre, spatial models are used to depict patterns of competition among the products or brands. The product space then serves as the principal means for identifying submarkets, determinant attributes, and potential opportunities for new products or brands.

A variety of different methods are used to empirically construct the product spaces and to interpret the resulting configurations. There are two basic types: *decompositional* and *compositional* approaches. Compositional methods start with the scaling of products or brands on a set of prespecified attributes, using factor analysis or discriminant analysis to determine the spatial model from the interrelationships of the attribute scales (Hauser and Koppelman 1979; Osgood et al. 1957; Pessemier 1977). Decompositional techniques, on the other hand, start with scaling products or brands on a global question (e.g., similarity or preference), using multidimensional scaling techniques to discover a small set of dimensions that characterize the set of products or brands (Green 1975; Stefflre 1972).

Each methodological approach has advantages and disadvantages. Decompositional methods do not require the analyst to know the determinant attributes prior to conducting the study, so there is a greater assurance that the "true" attributes will be identified. Moreover, data collection is more natural and less fatiguing to respondents. This, and the smaller number of parameters that need to be estimated, increases the reliability of the instrument. The principal disadvantage with decompositional methods is the difficulty in interpreting the dimensions in the spatial model. Various empirical techniques exist to aid the analyst in interpreting the dimensions, but interpretation remains very subjective and idiosyncratic.

Compositional methods permit the analyst to be more confident that he knows what dimensions underlie the product space. Furthermore, the configuration of points in the model is less sensitive to the number and nature of the objects included in the analysis. It is possible that the addition of a small number of objects can radically transform the dimensionality of the spatial model in either method, but this is somewhat more likely with decompositional methods. Compositional methods are also more widely available as part of standardized packages of computer programs, while decompositional methods are less widely available. For further discussion of the merits of various empirical approaches to constructing spatial models see Huber and Holbrook (1979) and Hauser and Koppelman (1979).

Individual Preference Model

Central to recently developed analytical procedures is the use of multi-attribute models to describe individual preferences. Prior to the construction of aggregate models, these procedures model individual preferences for products and brands for each and every consumer in the sample. Consumer preferences are described using variations on the compensatory model, where individual preferences for products are viewed as some (typically linear) function of the determinant attributes.

There are two principal types of compensatory models used to characterize individual preferences: the "ideal point" model and the "vector" model. The ideal point model represents individual preferences by locating an ideal object among the set of objects in such a way that preferences are inversely proportional to the distance in the attribute space between each object and the ideal point. Individuals are seen as preferring objects close to their ideal point over those further away. The ideal point need not correspond to any actual or feasible product, but typically it has been used as an indication of what types of products individuals might prefer if they were available. The "vector" preference model characterizes individual preferences as a linear function of the increasing (or decreasing) level of each attribute in the product space. The vector model can be seen to be a special case of the ideal point model by imagining that the ideal points have been projected to the extreme ends of the attributes, so that individuals always prefer more (or less) of each attribute. In both ideal point and vector preference models individual differences are modeled by allowing attribute weights to vary across individuals. These weights may be viewed as reflecting the differences in attribute "importance" or "salience" to individuals.

Evaluation

Stefflre's approach may now be compared with the approach that models individual consumer preferences. Since both approaches use the same basic six analytical stages to construct product spaces and to identify new product opportunities, the two approaches will be compared stage by stage. Table 3.2 shows a few selected procedures.

The first stage involves empirically delimiting the set of products or brands to be studied in the target market. Stefflre's "item-by-use" technique uses cultural notions of "what goes with what" to identify classes of products that have similar uses, while some of the other approaches rely upon the individual's "evoked set"—those brands or products that they have recently used or are familiar with. While both approaches aggregate individual responses to identify classes of similar products, Stefflre's approach has an anthropological bent, in that it stresses cultural communalities in market definition, while the other approaches are psychological in orientation, in that individuals are viewed as more independent of each other, or atomized. In practice, Stefflre also includes "outliers"—little known but promising products—to probe the market boundaries for possible opportunities.

The second stage, that of identifying the determinant attributes, is approached somewhat differently by Stefflre than by the others. While both approaches involve interviewing respondents to elicit the determinant attributes, the specific approach used to elicit attributes differs somewhat as well as the specific uses to which determinant attributes are put. Stefflre uses the judged similarity technique, coupled with an MDS model, while others use direct questioning, Kelly's Repertory Grid, or simply the analyst's judgment. Stefflre constructs a preliminary spatial model of consumers' perceptions of the products or brands using the similarity judgments. This spatial model aids in identifying the determinant attributes and in generating hypotheses about combinations of features that might represent successful new products or brands. Such hypotheses are tested at the next stage of the process. Typically, the other approaches skip the construction of a preliminary spatial model, preferring to construct rating scales directly from the determinant attributes, which are then used in the next stage to develop a spatial model.

In the third stage, the formulation of a spatial model of the market, Stefflre's approach contrasts strikingly with alternative approaches. Stefflre uses an aggregate decompositional approach (e.g., multidimensional scaling techniques) while almost all other researchers prefer compositional approaches, based on the determinant attributes, which permit individual consumers to be modeled (e.g., factor analysis). In contrast with other approaches, Stefflre's approach is the only one that permits the testing of hypotheses, at this step, about which features determine the positioning of objects in the space and their patterns of competition. These hypotheses are generated in the previous step by inspecting the preliminary spatial model based on consumers' perceptions. The alternative approaches, which do not model perceptions and preferences separately, cannot empirically check on the interrelationships between perceptions and preferences. Compositional

TABLE 3.2. Alternative Procedures for Strategic Market Analysis

Stages	Stefflre (1968)	Shocker and Srinavasan (1974)	Pessemier (1975)	Urban (1975)	Hauser and Urban (1977)
1. Market definition	• Item-by-use analysis	• (Stefflre's) Item-by-use analysis	• Evoked set of products	• Evoked set of products	• Evoked set of products
2. Identification of determinant attributes	• Judged similarity • MDS • Hypotheses about attribute bundles	• Kelley's Repertory Grid • MDS • Direct questioning • Regression	• No specific techniques suggested	• Direct questioning • Kelley's Repertory Grid • MDS	• Direct questioning • Kelley's Repertory Grid • MDS
3. Creation of model of aggregate product space	• MDS • Test of positioning of attribute bundles	• Direct measurement of attribute levels	• Multiple discriminant analysis	• Factor analysis • MDS	• Factor analysis • MDS
4. Modeling individual or segment decision making	• Ordinal preferences • Comparison with competitive array	• Ordinal preferences • LINMAP • First choice model • Probabilistic choice model (Luce)	• Ratio (dollar metric) preferences • PREFMAP • Probabilistic choice model (Luce)	• Ordinal preferences • PREFMAP or LINMAP • Prediction of long run market share	• Ordinal preferences • PREFMAP or LINMAP • Utility theory • Probabilistic choice model (multinomial logit)

5. Evaluation of and search for new product concepts	• Heuristic search • Incorporates managerial intuition • Many diverse alternatives included • Empirical test of share-of-choice	• Gradient method • Heuristic search through course and fine grids • Modified gradient search • Costs explicitly considered	• Heuristic search (STRATOP) gradient procedure • Costs explicitly considered	• Subjective (product refinement)	• Subjective (product refinement)
Remarks	• First practical procedure to include all steps in this framework; extensive use of consumer input to validate procedures	• First procedure to emphasize importance of modeling individual preferences in conceptual framework	• Mentions need to consider competitive reactions to moves by the firm	• Uses multistage data collection to predict ultimate trial, brand, switching, and long term market share	• Models manager's decision process as well as customer's and integrates the two

Source: Adapted from Shocker and Srinavasan (1979).

models are forced to assume that perceptual categories precisely correspond to those found in the preference analysis.

The fourth stage, that of modeling individual consumer preferences, is also approached quite differently by Stefflre than by the others. Stefflre assumes that individual consumers follow a variant of the ideal point model, that he calls an "astronomical" model, but he does not construct an explicit model of individual preferences nor does he attempt to show how the aggregate model can be derived from the individual models.[9] The distinguishing features of compositional approaches are the construction of individual models and the development of a set of parameters to derive each individual model from the aggregate model. Perhaps the best known model is that of INDSCAL (Carroll and Chang 1970), but some researchers prefer PREFMAP, LINMAP, or other models.

There are two crucial questions to consider in comparing these two approaches. First, how important is it to model individual consumer preferences? The principal justification of INDSCAL, and similar procedures, is that individual differences are so great that attempts to model aggregates without constructing individual-level models seriously distort the aggregate model. This is debatable and will be taken up at greater length in Chapter 11. It can be argued that compositional approaches are overly complicated and unnecessary. Moreover, such models may also introduce serious errors into aggregate estimates through their reliance on inappropriate assumptions, such as interval or ratio scaled preference measures. This point is discussed in Chapter 9.

The second question is how to interpret the dimensions that emerge in the spatial models of market competition? Stefflre, who uses decompositional methods, prefers to test empirically the importance of attributes that he identifies in the analysis by inserting concepts of hypothetical products described using the attributes and seeing where they position in the model when presented to respondents. Other researchers prefer compositional approaches because each dimension in the space is composed of more specific, directly scaled attributes.

The fifth stage, that of searching for new product opportunities, contrasts Stefflre's heuristic approach with the algorithmic approach favored by many other researchers. Stefflre relies primarily on psycholinguistic rules to systematically explicate alternative strategies in the market. For this approach to work a large number of diverse alternatives need to be generated and then subjected to empirical test. Certain other researchers prefer to develop algorithmic search routines that can be computerized to systematically search throughout the market space for promising locations (Albers and Brockhoff 1977; Pessemier 1977; Zufryden 1976). Computerized approaches are still in their infancy, but as yet they are only feasible when the number of attributes are small and must use simplifying computational heuristics in order to be able to search a large volume of space. There is no support for the superiority of the algorithmic approaches over the psycholinguistic or heuristic approach.

The sixth and final stage, that of evaluating new product alternatives, involves estimating the marginal contribution that the new product candidate would contribute to the firm's market share or total profits. Stefflre relies on determining the marginal increase in market share, after accounting for possible cannibalization effects between the new product candidate and the firm's older product line. He uses share of first choice to estimate market share. Some other researchers have suggested estimating quantity purchased or dollar equivalents rather than simple share of first choice (Lehmann 1971; Shocker and Srinavasan 1974). Hauser and Urban (1977) attempt to model the ultimate market share assuming market familiarity with the new product concept.

SUMMARY AND CONCLUSIONS

This chapter reviewed analytical procedures for assessing market opportunities for new products. Two distinct approaches were identified, management science and consumer behavior. Management science attempts to improve the quality of managerial decision making by objectively analyzing the problem. Unfortunately, much of the effect in this vein has neglected the problem of estimating consumer response to the firm's actions. Marketing research, in contrast, focuses on understanding consumer behavior, but, by and large, has not addressed the problem of how such knowledge may be best used by practical decision makers.

However, a new research mode has emerged in the past decade, the strategic positioning approach, which integrates these two previously distinct research traditions. This new research mode, exemplified by Volney Stefflre's work, attempts to aid management in generating and screening concepts for new products. One of the distinguishing features of this approach is its use of spatial models, based on consumer perceptions and preferences, to show the patterns of competition among the products and brands in a market. The use of a spatial model to display the competitive situation permits management to recognize strategic opportunities (and threats) easily. Management can have confidence in the validity of the spatial model since it is derived from consumer perceptions and preferences, not from arbitrary assumptions.

The strategic positioning approach can readily be applied to political campaigning. Spatial models of political competition may be used to identify strategic opportunities for political candidates as well as new products. These procedures permit a political candidate to identify his image in the electorate, compare it with the images of his competition, examine the impact of alternative claims and postures he might take, and select those that position him to his strategic advantage.

Stefflre's procedure for strategic positioning of new products stands out from the others. First, it has the strongest track record of success under actual use. In 1967, when the first study in this book was conducted, Stefflre's procedure was the *only* one of its kind available. Fifteen years later it still defines the standards in the field. Second, Stefflre's procedure is designed to screen a large number of diverse strategic alternatives. Few techniques of this type can consider as wide a range of alternatives. Third, only Stefflre's procedure permits hypotheses about which features determine positioning in the competitive space to be empirically tested, since only he models both perception and preference separately. Finally, his procedure is designed for maximum participation by management in the decision-making process, which minimizes problems in use as well as allowing a high degree of flexibility to fit management's requirements.

The next chapter describes a procedure for empirically analyzing political campaigns that is designed to identify and screen strategic opportunities for political candidates and parties. It is derived from Stefflre's procedure for strategically positioning new brands and products in commercial products. Subsequent chapters present examples of how this procedure was applied by political candidates in particular elections.

NOTES

1. The terms "brand" and "product" will be used interchangeably here since the analytical procedures discussed in this chapter may be used to analyze any set of competitive alternatives, whether brands in a selected product class (e.g., brands of cigarettes or beer) or products drawn from various product classes (e.g., the snack market—fruit, nuts, sandwiches, candy bars; or cold remedies—aspirin, decongestants, hot rum toddie's, cough syrup).

2. Management decisions made in the early stages about which ideas are worthwhile to pursue determine the fundamental orientation of the entire new product development process. Several authors have pointed out that internal political considerations often play a more substantial role than do external market conditions in shaping management decisions (Alexander 1979; Jay 1967; Stefflre 1979a).

3. In the political realm, the most common development process resembles that of the "prototype" more than the "concept," because the most typical situation involves a political candidate searching for a marketing program that will position him to his best advantage. Less often do political organizations start with a concept of the kind of candidate they would like to support and then go out searching for a candidate who fits.

4. This review is loosely based on the more comprehensive review by Shocker and Srinavasan (1979). However, Stefflre's work will be more pivotal here than it was in the earlier review. This emphasis reflects my concern with identifying procedures that have a proven track record of actual use in the field rather than those designed as an academic exercise.

5. While Stefflre has not published complete descriptions of his approach in marketing or management journals, he has occasionally contributed papers to conferences where he discusses his methods (Stefflre 1968, 1972, 1979a, 1979b). Despite his relative obscurity, Stefflre's work has had a powerful impact on the work done in this area. This can be seen in the breadth of his citations (Aaker and Myers 1975; Brown et al. 1968; Day 1970; Day, Shocker, and Srivastava 1979; Green 1975; Green and Carmone 1970; Green and Tull 1970, 1975, 1978; Frank, Massy,

and Wind 1972; Montgomery and Urban 1969; Myers 1980; Myers and Tauber 1977; Silk 1969; Shocker, Gensch and Simon 1969; Shocker and Srinavasan 1979). Stefflre's work remains at the forefront of the discipline. Recently several leading researchers have credited Stefflre with inspiring their current work (Myers 1976; Shocker and Srinavasan 1974; Silk and Urban 1978; Urban and Hauser 1979).

6. Multidimensional scaling techniques had just recently been developed in mathematical psychology at the time that Stefflre first formulated his approach to generating and screening new product concepts (Kruskal 1964a, 1964b; Shepard 1962a, 1962b; Torgerson 1958). Stefflre's early use of multidimensional scaling techniques sparked a flurry of interest in such techniques in marketing (e.g., Green and Carmone 1970; Green and Rao 1972). Chapter 4 in this book contains a discussion of multidimensional scaling techniques and shows how they are used to determine market strategy.

7. As Stefflre puts it: "At this stage we build 25 or 30 descriptions including:
   1. descriptions representing features of some of the products currently in the class;
   2. descriptions representing products we particularly care about testing our understanding of;
   3. descriptions representing new combinations of features currently in the product class;
   4. descriptions bringing in new features found in products near the class; and
   5. descriptions bringing in words not used currently in describing this type of product but implied as suitable for this area by Spurber's Law.

Spurber's Law suggests that when one word in a semantic field takes on a new meaning, other words in the same field will come following along into this new domain." (Stefflre 1971, p. 51)

8. Stefflre describes the procedures involved in his Phase II in a lengthy manuscript (1971) and in a more succinct paper (1979a). The outline of Phase II presented here is very brief and cursory, since the principal thrust of this book is the identification and screening of new product concepts, not the development of a physical product to match a predetermined description. Stefflre is one of those authors who should be read in the original.

9. Stefflre's "astronomical" model posits that an individual's preference for an object would be a function of both its position in a space (as in the ideal point model) as well as an independent factor that Stefflre calls "gravity" (Stefflre 1982).

4

AN APPROACH TO POSITIONING CANDIDATES

Propter necessitatem inventa est mechanica.
                                    Anonymous medieval churchman

What could be more astute or in tune with [Machiavelli's] *The Prince* than a denunciation of it?
    De Lamar Jensen, *Machiavelli: Cynic, Patriot or Political Scientist*

This chapter presents a procedure for strategically positioning political candidates (or parties) in electoral contests. The method is a straightforward extension of Volney Stefflre's procedure for identifying and screening concepts of new brands and products in commercial markets. In this procedure, an integrated series of techniques empirically map the patterns of competition in the selected political contest and identify strategic opportunities and threats. This permits campaign strategies to evaluate the impact of the introduction of any new candidate to the campaign, and to position candidates strategically so that they might take advantage of their own strengths or opportunities that arise during the campaign.

Political campaign decisions of many kinds depend upon implicit and explicit assumptions about the patterns of interparty or intercandidate competition and the electorate's perceptions of (and preferences for) the candidates and parties in the contest. One of the major problems confronting political candidates is how to identify a suitable image that not only embodies their beliefs and values, but that can also position them effectively in the electoral contest.

The strategic positioning approach is designed to help candidates determine campaign strategy by evaluating alternative positions and postures that they are considering adopting. By organizing their campaign activities around a small set of interrelated issue-positions or postures, candidates can have a better chance of winning by running an effective and efficient campaign.[1] Campaign activities can be effective, since the candidate's efforts are based on positions that have been shown to be popular and believable. Candidates can make efficient use of their scarce resources of time, money, and skilled personnel by organizing the campaign around a set of positions, seen by the electorate as mutually consistent.

The goal of this procedure is to identify positions and postures that meet the specifications set out by the candidate. The candidate has two essential tasks in attempting to win elections: beating the opposition and appealing to his supporters. Ideally, both of these tasks should be accomplished simultaneously. While the second task is extremely important, it is often overlooked. A candidate's supporters need to be motivated, if they are to be expected to work for his election or even just to turn out to vote on election day. Candidates who wish to establish a firm basis for a political career, rather than just to win a single election, cannot ignore the importance of building and maintaining a bloc of supporters. The procedures described in this chapter stand out from other analytical methods in that they comprise the only approach that explicitly considers the importance of a candidate's supporters in screening strategic alternatives.

There are four steps in the strategic positioning procedure (see Figure 4.1). Each step builds on preceding steps and provides empirical tests for earlier steps. It is assumed that a candidate, before deciding to employ this procedure, knows where he stands on the major issues facing his constituents, can raise adequate campaign funds, and can staff a viable campaign organization.

To use this approach, one must:

First, identify the competition. Elections are not held in a vacuum but take place in the context of contemporary events. Voters' views of the candidates in any contest depend upon whom they see as desirable or as prospective candidates. Indeed, some elections may even be dominated by leaders who dropped out of the race, who chose not to run, or who died recently. In order to understand voters' perceptions and evaluations of political candidates, the first step is to determine the full range of desirable or possible candidates. An effective way to do this is to interview a small sample of voters.

Second, map voters' perceptions. Once a list of the prospective candidates has been compiled, it is possible to begin to map voters' perceptions of those leaders by interviewing a second small sample of voters. The goal here is to identify the ways in which voters classify candidates, and the features (or characteristics) of the candidates that are important to the voters. In multiparty contests, it may also be important to identify voters' perceptions of political parties in addition to political candidates. Knowledge of voters' perceptions permits hypotheses (guesses) to be made about which candidates will compete more with each other than with remaining candidates, which

FIGURE 4.1. An Approach to Strategically Positioning Candidates.

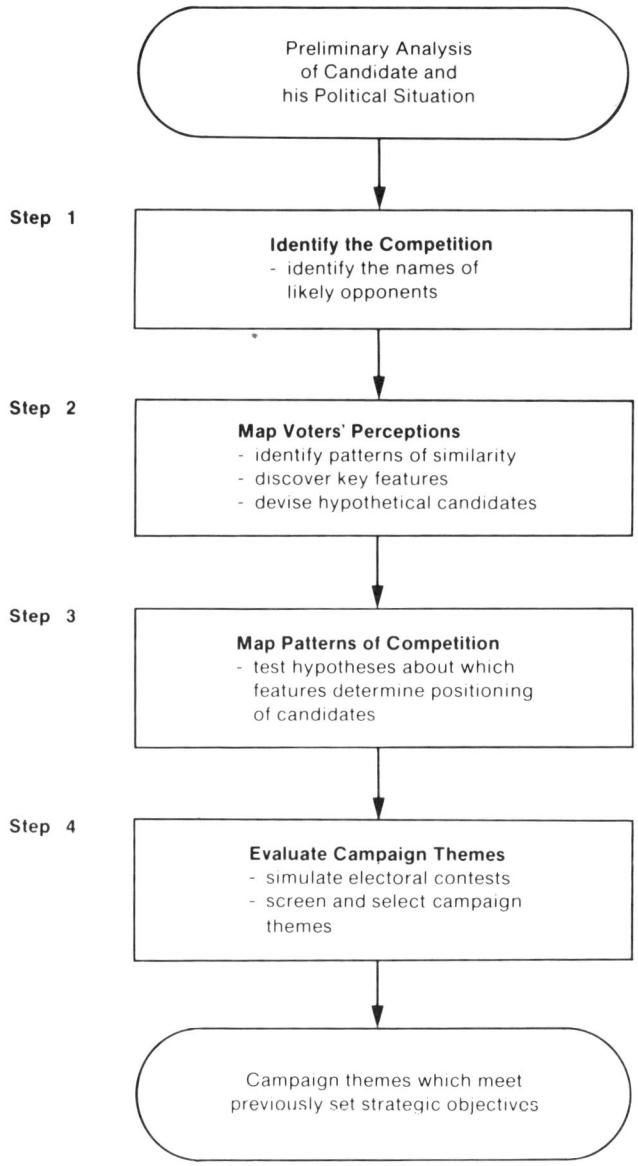

features determine positioning of candidate, and how to position (or reposition) candidates to take best advantage of the political situation. These hypotheses may then be tested in the next step by examining voters' political preferences.

In order to understand voters' perceptions, spatial models are constructed using MDS techniques.[2] In these models—or "maps"—similar candidates position close to each other, while dissimilar candidates position farther apart. Such maps permit campaigners to see complex relationships more easily than is possible with tables of data, and therefore they greatly facilitate the task of developing campaign strategy.

Third, map patterns of competition. The objective in this step is to map voters' preferences so that the patterns of competition among candidates (or parties) may be determined. It is based on a third and larger sample from the same target population. Hypotheses are tested in this step about which candidates compete more with each other for the same votes, and about which features determine the positioning of candidates. Once a candidate thoroughly understands the patterns of competition, he can begin to experiment with alternative ways to position himself by examining where various issues and slogans position in the structure.

Spatial models are then fashioned from voters' preferences, using MDS techniques, to show patterns of competition among the candidates in a parallel manner as has been done with voters' perceptions. The preference model is then compared with the perceptual model to test hypotheses about which features are the most important in determining where candidates position in the model. Confidence in the analysis, and in the strategic recommendations, is increased through the use of independent measures and independent samples to confirm the initial hypotheses.

Fourth, assess alternative campaign strategies. This step is designed to evaluate the impact of the adoption of any position or posture by any candidate in the contest, and the introduction of any new candidate to the race. The goal is to assist candidates in positioning themselves strategically in the campaign.

Hypothetical candidates are introduced in this step to represent the positions and postures being considered by the candidates. A wide range of strategic options are considered in order to identify the most suitable image for each candidate.

Interviewing techniques have been developed for collecting preferences for large numbers of objects. Up to 50 items can be accurately rank ordered using these procedures in personal interviews, and up to 8 items in telephone interviews. Once the respondents' preferences have been obtained, other techniques are used to evaluate the positions and postures under consideration.

Candidates, by following the four steps above, can generate and screen a wide variety of positioning strategies in any given political contest. This procedure removes much of the uncertainty involved in fashioning political strategy for it allows candidates to identify the most effective positions and postures to adopt. Once a candidate has decided upon his basic posture or image, he can begin to organize his campaign around that base.

In the next few sections of this chapter these steps will be discussed in detail in order to show what specific techniques are involved and how they fit together in a general approach to position candidates strategically. The concluding section describes the scaling techniques used for mapping voters' perceptions and preferences.

The second section of the book (Chapters 5, 6, 7, and 8) shows how the strategic positioning approach has been used in a variety of political contests. Each chapter in this section describes a specific electoral contest where this approach has been used: these include executive and legislative elections; two-party and multiparty contests; and French as well as U.S. political systems.

THE FRAMEWORK FOR AN APPROACH

Identifying the Competition

The development of effective campaign strategy depends upon understanding how voters evaluate candidates. In assessing these evaluations, it is important to include the full range of political leaders that are seen as possible or desirable candidates in the contest. It is vital to include the full range since voters' views of the candidates in any particular contest are shaped by voters' evaluations of other well known political leaders. For example, in any given election, voters might yearn for recent martyrs or religious leaders to enter the contest. Also, well known advocates or symbols of social causes are important to include as they may attract (or repel) many voters (e.g., environmental activists, religious leaders, controversial opponents of nuclear power, actors, entertainers, and astronauts).

The first step in this approach is to identify the full range of political and social leaders that voters see as desirable or possible candidates. This set of names can be determined by borrowing a technique from anthropology "ethnographic eliciting." This technique was developed in order to identify the objects seen to belong to any given domain (Black and Metzger 1965; Tyler 1969). Ethnographic eliciting techniques are open-ended, but they are structured interviewing techniques, designed to probe respondents' views of the world. To discover the names of the full range of candidates, a small sample of voters (N = 20) is selected from the target population and interviewed using these eliciting techniques. This sample need not be statistically representative, considering its extremely small size, but it should reflect the major cleavages in the electorate. Names mentioned in this interview as either "desirable or probable candidates" in the contest form the basis for all subsequent analyses.[3]

Mapping Voters' Perceptions

The next step is to map the electorate's perceptions of political candidates (or parties in multiparty contests). This involves primarily two steps: determining how voters categorize or classify politicians (or parties), and identifying the features of the politicians (or parties) that voters use in classifying them. Both of these tasks may be accomplished by conducting small-scale interviews using open-ended techniques. The sample size is approximately 60 respondents.

In these interviews, respondents are asked to judge the similarity of political leaders (or parties) and to indicate what features or characteristics they share in common. For example, the list of candidates developed in the previous step is shown to the respondents and they are asked to go through it in a systematic way pointing out which leaders they think are similar to each other. Initially, no justification is required for their choices. After they have finished this task they are asked to say in what way they saw each pair of similar candidates as being similar. All responses are recorded verbatim.

There is a surprisingly high degree of agreement in a society about what is similar to what, even though there is widespread disagreement about what is preferred and even about why the objects are similar (Converse 1964; Stefflre 1965). Apparently disparate groups have been consistently found to share common perceptual structures (Abelson 1955; Messick 1961; Osgood, Suci and Tannenbaum 1957; Snider and Osgood 1969). This homogeneity permits the use of very small samples in determining voters' perceptions of candidates in most elections, although larger samples are always necessary when estimating voters' preferences. However, homogeneity of perceptions should not be blindly assumed. Problems can arise when the electorate contains social groups that historically have had little contact with others and which do not share the same outlook. Whether or not such deep cleavages exist in any electorate is an open empirical question. The question of homogeneity is taken up again in Chapter 10 and discussed more fully at that time.

Spatial models of voters' perceptions are built using multidimensional scaling techniques. These models are based on the frequency with which political leaders (or parties) are judged to be similar to each other.[4] Direct inspection of the model permits campaigners to devise hypotheses about why certain leaders tend to be clustered together and why others do not. The verbatim statements suggest still richer hypotheses about which aspects of leaders (or parties) are salient to the electorate. At this stage all such hypotheses are, of course, pure speculation. The challenge is to find clues for strategically positioning candidates in upcoming elections.

It is not a simple task to interpret MDS models nor to identify positions in the structure that are attractive to voters. The approach adapted here views political leaders as bundles of complex attributes (Mauser 1972; Stefflre

1972, 1979a). Each leader consists, according to this view, of a large number of discrete values, which determine where the candidate positions in the MDS model. An alternative approach, which appeared quite promising ten years ago, assumes that there are only a small number of dimensions, which can be found using MDS techniques, and attempts to identify "ideal points" in the space (e.g., Carroll and Chang 1970; Green and Carmone 1970). Some early researchers took the concept of an ideal point literally. Recent work, however, argues that hypothesizing the existence of an ideal point is not a very useful way to think about the problem (Stefflre 1979b; Tversky 1972, 1977).

The fundamental questions underlying the interpretation of MDS models have to do with how voters acquire and process information about political leaders. A large and complex literature has developed that is concerned with understanding "person perception" (Bruner and Tagiuri 1954; Tagiuri 1969; Wyer and Carlston 1979). Given the complexity of inferential processes in this domain and the failure of simple mechanical schemes, such as ideal-point models, perhaps the most effective approach to discovering effective strategies is to screen a wide variety of plausible alternatives by presenting them to the voters.

Hypotheses about which features determine how political leaders position in the model and in upcoming political contests may be tested by devising hypothetical candidates and including them in subsequent waves of interviews. Hypothetical candidates consist of short, simple descriptions of plausible candidates. These descriptions may be derived from the voters' own vocabulary, from slogans, or from campaign themes expected to emerge during the course of the coming campaign. Descriptions of hypothetical candidates may be composed of stands on campaign issues, alternative leadership postures, party labels, links with well known groups, or variations on selected campaign themes.

Mapping Patterns of Competition

In order to map patterns of competition in a political contest, somewhat larger representative samples of voters (containing at least 200 respondents) must be drawn from the target population and interviewed concerning political preferences. In this wave, respondents are asked to rank a set of political leaders (or political parties) in the order that they prefer them. Hypothetical candidates are included to be ranked in addition to the original list of names.

Spatial models of the patterns of competition among the political leaders (or parties) are constructed by first intercorrelating the respondents' preference rankings. The correlation is an index of the extent to which candidates (or parties) appeal to the same people in the target population.[5] For example, Republican candidates will tend to correlate highly with each other since they appeal to Republican voters and to be disliked by Democratic voters. Similarity with Republican postures or positions on issues. These correlations are then scaled using multidimensional scaling techniques.

Patterns of competition are immediately evident in spatial models based on intercorrelated preferences. Political leaders (or parties) will cluster together to the extent that they appeal to the same voters. It is important to point out that such correlations are *not* direct measures of candidate similarity.[6] However, similar candidates are hypothesized to be highly intercorrelated. If the hypothesis is supported that objects compete with each other to the extent that they are seen to be similar, then the same patterns should be found in the preference model as were found in the perceptual model. This hypothesis may be tested in two separate ways: by comparing the structure in the two different models, and by determining if hypothetical candidates position where they were predicted to position.

It is worth pointing out that in both of the models (the perceptual and preference maps), objects of very different *levels* of preference may position close to each other. For example, the local Republican mayor or congressman will tend to position close to Republican candidates for president—because they share the same essential features and they appeal to the same type of voter—but presidential candidates are typically much better known and more popular than mayors. In order to measure the popularity of a candidate (or party) we must turn to other techniques besides spatial models.

Evaluating Campaign Strategies

The final step in this approach is to evaluate the positions and postures that the candidates might adopt. This is done by including hypothetical candidates, which consist of short verbal descriptions, in the preference interviews to be ranked alongside the names of prominent political leaders.

A particularly powerful way to develop campaign strategy is to recognize that the problem consists of two distinct stages: first, generating a wide variety of basically different strategic alternatives, and, then, empirically screening the alternatives using predetermined criteria. Such a procedure reduces to a minimum the chance of overlooking a significant strategic opportunity and increases the likelihood of identifying effective positions and postures.[7]

A large number of alternative positions and postures may be screened, without incurring too large a cost, by submitting all alternatives to a series of increasingly rigorous tests. Those positions or postures that survive early tests are subjected to more intense scrutiny in later phases to identify the most suitable strategy. These tests will now be described.

As was mentioned earlier, there are two important criteria for a candidate to consider in deciding which positions and postures to adopt: can the position or posture help him beat his opposition, and does it appeal to his present supporters? The first consideration for any candidate is identifying issue-positions or postures that permit him to win the election. One of the goals of this step is to estimate the drawing power of each issue-position or posture that the candidates are considering adopting. In the strategic positioning procedure this is done by simulating the number of voters who would support the position in selected mock elections. These procedures are discussed more fully in Chapter 9.

The second criterion, that of picking positions that appeal to one's supporters, is important on two levels. First, in the short term, candidates need to motivate their supporters in order to win any election. By selecting positions and postures that are attractive to one's supporters, candidates can stimulate them to work in the campaign, contribute money, and turn out to vote (Lazarsfeld et al. 1944; Berelson et al. 1954).

All too often, candidates take their supporters for granted in favor of courting the undecided voter. This can be foolish, as candidates risk losing their public credibility. In contemporary political contests, electorates are quite volatile. Candidates for highly visible offices cannot always count on party loyalty or indifference to weld their supporters to them, despite their stands on the issues. The classic problem is that candidates are forced to risk their base of support in order to attract the swing vote, since they lacked an effective way to determine the risk (Downs 1957; Scammon and Wattenberg 1970).

Moreover, in the long term, political candidates should pick positions that appeal to their supporters in order to establish a core of loyal voters who remember them from election to election. While the candidate running for reelection has greater freedom of maneuverability than does the candidate running for the first time for a political office, it is still important for him to select issues that appeal to his core supporters to maintain his public credibility. Many established candidates have overestimated the loyalties of their supporters and been turned out of office. The strategic positioning approach enables candidates to measure the importance of any issue-position or posture to their supporters. This may be done simply and quickly by inspecting the MDS model. Issue-positions found close to a candidate in the model are preferred by his supporters.

Part II of this book presents examples of how the strategic positioning approach has been used in a variety of political contests. Seeing how this methodology works in practice should give the reader a better idea of the power of this approach. Those readers who wish to see the empirical support for the approach are urged to skip ahead to Part III (Chapters 9, 10, and 11), where the assumptions underlying the technical procedures are examined in detail.

MULTIDIMENSIONAL SCALING

This section briefly describes multidimensional scaling techniques (MDS). It is written for the nontechnical reader and focuses on how to use MDS techniques.[8]

Multidimensional scaling techniques are useful for representing the structure hidden in tables of data since the objects are displayed in a spatial model. MDS is powerful tool for decision makers. There are primarily three reasons for this. First, spatial models permit a visual examination of the structure, which means that complex patterns may be grasped more easily. This is an invaluable aid in formulating strategies. Second, in MDS there is no necessity to know all of the important variables before one starts. MDS, like factor analysis, is principally a tool for discovering relationships and hypotheses. Third, MDS is very flexible. It can handle a wide range of data and can display a large variety of types of structures.

Mapping or Scaling Procedures

To use MDS, one starts with measures of the similarity or proximity of objects with each other. For example, measures may be respondents' judgments of the similarity of political candidates or indices of the extent to which candidates or parties appeal to the same voters, such as can be obtained by intercorrelating respondents' preferences. Since MDS techniques can accept a very wide range of proximity indices, the user must pay particular attention to selecting indices that measures what they are supposed to.

The input to MDS is a set of proximity measures for all pairs of objects. For ten politicians, there are $n(n-1)2 = 45$ such pairs, and for 25 politicians there would be 300 pairs. Obviously, such large data sets may only be analyzed by computer routines. Several MDS programs have been written; all of which work in essentially the same manner (e.g., MDSCAL, KYST, TORSCA, POLYCON, and SSAI).[9]

The goal of MDS procedures is to find a spatial model that best displays the patterns in the proximity measures. A spatial model is sought where the interpoint distances in the model correspond inversely to the order of the original proximities. That is, in the spatial model, similar objects are placed close to each other and dissimilar objects position further apart. MDS procedures use an iterative algorithm to find the best fit between the proximity measures and the interpoint distances (Kruskal, 1964a, b).

In using MDS to discover the basic structure in a data set, the analyst must deal with three fundamental questions:

1. What is the best dimensionality to represent the underlying structure (i.e., what is the most appropriate number of dimensions)?

2. How can he evaluate the quality of the MDS solution?
3. How can he interpret the spatial configuration?

Determining dimensionality

MDS procedures are designed to work in a space of fixed dimensionality. That is, the procedures find the best spatial solution once the analyst chooses the number of dimensions. Since the true dimensionality of the structure often is not known, the analyst must find MDS solutions for a range of dimensionalities and then select the best solution from among them.[10] Typically, analysts start with five-dimensional solutions and work down to one-dimensional solutions.

The analyst's goal is to identify that dimensionality that best displays the natural structure of the data. In making this decision, he is faced with a tradeoff between clarity and explanatory power. The greater the dimensionality he selects to display the data, the greater the explanatory power he has. But at a price: beyond two or three dimensions, the model becomes too complex to interpret readily. On the other hand, the smaller the dimensionality, the less accurately the MDS model reflects the natural structure of the data. One-dimensional models are the easiest to interpret, but they risk being overly simplistic.

FIGURE 4.2. Illustrative Plot of Stress versus Dimensionality, Showing an Elbow

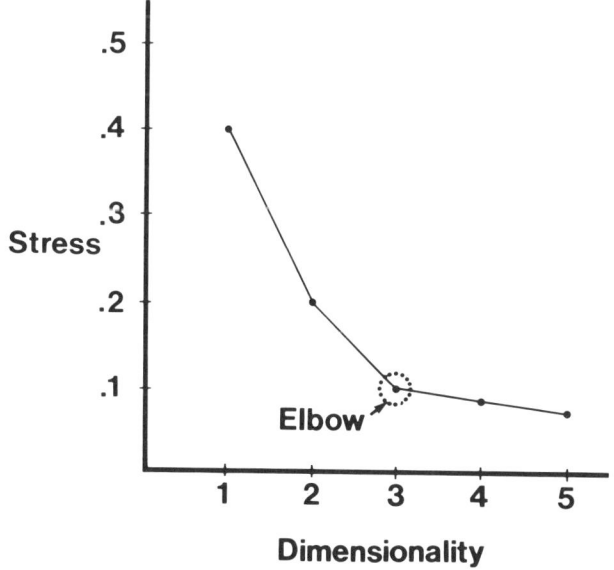

It is often useful in selecting the best dimensionality to plot the stress against the dimensionality. Figure 4.2 shows such a plot for an illustrative set of solutions. Stress, an index of the extent to which the solution deviates from the original data, usually decreases as the dimensionality (that is, the number of dimensions used in the spatial model) increases. In this example, after the third dimension, additional dimensions do not decrease the stress appreciably. When this occurs, it is called an "elbow" and it indicates that the maximum explanatory power, with the minimum number of dimensions, lies in the three-dimensional solution.

If no elbow can be found in the stress-dimensionality curve, as often happens in survey studies, the analyst is left to look for other criteria. Independent theoretical or empirical support may exist for specifying a dimensionality. If not, the analyst may simply pick the dimensionality he finds as the most useful for his purposes.

Evaluating the MDS Solution

MDS techniques guarantee solutions. Even if random data were analyzed, the procedures would yield spatial solutions that imaginative, if unsuspecting, analysts might find illuminating. How can one determine if the MDS solution satisfactorily represents anything in the "real world?" This problem is particularly troublesome in practical situations, since there may be no independent structure to compare with the MDS solution. When this is the case, the analyst is dependent on statistical analysis. There are three approaches to this problem that are widely used: *ad hoc* guidelines, Monte Carlo simulations, and cross-validation.

A few researchers have published guidelines for determining acceptable and unacceptable levels of stress (Krushal 1964a; Rabinowitz 1975). While easy to use, such guidelines have two problems: there are a variety of different indices available for measuring stress, but guidelines have been determined for only a few of them, and, even more importantly, stress measures have the unfortunate property of increasing with the number of objects scaled, so that a high level of stress may indicate either a poor quality solution or that a large number of objects has been scaled. This fact is ignored in the guidelines. Consequently, it is difficult to recommend their use particularly for applied studies, where typically a large number of objects are involved.

An alternative is to compare the stress levels observed in the MDS solution with those found by scaling random data sets with the same number of points. Several researchers have used this approach, called "Monte Carlo simulation," to develop tables for a variety of indices and for sets of objects ranging from 7 to 50 (Klahr 1969; Spence 1972; Spence and Oglivie 1973; Stenson and Knoll 1969). This approach is quite popular among academics. Unfortunately, it involves a tremendous amount of computer time to calculate the large number of simulations necessary to estimate the stress values for random data sets. Another, more serious problem with this procedure is that it is primarily designed for laboratory studies where there is very little "noise" in the data. Empirical data may be as noisy as random data but may contain definite structure.

The third method for evaluating MDS solutions is to independently analyze subsamples of the original data set. This is the cross-validation approach. If the same configuration can be found in each subsample, the analyst can have confidence that his model represents something besides noise; if not, his data is suspect.

The cross-validation approach is clearly the best of the three statistical procedures for evaluating MDS solutions. Its advantages are particularly evident in practical situations where the data is often noisy. Of course, if there are independent structures to compare the MDS solution with, then that would dominate any of these approaches.

Only a little extra effort is required to analyze a few selected subsamples. But by so doing, the analyst can discover if his model holds for specific groups in the target population (e.g., Democrats or Spanish-speaking groups). It is also useful to analyze random subsamples from the target population in order to get an idea of the inherent stability that exists in the data. By analyzing a very small number of random subsamples, the analyst can estimate how widely each object will stray from its observed position in the model. Despite the extra effort required by this approach, which is not as great as with the Monte Carlo approach, the cross-validation approach is strongly recommended for use in applied studies.

Interpreting the Configuration

MDS techniques simply display the data in a spatial configuration. It remains for the analyst to interpret the patterns that he sees in the data.

There are two ways to think about the kind of patterns that may be found in the data: discrete combinatorial frameworks or continuous dimensions. That is, the data may be interpreted using either a large number of dimensions with only a few discrete values on each, or alternatively, a few dimensions with a large number of values on each. This choice is not forced on the analyst by the choice of MDS procedures as a wide variety of structures may be embedded in multidimensional space (Degerman 1972).

The traditional approach, which is widely used in both political science and marketing, is to interpret the structure using a small number of continuous dimensions (Green and Carmone 1970; Riker and Ordeshook 1973; Weisberg and Rusk 1970). Following this approach, the analyst must search for ways to discover the primary dimensions that span the MDS configuration. This may be done intuitively, by inspecting the configuration, or by reference to external criteria, that is, by correlating other data with the configuration. For example, axes may be identified that pass through the structure. Then, by projecting the candidates' (or parties') position onto these axes, the dimension can be interpreted by looking at the order of their positions. Figure 4.3 shows how this approach has been used to identify a liberal-conservative dimension in an illustrative model of U.S. presidential candidates.

It is important to note that, while candidates are shown occupying only a very small number of points along this dimension, they could position anywhere along its length because the dimension is considered to be continuous (or at least to have a large number of positions).

Unfortunately, the traditional approach offers very few clues to a strategist trying to determine why a particular candidate positioned where he did. What does it mean to be two-thirds of the way between Carter and Connally? The traditional approach based on continuous dimensions is not very helpful because it is based on very general concepts such as liberalism or conservatism, which provide no clear guide to differentiating among positions along the axis.[11] This problem has long vexed marketers searching to position new products at exact locations in an MDS's configuration (Green 1975; Myers 1979; Shocker and Srinavasan 1979). How could one find out

FIGURE 4.3. Illustrative Multidimensional Scaling Configuration for Selected Candidates for President in 1980.

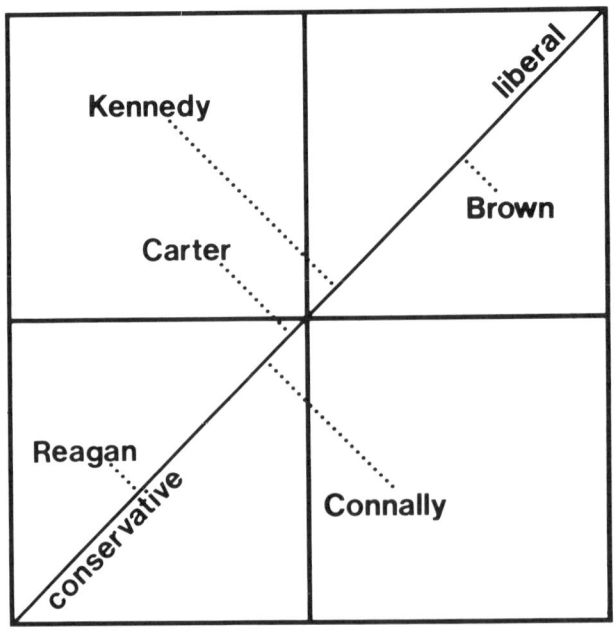

how to build a product so that it would position precisely at x = 8.6 units and y = 4.4?

An alternative approach is to view the structure as being generated by a large number of dimensions, where each of the dimensions has only a few discrete values (Stefflre 1972, 1979). This kind of data is often collected in political science to understand voters' images of political leaders, but it is rarely used to interpret spatial models (Campbell et al. 1960; Patterson 1980).

Discrete dimensions are used in linguistics with success to characterize the different speech sounds that occur in natural human languages (Jakobson and Halle 1956). It is also widely used in cognitive psychology and anthropology to characterize human information processes (Tyler 1969; Miller 1956; Bruner et al. 1956). Linguists find, for example, that each human language employs about 7 to 10 dimensions (distinctive characteristics) in identifying the speech sounds (phonemes) that are meaningful in that language. Typically, the distinctive characteristics are binary—although some are thought to be trinary (that is, to have three distinctive values rather than two). The alphabet (phonemic set) in a language consists of about 25-30 elements identified by various combinations of the 7 to 10 binary dimensions.

The discrete type of classification system appears to be quite powerful. It is spontaneously adopted by lay people (that is, not academics) in a wide range of situations (Miller 1956). Anthropologists and psychologists both have found discrete combinatorial frameworks useful in representing how people normally process information pattern recognition (Tulving and Donaldson 1972), kinship (Goodenough 1964), perception (Minsky 1975), semantic networks (Tyler 1969; Berlin and Kay 1969; Black and Metzger 1965), and choice behavior (Tversky 1972, 1977; Tversky and Sattath 1979).

Stefflre (1972, 1979b) has argued strongly that MDS models should be interpreted using discrete combinatorial frameworks. This approach would lead to a search for a number of discrete features that can discriminate among the objects rather than looking for two or three continuous dimensions that span the entire structure. Once such features have been identified, the analyst has a way to position each object in the space in relation to the other objects. For example, taking up the U.S. presidential candidates again, Table 4.1 shows several distinctive features that may be identified. (These particular features are merely for illustrative purposes; a better set could be developed by systematically analyzing respondents' comments.)

Regardless of how the MDS configuration is interpreted, the hypotheses about which features determine positioning in the structure should be tested in order to winnow down the alternatives. Hypotheses may be put to test by fashioning hypothetical candidates exhibiting the selected characteristics, presenting them to respondents in an independent sample, and determining where they position.

TABLE 4.1. Distinctive Features for 1980 U.S. Presidential Candidates (illustrative only)

	Party	Nuclear-Energy	Shah of Iran	Charisma
Brown	Dem.	anti	?	No
Carter	Dem.	pro	pro	No
Connally	Rep.	pro	pro	No
Kennedy	Dem.	?	anti	Yes
Reagan	Rep.	pro	pro	Yes

Note: Four binary features like those shown above are capable of discriminating among $2^4 = 16$ objects.

Perception and Preference Measures

The proximity measures used as input to the MDS analyses in this approach are described in this section. The choice of proximity measure is perhaps the most important decision facing the user of MDS techniques because of the fundamental role of input data in any analysis.

The strategic positioning approach depends upon two distinct proximity measures: an index of judged similarity to measure respondents' perceptions of candidates and parties, and intercorrelated preferences to measure the patterns of competition. These measures are described briefly in the following section. Readers interested in additional technical details are directed to an earlier article where these techniques are fully described (Mauser 1972).

Each of these measures are designed to be used in relatively large interviews (60-500 persons) and to include large numbers of stimuli (25 to 60 objects). Measures are designed to determine patterns in perceptions or preferences at the aggregate level rather than at the individual level. While a certain amount of information is lost concerning individual behavior by focusing on aggregate structures, models of aggregate structure are more useful to decision makers. Moreover, aggregate measures are more stable than are individual level measures. Early researchers in psychology, for example, were surprised at the consistently high level of agreement that they found in the aggregate structures (Messick 1956, 1961; Osgood and Suci 1955; Osgood, Suci, and Tannenbaum 1957).

Judged Similarity

This particular measure is a variant of what has been called pick $k/(n-1)$ data collection methods (Coombs 1964; Rao and Katz 1970). Respondents are presented with a list of objects (n) and requested to indicate for each object the other objects they think that it resembles. Respondents are asked in turn about each object on the list and are allowed up to a maximum number (k) of judgments per object.

The similarity judgments are then aggregated to yield a Judged Similarity Index for each pair of objects for the sample as a whole as well as for selected segments. The index, s_{ij}, may be expressed as

$$s_{ij} = \frac{2(f_{ij} + f_{ji})}{f_{i\text{-}} + f_{j\text{-}} + f_{\text{-}i} + f_{\text{-}j}}$$

Where f_{ij} is the frequency with which object i is judged to be similar to object j, f_{ji} is the frequency with which object j is judged to be similar to object i, and $f_{i\text{-}}$ is the marginal frequency that object i was judged to be similar to all other objects. $f_{\text{-}i}$ is the marginal frequency that all other objects were judged to be similar to object i. In similar fashion $f_{\text{-}j}$ and $f_{j\text{-}}$ are defined for object j. This expression yields a number ranging between 0 and 1.0 to indicate the relative similarity of objects in the domain. A symmetric proximity matrix is then fashioned using this index for the domain of objects for the full sample and for selected samples.

Pattern of Competition

The approach to measuring competition adopted here is based on estimating the extent to which objects tend to be preferred by the same people in a population. The precise measure used is the correlation of the preference rankings of pairs of objects across the sample of respondents using the Spearman *rho* correlation coefficient. The resulting correlations range between −1 and +1 and may be transformed into a suitable proximity index by adding 1.0 so that the range is positive. This transformation has the additional desired effect of reducing the importance of large disparities in the resulting scaling configuration.

Although imperfect, this index has several desirable properties. First, it only involves ordinal information so it avoids the stricter requirements of rating scale data, such as is used by the Survey Research Center at the University of Michigan. The use of rating scales forces respondents to adopt an artificial frame of reference, which introduces biases, and also requires assumptions about the comparability of interpersonal preference intensities. This assumption that preferences are interval-level (cardinal) data is unwarranted and leads to serious misrepresentation of voters' preferences. This issue is taken up again in Chapter 9.

Second, the use of Spearman's *rho* eliminates the evaluative component of preference, so that an object's position in the spatial model is not dependent on its relative level of preference. The elimination of the evaluative component is desirable in that the structure found in spatial analyses tends to be closely correlated with that identified in perceptual models based on samples from the same target population. The close relationship between preference and perceptual structures means that the features identified in these analyses tend to be more "actionable" (Huber and Holbrook 1979). This issue is taken up again in Chapter 10.

In these studies, preference rankings were obtained separately for political parties, names of political figures, and for concepts of new candidates or campaign themes. In each case, respondents were asked to rank them in the order that they preferred to see each hold the target political office (e.g., president, governor). Objects that share the same key features should position close to each other in the structure, since it is assumed that objects position in the underlying structure according to their key features. The positioning of the concepts and campaign themes permits hypotheses to be tested about the nature of the key features underlying the positioning of the politicians and the parties.

SUMMARY AND CONCLUSIONS

Procedures were described in this chapter for analyzing patterns of competition in political contests that were designed to help political candidates generate and screen alternative positions and postures that they may be considering adopting. This approach to positioning political candidates strategically is based on state-of-the-art procedures to develop new products and was originally developed by Volney Stefflre and was described in Chapter 3 (Brown et al. 1968; Stefflre 1968, 1972, 1979a; Silk 1969). The procedures are quite generally applicable and have been applied to a wide range of problem situations (e.g., a variety of consumer-goods markets, vacation opportunities, demands for health services, electoral strategy, and alternative living environments), and in a variety of countries (e.g., the United States, Brazil, Canada, France, Great Britain, Guatemala, Japan, Korea, Nigeria, and Mexico).

In politics, this approach to electoral analysis is unique. It is the only pragmatic approach for strategically positioning candidates that is based on an integrated set of marketing research techniques. While there are a large number of marketing research techniques being used at the present time in political campaigning (e.g., sample surveys and even MDS techniques), typically, such techniques are used on an ad hoc basis, and are often used without a full understanding of their limits. The approach described here has been applied in several political contests, subjected to repeated testing, and found to be useful in developing campaign strategy by the political candidates.

Moreover, the analytical framework underlying this approach is also unique. While the bulk of the work on elections has focused on understanding individual voting behavior, and has ignored political campaigning for the most part, the approach outlined here takes political campaigning as its central concern. This approach concentrates on modeling patterns of intercandidate (or interparty) competition rather than individual voting behavior. In common with only a small number of other studies, this approach relies on empirically developed spatial models to explain patterns of competition. However, in contrast to other approaches using spatial models, this approach does not take the spatial metaphor literally, but instead relies upon a discrete combinatorial framework to interpret the patterns of competition. Such an interpretive framework is particularly useful in positioning candidates precisely where desired in the competitive structure.

The approach described in this chapter should prove to be powerful primarily in highly visible political contests, where all candidates are equally matched with respect to campaign funds and organization, and are well known to the electorate. Such conditions are obviously not met in all elections. In low-level political contests that receive relatively little media attention (e.g., congressional races), strategic positioning may be less important than name recognition or organizational strength. However, even in such contests, positioning can play an important role in a candidate's strategy, and procedures similar to those presented here may be used to generate and screen alternative strategies under consideration.

The rest of the book examines these procedures more closely. Part II presents detailed case studies where this approach was used. A variety of elections are included. The first study looks at a U.S. presidential contest, while the other studies concern less visible contests—races for California governor and the French National Assembly.

After considering how these procedures can be used to develop campaign strategy, questions will naturally arise as to the validity of the procedures. These questions are taken up in Part III (Chapters 9, 10, and 11). The principal questions examined are: the validity of procedures for estimating the share of vote of candidates, the ability of the procedures to predict where new candidates and new issues will position in the competitive structure, and the stability of perceptions and preferences across time and across social groups.

NOTES

1. Political pros widely agree that campaigns should be kept simple if they are to be effective (Greenfield 1980; Kelley 1956, 1960; Leuthold 1968; Napolitan 1972; Nimmo 1970; Shadegg 1964, 1972; Steinberg 1976a). Dunn and Barban, in their excellent advertising text, succinctly explain why advertising campaigns should be organized around a simple coherent concept for maximum effectiveness (1978, Chapter 17). See also Kotler's (1982) description of the importance of maintaining a simple, easy to grasp "unique selling proposition" in competitive contests.

2. Multidimensional scaling techniques are discussed briefly in a nontechnical manner in the concluding section of this chapter. The reader who desires a more technical discussion of MDS procedures is urged to see Green (1975); Green and Carmone (1970); Jones (1974); Myers

(1979); Rabinowitz (1975); Romney et al. (1972); Schiffman et al. (1981); Shepard et al. (1972); Stefflre (1979b).

3. The use of ethnographic eliciting techniques differs somewhat from the standard approach in marketing and deserves discussion. Typically, academic marketers have focused on explaining individual decision making and have been concerned with identifying the "evoked sets" or the "relevant sets" of individual respondents (Howard and Sheth 1969; Silk and Urban 1978). Ethnographic techniques are less concerned with what any particular respondent finds acceptable, or is familiar with, as the goal is to model aggregate rather than individual decision making. The ethnographic approach is designed to ensure that no items are included in the domain that are not seen as belonging to that domain (in either a central or peripheral fashion) by voters as a group.

4. The index used here to measure judged similarity is described fully in a later section of this chapter. However, two characteristics of this index should be mentioned before going any further. First, it is designed to minimize problems arising from the different levels of familiarity among the political leaders. This is done by "double centering" the matrix (that is, by dividing the raw similarity of a pair of objects by the marginal totals for those objects). Double centering removes familiarity effects since the marginal totals are directly proportional to an objects' familiarity in the target population. Second, while this index forces symmetry, it does not force conformity with the triangle inequality. For further details see Mauser (1972) or Beals, Krantz, and Tversky (1968).

5. This index is similar to that used by the Survey Research Center at the University of Michigan (e.g., Weisberg and Rusk 1970) except that my index is based on preference rankings rather than "Feeling Thermometer" rating scale scores. Preference rankings, since they involve ordinal comparisons rather than absolute judgments as do rating scales, do not involve internal level measurement. As recently noted by Beniger (1979), interval level measurement requires that individual preference intensities be comparable across respondents, which cannot be done accurately.

6. Some researchers in political science have used *preference* correlations to indicate voters' *perceptions* (Converse 1966; Weisberg and Rusk 1970). This approach presumes that candidates who are preferred by the same voters are seen as resembling each other. Such an assumption needs to be subjected to empirical examination. This question is discussed further in Chapter 10.

7. The fundamental assumption of this approach is that the probability of finding a successful alternative is maximized by including a variety of distinct options to be considered. This variety should include distinct strategic options and not just different variants of the same basic strategy. This point was discussed in Chapter 3.

8. This discussion is freely adapted from the excellent article on multidimensional scaling techniques by Rabinowitz (1975). However, the insistence on discrete combinatorial frameworks, rather than continuous dimensions, to interpret spatial models, as well as the emphasis on cross-validation, is my own. In this respect, I have followed Stefflre (1979b).

9. These programs are available from their authors. For an up-to-date survey of these techniques, which also includes addresses at which to write for them, the reader is urged to see Rabinowitz (1975).

10. It is worth pointing out that there may not be a *true* dimensionality. This will pose a problem for the analyst if a large number of features are necessary to adequately describe the set of objects, or if the features have only a few distinct values (that is, if they are discrete), or if different features are required to discriminate objects in distinct regions of the space. Such characteristics are clearly nonspatial. In this case, the "best" MDS solution may be only a rough approximation of the underlying structure. Unfortunately, there is no reason to think that political perceptions or preferences should be inherently continuous. More about this point later.

11. The argument being made here is that global dimensions—of any type—may not be very useful in explaining local differences. Whether distance in the MDS model is measured using an interval or ordinal metric is irrelevant. There is no necessity that global dimensions exist in the MDS model. Positioning objects in the model precisely where one intends them to go requires a detailed knowledge of the local structure rather than the global dimensions.

PART II
POSITIONING POLITICAL CANDIDATES

The next four chapters illustrate how the strategic positioning approach described in Chapter 4 has been applied in a variety of political contests. This approach has been designed to assess strategic alternatives in any competitive political contest in any electoral system in the world—as long as the votes are honestly counted and reported. The campaigns analyzed here are quite diverse: multiparty and two-party contests, presidential, gubernatorial, and parliamentary elections, France and the United States, and contests that entail a high level of interest for citizens as well as those that citizens find much less interesting.

Each chapter briefly identifies the political context and then analyzes the electorate's perceptions and preferences. Two of the studies were conducted for political groups (see Chapters 6 and 7) and two (see Chapters 5 and 8) were academic projects. The reader concerned with political strategy may wish to skip the more academic chapters in preference for the more applied studies. For those readers interested in determining how the procedures work, or who have some statistical training, the academic chapters may prove to be more rewarding, as they are more technical.

The first two chapters look at American politics. Chapter 5 introduces the reader to the general principles behind the use of the strategic positioning approach to analyze political campaigns. This chapter examines a U.S. presidential contest to illustrate how candidates can be positioned to split the vote of preselected target candidates. This study was jointly funded by the National Science Foundation and the University of California at Irvine. Chapter 6 shows how this same approach was used as a pragmatic tool to identify strategic alternatives for the Democratic candidate for governor in a closely fought contest in California. This chapter discusses how campaign strategy was developed by the candidate and his staff.

The final two chapters in this section focus on French elections. Despite the differences between the French and American political systems, the strategic positioning approach is shown to be able to aid political candidates assess strategic opportunities. Chapter 7 examines how this approach was used by one of the major political parties to formulate strategy at the national

108 • POLITICAL MARKETING

level in the 1973 legislative elections. The strategic problem facing our client was to identify effective issue-positions in each of the constituencies where the party was fielding candidates. This problem was complicated by the need to find a small set of mutually consistent positions that could be effective against different sets of opponents. Chapter 8 selects a single legislative constituency and focuses on how the strategic positioning approach can be used to identify and screen strategic alternatives for legislative candidates in this constituency. This study was generously supported by the *Institut d'Etudes Politique* at the *Université de Grenoble* and provides a glimpse into citizens' perceptions and preferences in the French multiparty system.

5
THE ART OF STRATEGIC POSITIONING

> The American people have not been governed by political theory, but purely by opportunism. . . . Because of this plasticity we have been spared violent and bloody convulsions.
>
> Arthur M. Schlesinger, Sr.

To position candidates in an electoral contest requires an intimate knowledge of patterns of competition and vote-splitting. Vote-splitting refers to the tendency of certain candidates (or parties) to compete for the same voters and therefore to divide their common support. The strategic positioning approach, as described in the preceding chapter, provides detailed maps of the patterns of competition.

This chapter shows how the strategic positioning approach was used to predict patterns of competition and vote-splitting in a multicandidate U.S. presidential contest. To illustrate how this approach can be used to position candidates to split the vote of any preselected target candidate, this study examines how a wide variety of hypothetical candidates could be positioned in this contest.

Underlying the strategic positioning approach is the hypothesis that political candidates (or parties) will split each others' vote (or compete with each other) in any given election to the extent that voters see them as being similar to each other.[1] To the extent that this is true, patterns of vote-splitting for any candidate, actual or hypothetical, as well as alternative stands on issues, may be predicted from knowledge about voters' perceptions of political leaders and issues. Such an hypothesis may seem obvious to some readers and not worth empirical examination. Indeed, it is implicit in a variety of models of electoral phenomena (e.g., Downs 1957; Key 1964; Nie et al. 1976;

Scammon and Wattenberg 1970). However, other readers, perhaps those less persuaded by the rational capabilities of voters, would disagree, arguing that voters' perceptions and their preferences need not be intimately linked together. Candidates not seen as similar might split each others' vote for historical or organizational reasons. For example, during the 1968 presidential primaries, both George Wallace and Robert Kennedy were said to appeal to the same segment of the electorate, and thus to split their vote, even though few people thought they resembled each other (Converse et al. 1969).

In order to test this hypothesis, patterns of candidate similarity must be determined independently from measures of vote-splitting, otherwise the assertion is circular. This can be done, using the measures described in the preceeding chapter, if separate samples are drawn for measuring perceived similarity and for determining patterns of vote-splitting.

One of the objectives of this chapter is to examine the hypothesis that political candidates split their vote to the extent that they are seen as similar to each other in a U.S. election. The election chosen is the 1968 presidential contest, which was a three-way race between Richard M. Nixon, Hubert H. Humphrey, and George C. Wallace.[2] According to the hypothesis, George Wallace should draw more votes from either Nixon or Humphrey depending upon whom he is seen as resembling more.

In principle, this hypothesis holds for any third-party candidate who might enter the contest, and is not limited to George Wallace alone. This chapter, using simulation techniques, examines the extent to which similar candidates split their vote for a wide range of hypothetical third-party candidates in the 1968 presidential election, including verbal descriptions of various positions and postures as well as the names of a variety of contemporary figures.

This chapter is divided into three main sections. First, the importance of vote-splitting is discussed and some of the strategies to exploit its effects are touched on. Next, the critical, if sporadic, role of third-party candidates in U.S. elections is commented on, with special attention shown to the 1968 election. The balance of the chapter describes a study of the 1968 presidential contest that was undertaken to examine the hypothesis that political candidates split their vote to the extent that they are viewed as similar to each other.

VOTE-SPLITTING

Vote-splitting is a wide-spread but poorly understood phenomenon. A few campaigners have learned how to benefit from it, while others continue to lose elections because of it, never knowing what happened to them. Vote-splitting occurs in multicandidate contests whenever a few candidates appeal more to one segment than they do to the rest of the electorate. This common

Strategic Positioning • 111

appeal may, of course, be unintentional. By appealing to the same voters, these candidates compete more with each other, and draw votes away from each other—more than any of them do from the other candidates in the contest. An example will illustrate the phenomenon.

Consider a contest between three candidates: two are conservatives and one is liberal. If the electorate is evenly divided between liberals and conservatives, the liberal candidate clearly will win, since the two conservative candidates will split the conservative vote. Vote-splitting frequently occurs in multicandidate contests, such as presidential primary races and multiparty elections. It is not limited to any type of multicandidate contest, as candidates and electorates may be divided along any of a wide range of possible ways; cleavages in the electorate may exist along ethnic, religious, partisan, or ideological lines.

The phenomenon of vote-splitting has been recognized for a very long time. Political theorists since ancient Greece have been concerned about it and have devised a variety of voting systems to avoid or minimize its effects (see de Borda 1781; Farquarson 1969; Hare 1859; Nanson 1883; Lakeman and Lambert 1955). Vote-splitting is particularly strong in the "first past the post" system that is used in the United States, the United Kingdom, Canada, and in France (Rae 1971). Under this system, the candidate with largest number of votes (a plurality) is elected from each electoral district (e.g., state, riding, *circonscription*). Regardless of how many candidates are in the contest, voters cast only one vote, presumably for the candidate that they most prefer.

Politicians have not been slow in attempting to use vote-splitting to their advantage. There are a number of well known ways to do this, some of which may be used during the political campaign itself, while others are employed before the campaign even starts. One approach is to encourage additional opponents to enter a political contest, in order to draw votes away from the opposition. This tactic is most obvious in ethnically mixed districts. For example, a white candidate, facing a strong black opponent, may attempt to encourage a second black candidate to enter the race. In an effort to split the black candidate's vote, he may even go as far as indirectly funding the second black candidate's campaign. Of course, such ploys must be attempted very discretely.

Occasionally, a campaigner may wish to discourage a particular opponent who is politically too similar to him from entering a contest, if he suspects that the opponent would pull too many of his key supporters away from him. For example, the black candidate in the previous example might see if he could convince his black colleague not to enter the race. In addition to directly confronting the fellow, there are basically two types of approaches that he might use to do this: the carrot or the stick. A potential opponent might be lured away from entering the contest by indirectly arranging an offer for him of a better job. A job, of course, that would make it impossible for him to enter the contest. Alternatively, there is the stick. It may be possible to create difficulties for the potential opponent to mount a credible campaign, which would discourage him from entering. A variety of tactics exist to do this. For example, a potential campaign manager might be persuaded not to work for him, or perhaps, rich campaign contributors might be turned against him.

Once the campaign is under way and the list of candidates has been determined, more subtle ways must be found to take advantage of vote-splitting. To do so, detailed knowledge is required about the patterns of intercandidate competition (i.e., who competes with whom), and the perceived features of the candidates, which determine these patterns of competition. Once armed with this knowledge, a campaigner can select the issues or postures that position him against his competition in such a way that he can benefit from cleavages in the electorate to his advantage.[3]

The techniques described in the preceding chapter for mapping the electorate's perceptions and preferences have been designed to help campaigners discover and make effective use of patterns of competition (or vote-splitting) in multicandidate political contests. These techniques may be used to: evaluate alternative positions and postures that candidates are considering, position themselves strategically in the contest, and evaluate the impact on the election of the introduction of any new candidate.

This chapter examines how these techniques were used to predict patterns of vote-splitting in a multicandidate contest, while the next chapter takes up the use of these techniques to determine campaign strategy by evaluating alternative stands and postures for a candidate.

THIRD-PARTY CANDIDATES

U.S. politics traditionally has been dominated by the two major parties. While primary contests often involve three or more candidates, typically the only candidates on the ballot in the November general election are the nominees of the Democratic and Republican parties.[4] Occasionally, however, minor parties field candidates for state or federal offices, but such efforts rarely succeed in drawing even as much as 5 percent of the vote. Despite their meager share, however, in a close race candidates of minor parties can determine the outcome of the election by splitting the vote of one of the major candidates.

Several times in U.S. history, third-party candidates have had an impact on presidential elections.[5] In 1980, John Anderson frightened both Reagan and Carter by his strong early showing in the polls and primaries, but his support faded as the election drew closer.[6] Twice this century, Progressive party candidates have played a crucial role in presidential elections. In 1912 and again in 1924, Progressive party candidates were credited with drawing enough votes away from one of the major-party candidates to throw the election to his rival. In 1912 Theodore Roosevelt split the Republican vote to permit Woodrow Wilson, a Democrat, to become president; and in 1924, another candidate running under the Progressive banner, Robert LaFollette, drew enough votes from the Democratic candidate to permit the Republican, Calvin Coolidge, to win. More recently, Southern conservatives have twice tried to deadlock the electoral college by running third-party candidates. In 1948, the Dixiecrats almost threw the election to Republicans in their efforts to keep Harry Truman from being elected. Again in 1968, George Wallace's avowed purpose was to split the Democratic vote.

No doubt, the future will hold other important challenges by minor-party candidates in U.S. presidential elections. Not only have third parties periodically arisen throughout U.S. history, but the increasing volatility of public opinion during the 1970s and 1980s suggests that the time is ripe for new third-party movements. Two factors particularly contribute to this situation; the systematic decline of party loyalty since World War II and the increasing power of single-issue activist groups in U.S. politics.[7]

While the minor parties that have had the most success have typically split off from one of the major parties, it is very difficult to predict the nature of their impact on the contest (*The Wall Street Journal* 1964). For example, the Progressives, essentially a Republican splinter group, drew more votes from the Republican candidate in 1912 but drew more from the Democratic candidate in 1924. Also, in 1968, it was difficult to determine during the campaign whether George Wallace would hurt the Republican candidate (Richard Nixon) more or the Democratic candidate (Hubert Humphrey). The problem is compounded by the tendency of many political observers to ask the wrong questions about the nature of third-party contests. The key question is to ask about third-party candidates is not what type of voters favor them, but who are their supporters' second choices (that is, who their supporters would have voted for if that candidate had not been in the race).

In general, the entry of minor candidates into a normal two-party electoral contest can influence the outcome of the election in any of three distinct ways: by influencing who turns out to vote, by altering individual voters' preferences for the candidates, or by splitting one or more of the major candidates' vote. Each of these factors can operate independently of the others so that any combination of the three may be present in any one electoral contest.

First, including minor party candidates on the ballot might influence which voters, or how many of each kind, come to the polls on election day. The entry into the political contest of minor candidates might motivate some citizens to vote who might otherwise have not bothered, while other citizens might be discouraged from turning out to vote. Such a change in the composition of the voting population could alter the election results, even if the minor candidate failed to win the election. For example, blacks in the

South are voting in increasing proportions, drawn to the polls, in part, by the presence of black candidates on the ballot. Even if black candidates do not win, these new voters may determine which white candidate does. The Dixiecrat challenge in 1948 is credited with motivating blacks to turn out to vote in that election at record levels in order to vote against them (Key 1964). However, the belief in the existence of a significant segment of the electorate, untapped by the existing candidates, that would rally to the banner of a new and different candidate, proved illusory both for Goldwater in 1964 and for McGovern in 1972 (Converse et al. 1965; Miller and Miller 1976).

Second, minor party candidates might influence voters' political preferences directly so that voters' opinions differ from what they would have been in a normal two-party contest. Political preferences might be altered in any of several ways: issues might be raised that otherwise would not have been raised (or at least which would have been minimized), the importance of the differences among the major candidates might be reevaluated if minor candidates take an extreme position on an old dimension,[8] opinions about who the voters think could win the election might change, and the major candidates might change their campaign strategy in some way to attract the supporters (or the opponents) of the minor candidate. All of these effects can operate directly on the electorate through the media, or indirectly through changes in the ability of the major candidates to campaign effectively by inhibiting their ability to raise campaign funds or volunteers.

Third, minor candidates might draw votes directly away from one or more of the major candidates. Independently of any other effect that they may have on the election, minor candidates, by entering the contest, might siphon off votes from the major candidates. This can occur even if voters' political preferences are fixed and do not change during the election campaign. As discussed earlier, minor candidates can swing the election by drawing disproportionately from the vote of one of the major candidates in the contest.

This section has discussed the importance and difficulty of predicting the impact of minor party candidates on the normally two-party U.S. elections. In the next section we show how the techniques described in the previous chapter were successfully used to predict the patterns of vote-splitting in a recent presidential election.

THE SETTING OF THE ELECTION

In 1968, George Wallace launched an audacious drive to deadlock the electoral college; he was almost successful in his attempt. Wallace posed a greater challenge than the Dixiecrats had in 1948, because he was on the ballot in almost all 50 states as the nominee of the American Independent Party. His avowed goal was to split the Democratic vote in the important industrial states in the North. He hoped that, by denying key states to the Democratic candidate, no candidate would be able to win a clear majority of the vote in the electoral college.[9] In such circumstances, the Constitution provides that the House of Representatives must decide which of the presidential candidates will be elected president. Once the election had been thrown in the House, Wallace could have negotiated with Democratic and Republican party leaders for major policy concessions in return for his support. At the worst, Wallace figured his candidacy would throw the election to the Republican candidate. Since the Republican party's views on racial integration, states' rights, and the Vietnam War were much closer to Wallace's views than were those of the Democratic party, such an outcome would not have been seen as a complete failure by Wallace or by his supporters.

Wallace's plans, however, depend on his splitting the Democratic vote. His candidacy would help keep the Democrats in power if he actually drew more votes from the Republican candidate than from the Democratic candidate. Wallace ignored such a possibility, but some political observers were not so confident. During the campaign, it was an open question whether Wallace would draw more votes from Hubert Humphrey, the Democratic candidate, or from Richard Nixon, the Republican. Plausible arguments were made supporting both contentions. Nixon feared losing "the Goldwater vote" in the deep south and elsewhere. Since their positions were similar on several important issues, Wallace was seen as attracting the votes of ideological conservatives that Nixon needed to win. Humphrey, on the other hand, focused on Wallace's strong appeal to blue-collar workers and union members. Since these groups overwhelmingly vote Democratic, Humphrey was alarmed at the prospective loss of the support among traditional Democratic segments. He too feared that Wallace would split his vote.

Public opinion polls provided support for the concerns of both candidates. The two best known pollsters, George Gallup and Louis Harris, supported conflicting conclusions about Wallace's impact on the election. While they agreed that most of Wallace's supporters were nominal Democrats, they disagreed on the implications of this support. Harris, in two separate surveys, found that most of Wallace's supporters reported that they had voted for Goldwater in 1964, and that they would have voted for Nixon if Wallace had not been in the race (August 24 and September 13, 1968). Gallup, however, was less incisive in his questioning. Gallup's surveys were limited to an examination of the social and economic groups that supported each of the candidates. Gallup's findings, that Wallace drew most of his support from blue-collar workers and from unionized labor (e.g., 1968), were widely cited as supporting the contention that Wallace would split the Democratic vote.

In addition, the size of the Wallace vote was difficult to estimate. During the campaign, estimates of his nationwide support ranged from 9 percent

(Gallup, 1968) to 21 percent (Harris, September 1968), and averaged around 14 percent throughout September and October. The size of his electoral vote was much harder to estimate, as it depended on Wallace's share of vote in each of the 50 states. Nevertheless, the fear of a deadlocked electoral college were taken seriously enough to provoke a spate of concern about reforming the electoral system (Sperling 1968; Converse et al. 1969).

METHODS

This section identifies the reasons that lay behind selecting California as a site for this study, shows how the list of political and social leaders used in the study was determined, and describes the samples that were drawn of the California electorate.

Selecting the Site

The study was conducted in California for three reasons: states are the natural political unit in U.S. presidential elections, California is a uniquely interesting state because of its political volatility, and it was convenient, as I had already conducted electoral studies in that state, which could be used to look at the evolution of political preferences and perceptions over a span of time not usually covered in studies of political campaigns.

The state, not the nation, is the most appropriate unit for studying the impact of vote-splitting in U.S. presidential elections. Under the U.S. Constitution, presidents are elected by the electoral college rather than by direct popular vote.[10] The electoral college is composed of delegations from each of the 50 states, where the size of each delegation is proportional to state's population. Since a state's electoral vote goes to the candidate who managed to win a plurality in that state during the election, traditionally on a "winner take all" basis, presidential campaigns are organized on a state-by-state basis.[11] Consequently, surveys should be conducted at the state level in order to understand the influence of vote-splitting on presidential politics.

Identifying Presidential Candidates

To understand the electorate's perceptions of the candidates in any given political contest, it is necessary to identify the full range of political leaders that voters see as relevant to that contest. This permits a comprehensive analysis of the patterns of similarity and competition that exist in the particular electoral contest for the full-range of contemporary leaders.

By using the eliciting techniques described in the previous chapter, a comprehensive list of 25 names of political, social, and religious leaders was compiled in the 1968 presidential contest. This list includes every major candidate for president as well as candidates representing important minor constituencies. Table 5.1 presents this list.

Drawing Samples

Following the approach described in Chapter 4, four independent samples of California voters were drawn and interviewed prior to the November 1968 presidential election. The first sample consisted of ten respondents who were interviewed, using an "eliciting technique," to determine the appropriate set of political and social leaders to include in the study. This interview determined the names of 25 leaders that were used in the study. In the second sample, 65 respondents were asked about their perceptions of these 25 political and social leaders (the Judged Similarity Sample). Interviewing in the second sample was conducted in two separate waves to look at how perceptions evolved during the campaign. First, 36 respondents were interviewed in July, before the Democratic and Republican parties held their conventions to choose their party's presidential nominee; then 29 respondents were interviewed in September, after the presidential nominees had been determined. Voters' perceptions were analyzed using MDS techniques and hypotheses formulated about how voters categorize politicians, the features of politicians that voters see as being the most important, and which politicians would split their vote in multicandidate contests.

Very small samples were drawn for the first two types of interviews because of the homogeneity that was expected in people's political perceptions (Abelson 1955; Messick 1956; Osgood, Suci, and Tannenbaum 1957;

TABLE 5.1. Political and Social Leaders Included in Judged Similarity and Small Scale Preference Interviews

1. Edmund G. "Pat" Brown	14. Maxwell Rafferty
2. Stokely Carmichael	15. Ronald Reagan
3. Everett Dirksen	16. Nelson A. Rockefeller
4. Dwight D. Eisenhower	17. John G. Schmitz
5. Barry M. Goldwater	18. Dr. Benjamin Spock
6. Hubert Humphrey	19. Adlai Stevenson
7. Lyndon B. Johnson	20. Jesse M. Unruh
8. John F. Kennedy	21. George Wallace
9. Robert F. Kennedy	22. Earl Warren
10. Martin Luther King, Jr.	23. Lawrence Welk
11. John V. Lindsay	24. Gen. William C. Westmoreland
12. Eugene J. McCarthy	25. Samuel Yorty
13. Richard Nixon	26. My ideal candidate for president

Note: The "my ideal candidate" category was included only in the Judged Similarity Interviews.

Stefflre 1965). A loose quota system was used to collect these samples. An effort was made to include people of different sexes, races, religion, and party affiliations.

To test the hypotheses listed above, two other samples were drawn from the same target population. First, the Small Scale Preference Sample was drawn. In October, 193 respondents were asked to rank order a list of hypothetical candidates for president. This list of candidates included the names of political and social leaders used in the Judged Similarity Interview as well as 25 other candidates identified by verbal descriptions. This sample, like the two earlier samples, was only crudely representative of the California electorate, as only quota sampling methods were used to select respondents. The primary variables considered in this sample were race, religion, party affiliation, county of residence, and income level.

The fourth and last sample (the Large Scale Preference Sample) was drawn to estimate the share of the vote candidates would receive in the presidential election and to test hypotheses developed from the earlier samples. Respondents were interviewed over the telephone during the four days immediately preceeding the November general election. Using a balanced lattice procedure, respondents were asked to rank order eight candidates for president according to their preferences.

A multistage probability sampling method was used to select 1,500 registered voters from California for the fourth sample. This survey was conducted in two stages. First, four replicated samples of telephone numbers of private households throughout California were selected using multistage probabilty procedures (Kish 1965). Next, interviewers called the selected households in search of a registered voter. The exact procedure that was followed is described more fully elsewhere (Mauser 1972). Table 5.2 shows the key features of each of these four samples.

RESULTS

The central objective of this study was to examine patterns of vote-splitting for alternative third-party candidates. Since it was hypothesized that similar candidates would compete more with each other than with other candidates, the first step was to carefully map the electorate's perceptions and preferences. The results of this study fall naturally into three topics: the electorate's perceptions of the political and social leaders, the patterns of competition among these leaders, and an examination of the hypothesis that political candidates compete with each other (split their vote) to the extent that they are seen by the electorate as being similar to each other.

Political Perceptions

Spatial models were constructed of the electorate's perceptions of the political and social leaders using MDS techniques as described in Chapter 4.

TABLE 5.2. Samples Drawn in 1968 California Study

Sample	Stimuli	Date Interviewed	Sample Sizes
Eliciting technique	—	May	10
Judged similarity	25 names	June/September	65
Small scale preference	25 names 25 descriptions	October	193
Large scale preference	5 names 3 descriptions	November 1–4	1,161

Figure 5.1 shows the two-dimensional solution (perceptual map) that was found when all respondents are grouped together, and Figure 5.2 shows the three-dimensional solution for the same respondents.[12]

As can be easily seen, the Democratic or liberal leaders are found on the left side of the structure, while the Republican or conservative leaders are on the right side. Interestingly enough, the "extremists' or "radicals," of both the right or the left, are clustered together in the upper-center of the figure. Moreover, well-known national and state-level office holders of both parties tend to cluster together at the bottom of the figure.

The overall impression of the figure is that of a doughnut or bagel—that is, all the items are distributed around the rim of a circle with none in the center (or hole). The same phenomenon is seen in the three-dimensional model, where items take the shape of a hollow basketball since all items are found on the surface or rough sphere. The circular structure stems from the electorate's perceptions of the leaders, not from any artifact in the data analysis (Mauser 1970, pp. 128-29).

The first step in analyzing the electorate's perceptual map is to locate clusters of similar leaders. Five clusters immediately fall out, either by "eyeballing" the spatial map or by using clustering techniques (Johnson 1967):

1. Johnson, Humphrey, Brown, Unruh, (Dirksen)
2. Eisenhower, Westmoreland, Dirksen, Welk, (Nixon)
3. Wallace, Rafferty, Reagan, Schmitz, Yorty, Goldwater, Nixon,
4. Carmichael, Spock, King, (Wallace), (Rafferty)
5. John Kennedy, Robert Kennedy, The Ideal,[13] Rockefeller, Lindsay, Stevenson, McCarthy, Warren

The most succinct way to think of this structure is to imagine two underlying dimensions: political party and ideology combined together, which runs from liberal Democrats (John Kennedy) to Republican conservatives (Barry Goldwater); and political style, running from the extremists

FIGURE 5.1. Two-dimensional Perceptual Map (M-D-SCAL Solution for Judged Similarities, All Respondents, N = 63, Stress = 0.259)

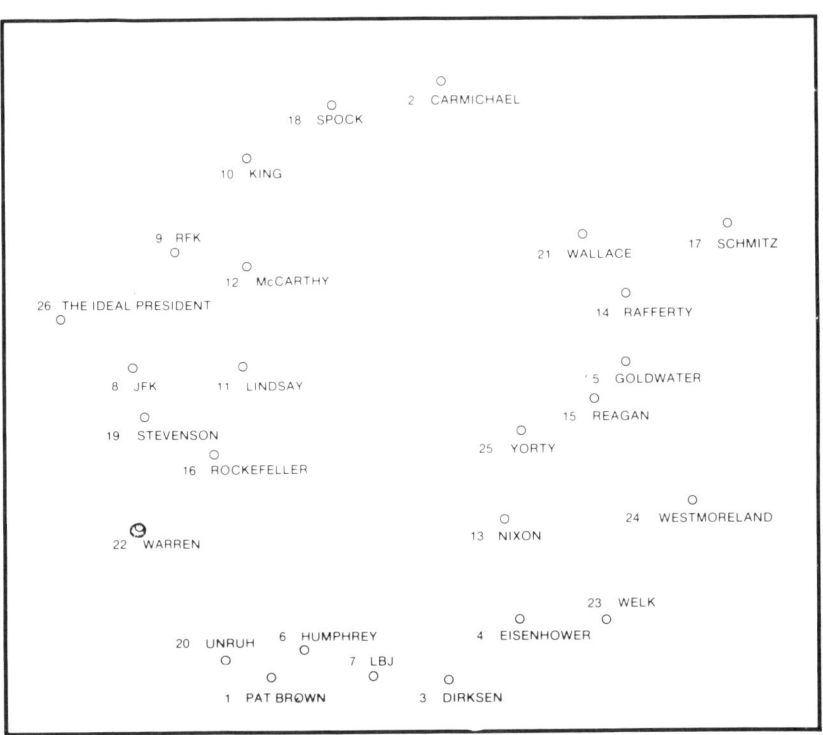

(Carmichael or Wallace) to the moderate leaders (Lyndon Johnson and Everett Dirksen). The first dimension appears to be essentially dichotomous, in that Democrats (or liberals) and Republicans (or conservatives) tend to cluster at opposite ends of the configuration. In contrast, the second dimension has leaders scattered all along its length without separate clusters being too evident (see Figure 5.1).

These two underlying dimensions are sufficient to explain the basic patterns of political leaders that are found in both the two- and three-dimensional configurations. Various interpretations of the third dimension may be made, but none are very satisfactory. Rather than artificially concoct a third dimension, it seems wiser to abandon the search. Moreover, these are the only two dimensions that reappear in the preference data.

To interpret this map of political perceptions, respondents' comments about the leaders in the Judged Similarity Interview were content analyzed. The objective was to identify the features that these leaders were seen as

FIGURE 5.2. Three-Dimensional Perceptual Map (M-D-SCAL Solution for Judged Similarities, All Respondents, N = 63, Stress = 0.183)

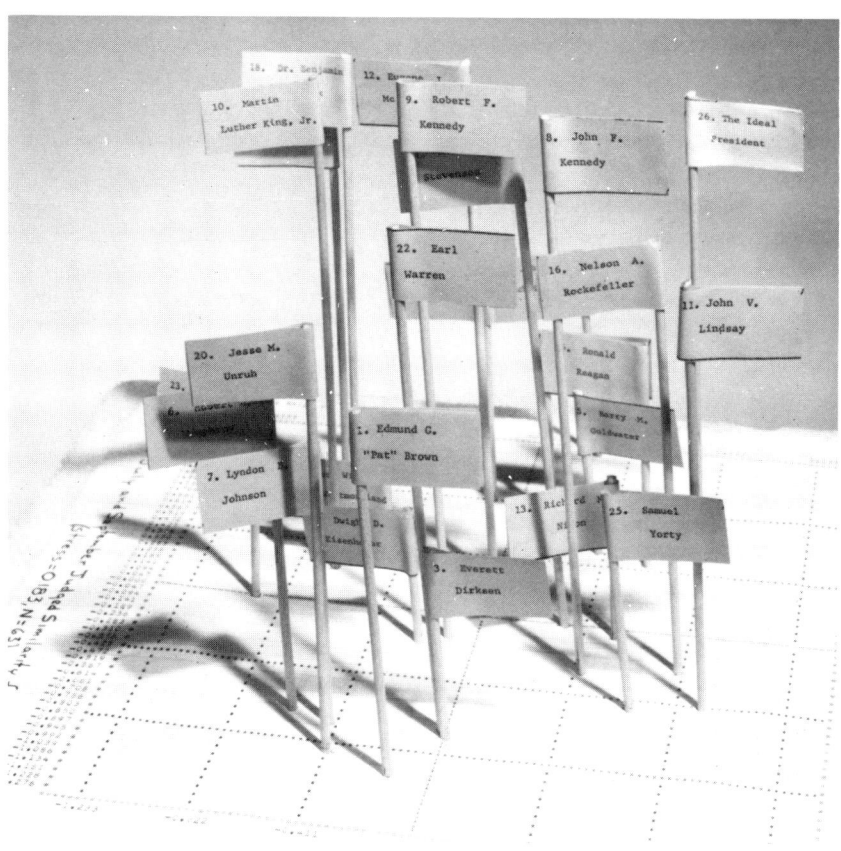

Source: Mauser (1972).

having by the electorate, which presumably caused them to position as they did in the structure. An ethnographic approach was used to ensure that the data were analyzed from the point of view of the voters rather than from that of the political leaders (Frake 1962; Metzger and Williams 1963; Black and Metzer 1965). Such an approach emphasizes the importance of using analyses that respect the respondents' natural organization and their terminology as much as possible (Tyler 1969). Tables 5.3 and 5.4 illustrate respondents' comments about George Wallace and Robert Kennedy.

TABLE 5.3. Characteristics of George Wallace Mentioned by Republican Voters in Judged Similarity Interview (September 1968)

Carmichael:
Wallace is an intelligent radical, Carmichael is a basic radical. Intelligent radical—gilds the lily. Basic radical—stands with might, like going to "switch you."
Extremists—polarized—want to use violent means to achieve an end or change something they don't like.
Both are racists. Neither one tries to see any good in opinions other than their own.
Both want to take all our freedom starting a little at a time. Both are too extreme in the measures they are trying for.
Trying to wreck the country—Carmichael the blacks—Wallace through the whites.

Goldwater:
Straighten things out instead of fooling around. Believe in strong armed riot control. Both believe in upholding the police and cutting out a lot of this foreign spending.

Humphrey:
Both running for president. Both losing.

King:
Both want to rule, take a little freedom away and slowly work to take it all. Both are two-faced as can be.
King was for the blacks and stirred them up. Wallace stirs up whites.

McCarthy:
Strongly opinionated about platforms. Wallace is going to save South for whites by not putting up with civil rights movements. McCarthy is unyielding, like when he lost to Nixon, like Wallace is going to lose to Nixon.

Nixon:
Running for president. Dislikes Humphrey.
They don't have showmanship. In person they give out a warmth, but on TV they just don't have it. They have loyal supporters in groups of people who know them personally, but on TV they don't come across.
Republicans. Running for president. Stronger domestic law enforcement.

Rafferty:
Excel in their ability to confound masses of middle-class voters. Emotions and distortions of fact seem to be the vanguard of their attacks on other opinion.
Does the same things as Rafferty in an unsophisticated way. He thinks he is right. Wallace does not have the worldliness to lead the country. The way he handled his state would indicate he could not gain respect of world for any higher office, being so dictatorial—but not sophisticated.

Rockefeller:
Running for president.

Schmitz:
In that they represent some of the narrowest and dangerously conservative thinking of any politicians in the United States today. Both have immediate and oversimplified solutions to problems of today.

TABLE 5.3. (continued)

Unruh:
   Both are power-hungry for political office.
   They take opposite sides in their political opinions, they take opposite sides of a situation.

Warren:
   Both are men that will say what they think regardless of whether they'll be popular or not, they'll still do what they want to do.

Yorty:
   Against some of this integration. Believe in a little bit more law and order. At least they'll come out and say it whether they're popular or not.
   Both believe in enforcing law and order.

Ideal:
   (If he lives up to what he says, and I believe he would) to get back law and order in this country to where it should be, so you can walk down the streets safely anytime.

Source: Mauser (1972).

Each of the five clusters seen in the perceptual map can be characterized using the respondents' comments. Despite painstaking efforts to identify features that apply to all members of a given cluster, it was not always possible to do so. Occasionally, some of the features will not apply to one or two members of a cluster, even though such features distinguish the other members of that cluster from all the remaining leaders. It is not clear how to treat such deviant cases. Perhaps the feature in question should not be thought of as characterizing that cluster. Perhaps the deviant member does not belong to that cluster despite appearances. Or, perhaps the best way to think of these clusters is using the notion of "family resemblence" (Wittgenstein 1966), rather than the Aristotelian notion of "essential" characteristics. Whatever, hypotheses about which features determine positioning in the structure may be tested empirically by devising hypothetical candidates and inserting them in the preference interview.

The Johnson cluster—which includes Johnson, Humphrey, Brown, Unruh, and more weakly, Dirksen—is primarily described as "experienced," "partisan politicians," and "expedient." The members of this cluster are identified as the men who control the national political parties and are seen as putting the interests of their political parties ahead of their own interests. Thus, they are described as expedient rather than "idealistic" or "standing up for what they believe." Their role as "brokers" within the political parties is recognized but not seen as a positive attribute in a presidential candidate. Except for Dirksen, all of these candidates are clearly identified as Democrats.

The Eisenhower cluster—Eisenhower, Westmoreland, Dirksen, Welk, and to a lesser extent, Nixon—is closely identified with the features "conservative" and "Republican." With the exception of Lawrence Welk,

TABLE 5.4. Characteristics of Robert Kennedy Mentioned by Democratic Voters in Judged Similarity Interview (September 1968)

Brown:
   RFK being young had the potential to become a Pat Brown in terms of his accomplishments—help unify the country like Brown did for California. RFK was starting and Brown was the end; young and old.

John Kennedy:
   They are from the same family. Have the same family feeling. Bring up kids broadly. Dynastic idea.
   Brothers, Catholics, Democrats.
   Idealistic, charismatic quality. Leadership.
   Had a real interest in helping their country. At least if they were competitive, they had something to give to their country.
   Brothers, popular, charismatic; good politicians; know how to work with and manipulate people; progressive urban concerned Democrats; liberal and peace loving.
   Dedicated public servants. Sacrificed their talents and capabilities for the improvement overall of the country.
   Peace in Vietnam. Equality for all races.

King:
   Crusaders, had a great deal of potential that was never tapped; both were willing to take a chance against public feeling or pressures.
   Leadership quality. Care about people.
   Both men of peace. Peaceful solutions to Negro problems.
   Workers. Go beyond the system (beyond the framework) right to the people—to the problem.

Lindsay:
   They've so many abilities, but more than that, it comes out and hits you. Charisma.

McCarthy:
   Believe in idea of peace in Vietnam.

Rockefeller:
   Looking for a new liberalism in their parties. Out for discovering new and better ways of doing things.
   Use personality, (theirs) well. They exploit it. Advertising image. Opportunistic.
   Having a female reaction—give me the impression of being able to influence the female population. Both men of wealth.

Spock:
   Both say what they believe in gut level—whether it's popular or not.

Stevenson:
   Idealistic. They have-updated New Deal liberalism by expanding foreign policy with more of an international concept of coexistence.
   Both had greatness—statesmanship. Don't just think of the country, but for the people, the individuals. They had love.

TABLE 5.4. (continued)

Unruh:
Both peace advocates and try to further their political well-being.
Worked together in RFK's campaign—try hard at being politicians; sometimes have a ruthless image—willing to compromise for party expediency and personal gain; progressively liberal democrats.
Unruh announced JFK for president. Both liberal. Both against war in Vietnam. For equality for all.
Organizationalists—believe in planning everything.

Warren:
Humanitarian interest—give equal opportunity to all people.
Criticized for divergent views from mainstream of American thought. Controversy—always in the eye of the public, so they just retreated.
Liberal views. Fair, sincere. Against discrimination. For equality for all.
Secure, fair, unbiased, sincere.
Realization of legal thoughts of minorities. Far-sighted—can see where things will lead.

Yorty:
Disliked by large segments. Pragmatists.

Ideal:
Because like his brother John, took stance on issues. Had convictions. Tried to get at causes behind riots, give Negroes some self-respect, don't just put them on welfare.
He seems to have had real empathy for people who were down-trodden today. He really seemed to care.
Capable of achieving idealistic ends with practical means. Farsighted.

Source: Mauser (1972).

they are also described as "patriotic" and "experienced." While Welk is definitely identified as a Republican, and patriotic, he is not seen as politically experienced. He is probably placed in this cluster because his personality is seen as similar to Eisenhower's and Dirksen's, and thus it is inferred that he would share their partisan affiliation and ideological characteristics.

The first two clusters (Johnson's and Eisenhower's) are both seen as being older and more experienced, and as containing the leaders of the national political parties. The two names judged to be the most similar of all of the possible pairings were Eisenhower and Westmoreland. This strong similarity appears to be due to the wide recognition that both men are, or were, army generals. In addition, both are seen as "very patriotic" and as being "strong leaders." Despite this powerful similarity, this does not imply that Westmoreland could have inherited Eisenhower's mantle of popularity. At the very least, "Westy" would have had to return home as a victorious, military hero, as did Eisenhower, and this did not happen. Nevertheless, in 1968, people who were strongly attracted to Ike were attracted to Westy more than most voters because of their similar images. It is interesting to note that

Westmoreland did try for political office in Virginia (as a Republican), after retiring from the military, but he was not successful.

The Kennedy cluster, which includes John Kennedy, Robert Kennedy, Rockefeller, Lindsay, Stevenson, McCarthy, Warren, and the "ideal president," is primarily identified as "sincere and honest," "willing to stand up for what they believe," "crusaders," and as being "compassionate." Sincerity and high-mindedness are their most salient features. To a lesser extent, this cluster is seen as being "of high leadership quality," "experienced," and as either presidential candidates or former presidents. Except for McCarthy, all are seen as being "liberal" and to "believe in equality for all"; and except for Rockefeller and John Kennedy, all are seen to favor pulling out of Vietnam. Finally, there is a tendency to consider these candidates as "sophisticated Easterners."

The Carmichael cluster, including Carmichael, Spock, King, and to a lesser extent, Wallace and Rafferty, is described as "extremist," "racist," prone to "violence," and as "demagogues." Despite the substantial difference in the substance of the political views of these men, their political styles tend to set them apart from the other candidates, even those with similar views. The similarity between Carmichael and Wallace is one of the strongest in the entire set. Except for Wallace and Rafferty, the others are described as "for Negroes," and as wanting to pull out of Vietnam. The tendency for the extremists of the left and right to be seen as similar to each other suggests the existence of a political circle, rather than a one dimensional spectrum, to represent the underlying structure.[14] It was hypothesized that this circular structure would not be strongly reflected in the pattern of preference structure.

The final cluster is the Wallace grouping (Wallace, Rafferty, Reagan, Schmitz, Goldwater, Yorty, and Nixon). It is described primarily as "advocating 'law and order' policies," and as being "aggressive," and "anti-Negro." They are also seen as wanting to increase military activity in Vietnam in order to win the war. Except for Wallace and Yorty, all the members of this cluster are clearly described as Republicans, and even Wallace and Yorty are described as Republicans as often as they are described as Democrats. In general, this cluster contains those candidates who are seen as willing to use armed forces (either police or military) to enforce governmental authority.

To test hypotheses about which features determined positioning, a wide variety of hypothetical candidates were concocted from voters' comments in the Judged Similarity Interview. Candidates were devised to take clear stands on salient policy questions, to exhibit definite personalities, to mouth selected campaign slogans, to appeal to certain social groups, and to match actual politicians.

It should be possible to infer a political leader's most important features from the hypothetical candidates that position close to him in the structure, since the hypothetical candidates should position near to the leaders with whom they are seen as sharing essential characteristics. Table 5.5 shows the hypothetical candidates that were introduced in the preference interview.

Patterns of Competition

If candidates judged to be similar are preferred by the same kinds of people as hypothesized, then the basic structure should be the same for both

TABLE 5.5. Hypothetical Candidates Included in the Small Scale Preference Interview

26. A president we could be proud of who would set a fine example.
27. An experienced, mature Republican who is running for president again.
28. A candidate who wants to eliminate poverty and slums in the United States.
29. A good Christian American who could set a good example for the country as president.
30. A candidate who wants an honorable end to the Vietnam War.
31. A president who guarantees a job with a decent wage for everybody.
32. A patriotic American who would be a strong leader as president.
33. A liberal Democratic nominee who supports organized labor.
34. A president who can win the Vietnam War.
35. A president who would support the police and stop the courts from coddling criminals.
36. The vice-president of the United States and the Democratic nominee for president.
37. A candidate who wants the United States to immediately withdraw from Vietnam.
38. A president who could unite the nation and heal our troubled cities.
39. A president who wouldn't be afraid to stop Negro rioters and student anarchists.
40. A man who is willing to stand up for his beliefs regardless of the consequences.
41. A Republican nominee who supports the free enterprise system and fiscal responsibility in government.
42. A candidate who would use nuclear weapons if necessary to win the Vietnam War.
43. A president who will sincerely search for peace.
44. A candidate who will work to end white racism in the United States.
45. The incumbent president who is a shrewd politician and who would continue pretty much the same policies as before.
46. A candidate who will enforce law and order in our cities.
47. An idealistic intellectual who wants the United States to unconditionally stop bombing North Vietnam.
48. A candidate who believes in states' rights: that the states should be able to handle their own racial problems.
49. A president who would cut federal spending and reduce taxes.
50. A young, dynamic senator who believes in civil rights and who appeals to the youth and to the minorities.

the Judged Similarity and the Pattern of Competition data. The same clusters should be observable in both MDS configurations and the same dimensions should span them. This should be true even though the structures were derived from independent samples of California voters, and different types of measurements were made on each. The relative importance of the features might differ, causing clusters to be stretched or compressed, but any other difference in pattern would indicate that some new factor, not present in the similarity structure, was operating in the Pattern of Competition structure.

The Pattern of Competition structure can be inferred from either Figure 5.3, the three-dimensional MDS configuration, or from Figure 5.4, the two-dimensional MDS configuration.

The most salient aspect of the Pattern of Competition structure is its polarization. Almost all of the candidates—names and descriptions—are tightly grouped into two clusters situated at opposite ends of the configuration. Only 6 of the 50 candidates can be found between these two clusters. This contrasts with the circular or basketball structure observed in the Judged Similarity configuration where no tendency was observed for it to break up into polar groupings.

The first cluster contains all of the Democrats except Yorty and only two Republicans (Lindsay and Warren). Inspecting the Judged Similarity verbatims shows that almost all of these candidates are described as "liberal" in terms of their foreign or domestic policies. The descriptions that position in this cluster may also be used to infer its important features.

Only the descriptions that are "liberal" in some sense, or refer to Democrats, position in this cluster. For example, some of the descriptions that cluster here are, "a candidate who wants the United States to immediately withdraw from Vietnam," "a candidate who wants to eliminate poverty and slums in the United States," and "The vice-president of the United States and the Democratic nominee for president."

The other cluster contains all of the Republicans (except Lindsay, Rockefeller, and Warren), a single Democrat (Sam Yorty), and George Wallace, an ex-Southern Democrat and founder of the American-Independent splinter party, and General Westmoreland—who is identified as a Republican by most respondents. Inspecting the Judged Similarity verbatims shows that these candidates are described as either "Republican," "conservative," or "hawkish." Looking at the descriptions that cluster close to these candidates we find that all of the descriptions matching these labels position in this cluster. For example, "a President who can win the Vietnam War," "a president who would cut federal spending and reduce taxes," and "a candidate who will enforce law and order in our cities."

The remaining candidates were scattered throughout the area between the two major clusters. Only six candidates—two names and four descriptions—escaped being polarized, as they appealed equally to Republicans and

Strategic Positioning • 129

FIGURE 5.3. Three-dimensional Map of Patterns of Competition (M-D-SCAL Solution for Preference Correlations in Small Scale Preference Interview, All Respondents, N = 193, All 50 Political Figures, Stress = 0.113)

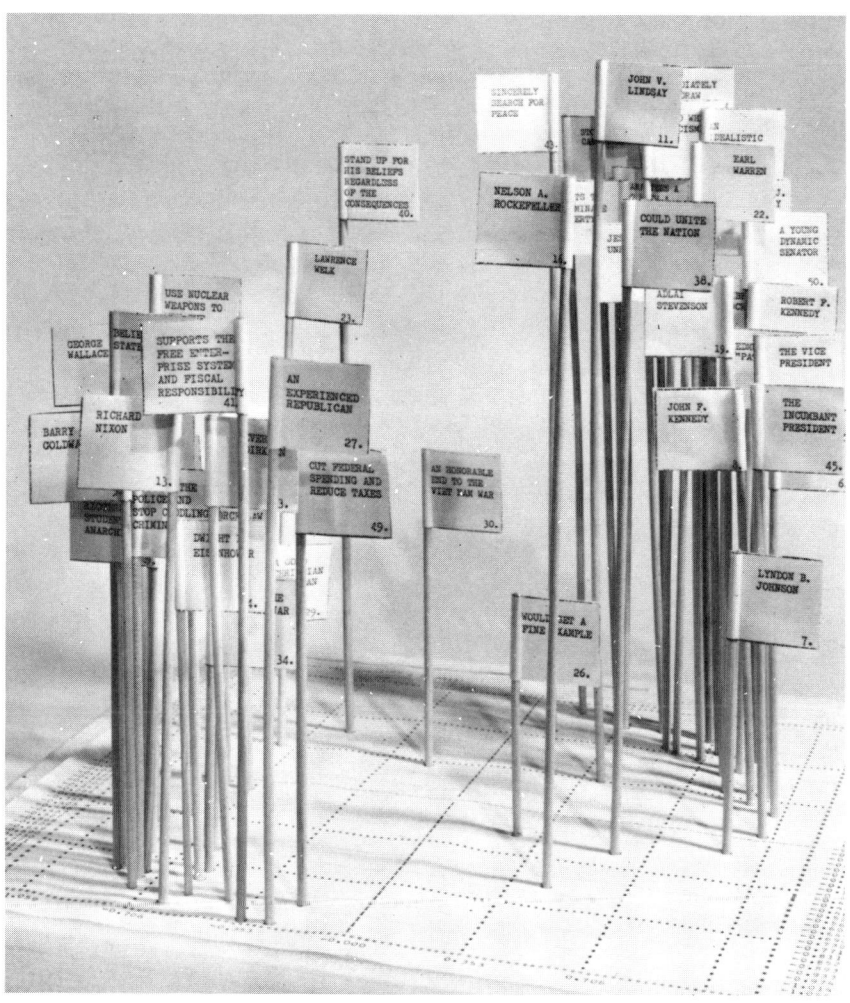

Source: Mauser (1972).

Democrats alike. Only Rockefeller and Lawrence Welk out of the 25 candidate names included had a nonpartisan appeal, while only 4 out of 25 descriptions elicited general agreement across all voters about their desirability:

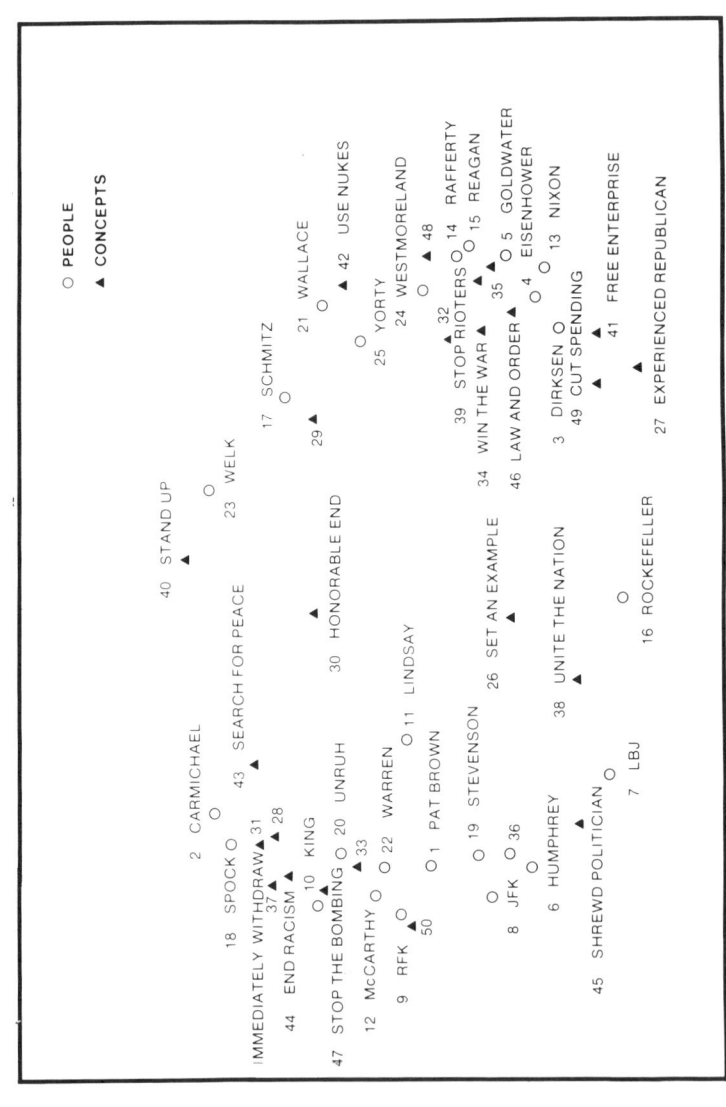

FIGURE 5.4. Two-dimensional Map of Patterns of Competition (M-D-SCAL Solution for Preference Correlations in Small Scale Preference Interview, All Respondents, N = 193, All 50 Political Figures, Stress = 0.160)

"A president we could be proud of who would set a fine example."
"A candidate who wants an honorable end to the Vietnam War."
"A president who could unite the nation and heal our troubled cities."
"A man who is willing to stand up for his beliefs regardless of the consequences."

The critical feature that determines placement in the neutral area—between the two polar extremes—is that candidates elicit general agreement from Democratic as well as Republican voters. Of course, such agreement could be at any level of popularity. Candidates who positioned in the neutral area ranged in popularity from "a candidate who could unite the nation and heal our troubled cities," who had the *highest average ranking* of all 50 candidates, through Rockefeller (with the tenth highest average ranking), to Lawrence Welk, who had the next to last average ranking (49th)—only Stokely Carmichael had a lower preference ranking.

The competition structure is polarized around a "liberal-conservative" dimension, in terms of both domestic and foreign policy issues, with Democratic candidates positioning on the more liberal side of these issues and Republican candidates positioning on the conservative side. This dimension is a collapsed form of the two major dimensions found in the perceptual map based on the Judged Similarities data.

The second dimension that spans the competition structure, orthogonal to the first, extends from Carmichael to Johnson, on the Democratic side, and from Wallace to Dirksen, on the Republican side. Spread out along this continuum one finds the full range of political postures, from the outspoken critics (of both the right and the left) to the reserved and diplomatic styles of the nation's leaders. While this dimension can be seen in the similarity structure, it did not emerge in voters' perceptions as an independent dimension.

Comparing the similarity and competition structures, the same clusters can be identified. The five clusters of candidates found in the similarity structure group together in the competition structure also, with Rockefeller and Welk being the only exceptions. Moreover, the members of the original five clusters remain closely grouped together, for the most part, in the preference data.

The two structures then appear to be basically similar at the global level: the same dimensions span both of them and the same clusters are observable in both. The next section examines the hypothesis that similar candidates compete with each other more vigorously by correlating patterns of perceived similarity with patterns of competition.

Similarity and Competition

Predicting patterns of competition, or vote-splitting in multicandidate contests, on the basis of voters' perceptions, depends upon the existence of strong empirical support for the hypothesis that political candidates will split each other's vote, or compete with each other, to the extent that the electorate sees them as being similar to each other. This hypothesis will now be empirically examined.

The assertion that similar candidates split their vote remains tautological unless independent measures are used to determine the extent to which candidates are judged to be similar to each other, and the extent to which candidates split their vote, or compete with each other. In this study, each of these concepts was measured using separate samples drawn from the target population in order to test this proposition. One sample determined perceived similarity, a second sample measure patterns of competition, while a third sample determined patterns of vote-splitting.

The first step in testing this hypothesis is to examine the extent to which similar candidates compete for the same votes. This may be done by simply intercorrelating the measures of candidates similarity (as found in the Judged Similarity Sample) with the patterns of competition (as found in the Small Scale Preference Sample). A correlation of 0.534 is found for the full set of 25 political leaders included in both interviews. This indicates that there is a substantial, but not an intimate, relationship between candidate similarity and pattern of competition.

However, the correlation coefficient is notoriously sensitive to the values of a few extreme cases. To ensure that the observed correlation is not just a statistical artifact, the correlation was recalculated after eliminating the lesser known political figures. Unfamiliar figures were eliminated by setting a minimum value for the expected cell frequencies (MEV). The higher the minimum set, the greater the level of public visibility that was required for a figure to be included in the correlation. Table 5.6 shows the results of progressively raising the MEV from zero (no minimum, that is, all figures are included) to seven (where only the best-known political figures are compared).

As is immediately evident, the correlation between similarity and pattern of competition remains substantial, even when the more "unfamiliar" figures are eliminated. Clearly, there is a robust relationship between candidate similarity and the pattern of competition.

Interestingly, the correlation collapses to zero when calculated separately for Democratic and Republican respondents. Standard sociological analysis argues that the observed relationship between similarity and pattern of competition was due to party affiliation (Rosenberg 1968, Chapter 2). If so, Democratic and Republican leaders should form partisan clusters only when respondents are pooled together. Examining the MDS configurations for Democratic and Republican voters separately supports this conjecture. Partisan clustering cannot be seen in the patterns of preference structures, when Democratic respondents are examined independently from Republican respondents. This suggests that the major factor accounting for the relationship between similarity and patterns of competition is political partisanship.

TABLE 5.6. Correlation between Judged Similarity and Patterns of Competition for Political Leaders

	Minimum Expected Value (MEV)[a]							
	0	1	2	3	4	5	6	7
Total Sample	.534 (300)	[b]	[b]	[b]	.635 (201)	.718 (117)	.758 (60)	.846 (25)
Democratic Respondents	−.028 (300)	−.030 (266)	−.016 (145)	−.416 (21)				
Republican Respondents	−.014 (300)	−.027 (253)	−.017 (106)					

Note: Entries in this table are Spearman Correlation Coefficients calculated between 25 × 25 matrices. The number of cells included in each correlation is indicated in parentheses.

[a]The minimum frequency accepted per cell for judged similarities. Unfamiliar candidates are eliminated by raising the MEV.

[b]Not calculated.

Source: Mauser (1972).

Predicting Patterns of Vote-Splitting

The central problem under consideration in this chapter is that of predicting the patterns of vote-splitting in a multicandidate contest from voters' perceptions of the candidates. So far it has been shown that candidates tend to compete for the same votes to the extent that they are judged to resemble each other. It remains to be shown, however, that patterns of vote-splitting can be predicted for particular candidates in any given election.

The three-way contest for president in 1968 offered an opportunity to test this hypothesis in a major election. If similar candidates split their vote more than dissimilar candidates, it should be possible to predict for any third-party candidate whether he would, by entering the race, draw more votes from the Democratic candidate or from the Republican candidate, by simply determining whom the third-party candidate was seen by the electorate as resembling more.

Before this hypothesis may be put to test, we need to define a few terms more precisely. The criterion that we wish to predict is vote-splitting, which is defined as the extent to which any given candidate in an electoral contest draws votes disproportionately from the other candidates in the contest. No vote-splitting can be said to occur if vote are drawn from candidates in direct proportion to their share of the vote. *Draw* is defined as the proportion of the vote that a particular candidate loses to another. Table 5.7 shows an illustrative example to clarify these concepts. In the two-candidate race, Candidates A and B get 60 percent and 40 percent of the vote respectively. If Candidate C enters the race, he pulls 25 percent of the total vote: 15

percentage points from A and 10 percentage points from B. Candidate C draws equally from both candidates because the share-points he pulls away from each candidate is proportionate with their share of the vote. Candidate C would have to draw disproportionately from the other two candidates before we can see that vote-splitting has occurred. Such a situation can be seen in Table 5.8 where Candidate N draws 33 percent of Candidate K's vote, but only 12 percent of Candidate L's vote.

Turning to the 1968 presidential contest, we can determine if George Wallace could be said to have split the vote in the California state contest. Table 5.9 shows the results of mock elections that were simulated to estimate George Wallace's impact on this contest. These contests were simulated from respondents' preference rankings.[15] As can be seen, Wallace draws just slightly more from Nixon than he does from Humphrey. Such a small difference may not appear very important, but it suggests that Nixon would have beaten Humphrey by an even larger margin had Wallace not been in the contest. To put this point a little differently, if Wallace could have drawn even more votes than what he actually did, say as much as 30 percent of the total vote, given this draw ratio, Wallace would have swung California from Nixon to Humphrey.

TABLE 5.7. Illustrative Three-Way Contest Showing Proportionate Draw—No Vote-Splitting

	Candidate A	Candidate B	Candidate C
Two-way race	60%	40%	—
Three-way race	40%	30%	25%
Difference	15%	10%	
Draw	$\frac{15}{60} = 25\%$	$\frac{10}{40} = 25\%$	

TABLE 5.8. Illustrative Three-Way Contest Showing Vote-Splitting Due to Disproportionate Draw

	Candidate K	Candidate L	Candidate M
Two-way race	60%	40%	—
Three-way race	45%	35%	25%
Difference	20%	5%	
Draw	$\frac{20}{60} = 33\%$	$\frac{5}{40} = 12\%$	

TABLE 5.9. George Wallace and the 1968 California Presidential Contest

	Humphrey	Nixon	Wallace	Total
Two-way race	48.1%	51.9%	—	100%
Three-way race	44.7%	47.3%	8.0%	100%
Draw by Wallace	7 %	9 %		

Source: Large Scale Preference Sample, N = 1,161, which was drawn the weekend prior to the election using multistage probability sampling techniques and telephone interviews by Hooper, Inc.

Could George Wallace's pattern of draws in this election have been predicted? Despite the small differences in the draws, the answer appears to be yes. George Wallace was judged to be more similar to Nixon than to Humphrey (0.019 − 0.034 = − 0.015) by respondents in the Judged Similarity interview conducted in the summer of 1968; Wallace's pattern of competition was more similar to Nixon's than to Humphrey's, as was determined in the Small Scale Preference Sample in October (0.661 − 1.161 = − 0.500). Even the Judged Similarity interview conducted as a pilot study, during the summer of 1967, over a year before the November 1968 election, estimated that Wallace was seen as more similar to Nixon than to Humphrey (Mauser 1969). Hence, all indices pointed to Wallace drawing disporportionately more votes from Nixon than from Humphrey.

A wide variety of third candidates may be examined in the same fashion. In the final sample, conducted the weekend prior to the election, 1,161 respondents were asked to rank five "other" candidates for president besides Nixon, Humphrey, or Wallace. In the Small Scale Preference Sample, 193 respondents were asked to rank 22 "other" candidates for president. Each of these other candidates may be considered as a hypothetical "third candidate" in the 1968 presidential contest, against Nixon and Humphrey, and used to examine the hypothesis that similar candidates tend to split their vote.

In fact, it is now possible to test the entire chain of hypotheses interrelating similarity and vote-splitting: candidates judged to be similar should tend to compete more for the same voters than less similar candidates, candidates that compete more for the same voters should tend to split their vote more than other candidates, and similar candidates should tend to draw votes from each other more. Each of these three concepts (judged similarity, patterns of competition and vote-splitting) were measured independently using different samples of respondents. Table 5.10 shows the results for the third candidates included in all three interviews.

As can be seen in Table 5.10, the scores tend to keep the same sign across rows. This indicates that a third candidate, in general, draws more votes from the candidate that he is seen as resembling, and with whom he tends to

TABLE 5.10. Predicting Vote-Splitting for Third Candidates from Indices of Judged Similarity and Pattern of Competition

Hypothetical Third Candidate	Judged Similarity ($N = 65$)[a]	Pattern of Competition ($N = 193$)[b]	Relative Draws ($N = 1,161$)[c]
Lyndon Johnson	+.149[d]	+.980	+27%
Nelson Rockefeller	−.004	−.001	+15%
George Wallace	−.015	−.500	− 2%
Robert Kennedy[e]	+.010	+.083	+41%
Stop rioters[f]	h	+.017	+ 2%
End the war honorably[g]	h	−.061	+ 9%

[a] Based on the Judged Similarity Sample.
[b] Based on the Small Scale Preference Sample.
[c] Based on the Large Scale Preference Sample.
[d] A positive score indicates that the third candidate is more similar to (or competes more) with Humphrey than Nixon; a negative score indicates a greater similarity to (or competitiveness with) Nixon than to Humphrey.
[e] "A candidate like Robert Kennedy." This study was conducted after his assassination on the eve of the California primary election.
[f] "A candidate who would not be afraid to stop Negro rioters and student anarchists."
[g] "A candidate who wants an honorable end to the Vietnam War."
[h] Only names were included in the Judged Similarity Sample.
Source: Mauser (1972).

compete more for votes. Nelson Rockefeller and "a president who would end the war honorably" were exceptional in that they violated this pattern.

A stronger hypothesis may be tested. We can hypothesize further that third-party candidates will not only *draw more* votes from the candidate that they are seen as resembling more, but also that third candidates will draw votes from candidates to the extent that they are seen as similar to them. To test this hypothesis the columns in Table 5.10 can be intercorrelated. These results are shown in Table 5.11.

The hypothesis is solidly supported. All correlations in the table are significantly different from zero and show a very strong and reliable relationship. Whether the correlations are calculated for the 6 possible third

TABLE 5.11. Predicting Patterns of Draw for Hypothetical Third Candidates

	Relative Similarity[a] (N = 65)	Relative Competition Patterns[b] (N = 193)
Relative Competition Patterns (N = 193)	.830[d]	—
Relative Draws[c] (N = 1,161)	.800[e]	.657[e]

[a] The extent to which the third candidate is perceived to resemble Nixon or Humphrey, based on the Judged Similarity Sample (N = 65).

[b] The extent to which the third candidate appeals more to Nixon's supporters or to Humphrey's. Calculated from patterns of correlations in Small Scale Preference Sample (N = 193).

[c] The extent to which the third candidate draws votes more from Nixon or Humphrey in a three-way contest calculated from draw patterns in Large Scale Preference Sample (N = 1,161).

[d] Spearman *rho* correlation for 23 politicians in both the Judged Similarity Sample (N = 65) and the Small Scale Preference Sample (N = 193). For the Judged Similarity Sample and the Large Scale Preference Sample (N = 1,161), which included only 4 politicians, Spearman's *rho* is 1.0.

[e] Spearman *rho* correlation for the four politicians shared by Large Scale Preference Interview and Judged Similarity Interview. Considering all 23 politicians shared in the Judged Similarity Interview and the Small Scale Preference Interview there is a *rho* of 0.680.

[f] Spearman *rho* for six politicians and campaign themes shared by Large Scale Preference Interview and Small Scale Preference Interview. If both draws and intercorrelations are calculated using the same sample, the relationship between them is much stronger. For the campaign themes in the Small Scale Preference Interview *rho* equals 0.910. For the 23 politicians in the Small Scale Preference Interview *rho* equals 0.825.

Source: Mauser (1972).

candidates in the Large Scale Preference Interview or the 23 possible third candidates in the Small Scale Preference Interview, strong positive correlations are observed between the perceived similarity of the third candidate, his relative pattern-of-competition, and the extent to which the third candidate draws votes away from the Republican or Democratic candidate in the contest.

Patterns of vote-splitting for candidates in multicandidate contests have been shown to be predictable from patterns of perceived similarity, as judged by the voters. It is even possible to predict patterns of vote-splitting up to a year in advance.

CONCLUSIONS

This chapter showed how the 1968 presidential contest in California was analyzed using the approach described in Chapter 4. It was argued that detailed knowledge of the electorate's perceptions of the candidates, and their preferences for them, would enable campaigners to harness the patterns of vote-splitting to their advantatge. Consequently, spatial maps were developed using MDS techniques for voters' perceptions of, and preferences for, contemporary political leaders.

It was hypothesized that political candidates compete with each other and will tend to split their vote in any given election to the extent that the electorate sees them as being similar to each other. Such an hypothesis is circular unless patterns of perceived similarity are measured independently from patterns of competition and vote-splitting. To test this hypothesis, the patterns of vote-splitting that would be expected for a variety of third candidates (both real and hypothetical) in the 1968 presidential contest were predicted from independent measures of their perceived similarity and their patterns of competition.

The results strongly support the hyothesis. Consider first the case of the third-party candidacy of George Wallace. Wallace was seen as resembling Richard Nixon more than Hubert Humphrey by the California electorate, and he appealed more to Nixon voters than to Humphrey voters. Thus, Wallace was predicted to draw more votes from Nixon than from Humphrey. That is exactly what happened. Despite Wallace's belief that his candidacy would tend to split the Democratic vote, just the opposite proved to be the case. George Wallace drew slightly more votes from Nixon than he did from Humphrey, which acted to reduce Nixon's margin of victory in the California contest.

The hypothesis was also tested for a variety of hypothetical third candidates who might have run against Nixon and Humphrey in place of George Wallace. Such contests did not occur, of course, but it is nevertheless interesting to speculate how the hypothesis would have fared. If it is supported, then confidence would be increased that the hypothesis would hold across the full range of possible third candidates who might have entered the contest. Strong reliable correlations were found between judged similarity of hypothetical third candidates, their patterns of competition, and their tendency to draw votes from either Nixon or Humphrey. Particularly striking was that the hypothesis held for verbal descriptions of hypothetical candidates as well as for names of contemporary political leaders.

This approach offers a powerful technology for strategically positioning political candidates in that it contains a realistic model of electoral competition as well as an integrated set of measures. Politicians have long recognized instinctively the importance of vote-splitting in multiple-candidate contests, but they have lacked the tools to take advantage of this knowledge. The technology described here can unambiguously identify which candidates will tend to split their vote, and why. This capability allows political strategists to anticipate the effects of candidates entering (or changing their appeals) during a political campaign.

In contrast with traditional approaches to understanding vote-splitting, which rely on voter differences, the approach used here focuses on perceived differences among the candidates to explain patterns of switching between candidates during an electoral contest. The traditional approaches assume that the voters' interests can be unambiguously determined by their group affiliations, and that these interests are clearly reflected in the positions taken by the candidates in the contest. Such is rarely the case. Voters often have conflicting interests and opinions, which candidates may deliberately attempt to capitalize upon by avoiding clear stands on the issues, or by adroit posturing. Moreover, the declining importance of partisan loyalty, and the emergence of new issues that cut across traditional alignments, erode even further the usefulness of the traditional approaches based on voter groups. The great advantage of the approach presented here is that it is designed to measure, and to explain, the patterns of competition in the contest.

The strategic positioning approach is not limited to multiple-candidate contests. In contests between two or more candidates, this approach can be used to simulate the electorate's response to alternative postures or positions that any of the candidates might adopt. This capability permits candidates to develop campaign strategy for a greater number of contingencies than is now currently possible. The next few chapters show how this approach may be used to develop and to screen campaign strategies in political contests.

NOTES

1. Strictly speaking, this hypothesis would be expected to be limited to single-choice situations (e.g., elections, markets, contests) that is, those choice situations where people indicate their first choices only from among a set, containing more than two elements, such that one and only one element is designated as the group's choice the winner

2. This chapter draws upon work published earlier, particularly Mauser (1970, 1972) and Mauser and Stefflre (1974).

3. A recent article in the *California Journal* cites several attempts of candidates in California covertly sponsoring minor candidates to harass the opposition and to split their vote (Walters 1981).

4. Perhaps New York State is the most striking exception to this statement. In New York, there are four parties: the Liberals and the Conservatives regularly contest elections, in addition to the Democratic and Republican Parties. Moreover, these two parties have been successful in electing their candidates to major offices. The Conservatives elected James Buckley to the U.S. Senate in 1970 (for one term only), and the Liberals' John Lindsay was mayor of New York City for a few terms during the 1960s and 1970s (Jewell and Olson 1982).

5. See Mazmanian (1974) for a thorough discussion of the role of third parties in U.S. presidential elections.

6. Early in the 1980 presidential campaign, John Anderson's national support was over 20 percent of registered voters, compared with the 34 percent who preferred Reagan and the 40

percent who preferred Carter. The percentage of people indicating Anderson as their first choice steadily declined to election day when he drew less than 7 percent of the popular vote. While Anderson drew more than 10 percent of the vote in ten states, winning almost 19 percent in Alaska, he did not control the balance of power in any state. Even if of his support had gone to Carter, Carter would have won only five more states, for an additional 70 electoral votes, leaving Carter still trailing far behind Reagan, losing by 419 to 110 rather than 489 to 49 electoral votes (Pomper, et al. 1981). Despite Anderson's fizzling out, his candidacy shows there is a sizable bloc of support that would support independent candidates. This potential is there for the future.

7. For a discussion of recent political trends in U.S. politics, readers are urged to read Fishel (1978), Goldwin (1980), or Ladd (1977).

8. This phenomenon is called "defining the anchor point of a dimension" and is discussed more fully in Sherif and Hovland (1961).

9. Candidates need to win a majority (not just a plurality) of the vote in the electoral college to be elected president. Since there were 538 electoral votes in 1968, Wallace had to keep either candidate from winning more than 269 votes. To do this, he needed all the votes in the deep South, plus those of the border states, or a few of the large northern states. But most important, Wallace had to arrange it that the major candidates split the remaining electoral vote nearly equally.

10. Strictly speaking, the nationwide popular vote has nothing whatever to do with determining who is elected president. For example, in three out of the nine presidential elections since World War II, the winner failed to receive a majority of the popular vote: Harry Truman got 49.6 percent in 1948, John Kennedy drew 49.7 percent, and Richard Nixon managed to get elected to his first term in 1968 with only 43.3 percent of the popular vote.

11. A state's electoral vote should not be confused with its delegations to the Democratic and Republican parties' nominating conventions. Rules governing voting at the party conventions are made by each party's rules committee in addition to relevant state and federal statutes. The Democrats severely restricted "winner take all" primary votes in 1976, while the Republicans narrowly voted to keep this rule in 1976. Throughout this tumult, the rules in the electoral college have remained fixed. For a discussion of recent rules changes in presidential politics, the reader may wish to consult Asher (1980), Lengle and Shafer (1980), Marshall (1981), Ranney (1974), or Wayne (1980).

12. Kruskal's multidimensional scaling program, M-D—SCAL-3, was used to generate all MDS models in this chapter (Kruskal 1964a and b). The stress values for these configurations may appear to some researchers to be rather high, but this is an artifact of the large number (25 to 50) of items being scaled since Kruskal's measure of stress, unfortunately, increases with the number of items being scaled (Spence and Ogilvie 1973; Stenson and Knoll 1969). The four MDS configurations reported here can be shown to be stable, despite the high levels of stress. All configurations were submitted to two independent tests: the observed stress levels were compared with random data using Monte Carlo procedures, and the configurations for distinct subsamples were compared with each other. For further details concerning the M-D-SCAL parameters used here or these tests, the reader is urged to consult Mauser (1970).

13. The "ideal candidate for president" category was included in this study as a means of eliciting comments of desirable attributes of candidates. As discussed in Chapter 4, early marketing researchers thought that such an item could literally be used to discover ideal positions for locating new products. More recent work suggests that this was an ill-founded hope (Tversky and Kahnemann 1981; Stefflre 1972, 1979b).

14. In addition to these verbatims, support for the essential circularity of the electorate's perceptions was also found in the MDS analysis and by directly observing the raw judged-similarity data matrix. Circular structures of this sort appear occasionally in data drawn from a wide variety of fields, for example, the color circle (Ekman 1954; Shepard 1962), circular tones

(Levelt et al. 1966; Shepard 1964), and are consistent with multidimensional structures of political preferences of electorates or voting patterns of parliaments (Sartori 1976). Guttman (1954) has called data structures that are continuous and that form a closed circular structure reflecting qualitative differences as the *circumplex*. The parallel with the color circle is instructive. Psychologists have found that when human observers are presented with colors that vary only in hue, judgments about interobject similarity fall in a circular pattern, even though hue may be fully characterized by the wave length of light, a unidimensional variable. See Degerman (1972) and Shepard (1974) for a full discussion of this point.

15. The share of vote can be simulated for any subset of candidates (or parties) if voters' ordinal preferences are known for the full set of candidates. The method for accomplishing this is described and empirically evaluated in Chapter 9. It is shown that share-of-vote can be predicted quite accurately from ordinal preferences.

6

PRAGMATISTS VS. PURISTS IN CALIFORNIA

> Never attempt to beat the other man at his own game.
> Stephen Shadegg, *How to Win an Election*

Over the past few decades political campaigners have adopted an increasing number of marketing concepts and techniques. Nevertheless, the determination of campaign strategy remains a difficult and challenging undertaking. Strategy formulation is particularly challenging because it must be made on the basis of very little information.

This chapter shows how the strategic positioning approach, originally designed to evaluate concepts of new products, was used to generate and screen strategic options for the Democratic candidate for governor of California. This approach was not only capable of evaluating alternatives positions and postures that the candidate had been considering, but also it was able to discover a new strategy, not previously anticipated by the candidate's advisors, which was superior to those suggested.

The strategic positioning approach was described in Chapters 3 and 4. The same approach is used in Chapters 5 and 6 to map voters' perceptions and preferences. The replication demonstrates the general applicability of the approach and permits the reader to judge its usefulness as a practical tool.

The goal of this study was to identify a small number of campaign themes that could serve as the central focus of the candidate's advertising campaign. The study was designed to identify campaign themes (or issue-positions) which

---

This chapter is an expanded version of my article, "Positioning Political Candidates: An Application of Concept Evaluation Techniques," *Journal of the Market Research Society* 22 (1980), pp. 181-91. Permission to excerpt heavily from this article is gratefully acknowledged.

met two criteria: they beat the opposition in a head-to-head choice situation, and they appealed to the candidate's supporters in the electorate. While pre-election polls are routinely used to identify which issues are important to voters, procedures are not typically available to permit political strategists to evaluate specific positions on the issues.

Both of the criteria mentioned above are crucial in selecting issue-positions. If a candidate chooses positions or postures that can beat the opposition, but that do not appeal to his supporters, he risks losing his credibility and his base of support. Credibility is particularly valuable for the candidate who intends to establish a political career, rather than just to win a single election. By restricting himself to positions that appeal to his bloc of supporters in the electorate, a candidate ensures that he maintains his credibility. The procedures outlined in this chapter permit candidates to screen issue-positions on both of these vital criteria.

This chapter is divided into four sections. First, the political situation in California is briefly outlined. Next, the discussions with the candidate's campaign staff are covered showing how the goals for the empirical study were set. The study we conducted is then described and our strategic recommendations presented. In conclusion, the impact of our involvement in the campaign is evaluated.

THE POLITICAL SITUATION

Elections in California, like in most states, are essentially contests between the Democratic and Republican candidates.[1] While Democrats outnumber Republicans in the California electorate by a considerable margin, Republican candidates have not done badly at all in statewide contests. For the past 20 years, the state has kept one Democrat and one Republican in the U.S. Senate. Moreover, Republicans have alternated with Democrats in the governor's mansion in Sacramento, the state capital since the 1950s when "Goodie" Knight, a Republican, was governor.

In 1958, the Democrats won a sweeping victory, winning control of the state assembly, electing a U.S. senator, and putting Edmund "Pat" Brown in as governor. Brown easily won reelection in 1962, running against former vice-president Richard M. Nixon, but he was stymied in his try for a third term as governor in 1966 by Ronald Reagan, a political novice and former Hollywood actor. That year Ronald Reagan claimed the governor's mansion, promising a return to fiscal conservatism and "law and order." After the turbulent events of the late 1960s, including race riots, student demonstrations, and the assassination of presidential candidate Robert Kennedy in Los Angeles on the eve of his California primary victory, Reagan ran for a second term in 1970. He saw no need to change the successful platform that he had campaigned on before.

The Democratic candidate for governor in 1970 was Jesse Unruh, who had recently resigned his position as speaker of the California state assembly to run against Ronald Reagan. Unruh had been speaker for a number of years and was widely known as the most powerful man in state politics. Since 1958, he had used his power as assembly speaker to build the assembly into one of the most respected state legislatures in the country, and to firmly implant himself in control of both the assembly and of the Democratic party, which held the majority of the seats in the assembly. Unruh was widely known in California as "Big Daddy," as much for his imposing physical size (over 300 pounds) as for his political strength. Perhaps one of his best known anecdotes, that "money is the mother's milk of politics," typifies the popular view of Unruh as a tough professional politician.

Political parties are strikingly weak in California. Historically, this is due in large part to the "reforms" instituted by the Progressives in the first few decades of this century. Hiram Johnson, the crusading Progressive governor, led the fight against the political parties as they were seen as corrupt, attempting to return control of government to the "good citizens" of California. In the interest of "good government," patronage opportunities for the political parties were systematically reduced as much as possible. Government positions, which before the Progressives had came to power had been filled by political patronage, were incorporated into the civil service or opened up to competitive "nonpartisan" elections. In nonpartisan contests, political parties are prohibited from either officially supporting or nominating candidates. For example, all elected officials at the municipal level in California, and many at the state level, are selected through nonpartisan elections.

Even more important, nominees for all major partisan offices must be selected in primary elections, where political parties are explicitly forbidden from supporting candidates. This effectively removes political parties from control of the nominating process, moving nominations out of "smoke filled rooms" and forcing candidates for partisan offices to run in open primary elections.

In conjunction with the mobility of the electorate, the reforms of the progressive era have produced a very volatile situation. Candidates must construct their own personal organizations, outside of the traditional political parties, in order to contest any election. The large, heterogeneous California electorate is also relatively disinterested in politics, partly because of the ready availability of other distractions, but also due to the difficulty of becoming involved in practical politics.

There are two principal means for reaching the California electorate: through the mass media or by using volunteer workers. While complementary, these alternative campaigning methods are also antagonistic in that all candidates, whether Republican or Democrat, have to decide the extent to which their campaign will rely on each of these campaigning methods.

If candidates wish to use the mass media to reach the voters, they must somehow attract the attention of the news media, or else purchase expensive advertisements. Gaining news coverage in direct competition with other "newsworthy" events, such as sports, sensational crimes, or crises of national or international importance, is by no means an easy task (Leary 1977). To handle this problem, imaginative campaigners have dreamed up a variety of dramatic "pseudo-events" in an effort to get free TV coverage on the evening news programs.

On the other hand, political advertising, while effective, is very expensive. Cost considerably limits the extent to which candidates can take advantage of the direct access to the electorate that is offered by the mass media. Television dominates the other mass media in terms of its political significance. Nevertheless, other media should not be ignored. Traditionally popular media, such as radio and newspapers, as well as nontraditional media, such as direct mail and automatic telephone messages, hold tremendous potential. In the late 1960s candidates for major statewide offices in California, such as governor or U.S. senator, spent approximately $500,000 on media expenses alone in the general election. If they had faced a competitive primary contest to win their party's nomination, they had to count on spending an equivalent sum for the primary contest as well. For example, John Tunney is estimated to have spent $1,600,000 in his successful bid for the U.S. senate against George Murphy in 1970. Approximately half of this sum went for purchasing broadcast time on TV alone. The cost of developing the advertisements is not included in this figure, nor are expenses for either radio or newspaper advertisements (Hiebert et al. 1975, pp. 42-44). Media costs have more than doubled since 1970.

An alternative campaign tactic is the volunteer organization. Instead of relying on the mass media to reach the voters, candidates can use volunteers to canvass precincts. Volunteers can identify potential supporters, distribute campaign literature, and, returning on election day, turn out the vote. All candidates must have a campaign organization of some size. In some states, such organizations are composed primarily of paid party workers. This is the famed "party machine," and in such a framework, volunteers typically constitute only a very small part of a candidate's campaign organization. In California, however, party activists have been supplanted by unpaid volunteers to a degree entirely unknown in the rest of the United States.

Although unpaid, volunteers do not come without cost, exacting as they do a high degree of autonomy in choosing and carrying out their tasks. Volunteers also demand a large amount of "stroking" or "care and feeding" before they consent to do their tasks. Because of the demise of political parties in California, many of the volunteers are motivated by ideological conviction rather than by partisan loyalty. This means that, to get their support, candidates must adopt positions that the volunteers view as compatible with their own. Much of the seemingly bizarre behavior that politicians sometimes engage in can be explained by their need to attract and to motivate a corps of volunteer workers. As single-issue activists become more and more powerful throughout the United States, this type of political campaigning will become even more common.

This was the political situation in California going into the 1970 elections. Ronald Reagan, the popular Republican incumbent, was attempting to win reelection to a second term on essentially the same platform as he had adopted in his first campaign. Facing him was Jesse Unruh, the Democratic nominee and former speaker of the assembly, who was well-known in California but was not particularly popular. The lack of strong political parties in California meant that both candidates had to find ways to reach the voters independently of party organizations. Traditionally, the Republicans have relied more on mass media, because of their bigger campaign chests, while the Democrats have depended more on volunteers as they have not been as well-heeled.

IDENTIFYING THE PROBLEM

During the summer of 1970, our marketing research firm was contacted by one of the staff members for the Democratic candidate for governor of California. Plans were being finalized for the candidate's advertising campaign that they intended to mount during the last, crucial months before the election. Prior to determining their strategy, the staff was considering surveying voters' political opinions and perceptions of the candidates.

After a series of meetings with the campaign staff, in which the candidate's strategic opportunities and problems were explored, the outlines of a campaign strategy began to emerge. The candidate and his staff, recognizing the importance of coordinating their campaign activities around a coherent strategy, agreed that the fall campaign should focus on a small number of interrelated campaign themes. They reasoned that the impact of the campaign would be maximized by orienting the candidate's speeches, his radio spots, billboards, and all other campaign efforts around a few, well-chosen campaign themes. As might be expected, there was some disagreement among the staff over the best direction to pursue in the fall campaign, and more precisely, over which campaign themes should be emphasized. Two main factions emerged on the campaign staff.

The pragmatists argued that the most crucial segment of the electorate consisted of those Democrats who presently were leaning toward supporting the Republican candidate. They observed that this segment could swing either way, while voters whose voting intentions were consistent with their registration would probably not be influenced by the election campaign. Therefore, they argued, this undecided segment would determine the outcome of the election. In order to get their votes, the candidate was urged to adopt those campaign themes that appealed to "the swing vote." This meant, they said, adopting conservative Republican positions on key issues. While such positions would not be viewed favorably by loyal Democrats, who were on the liberal side for the most part, their grumbling could easily be discounted. Loyal Democrats would have no other option on election day but to vote for the Democratic candidate for governor. Democratic voters who leaned toward Reagan should be surveyed, they argued, in order to identify the issue-positions that would have to be adopted. (See Table 6.1.)

By focusing on the undecided voter or the swing vote the pragmatists based their approach on the triage concept. This concept was supposedly first used by a field doctor in the Napoleonic army who had the difficult task of deciding how to allocate his scarce medical resources efficiently in order to treat the battlefield casualties. He is said to have dealt with this problem by identifying three classes of wounded: those who would probably not be able to fight again regardless of medical aid, those who soon would be able to resume fighting without medical intervention, and those who would be able to return to the front line only with appropriate medical aid. He argued that, Christian charity aside, battlefield medicine should focus exclusively on the third category for maximum effectiveness.

In the political context, the pragmatists' use of this approach ignores already committed partisans in favor of the swing vote. This approach sounds sensible, but by implicitly assuming that political campaigning cannot greatly influence the partisans, it does not take advantage of the reinforcing and activating effects of political campaigning on the committed voter that was documented in the early voting behavior studies (Lazarsfeld et al. 1944; Berelson et al. 1954).

Opposing this point of view was another faction, the "purists," who asserted that winning the election was less important than remaining true to one's own beliefs. The candidate should not adopt a campaign theme merely because it appealed to a certain segment of the electorate, however crucial

TABLE 6.1. The Pragmatist's View of the Electorate, by Party Affiliation of Voter

		Democratic	Republican
Candidate Preference	Unruh	*ignore:* already committed	*ignore:* too few voters of this type
	Reagan	*target:* swing voter	*ignore:* already committed

that segment might be. They argued that he should take forthright stands on those issues that he felt were the most important facing the state. Anything less would be immoral.

If the candidate adopted this approach, only his most loyal supporters could be counted on to vote for him. While it was likely he would lose the election, at least he would have raised the issues that needed to be raised. Obviously, the purists saw no need for a voter survey, since the candidate and the staff could identify the most pressing issues for themselves. Scarce resources, they argued, should be devoted to communicating the candidate's positions on the issues to the voters rather than squandering them on useless surveys.

The purist's position is somewhat practical, despite his line of reasoning. This moralistic stance strongly appealed to the volunteer workers who staffed the campaign organization. Volunteers traditionally play an important role in the Democratic campaign, canvassing precincts, distributing literature, and, on election day, turning out loyal voters. Their enthusiastic support for the candidate is often crucial in attempting to win the election.

We pointed out that this was a false dichotomy—that it was not necessary to have to choose between virtuously losing the election or cynically winning it; or, even between appealing to loyal Democrats or to the swing vote. Defining the problem in this way excluded the possibility that campaign themes might exist that appealed to the candidate, his loyal supporters, and that were highly popular in the electorate at large. We argued that it was an empirical question whether or not such campaign themes could be found. This question should not be decided by the campaign staff. We suggested that a survey should be conducted of the full electorate, just not the swing vote, in order to evaluate alternative positions and postures that the candidate was considering adopting. Because so little was known about how voters perceived the major candidates, a preliminary study should be conducted, we went on, in order to facilitate the formulation of alternative campaign themes.

The candidate and his staff decided to support our proposal for two separate surveys of the full electorate. The survey procedures adopted were similar to those described in Chapter 4. This approach has several advantages over the typical survey of voters' perceptions and opinions: it generates rich descriptions of voters' perceptions, it tests a wide range of alternative campaign themes, and it permits the internal consistency of the approach to be empirically examined, since it involves separate samples.

THE STUDY

Two separate and independent samples of registered voters in Los Angeles County were drawn for this study. The objective of the first sample was to determine voters' perceptions of the major candidates for governor, permitting an examination of the images of the Democratic and Republican candidates, their positive and negative aspects. These data offer rich opportunities to formulate campaign themes. In the second sample, voters were asked about their preferences for the political candidates and campaign themes.[2]

The study was limited to Los Angeles County because resources were severely constrained. We decided to conduct a small, restricted study, that we could tightly control, rather than attempt a larger, less manageable study, given our resources. While the results would not be strictly representative of the statewide electorate, Los Angeles County contained almost 40 percent of all eligible voters in California, and it was the key area for Unruh to win in the general election.

Both samples were drawn in the same manner, using multistage cluster sampling techniques. First, weighted probabilistic sampling techniques were used to select a small number of precincts out of Los Angeles County, and, once the precincts had been chosen, to select households within these targeted precincts. Swing precincts were defined and oversampled in a way that allowed sample estimates to be made for both this segment and for the entire electorate. Respondents were drawn from households, using sex and age quotas, and personally interviewed.

To disguise the partisan nature of the study, interviewers were identified only as working for our marketing research firm. The name of the sponsor was not mentioned to the respondent.

Political Perceptions

During August a sample of 75 respondents was drawn and interviewed concerning their perceptions of California political figures. The Judged Similarity technique, described in Chapter 4, was used to determine the perceived similarity of 25 prominent political, religious, and social leaders (see Table 6.2 for the leaders included in this list). This allowed us to uncover the key dimensions that voters reacted to in judging political leaders, as well as to identify the categories of leaders that voters naturally used in judging the candidates in this particular campaign.

After respondents had indicated which leaders they thought were similar to which other leaders, they were asked to tell in their own words what the figures they had judged as being similar had in common. These free-response descriptions were important for determining what features, or aspects of these leaders, respondents thought were important to use in characterizing each of them. Respondents' comments were recorded verbatim and content-analyzed to identify critical features.

The similarity judgments were aggregated and scaled using the TORSCA multidimensional scaling program (Young and Torgerson 1967). Spatial

TABLE 6.2. The Political and Social Leaders Included in the 1970 California Political Study

Alan Cranston	Max Rafferty
Angela Davis	Nelson Rockefeller
Billy Graham	Norton Simon
Bill Cosby	Rachel Carson
Earl Warren	Ralph Nader
Edmund G. "Pat" Brown	Robert Finch
Edmund Muskie	Robert Kennedy
George Brown	Ronald Reagan
George Murphy	S. I. Hayakawa
Hubert Humphrey	Sam Yorty
Jesse Unruh	Spiro Agnew
John Tunney	Thomas Bradley
Lyndon Johnson	my IDEAL Governor

models were built in this way for Democratic voters and for the full electorate.[3] Figure 6.1 shows a two-dimensional TORSCA solution for the electorate's perceptions of the political leaders. As may be easily seen, almost all of the leaders fall into two clusters at opposite ends of the figure. Liberals are grouped together on the left side of the figure (all Democrats except Earl Warren) and the conservatives are on the right side (all Republicans except Sam Yorty).

The major dimension spanning these two clusters is quite similar to the principal dimension found in the 1968 presidential contest, although the clusters in 1970 are less distinct. Both the Democratic and Republican clusters tend to separate into two smaller groups, on the basis of their social activisim. (Mayor Yorty will be treated as a Republican in this analysis because, although he has maintained his Democratic registration, he has supported Republican candidates and he is seen as pro-Republican by Southern California voters.)

Jesse Unruh is nestled in the Democratic cluster, closely surrounded by other well-known Democrats, such as Robert Kennedy and Ed Muskie. His most frequent descriptions are "party Democrat," "powerful politician," and "for the little guy."

Ronald Reagan sits across the figure from Jesse Unruh, near the center of the Republican cluster. He is closely associated with law and order issues, such as cracking down on student demonstrators, welfare chiselers, and drug dealers. Other issues with which he is linked, mentioned less frequently, are the need to fight inflation and reduce taxes.

Close inspection of the respondents' descriptions of the political leaders indicated that, in addition to party affiliation, there were principally two kinds of issues that spanned these two clusters of candidates: social issues,

FIGURE 6.1. Perceptual Map of U.S. Political Figures. Two-Dimensional TORSCA-9B Solution for Judged Similarity Data (1970)

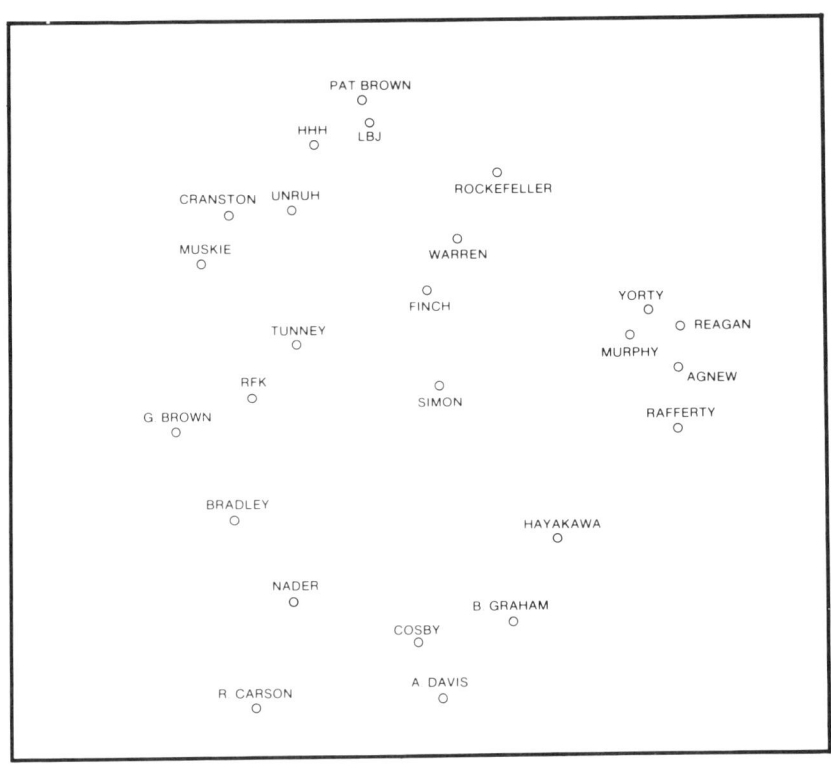

those relating to law and order; and those relating to economic issues, involving taxes and inflation.

The principal value of analyzing voters' political perceptions lies in the role it plays in developing alternative campaign themes. Both purists and pragmatists contributed issue-positions and postures that they wished to see used as the basis of the candidates' fall advertising campaign. Because the preference interview could easily accommodate a large number of alternative issue-positions, it was not necessary to have to make an administrative decision between the two warring factions on the committee. Twenty-five alternate issue-positions were retained for testing in the preference interview.

Political Preferences

As soon as the issue-positions to be evaluated had been determined, the second sample was drawn from Los Angeles County. Respondents were selected in a parallel manner as in the previous sample. The objectives for this part of the study were to determine voters' support for the two major candidates in the contest, to understand the source of this support by examining the structure of voters' political preferences in depth, and to evaluate the issue-positions that had been proposed by the candidate's staff.

In this interview, respondents were asked to rank the 25 political figures that had been included in the earlier interview, in the order that they would like to see them become governor of California. At the same time, respondents were also presented with 25 hypothetical candidates to be ranked. Each such hypothetical candidate was fashioned out of the issue-positions to be evaluated. Two hundred and thirty-nine interviews were successfully completed in two weeks of interviewing. Table 6.3 presents the hypothetical candidates that were constructed using the issue-positions submitted by the campaign staff. They are about evenly divided between those that appeal primarily to loyal Democrats and those that are designed to attract the swing vote. Roughly one-third deal with economic issues, while the remaining two-thirds exploit social issues. Table 6.4 shows how the issue-positions sort out according to these two factors.

The preference ranking procedure used here was the same as the one described in Chapter 4 and used in Chapter 5. Following this procedure, respondents are given a deck of index cards containing all 50 items to be ranked, instructed to become familiar with and consider all the items, including the issue-positions, as "hypothetical candidates for governor" about whom all that one knows is the description on the card.

Once respondents became familiar with all the items, they were requested to sort them into three piles according to their willingness to see them become governor of California: Pile #1 for the candidates they would most like to see elected, Pile #2 for those they do not feel strongly about, one way or the other, and Pile #3 for those they definitely would not like to see elected. Then respondents were asked to rank the items in each pile in the order of their preferences. Finally, after each pile had been ranked, all three piles were stacked together and the respondents were requested to look through all items one last time to verify if the final order agreed with their political preferences.

Ranking a set of items of this size is not an easy task for the typical respondent. It is particularly difficult to get respondents to rank the hypothetical candidates, since they are described by snippets of facts, or simply as proponents of one of the issue-positions. Nevertheless, if careful attention is paid to designing the instructions and to carrying out the interview procedures the rankings appear to meet reasonably rigorous standards of reliability and validity. These questions are taken up in greater detail in Chapter 9.

Spatial models were constructed for understanding voters' patterns of competition by first intercorrelating the preference rankings for all 50 items,

TABLE 6.3. Verbal Descriptions of Hypothetical Candidates

1. A governor who will fight inflation and the increased cost of living.
2. A governor who is a tough man of action.
3. A governor who would ban offshore drilling to reduce oil pollution.
4. A governor who will put some muscle into consumer protection.
5. A governor who would eliminate welfare from county property taxes.
6. A governor who favors liberalizing the abortion laws.
7. A governor who is his own man and is not controlled by big business and rich campaign contributors.
8. A governor who would restore the prestige of California's universities and colleges.
9. A governor who would insist upon tough antismog laws.
10. A governor who would go to Washington to bring more jobs to California.
11. A governor who would enforce rules of conduct for both the students and for the faculties in state schools.
12. A governor who will cut property taxes for low and middle income home owners.
13. A governor who will close tax loopholes like the oil depletion allowance and special deals for insurance companies.
14. A governor who would increase state support for local police.
15. A governor who would make the colleges fire teachers who take part in violent demonstrations.
16. A governor who will cut welfare costs no matter who complains.
17. A governor who will make businesses pay a bigger share of taxes.
18. A governor who opposes school busing.
19. A governor who would encourage college faculties to solve campus problems by themselves.
20. A governor who would crack down on drug abuse.
21. A governor who would fight to make our cities safer places to live in.
22. A governor who would abolish the property tax on homes.
23. A governor who will act now to improve the quality of public school education.
24. A governor who would fight the auto industry to eliminate smog.
25. A governor who will make the state pay at least 50% of public school costs.

and then scaling these correlations using TORSCA. This scaling procedure was described in detail in Chapter 4 and is identical to that used in Chapter 5 to analyze voters' preferences in the 1968 presidential contest. Spatial models were constructed for Democratic voters as well as for the full electorate. Figure 6.2 shows the two-dimensional TORSCA model for the electorate's preferences for political leaders and campaign themes.[4]

The spatial model is helpful in identifying the bases of support for each politician. The issue-stands that position close to each politician in the model are preferred by the same voters who prefer that politician. This follows since objects position close together in this model only if they are highly

TABLE 6.4. Types of Issue-Positions Included

		Issue Content	
		Social Problems	Economic Problems
Target Group	Loyal Democrats	3, 4, 6, 7, 8 9, 19, 23, 24	10, 13, 17
	Swing Vote	2, 11, 14, 15 16, 18, 20, 21	1, 5, 12 22, 25

intercorrelated. A positive correlation implies that voters who prefer one of the objects more than most voters, also prefer the second more than most voters.

In the perceptual model, in contrast, objects cluster together if they are seen to share similar characteristics. (This does not imply that they are *preferred* equally.) In the model for patterns of competition, objects that cluster together may not show common characteristics with each other beyond appealing to the same subgroup of voters (e.g., Billy Graham and Ronald Reagan). Tables 6.5 through 6.8 show the issues and public figures correlated with a few selected politicians.

The most fruitful way to interpret scaling models, as has been argued earlier, is to look for clusters rather than insisting on finding continuous dimensions. There are two principal reasons for this: the natural restrictions on the information processing capacity of individuals, and the implications for positioning objects in the model.

First, consider the information processing capacity of the typical person. A large variety of carefully executed studies support the argument that people are much more likely to use several different dimensions in discriminating among objects in any given domain, making only two or three reliable distinctions along each dimension, than they are to use a small number of dimensions but with a large number of distinctions on each one (Bruner 1956; Miller 1956; Tyler 1969; Stefflre 1972, 1979b).

For example, voters are more likely to think of politicians as differing in terms of party affiliation (either Democratic or Republican) and as being either for or against any of several particular issues, rather than thinking of politicians as being located at precise positions along a single liberal-conservative dimension. This is consistent with modern studies of voter behavior (Campbell et al. 1960; Nie et al. 1976).

Second, labeled regions (or clusters) help the strategist by explicitly recognizing the multiplicity of dimensions underlying placement in the model. This facilitates the identification and construction of objects that will position in the model where the strategist intends them to go—in developing

FIGURE 6.2. Map of Patterns of Competition for U.S. Political Figures. Two-Dimensional TORSCA-9B Solution for Preference Correlations (1970).

Source: Mauser (1979, 1980).

specific campaign themes for a particular bloc of voters, or in identifying the nature of support for a particular candidate. The model based on continuous dimensions is particularly difficult to translate into physical interpretations (Green 1975; Myers 1979).

As can be easily seen in Figure 6.2, the politicians fall naturally into two clusters: those preferred by Democratic voters on the left side of the figure, and those preferred by Republican voters on the right hand side. At the bottom of the figure, liberal Republican politicians tend to be intermingled with liberal Democrats. This contrasts with the more polarized structure seen in the 1968 presidential study, where two distinct clusters were identified with no overlap at all. It is impossible to tell from only two studies if this is due to the specific politicians included in these studies, or due to intrinsic differences between presidential and gubernatorial campaigns.

Interestingly enough, the hypothetical candidates are not as tightly clustered as are the politicians. A large number of issue-stands fall between

TABLE 6.5. Issue Positions Correlated with Jesse Unruh

Rank	Correlation		Issue Position
1	0.27	Issue 17	Make business pay a bigger share of taxes.
2	0.26	Issue 25	Make the state pay at least 50% of public school costs.
3	0.25	Issue 13	Close tax loopholes like the oil depletion allowance.
4	0.24	Issue 03	Ban offshore drilling to reduce oil pollution.
5	0.17	Issue 07	Be his own man and not be controlled by big business and rich campaign contributors..
21	−0.25	Issue 14	Increase state support for local police.
22	−0.26	Issue 18	Oppose school busing.
23	−0.28	Issue 11	Enforce rules of conduct for students and faculty in state schools.
24	−0.29	Issue 20	Crack down on drug abuse.
25	−0.31	Issue 15	Make colleges fire teachers who are involved in violent demonstrations.

Note: Correlations have been calculated from preference rankings for 25 issue positions and 25 political personalities. High positive correlations imply that the issue positions appeal to the same bloc of voters as does the personality of the political leader (total sample, N = 231).

158 • POLITICAL MARKETING

the two clusters of politicians. This indicates that these stands appeal to both Democratic and Republican voters alike. Of course, as was seen in the 1968 study, attracting bipartisan support is not synonymous with a high level of support. It is quite possible that certain issue stands might end up falling in the middle because they are rejected by both Democrats and Republicans. More typically, issue-stands position in the center because they receive support that cuts across party lines. Environmental and civil liberties issues, and an interest in increased consumer protection by governmental agencies appeal to certain voters within both the Democratic and Republican parties in California. This would appear to be fertile ground for campaign strategists, either Democratic and Republican.

Evaluating Issue-Positions

The primary goal of this study was to find a small number of issue-positions that could be used as campaign themes by the Democratic candidate for governor. For strategic reasons, positions or postures were sought that would not only be highly popular but that would also appeal to loyal Unruh supporters. In order to identify issue-positions or postures that met this goal, two specific criteria were set.

First, the issue-positions had to be chosen over the opposition by more than 50 percent of the respondents in a head-to-head choice situation.[5] This is a difficult criterion to meet, but it guarantees that any issue-position selected will be able to attract support. Moreover, it is particularly appropriate because the candidate himself must have met the same test in the general election: that is, he had to beat the opposition in a head-to-head contest.

TABLE 6.6. Personalities Correlated with Jesse Unruh

Rank	Correlation	Personality
1	0.51	Edmund G. "Pat" Brown
2	0.42	Hubert Humphrey
3	0.41	George Brown
4	0.38	John Tunney
5	0.37	Robert Kennedy
.		
.		
.		
20	−0.47	Billy Graham
21	−0.55	Max Rafferty
22	−0.56	George Murphy
23	−0.57	Spiro Agnew
24	−0.60	Ronald Reagan

Note: Correlations calculated from preference rankings for 25 well known personalities (total sample, N = 231). High-positive correlations imply that the political and religious leaders appeal to the same bloc of voters.

TABLE 6.7. Issue Positions Correlated with Ronald Reagan

Rank	Correlation		Issue Position
1	0.45	Issue 15	Make colleges fire teachers who are involved in violent demonstrations.
2	0.40	Issue 11	Enforce rules of conduct for students and faculty in state schools.
3	0.32	Issue 20	Crack down on drug abuse.
4	0.27	Issue 16	Cut welfare costs no matter who complains.
5	0.26	Issue 14	Increase state support for local police.
21	−0.23	Issue 07	Be his own man and not be controlled by big business and rich campaign contributors.
22	−0.24	Issue 19	Encourage college faculties to solve campus problems by themselves.
23	−0.25	Issue 13	Close tax loopholes like the oil depletion allowance.
24	−0.27	Issue 03	Ban offshore drilling to reduce oil pollution.
25	−0.28	Issue 06	Favors liberalizing abortion laws.

Note: Correlations have been calculated from preference rankings for 25 issue-positions and for 25 well-known political personalities. High positive correlations imply that the issue-positions appeal to the same bloc of voters that the personality of the political leader does (total sample, N = 231).

Second, the positions had to be preferred by the voters who currently preferred the Democratic candidate. This was determined by examining the extent to which preference rankings for issue-positions were correlated with preferences for Jesse Unruh. A high positive correlation between an issue-position and a politician implies that voters who prefer the issue-position also prefer that politician.

Table 6.9 shows how the issue-positions were evaluated in terms of the two criteria: high correlation with the Democratic candidate, and ranked higher than the Republican candidate by more than 50 percent of the respondents. First, issue-positions are arranged in this exhibit in terms of decreasing correlation with the Democratic candidate, and, in general, in terms of increasing correlation with the Republican candidate. Thus, the three issue-positions at the top of the table, #13, #17, and #7, appeal most strongly to the supporters of the Democratic candidate because they have the highest correlation. Thus, these three issue-positions satisfy the first of the

160 • POLITICAL MARKETING

TABLE 6.8. Personalities Correlated with Ronald Reagan

Rank	Correlation	Personality
1	0.70	Spiro Agnew
2	0.68	George Murphy
3	0.56	Max Rafferty
4	0.47	Sam Yorty
5	0.40	S. I. Hayakawa
.		
.		
.		
20	−0.43	Edmund Muskie
21	−0.48	Thomas Bradley
22	−0.52	George Brown
23	−0.56	Robert Kennedy
24	−0.60	Jesse Unruh

Note: Correlations calculated from preference rankings for 25 well-known personalities (total sample, N = 231). High-positive correlations imply that the political and religious leaders appeal to the same bloc of voters.

two criteria set out originally. Moreover, positions #13 and #7 have the highest degree of support of any positions in the study, being ranked higher than the Republican candidate by 65 percent and 64 percent respectively. Clearly, at least two issue-positions may be found that meet both of the two criteria established. All three of these issue-positions may be seen in Figure 6.4 tightly grouped together in the upper left—near Jesse Unruh and Robert Kennedy.

Issue-positions #4, #23, and #12 are also somewhat promising. While correlated less strongly with the Democratic candidate, these three issue-positions draw almost as many voters from the Republican candidate as do the first set of three positions. Issue-positions #23 and #4 are surprisingly powerful and draw their support from a hitherto unappreciated segment: a coalition of liberal Democrats and Republicans who desire increased consumer protection and improved quality of education in the public schools.

Issue-positions #20 and #21 may be clearly rejected because, while very popular, they have been preempted by the opposition. This may be seen by their strong negative correlation with the Democratic candidate. If these issue-positions were adopted by the Democratic candidate as his primary thrust in the campaign, it would be seen as being inconsistent with his previous image and it would damage his credibility with the electorate. At the very least these positions would do nothing as far as giving the voters reason to prefer him over the opposition. Support of these positions could cause loyal Democrats to turn their backs on the candidate of their own party. These defectors, while unlikely to vote Republican, would be certainly less likely to volunteer in the campaign or even to turn out themselves on election day.

TABLE 6.9. Evaluating Issue-Positions

Issue-Positions		Correlation[a] with Democratic Candidate	Correlation[a] with Republican Candidate	Preference[b]
Issue #17	Make businesses pay a bigger share of taxes.	.27	−.19	59%
Issue #13	Close tax loopholes.	.26	−.15	65%
Issue #7	Be his own man and not be controlled by business.	.18	−.19	64%
Issue #12	Cut property taxes for low- and middle-income homeowners.	.11	−.13	61%
Issue #23	Act now to improve public school quality.	.11	−.12	62%
Issue #4	Put some muscle into consumer protection.	.08	−.15	58%
Issue #24	Fight auto industry to eliminate smog.	.05	.00	58%
Issue #9	Insist upon tough antismog laws.	.00	.02	62%
Issue #21	Fight to make our cities safer places to live in.	−.23	.14	58%
Issue #20	Crack down on drug abuse.	−.28	.14	60%

[a] Respondents' preference rankings of 25 positions and 25 politicians were intercorrelated with each other. Issue-positions and politicians preferred by the same voters are correlated positively.

[b] This column shows the percentage of respondents who ranked each issue position over the Republican candidate. Percentages higher than 50 percent indicate that the position was preferred by more voters than the candidate.

Source: Mauser (1980).

The remaining two issue-positions are not yet seen as partisan issues. Neither position #9 nor #24 correlate with either gubernatorial candidate. It might be possible for the Democratic candidate to preempt these issues with adroit positioning.

We recommended that the candidate immediately adopt issue-positions #7 and #13 and use them as the keystone in his campaign. In addition, we urged careful consideration of issue-positions #4, #12, #17, and #23. They appeared somewhat promising, but further analysis seemed prudent before a decision could be made.

CONCLUSIONS

This study illustrated how the strategic positioning approach has been used to identify campaign strategy. This approach successfully found campaign themes that met the goals set at the beginning of the study, that is, to find a small number of campaign themes that simultaneously were highly popular and appealed to the candidate's present supporters. Finding such campaign themes had appeared difficult if not impossible prior to the study, as the campaign staff had seen the problem as one of having to choose between pragmatically copying the opposition or courting defeat by remaining pure.

It was not found to be necessary to choose between the Scylla or the Charybdis of the campaign staff's factions. The arguments of both the pragmatists and the purists rested on a shared oversimplified model of political behavior. Both factions erroneously assumed that voters' preferences were one-dimensional—stretching from liberals to conservatives. Consistent with such an analysis, they reasoned that it would be impossible to appeal simultaneously to both the undecided voter, who by definition is at the center of the political spectrum, as the pragmatists urged, and to the Democratic loyalist on the left, as the purists wanted, because these two groups were found at widely divergent locations on the ideological spectrum. As has been shown in this study, such a view was simplistic and excluded promising campaign strategies.

Voters' preferences were found to be multidimensional, rather than unidimensional, so that campaign themes could be identified that met both of the predetermined criteria at the same time. Thus the candidate was not forced to imitate the opposition in order to win the election. Our procedures identified issue-positions that, if adopted, would permit the candidate to appeal simultaneously to Democratic loyalists and to undecided voters.

Due to the lack of adequate information, campaign strategists often misread the political situation and unintentionally overlook powerful options. The widespread belief that political preferences are one-dimensional forces many campaigners unnecessarily to have to choose between maintaining their credibility and attempting to win the election. Improved procedures for generating and screening strategic alternatives will permit candidates to win elections in a more responsible manner.

In evaluating this approach, a crucial question to ask is did it enable the candidate to do better than he would have done without it? This is, of course, an extremely difficult question to answer, not only because of the inherent complexity of electoral campaigns, but also because of the way in which policy decisions are made. Nevertheless, a few observations are called for.

The reports of our voting studies were circulated among the key decision makers in the campaign. We know that out reports were read and understood by them. How influential our arguments or our reports were in shaping the policy decisions is more difficult to determine. However, it appears that the candidate reorganized his campaign strategy along the lines that we had advocated in our reports.

During October, Jesse Unruh ran a hard-hitting campaign, in which he stressed populist issues, contrasting his own support for the "little guy" with Ronald Reagan's "fat cat" supporters. His campaign was based on the voters' anger at high taxes and their resentment against tax loopholes available to big business. In many ways Unruh's campaign anticipated the populist fervor that eventually resulted in Proposition 13, the Jarvis-Gann initiative, a few years later.

The result of Unruh's decision to reorient his campaign was that the Democratic share of the vote, which had been declining steadily ever since the June primary elections, stopped falling and began to increase for the first time. As can be seen in Figure 6.3, the Democratic share of the vote increased

FIGURE 6.3. Evolution of Candidate Preferences during the 1970 Campaign

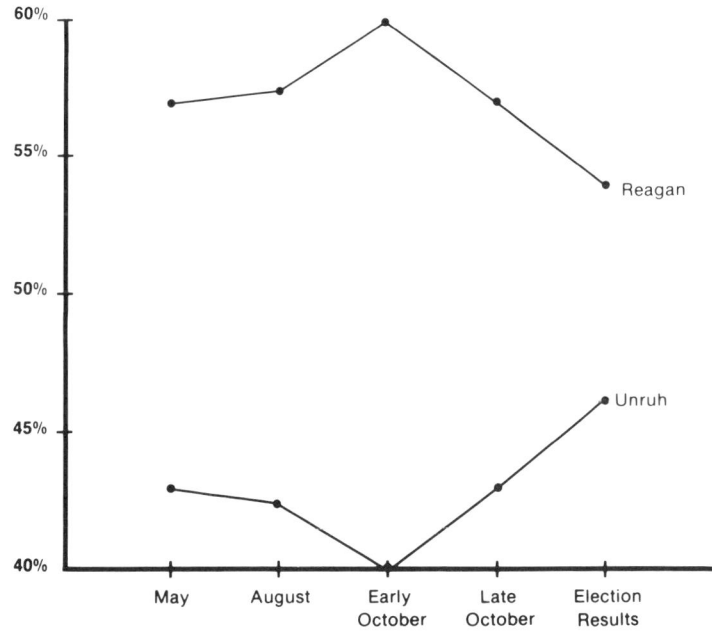

Source: Field (1970).

by six percentage points during the month immediately preceeding the election—the largest change during the entire year (Field 1970).

This reversal in the polls surprised many veteran political observers in California who had predicted a Democratic disaster in the November election. Not only was Ronald Reagan considered to be much more popular than Jesse Unruh, but the Republicans had a much larger political war chest: almost $5 million, according to some estimates, while the Democrats had to content themselves with less than $1 million. Reagan won reelection, but he came into office with a much smaller margin than had been predicted. Instead of sweeping in as he had in 1966, when he won by almost 1 million votes, Reagan defeated Unruh in 1970 by only 500,000 votes. More significantly, Reagan did not lead the ticket as he had in 1966; this time around, three statewide Republican candidates drew more votes than Reagan did.

In conclusion, the strategic positioning approach has been shown to be a powerful tool for developing campaign strategy. This approach permits strategists to identify highly effective issue-positions that meet the candidate's predetermined criteria. By so doing, it permits candidates to campaign more effectively and more efficiently. Campaigns can be more effective because candidates will be less likely to overlook powerful strategic options. Campaigns can be more efficient because by improving the information available to political strategists campaigners will be able to make better use of scarce campaign resources. Thus, the strategic positioning approach is cost-effective by helping candidates achieve a low cost-per-vote ratio.

NOTES

1. An excellent introduction to California politics is given in Bell and Price (1980).
2. Chapters 4 and 5 outline in detail the principles and procedures underlying this general approach.
3. The procedures involved in multidimensional scaling are described in Chapter 4. The two-dimensional configuration shown in Figure 6.1 has a stress of 0.253. Since this is rather high, the sample was divided along partisan lines (Democratic and Republican respondents) to examine the stability of the MDS configuration. A correlation of 0.64 was found between these two major political segments indicating a sufficient level of agreement to justify a single aggregate model for the entire electorate.
4. The two-dimensional configuration for all 50 items, issue-stands as well as political leaders, has a stress of 0.209, while the three-dimensional configuration has a stress of 0.153. The structure appears to be stable as there is a correlation of 0.75 between odd- and even-numbered respondents. Chapter 11 examines the general question of the stability of aggregate perception and preference structures.
5. Share-of-vote for issue-positions and political candidates were estimated using respondents' preference rankings. This procedure can yield highly accurate estimates, despite the large number of items that respondents had been asked to rank order. For example, the share-of-vote for the two major candidates in this contest, based on this sample, was very close to the actual

election returns. The two-party vote in Los Angeles County was estimated at 50 percent/50 percent while the actual returns were 48 percent/52 percent, which is well within sampling error estimates for a sample of this size. Chapter 9 examines this procedure in greater detail.

7
STRATEGIC ANALYSIS IN FRANCE

> The mercenaries and auxiliaries are useless and dangerous, and if any one supports his state by the arms of mercenaries, he will never stand firm or sure, as they are disunited, ambitious, without discipline, faithless, bold amongst friends, cowardly amongst enemies, they have no fear of God, and keep no faith with men.
>
> Machiavelli, *The Prince*

> France contains two fundamental temperments—that of the left and of the right; three principal tendencies, if one adds the center; six spiritual families; ten parties, large or small, traversed by multiple currents; fourteen parliamentary groups without much discipline; and forty million opinions.
>
> Jacques Fauvet

Earlier in this book, it was claimed that the strategic positioning approach could aid political candidates and parties to identify promising campaign strategies in any competitive election in the world. Some support for this sweeping claim may be found by examining how this approach fares in selected political contests in a few diverse countries. The two previous chapters examined U.S. elections: statewide contests for U.S. president and state governor. The next two chapters take a tentative step beyond U.S. politics and apply this approach to French elections.

This chapter shows how the strategic positioning approach was employed by one of the major political groupings in France to identify campaign strategies for candidates in selected legislative constituencies (*circonscriptions*) in the 1973 legislative elections. My goals here will be to present a general overview of how this approach was adapted to this particular political situation and to discuss the problems and pitfalls that were encountered in extending this approach to this French context. Chapter 8 selects a single *circonscription*, in order to focus on the methodology involved in the approach, and shows how it can be used to identify political options for legislative candidates.

The strategic positioning approach can be used in any political contest that is fairly and publicly conducted, in any country in the world. With appropriate modifications, this approach may be successfully applied in parliamentary as well as presidential systems, single- or multiple-member constituencies, two-party or multiparty contests, partisan or nonpartisan contests. While electoral systems vary greatly in terms of how individual votes are allocated to candidates, all democracies require candidates to compete for electoral support through public campaigning. In such elections, campaign strategy is directly related to voters' perceptions of the political parties and candidates. Thus, this approach, since it relies upon a close relationship between aggregate perceptions and patterns of competition, is applicable in any political system. Stefflre has argued that the principles underlying this approach hold across all languages and all cultures (Stefflre 1965; Stefflre et al. 1971). For example, the assertion that similar objects will substitute for each other to the extent that they are judged to be similar, which was empirically supported in U.S. elections, should also hold true for French politics. Similarly, the measurement techniques for mapping patterns of perceived similarity and patterns of competition and substitution have been devised to be independent of language and culture.[1] While there is no guarantee that principles and procedures, developed with a sensitivity for cross-cultural problems, will prove to be as robust as their authors believe, such an approach may be expected to have a greater hope of success than analytical techniques designed myopically for use in a particular context.

The application of this approach to any given electoral system, as with any survey approach, requires identifying the most appropriate electoral unit for conducting the study. In almost every popular voting scheme, however indirect, there is a readily identifiable electoral unit that is responsible for aggregating the popular vote; this is the unit required. The simplest voting scheme is that used in statewide elections where all citizens participate as a whole (for example, statewide elections of governor, or the French presidential elections).[2] Obviously, in this scheme the appropriate electoral unit is the state as a whole. Legislative elections, such as the French National Assembly or the U.S. House of Representatives, are slightly more complex since they are conducted constituency-by-constituency. To study the French National Assembly elections, for example, the most appropriate unit is the *circonscription*, which is the locus of elections for its members and corresponds to the U.S. congressional district. Thus, in the strategic positioning approach, as any survey approach, separate survey studies must be conducted constituency-by-constituency in order to interrelate adequately the electorate's perceptions with their preferences.

This chapter is divided into two principal sections. Since it is necessary to review French history and politics in order to make full use of this approach, the first section briefly describes the French electoral system and traces the recent history of the most important political parties and groupings.[3] The second section shows how the approach was used to identify promising campaign strategies for our client in the 1973 legislative elections. The methods used are critically described, identifying the major problems and pitfalls that were encountered, and selected results presented. Due to the extreme reticence of the client, it is not possible to present detailed results of this study. Nevertheless, partial results from a few *circonscriptions* are available. As in previous chapters, questions concerning the reliability and validity of the methodological procedures will be deferred to Part III of the book.

A BRIEF INTRODUCTION TO FRENCH POLITICS

The Electoral System

The present regime, the Fifth Republic, was formed in 1958 by General Charles de Gaulle at the request of the National Assembly. De Gaulle was invited to head the government and to revise the constitution by the National Assembly because the parliamentaary leaders feared civil war and hoped to avoid a *coup d'etat*, threatened by rebellious generals in Algeria. The Fourth Republic (1945-58) had chosen to abdicate rather than fight. Such an end was consistent for a regime that had stumbled from crisis to crisis throughout the 12 years of its existence. There was widespread agreement in France at this time that the Fourth Republic, crippled by internal divisions, could not confront issues or make forceful decisions; a new start was needed. (See Tables 7.1 and 7.2.)

The Fifth French Republic was designed by de Gaulle to overcome the weaknesses that he saw in the previous regime. He created a hybrid system, so that there would be a strong president, elected directly by popular vote, as well as a parliament, consisting of the National Assembly and the Senate. The separation of the executive and legislative branches of government, which is familiar to Americans, was clearly chosen by de Gaulle to reduce the power of the parliament by creating an independent seat of power. Parliament is organized in a manner not unlike the British model, with the striking exception that the president, not parliament, appoints the prime minister. In order to form a government, the prime minister must obtain the approval of parliament, but by virtue of his presidential appointment, he can operate much more independently of parliamentary coalitions than he could in the British model.

TABLE 7.1. Brief Synopsis of French History

circa	428	Monarchy
	1792	First Republic
	1804	First Empire (Napoléon I)
	1814	First Restauration
	1815	100 Days (Napoléon I and II)
	1815	Second Restauration
	1830	July Monarchy (Louis-Phillipe I)
	1848	Second Republic
	1852	Second Empire (Napoléon III)
	1871	Third Republic
	1940	Vichy Government (Marshal Pétain)
	1945	Fourth Republic
	1958	Fifth Republic (General de Gaulle)

The presidency is the center of power in the French Fifth Republic. The French president has much greater power than does any U.S. president. Not only can he dissolve parliament and call elections at any time he judges it opportune, giving him a powerful method to obtain popular approval for his policies, but, moreover, the checks and balances in the French constitution are much more limited than those of the U.S. presidential system. The only effective check on presidential power is the electorate, not parliament. Presidential elections and referenda are crucial in legitimizing the power of the presidency.

Since 1962, the president has been elected by direct popular vote for a seven-year term. Two rounds (*tours*) of balloting are held if no candidate can win an absolute majority of the vote (50 percent plus one) on the first ballot. In such a case, a second ballot is held two weeks after the first, between the two leading candidates in the first ballot. The authority of the president is greatly enhanced by these electoral procedures because they ensure that he must receive an absolute majority of the vote to take office.

De Gaulle reached back to the Third Republic (1871-1940) to find a method of electing deputies to the National Assembly, rejecting the system of proportional representation used in the Fourth Republic. Deputies are elected in the Fifth Republic by popular vote for five-year terms, in single member constituencies—*circonscriptions*—using two *tours* of voting if necessary. To win on the first ballot, a candidate must have an absolute majority of votes cast (50 percent plus one), including at least a quarter of all registered voters. If no candidate can meet these conditions, a second ballot is held the following Sunday, where only a plurality is required for victory. Any candidate receiving at least 10 percent of the vote can enter the second ballot.

Typically a large number of political parties field candidates in the first round. Because of the multitude of candidates, it is difficult to win an absolute majority. Less successful candidates, after negotiating concessions,

TABLE 7.2. Elections in the Fifth Republic for President and National Assembly

1958	President: de Gaulle elected
1958	National Assembly: UNR majority
1962	National Assembly: UNR majority
1965	President: de Gaulle reelected
1967	National Assembly: UNV^e majority
1968	National Assembly: UDR majority
1969	President: Pompidou elected
1973	National Assembly: narrow URP majority
1974	President: Giscard d'Estaing elected
1978	National Assembly: narrow RPR and UDF majority
1981	President: Mitterrand elected
1981	National Assembly: PS majority

often withdraw between rounds in favor of more successful competitors. French political coalitions often arrange to unite behind a common candidate on the second ballot, using the first ballot as a screening device. In this way the first ballot resembles a U.S. primary contest, serving to identify the most popular representatives of broad political groupings, who then face each other in the run-off election

Political Parties

As one of the oldest nations in Europe, France has a long and complex history. Past events have created deep divisions in the political culture, which still shape present day controversies, even as this common historical experience has created a strong sense of national identification. Basic political cleavages in France tend to be ideological and to be bound up closely with class differences. This contrasts sharply with the United States, where Americans, regardless of their political preferences, share much the same fundamental political beliefs, but tend to be divided more along ethnic and religious lines.

French politics is strongly polarized and appears to have been so since at least the time of the French Revolution in 1789. This polarization divides French citizens into two hostile camps, two large "political families," each inspired by a different political mood or temperament. The names used to identify these blocs of parties have changed throughout history, "Royalist" versus "Republican," or "Right" versus "Left," as have the political issues motivating the division, but the political alignment has remained surprisingly stable over a long period of history (see Table 7.3).

Since the founding of the Fifth Republic in 1958, the principal division in French politics has been between those who supported General de Gaulle and his policies, the *Gaullistes* (also called the *majorité*), and those who

TABLE 7.3. A Glossary of Political Parties and Factions in the Fifth Republic

Majorité (Majority)

CDP	*Centre démocratie et progrès* (split with the CD in 1969 to support UDR)
CNIP	*Centre national des indépendents et paysans* (a small right-wing group)
RI	*Républicains Indépendents*
RPR	*Rassemblement pour la République* (most recent name for UDR, adopted in 1976; led by Jacques Chirac)
UDF	*Union pour la Démocratie française* (coalition of RI, CDS, PR and other centrist factions in 1978 to support Valéry Giscard d'Estaing)
UDR	*Union des démocrates pour la République* (Known earlier as the UNR and the UDV^e)
UDV^e	*Union des démocrates pour la Ve République*
UNR	*Union pour la Nouvelle République*
URP	*Union des républicains de progrès* (electoral coalition in 1973 composed of UDR, RI and the CDP)

Centre

CD	*Centre démocrate*
CDS	*Centre des démocrates sociaux* (fusion of CD and CDP in 1976)
CR	*Centre républicain*
PR	*Parti radical-socialiste*
PSD	*Parti socialiste démocrate*
Réf	*Mouvement réformateur* (loose coalition among PR, CD, CR, and PSD in 1974, disbanded in 1978)

Gauche (Left)

FGDS	*Féderation de la gauche démocrate et socialiste* (electoral alliance of PS and MRG in 1967 and 1968)
MRG	*Mouvement des radicaux de gauche* (splinter group of PR in 1972)
PCF	*Parti communiste français*
PS	*Parti socialiste* (formerly the SFIO)
PSU	*Parti socialiste unifié* (split with the SFIO in 1958)
SFIO	*Section française de l'internationale ouvrière* (changed its name to PS in 1969)
UGSD	*Union de la gauche socialiste et démocrate* (electoral alliance of PS and MRG in 1973)

opposed him, the *gauche* (Left).[4] Until very recently, the *Gaullistes* constituted a majority of the deputies in the French National Assembly (hence their name), and won every presidential election, forcing the *gauche* into permanent opposition. Each of these political families includes several political parties and groupings that are constantly jockeying for power, forming coalitions, breaking up, and then regrouping into new coalitions.

General de Gaulle retired from politics in 1969, after losing a referendum, but the government remained in the hands of his supporters. In the National Assembly, the *Gaullistes* and their allies won a landslide victory that year, polling 46 percent of the votes cast, and controlling an absolute majority of seats in the Assembly. His second prime minister, Georges Pompidou, won the support of the Gaullist political barons and the presidential elections in 1969, held to replace de Gaulle.

In 1973, the Gaullist *majorité* consisted of three principal groups: UDR (*Union des démocrates pour la République*)[5] the RI (*Républicains indépendants*), and the CDP (*Centre démocratie et progrès*). To contest the legislative elections that year, these three groups formed a coalition to run candidates called the *Union des républicains de progrès* (URP). Prior to the 1973 elections, the UDR held the lion's share of the seats in the National Assembly (273 out of 483). Since they held an absolute majority, they could govern by and large without relying on the support of other groups. Nevertheless, two smaller parties were associated with the UDR in the majority: the RI, headed by Valéry Giscard d'Estaing, and the CDP, led by Jacques Duhamel. Of these two groups, the RI was by far the more important, as the RI held 61 seats in the Assembly and had been organized independently from the UDR since Giscard broke with de Gaulle's Algerian policy in 1967. The CDP was a more recent group, very loosely bound together; it included 27 centrist and independent members of the Assembly, and was fielding candidates for the first time in 1973 under its own banner.

The *gauche* formed the principal opposition to the *gaullistes*, which was, and still is, composed of two major parties and a scattering of smaller parties of varying significance. The two principal parties of the *gauche* are the *Parti socialiste* (PS), led by François Mitterrand, and the *Parti communiste français* (PCF), led by Georges Marchais. The PCF and the PS were formed in 1920, when the SFIO (*Section française de l'Internationale ouvrière*) split in response to the Russian revolution, and they have alternated between bitter rivalry and guarded cooperation ever since. In 1972, the two parties signed a historic agreement, *le programme commun*, which outlined their joint plans for governing France if the Left were to come to power.

Two other small but important parties on the French Left deserve to be mentioned: the *Mouvement des radicaux de gauche* (MRG) and the *Parti socialiste unifié* (PSU). The MRG had split off from the *Parti radical* in 1971 with the election of Jean-Jacques Servan Schreiber as the head of the *Parti radical*. Under the leadership of Robert Fabre, the MRG had decided to present candidates jointly with the PS under the banner *Union de la gauche socialiste et démocrate* (UGSD) in the 1973 elections and had joined with the PS in signing the *Programme commun*.

The PSU had been born in 1960 with the onset of the Fifth Republic by dissidents from both the PS and the PCF. Since its inception, the PSU has seen itself as a "laboratory of ideas" and has attracted young, diverse, and dynamic members. It has espoused some of the most controversial points of view in French politics. For example, it is associated most notably with the student uprisings in May 1968 and *autogestion* (industrial democracy). Neither the MRG nor the PSU has ever commanded more than a few votes or seats in the Assembly. Nevertheless, both parties play vital roles in leftist politics.

Despite the strong polarization of French politics, the center has attracted a small number of deputies in the National Assembly who spin a revolving kaleidoscope of tenuous groupings and coalitions. Prior to the 1973 elections, several centrist groups had formed the *Movement réformateur*, consisting primarily of the *Parti radical*, under the direction of Jean-Jacques Servan Schreiber, and the *Centre démocrate*, led by Jean Lecanuet. The *Centre républicain* and the *Parti social-démocrate* (PSD) were also involved, but only as minor players.

Despite the large number of seats held by the *majorité* in the National Assembly, public opinion was about evenly divided between the *gauche* and the *majorité* going into the 1973 elections. As can be seen in Table 7.4, both blocs could count on about 40-46 percent of the total vote. Control of the Assembly depended upon the distribution of the vote. In the past, the left had won fewer seats than the *majorité* because its vote was more highly concentrated in dense urban districts. Most of the deputies in the *majorité* came from sparsely populated and more competitive districts. Because of the unusual nature of the previous election, which had been held immediately following the 1968 disruptions, the left counted on winning back a few of its traditional seats (see Table 7.5).

TABLE 7.4. Political Preferences in 1973

Majorité (URP: UDR, RI, and CDP)	37%
Réformateurs	15%
Extreme Right	3%
UGSD (PS and MRG)	21%
PSU and Extreme Left	4%
PCF	20%
	100%

Source: Survey of Metropolitain France by SOFRES (February 21-24, 1973) as reported in *Le Monde*

TABLE 7.5. Division of Seats in the French National Assembly prior to the 1973 Elections

Elected March 1967		Outgoing Assembly (elected June 1968)	
Majority		*Majority*	
UDV[e]	244	UDR	273
		RI	61
		CDP	26
Center		*Center*	
Centre démocrate	27	*Réformateurs*	15
Diverse moderates	17	Diverse moderates	20[b]
Left		*Left*	
FGDS[a]	116	UGSD-PS[c]	41
		UGSD-MRG	8
PCF	73	PCF	34
PSU and extreme left	5	PSU and extreme left	1
Diverse left	5	Diverse left	4[d]
	487		483[e]

[a] *Fédération de la gauche démocrate et socialiste.*

[b] Consisting of 12 ex-UDR, four PDM (*Progrès et Démocratie moderne*), three unaffiliated, and one radical.

[c] *Union de la gauche socialiste et démocrate*, which involved the *parti socialiste* (PS) and the *mouvement des radicaux de gauche* (MRG).

[d] Consisting of three ex-socialists, and one extreme left.

[e] There were four vacant seats due to recent deaths and resignations (all formerly held by the UDR).

Source: *Les Forces Politiques et Les Élections de Mars 1973, Le Monde.*

THE STUDY

This section shows how the strategic positioning approach was adapted for use in the French legislative elections. As it was a contracted study, the client has the right to keep private certain sensitive material. Thus, my presentation, by necessity, will be somewhat programmatic. Nevertheless, a basic outline of the study will be presented, with attention to the modifications required by the French context, and illustrative results presented.

Prior to the 1973 legislative elections, plans were being laid by party leaders for the coming election campaign. I was contacted by a marketing research firm in Paris to help design and implement a nationwide survey for one of the major political groupings.[6] We proposed targeting 100 *circonscriptions* throughout France for extensive survey analysis: only the ones most needed for our client to win control of the National Assembly. All of the one hundred *circonscriptions* were to be surveyed, using this approach, in order to identify the most effective way to position candidates in those districts.

The goal of the study was to identify a small number of positions and postures that would position selected candidates most effectively in the targeted districts. Our task was complicated by two interrelated problems. First, we had to select positions that would be effective in both rounds of voting, but the nature of the competition would differ from the first to the second round of voting. In the first *tour*, the most dangerous competitors would be rival groups in the *majorité*, (that is, either the RI or the CDP), while in the second *tour*, competition would be most likely from the *gauche*, either a Socialist or a Communist, with the possibility that the *réformateurs* might also run a candidate to give a few three-way races. Thus, positions and postures need to be found that would be effective against rival groups in the *majorité* as well as against the *gauche*.

The second complicating factor was the difficulty of running a coherent national campaign with the wide variety of constituencies in the country. This variety necessitated tailoring the campaign to local conditions in each *circonscription*, but the demands of running a national campaign militated against too fragmented an approach. The kinds of problems that worried the voters differed across the country, as did their responsiveness to various claims and promises. If possible, positions and postures needed to be found that would be effective across the full range of *circonscriptions* in the country.

Our proposal was accepted, although in a somewhat scaled down form. Early in January 1973 we started interviewing in selected *circonscriptions* throughout France. *Circonscriptions* were chosen for the study in the following way. First, we identified those that appeared critical on the basis of previous legislative contests, that is, they had to be competitive with the UDR-URP having a reasonable, but not too solid chance of winning.[7] This followed from the triage concept: we wanted to find those districts where our intervention could make a difference. It would be useless to analyze in detail those districts where our client was either a shoo-in or had no chance of winning. Next, the client went through the list to identify those *circonscriptions* where the central party organization wished to give substantial support to candidates.

Interviews

After the preliminary screening, a number of *circonscriptions* were selected throughout France to be the target of further study. In each, a sample (of 150 to 250 respondents) was drawn, using probabilistic sampling procedures, and interviewed during January 1973, prior to the nomination of candidates and less than two months before the first *tour* of the election, which was to be held March 4, 1973.

Respondents were interviewed personally, in their homes, by professional interviewers. To qualify for the interview, respondents had to be French citizens of voting age. The interviews lasted approximately 45 minutes and covered a wide range of political questions. As a cost saving measure, this interview included both similarity judgments of French political leaders and questions about their preferences for leaders and selected positions and postures. Respondents were asked about their preferences for local candidates who appeared likely to enter the upcoming legislative elections, in addition to the national leaders of the major political groupings (e.g., Giscard, Mitterrand, and Chaban Delmas).

In hindsight, the decision to collect both perceptual (judged similarity) and preference data in the same interview was less effective than had been hoped before the study and would not be recommended under similar circumstances. The perceptual data are primarily valuable for generating hypotheses about who competes with whom and why. Such hypotheses are valuable sources of ideas for campaign themes and appeals. These hypotheses and ideas should be tested in the preference survey, if there is time to analyze the perceptual data prior to collecting the preference data. This is impossible, of course, when both perceptual and preference data are collected simultaneously. It would have been better to have drawn a much smaller, but earlier, pilot sample drawn in only one or two of the *circonscriptions* targeted for the study. This procedure would have improved the chances of identifying more effective ways to position the party's candidates.

Two very different, but complementary, approaches were taken to identify promising positions and postures. First, respondents were asked a series of open-ended questions about what they thought the election of each major political grouping would entail.[8] In this way, the hopes and fears of the voters were ascertained in their own words. Second, respondents were asked to indicate their preferences for 23 positions and postures that appeared likely to be used by one or more of the major political groupings, or that were being considered for use by our client. This permitted an evaluation of party strategy in each district

Finally, voters were asked about their level of political interest, their past votes, their voting intentions in the upcoming legislative elections as well as in selected hypothetical elections, and a variety of questions classifying them into standard political and social categories.

Strategic Analysis

The goal of the data analysis was the identification of the strategic options available to our client at both the national and individual constituency level. The report forwarded to our client included, at both levels:

1. Spatial maps of political parties, candidates, and postures.
2. The problems seen as most serious by voters of specified types.

3. The electorate's image of the three major political factions (the majority, the center, and the left).
4. The electorate's reaction to selected campaign positions, postures and promises.
5. Estimates of election outcomes for alternative candidates and strategies.

Each of these points will now be discussed in turn. To illustrate our approach to strategic analysis, as well as to give a flavor of this electoral contest, a few selected constituencies will be examined.

Spatial Maps

As in previous chapters, spatial maps were used to gain an overview of the competitive situation. In France, given the multiplicity of political parties, spatial maps must include political parties as well as political leaders and issue-stands. This permitted the identification of the source of support of each political party and each political leader.

Figure 7.1 shows the patterns of competition among French political parties and leaders in one *circonscription* going into the 1973 legislative elections.[9] Since this spatial map is based on intercorrelating respondents' preferences for leaders and parties, clusters in this figure represent items preferred by the same type of voter. Items position close together in this spatial map only if they are highly intercorrelated. A positive correlation implies that both items are viewed similarly to be liked (or disliked) by the same people, while a negative correlation implies that respondents who prefer one, dislike the other.

Spatial maps are useful in identifying the basis of support for politicians or political parties. As is easily seen, there are two readily identifiable groupings: on the left are the three major parties of the *gauche* (PS, PSU, and PCF), as well as the prominent leaders of those parties; on the right is a somewhat more diffuse cluster of parties and leaders, scattered around the *majorité* (the UDR and the RI). Immediately above and to the left of the *majorité* are the center parties (e.g., PDM, CD), with their leaders—Dunhamel, Lecanuet, and Poher. At the upper-right is Tixier-Vignancourt, a well-known proponent of the extreme right.

The principal strategic implications of this map are straightforward: the *majorité* and the *gauche* appeal to very different segments of the electorate and cannot expect to draw support from the other segment. This confirms the claim that the French electorate is fundamentally divided into two warring camps, and that the centrists primarily appeal to the followers of the *majorité* rather than the then-opposition parties of the left.

Only a few political leaders, Jean-Jacques Servan Schreiber (JJ SS) and Nicoud, and the *parti radical*, resist bifurcation and remain boldly in the center of the figure. JJ SS was at that time the leader of the *parti radical* (PR), which, despite its name, is a center-left party from the French Fourth

FIGURE 7.1. Map of Patterns of Competition for French Political Leaders. Two-Dimensional TORSCA-9B Solution for Preference Correlations (8 Political Parties; 21 Leaders; Stress = 0.179)

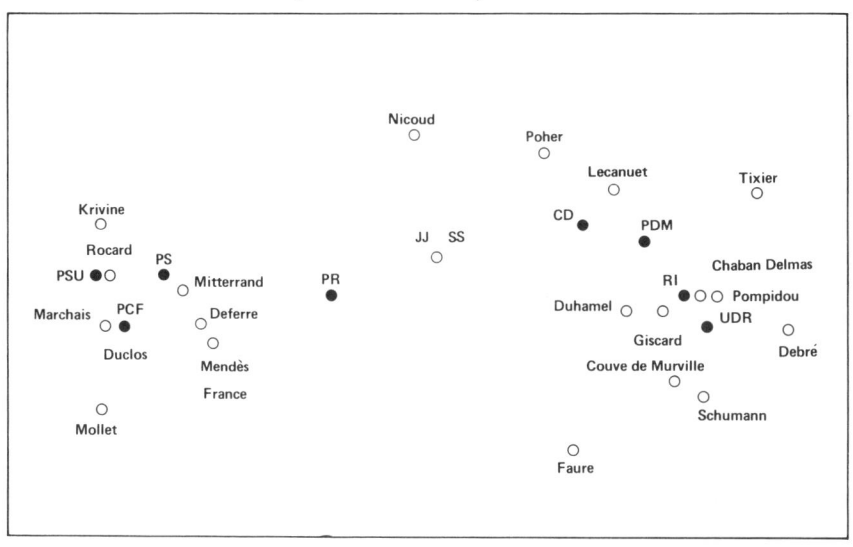

Source: Mauser and Stefflre (1974).

and Fifth Republics, which had been allied with the FGDS during the late 1960s. With the election of JJ SS to the leadership of the *parti radical* the party split open with a large fraction of its membership forming the *movement des radicaux de gauche* (MRG), in rejection of JJ SS's centrist orientation, to form an electoral alliance with Mitterrand and the *parti socialiste* (PS). JJ SS then took the rest of the party members and joined with Jean Lecanuet, of the *Centre démocrate* (CD), to launch the *movement réformateur* in preparation for the 1973 legislative elections.

Perceived Problems

Before fixing their campaign strategies, political parties must identify the major concerns of the voters. In legislative elections, this means assessing the electorate's concerns in each and every constituency. A standard method of doing this is to ask a sample of respondents what they think are the most serious problems facing them at that time.[10] In our survey, responses were recorded verbatim and coded to reveal the most frequently mentioned types of comments. Table 7.6 presents the results from one of the constituencies in the study. As can be readily seen, inflation and its attendant problems dominated the respondents' concerns, while international issues (e.g., world peace) drew many fewer comments. Given the bifurcation of the electorate, it

180 • POLITICAL MARKETING

might be expected that quite different problems would dominate the concerns of the supporters of the *majorité* and those who supported the *gauche*. This was found to be the case, although the patterns varied from *circonscription* to *circonscription*.

Images of Political Factions

The electorate's response to any campaign promise or posture depends on their image of the politician or political faction who takes that stand. Certain claims will be more believable depending on who says them or about whom they are said. Tables 7.7 through 7.9 show the images of the three major political factions as determined in one constituency on the outskirts of Paris (the 13th *circonscription* of the Hauts-de-Seine).

The *majorité* has a solid, but somewhat dowdy image. It is seen as providing "continuity," and "stable government," virtues that are not

TABLE 7.6. Most Serious Problems Seen Facing the French Public

	Frequency Mentioned	Percentage
Improve purchasing power	71	14.5%
Decent retirement	41	8.4
Increase wages	36	7.3
Housing conditions	36	7.3
Stable prices (value of the *franc*)	32	6.5
Job security	31	6.3
Age of retirement	26	5.3
Reform in education	25	5.1
Work conditions	19	3.9
Social security (public health)	18	3.7
Transportation problems	18	3.7
Fiscal reform	18	3.7
Welfare politics	17	3.5
Unemployment	16	3.2
Social reform	15	3.0
Jobs for women	14	2.8
Free speech	9	1.8
World peace	8	1.6
French military independence	6	1.2
Shorter work week	5	1.0
Cost of living	4	0.8
Government budget	3	0.6
Other	23	4.7
	491	99.9%

Note: These data are based on 150 respondents drawn from the eighth *circonscription* of the Hauts-de-Seine. Problems total more than 150 because respondents could mention more than one problem.

TABLE 7.7. Voters' Image of the *Majorité*

Potential Benefits

22%	Continuity (vs. 0%—G, 10%—R)
9.0%	Stable government (vs. 0%—G, 2%—R)
7.7%	Foreign policy (vs. 3%—G, 6%—R)
7.0%	Economic policy (vs. 4%—G, 8%—R)
3.9%	Price stability (vs. 1.8%—G, 1%—R)
3.2%	Freedom of the press (vs. 2.2%—G, 5%—R)
2.0%	Keep their promises (vs. 1.3%—G, 5%—R)

Potential Dangers

19.2%	Increase in the cost of living (vs. 1.8%—G, 2.9%—R)
8.3%	Social class differences (vs. 0.6%—G, 5.8%—R)
7.7%	Scandals (vs. 2.4%—G, 0%—R)
7.0%	Continuity (vs. 1.2%—G, 7.2%—R)
6.4%	Stagnation (vs. 1.8%—G, 5.8%—R)
5.8%	Social problems (housing, transportation) (vs. 1.2%—G, 0%—R)
4.5%	Unemployment (vs. 0%—G, 1.4%—R)

Note: These comments are based on a sample of 150 respondents drawn from the 13th *circonscription* of the Hauts-de-Seine. Percentages indicate the relative frequency with which each comment was made in reference to that grouping (e.g., 22 percent of all positive comments made about the *majorité* referred to "continuity," while there were no references to "continuity" for the *gauche* [G] and only 10% of such comments for the *réformateurs* [R].

unimportant in France, a country that still remembers the precarious Fourth Republic that tottered along after World War II for 12 years, but such virtues are not very exciting either. Since neither of the other two political factions, the *gauche* or the *réformateurs*, are seen as being able to provide "a stable government," this is a powerful attribute. In fact, the *majorité* has relied on this belief so strongly that they have made their governing ability a central theme in every election since the founding of the Fifth Republic in 1958. The drawbacks of being in power are also evident. The government is blamed for inflation, class differences, and for not solving important social problems, such as the need for better housing, transportation, and jobs for the unemployed. A series of scandals involving members of the government has not gone unnoticed either. Finally, there are even some voters who take the *majorité* to task for their primary virtue, continuity, evidently equating it with stagnation, and yearning for change.

The *gauche* is seen quite differently, almost a mirror image of the Gaullists. In a time when people's major worries are economic, a leftist government is viewed as meaning better working and living conditions. Where the Gaullist majority is seen as stable, respondents fear that electing the *gauche* would mean internal chaos and oppression. Since the *gauche* has not been in power since the founding of the Fifth Republic, it is an unknown

TABLE 7.8. Voters' Image of the *Gauche*

Potential Benefits

27%	Prices, salaries, cost of living (vs. 8.4%—M, 8%—R)
22%	Better conditions for workers (vs. 6.4%—M, 7%—R)
12%	Social reforms (vs. 7%—M, 13%—R)
5.3%	Transportation, public services (vs. 3.2%—M, 4%—R)
4%	Labor reforms (vs. 2%—M, 3%—R)

Potential Dangers

18%	Oppression (vs. 4.5%—M, 4.4%—R)
16.8%	Disorder, discontent, panic (vs. 5%—M, 7.2%—R)
10.2%	Fear of communism (vs. 0%—M, 1.4%—R)
8.4%	Monopoly, nationalization (vs. 6.4%—M, 1.4%—R)
7.8%	Poor foreign relations (vs. 1.9%—M, 0%—R)
5.4%	Decline of capital investment (vs. 1.9%—M, 0%—R)
2.4%	Poor budget decisions (vs. 1.3%—M, 0%—R)

Note: These comments are based on a sample of 150 respondents drawn from the 13th *circonscription* (Hauts-de-Seine). Percentages indicate the relative frequency with which each comment was made in reference to that grouping (e.g., 27% of the positive comments made about the left referred to "prices, salaries, or the cost of living," while there were only 8.4% and 8% of that kind of comment for the *majorité* [M] and the *réformateurs* [R], respectively).

and untested entity. The electorate appears to project both its hopes, as well as its fears, onto the left.

The *gauche* is seen as promising to solve the problems that the *majorité* has left unsolved: prices, salaries, and the cost of living, as well as bringing about desired social reforms, particularly for workers. On the other hand, many voters fear a change of regime. They fear government oppression, perhaps because they equate the *gauche* with Communism, or perhaps because they anticipate that the *gauche*, once in power, would act against their economic interests; witness the fears about nationalization, bad governmental budget decisions, and the decline of capital for investment purposes. It has been typical in France for years that immediately before every election there are front page stories concerning French citizens who have been caught fleeing to Switzerland with hundreds of thousands of French francs in cash in anticipation of the *gauche* coming to power.

The striking contrast between the images of the *majorité* and the *gauche* suggests that the best campaign for the *majorité* would be to promise some reforms (at least promise a rededication to "good government"), in order to combat their negative image, but to put the most stress in their campaign on frightening voters about the horrible consequences of a victory of the *gauche*. This is nothing new. The *majorité* has paraded the bogey man of the *gauche* for years with regular success.

The intense polarization of the French electorate, seen in the contest just discussed, is also reflected in voters' image of the *réformateurs*, who are seen

Strategic Analysis in France • 183

TABLE 7.9. Voters' Image of the *Réformateurs*

Potential Benefits

13%	Social reform (vs. 11%—M, 27%—G)
10%	Continuity (vs. 34%—M, 0%—G)
8%	Economic and political reform (vs. 2.6%—M, G)
6%	Foreign policy (vs. 7.7%—M, 3%—G)
5%	Keep their promises (vs. 3%—M, G)
3%	Reform of social security and family benefits (vs. 2%—M, 2.2%—G)

Potential Dangers

17.4%	Poor foreign relations (vs. 3.2%—M, 7.8%—G)
14.5%	Economic and political instability (vs. 5.8%—M, 4.2%—G)
7.2%	Do not keep their promises (vs. 0%—M, 2.4%—G)
7.2%	Continuity (vs. 7%—M, 1.2%—G)

Note: These comments are based on a sample of 150 respondents drawn from the 13th *circonscription* (Hauts-de-Seine). Percentages indicate the relative frequency with which each comment was made in reference to that grouping (e.g., 17.4% of all negative comments made about the *réformateurs* referred to their poor foreign policy, while there were only 3.2% and 7.8% of that kind of comment made about the *majorité* [M] and the *gauche* [G], respectively).

as having the drawbacks of both the *majorité* and the *gauche*. A government led by the *réformateurs* is seen as simultaneously maintaining continuity and provoking political and economic instability. The electorate's memory is still fresh of the unstable and inept governments of the Fourth Republic, when the centrists last held power. On the positive side, the *réformateurs* are seen as potentially being able to bring about needed reforms even while maintaining continuity. However, only rarely have the *réformateurs* been able to translate this hybrid image into votes.

Even as spoilers, the *réformateurs* are an important thorn in the side of the *majorité*. As was seen in Figure 7.1, the *réformateurs* appeal primarily to the same segment of the electorate as does the *majorité*. A careful inspection of the images of these three factions show why. The *réformateurs* offer an alternative to those voters who are dissatisfied with the lackluster performance of the *majorité*, and who desire the kinds of social reforms promised by the *gauche*, but who are still afraid of what the *gauche* would do once in power. Such a posture would appeal to a certain portion of the electorate that might otherwise vote reluctantly for the *majorité*, or not cast a ballot, which would split the vote for the *majorité*, in some *circonscriptions*, thereby electing candidates from the *gauche*. The possibility of the *gauche* coming to power haunted French politics in the mid-1970s.

Evaluating Positions and Postures

To assess the drawing power of political positions and postures, respondents were asked to rank a variety of slogans and promises in terms of

TABLE 7.10. Patterns of Draw for Campaign Positions and Postures in the 1973 Legislative Elections

Campaign Positions	Draw from Pompidou	Draw from Mitterrand	Total Draw
14. Better pay	43%	40%	83%
4. Find jobs	38	44	82
18. World peace	47	35	82
8. Purchasing power	40	41	81
6. Reduce the work week	34	37	71
15. Less specialized work	33	35	68
7. Protect nature	38	29	67
2. Social security	28	32	60
5. Participate in decisions	29	30	59
17. Defend consumers	29	29	58
11. Local sports facilities	28	29	57
23. Constituency problems	28	25	53
3. Freedom of the press	21	30	51
13. Fight corruption	26	24	50
21. Small businessmen, peasants	26	22	48
1. Economic superpower	23	18	41
9. An independent France	17	20	37
19. Educational policy	24	13	37
12. Less control by Paris	15	21	36
20. Continuity	24	11	35
16. Repress agitation	19	9	28
22. Heads of business	16	11	27
10. Illegal abortions	10	8	18

Note: Entries are percentage of respondents who prefer each theme over *both* Pompidou and Mitterrand, showing draw from Pompidou's supporters and from Mitterrand's. These results are based on a sample drawn from the third *circonscription* in the *Cher.*

their preferences for them. The results for one of the *circonscriptions* included in the study is shown in Table 7.10. The entries are the percentage of respondents who prefer each slogan or promise over these national leaders. For example, 43 percent of the sample preferred position # 14, "increase the revenue of the poorest paid workers," over Pompidou, while 40 percent preferred this same slogan over Mitterrand, giving a total of 83 percent of the respondents who preferred that slogan over both of the national leaders. As may be seen, the most powerful issues concern the national economy (# 14, 4, and 8), although "world peace" (# 18) and "improved working conditions (# 6 and 5) follow closely in voters' minds. The *gauche* would appear to have captured somewhat more appealing slogans than the *majorité*, in promising to improve wages and reduce unemployment, while the *majorité* is seen as "maintaining purchasing power" (# 8), which is important, but less immediate.

A few slogans drew more support than had been anticipated—"defending consumers" (# 17) and "protecting the environment (# 7) did not figure prominently in any bloc's campaign rhetoric, but did surprisingly well with voters.

On the basis of analyses like these in each of the *circonscriptions* included in the study, we recommended that the URP orient its campaign around combatting inflation, arguing that only "the party of de Gaulle" had the leadership to deal effectively with this problem while maintaining stability and continuity. People's fears of social disorder, if the *gauche* were to come to power, could be fanned in order to counteract their unrealistic promises of better jobs and wages for workers. Finally, we argued for initiating reforms of selected political and economic institutions in order to undercut support for the opponents of the *majorité*. Precisely which reforms should be made required further study.

CONCLUSIONS

When the dust had settled, after both rounds of voting, the *majorité* still retained control of the National Assembly but had lost nearly 100 seats.

TABLE 7.11. Impact of the 1973 Elections

	Outgoing Assembly	Elected		Total	Gains or Losses
		First Ballot	Second Ballot		
Parties or Factions					
URP-UDR	273	26	158	184	−89
URP-RI	61	13	41	54	− 7
URP-CDP	26	6	17	23	− 3
Réformateurs	15	—	31	31	+16
UGSD-PS	41	1	88	89	+48
UGSD-MRG	8	—	12	12	+ 4
PCF	34	8	65	73	+39
PSU & Extreme Left	1	—	3	3	+ 2
Diverse	24[a]	6	13	19[b]	− 5
	483[c]	60	428	488[d]	

[a] Consisting of 20 diverse moderates and four diverse left (see notes for Table 7.3).
[b] Consisting of 14 diverse majority, three diverse left and two unaffiliated.
[c] There were four vacant seats due to deaths or resignations.
[d] Three seats had been added to the National Assembly for the 1973 elections (all in the Bouches-de-Rhone), giving a new total of 490 seats in the National Assembly, but at the time of publication in 1973 the results were not available for two seats.

Source: *Les Forces Politiques et Les Élections de Mars 1973*, Le Monde.

Almost all of the gains of the last elections, held immediately after the student uprisings in 1968, had been erased. (Compare Tables 7.5 and 7.11.) But the Gaullists and their allies still controlled a comfortable majority in the Assembly. With 275 seats, they held 30 more than an absolute majority. While the *gauche* picked up almost all of the seats the *majorité* lost (the Socialists picked up 48 seats and the Communists 39), the big winners in the election were the centrists. For the first time in the history of the Fifth Republic, the UDR had to share power with other parliamentary groupings as it no longer held a majority of seats by itself in the Assembly. The RI and CDP, with 77 seats between them, now held the balance of power. Even though the UDR was the largest party in the Assembly, it could no longer govern without the assent of its smaller allies.

The dreams of the centrists were aroused by the success of the *réformateurs* in the 1973 elections. The *movement réformateur* doubled its numbers in the Assembly from 15 to 31 seats, so that they finally held enough seats to qualify as a recognized parliamentary group. This meant a significant increase in their rights and prerogatives in the Assembly, principal among them was the right to join legislative committees, a privilege long denied them. Their electoral success spurred many of the centrists, principally Giscard D'Estaing, to dream of creating a "new majority," one rooted in the center of the political spectrum, extending from Socialists of Gaullists.

Our study achieved its modest aims. In each of the *circonscriptions* we identified the positions and postures that would be the most effective for *majorité* candidates. In some cases, the URP did not have a good chance of winning. Our surveys confirmed this so that we recommended the URP candidate withdraw in order to use the resources more effectively elsewhere. Overall, our surveys confirmed the results of the national surveys by IFOP and SOFRES that voters were primarily concerned about economic issues, but were profoundly divided over whose leadership to accept, that of the *gauche* or the *majorité*. Our surveys did, however, find two issues to be important to voters that had been overlooked by most politicians and pollsters: defending consumers and protecting the environment. In the ensuing seven years, environmental concerns have become a significant political issue in France.

Due to the complexity of politics, it is difficult to say whether our particular study had an impact on the election outcome. Probably not much, if any. Perhaps we contributed to the victories of a few candidates by identifying the key positions to adopt. But these candidates most certainly had other information available to them that supported the same decision. The principal means left with which to evaluate the study is to evaluate the methods by internal reliability and validity checks. This is done to a limited extent in Chapters 10 and 11, where I pull together results for all four studies.

NOTES

1. See Stefflre (1968, 1972, 1979a) and Stefflre et al. (1971). From a practical point of view, one would expect that the approach would fare rather well in multiparty systems in light of its success in a wide variety of commercial markets in a number of countries, since commercial markets typically contain a large number and variety of products and brands (Stefflre 1979a).

2. In the U.S. presidential elections, the most appropriate unit is the state, rather than the nation as a whole, because of the role states play in the electoral college. For further discussion of this point, see Chapter 5.

3. Of necessity, this introduction will have to be extremely brief. For the reader hungry to explore French politics further, I would recommend starting with Henry Ehrmann's very readable book, *Politics in France*, now in its third edition. A valuable source of information concerning the 1973 legislative elections is the slim supplement *Les Forces Politiques et les Elections de Mars 1973*, published by *Le Monde*, March 1973. Moreover, my introductory comments focus on French politics in the mid-1970s. Much has happened in France during the past decade that cannot be discussed here. In 1981, for the first time, the Socialists won control of the government from the center-right coalition that had been in power since the founding of the Fifth Republic in 1958. François Mitterrand, running for president for the third time, beat Giscard d'Estaing by over one million votes out of over 30 million votes cast, after losing to Giscard by fewer than 450,000 in 1974. He immediately dissolved the National Assembly and called for the country to give the left a majority in the Assembly so he could adequately govern. France responded by giving him a stunning victory, with the Socialists winning an absolute majority in the Assembly. But this is another story. Chapter 7 and 8 look at French politics in the mid-1970s, so we must try to put ourselves back at that point, attempting to ignore what we know of recent events in France.

4. For want of better terms, the political groups that supported de Gaulle and his political successors, principally the UDR, RI, and CDP, will be referred to here interchangeably as the *majorité* or the *Gaullistes*, even though this coalition ceased to command a majority of seats in the National Assembly after 1973, and, in addition, many members of the RI or the CDP would categorically reject such a label, preferring to be called *modérés* or *centristes*. There simply is no good term that elicits general agreement for this group. Since this coalition opposes the *gauche* it might be thought reasonable to call it the *droit* (right), but ever since World War II, this term has been rejected by every significant French political group as an insult.

5. The UDR (*Union des démocrates pour la République*) is the original Gaullist party and has had a variety of names since it was hastily thrown together to support General de Gaulle's return to power in 1958. At its founding, it was known as the *Union pour la Nouvelle République* (UNR), but in 1967 became the *Union des démocrates pour la Ve République* (UDV^e). After the events of 1968, the party adopted the name *Union pour la défense de la République* (UDR) to contest the 1968 legislative elections. Soon afterward it adopted the present title, leaving its initials unchanged.

6. This study was a frustrating one for me for several reasons. First, I was never officially told who the client was, although it soon became obvious that it was a faction in the UDR. Not knowing the client made it difficult to develop effective strategy. Second, I had to work through intermediaries to analyze the data. Such an arrangement worked very imperfectly. As a result, I could not do as many empirical checks on the methods as I would have liked, which led me to have less confidence in the analysis than I would have wished.

7. Such districts are sometimes called "marginal" or "swing" districts (see LeGall and Riglet 1973).

8. "In your opinion, what would be the advantages of a government formed by the current majority [UDR, CDP, and the Independent Republicans]?" This was followed by "What would

be the disadvantages?" Similar questions were then asked in turn for the *gauche* and the *réformateurs*.

9. This particular figure is based on a sample of respondents drawn from a *circonscription* in the *Isère* in the French Alpes. While some readers may be surprised, the patterns of competition revealed here closely resemble those of the national combined sample in that the same polarization between the *majorité* and the *gauche* was found in *all circonscriptions*. Aggregate data of this sort is typically quite stable, even over quite diverse types of samples (Converse 1964; Messick 1961; Snider and Osgood 1969).

10. This question was "In your opinion, what would you say are the most important problems currently facing the French people?"

8
IDEOLOGY, IMAGE, AND POLITICAL STRATEGY

> In politics as elsewhere one must not love too much; it confuses; it lessens the clarity of one's view—and it is not always counted to one's credit.
> Charles-Maurice de Tallyrand

> *Suivez-moi, vous aurez un bien meilleur destin*
> La Fontaine, *Le loup et le chien*

This chapter shows how the strategic positioning approach can be used to develop campaign strategy in a multiparty contest in France.[1] Voters' political preferences were analyzed in a selected legislative constituency in order to identify strategic options facing political parties in that constituency.[2] The previous chapter gave a general overview of how the approach was used at the national level by one of the major political factions in the 1973 French legislative elections, but it did not examine the technical workings of the methodology in any particular constituency. That has been left to this chapter. By focusing on a single constituency, it is possible to show how this approach can identify and evaluate strategic options in electoral contests quite different from those in the United States.

As has been discussed, the strategic positioning approach, since it involves voter surveys, should be applied to the political unit responsible for aggregating the popular vote if it is to be used to develop electoral strategy. In legislative elections, that unit is the individual constituency.

Legislative elections, in effect, are not single elections, but rather many elections, each held simultaneously in separate constituencies. Thus, to link the electorate's perceptions or preferences to campaign strategy, survey analysis must focus, in legislative elections, on the individual constituency. Of course, as has been seen in earlier chapters, the most appropriate unit to study the popular vote in U.S. presidential and gubernatorial elections is the state. Were we to study the French presidential elections, the appropriate unit would be the nation as a whole, since, unlike U.S. presidents, the French president is elected by direct popular vote.

In contrast with the three electoral studies covered in preceding chapters, which were conducted prior to selected elections, this chapter describes a study conducted after the legislative elections. Since the goals of this study are illustrative and methodological, rather than pragmatic, timing is not important. No attempt will be made here to explain the 1973 election outcome; rather, efforts will be directed at analyzing voters' preferences at the time of the study and discussing the implications for strategy were elections to be held immediately following the study. The timing of the study, however, provided an opportunity to examine the extent to which opinion structures remain stable across time. The issue of temporal stability is taken up again in Chapter 11, where data from both the United States and France are discussed. A few months after this study was completed, France was plunged into another election. With the sudden death of then-president Georges Pompidou early in April 1974, a presidential election was hurriedly scheduled for May 1974. Even though this study was limited to a single *circonscription*, a few hints were sought in our data, nevertheless, about voters' preferences in this election.[3]

This chapter is divided into three major sections. The first outlines the political nature of the *circonscription* selected. Next, the methods used in this study are described, and the final section presents our analyses and recommendations. Two types of analyses are discussed. First, voters' preferences are analyzed using multidimensional scaling techniques in order to understand the basic patterns of competition. Hypotheses about why items position as they do in the model are tested using hypothetical candidates. Second, alternative campaign strategies are evaluated for selected candidates in this *circonscription*.

THE CONSTITUENCY

This study was conducted in the fourth *circonscription* of the *département* of the Isère, which is in the French Alps and extends from the outskirts of Lyon to just short of the Italian border.[4] Due to the availability of abundant hydroelectric power, the area is one of the fastest growing in France. The largest city in Isère is Grenoble, which lies in a broad valley at the intersection of two rivers, the Isère and the Drac.

The fourth *circonscription* was selected out of the seven in the *département* for several reasons. First, it is a politically competitive constituency where all the major political factions are represented. Next, it contains a diversity of social and economic groups, and it is divided, almost equally, between rural and urban regions. Finally, it was located conveniently close to the University of Grenoble for a class project.

The fourth *circonscription* of the Isère is located northwest of Grenoble following the curvature of the Rives river in the lower Isère valley. It is composed of seven cantons: Pont-en-Royans, Rives, Saint Egrève, Saint Marcellin, Tullins, Vinay and Voiron. The suburban part has been characterized as an "industrialized area which favours the extreme Left," while the lower Isère valley is rural and tends to support the right (Barral 1962).

Since they were first created in 1875, under the Third Republic, there has been a remarkable stability in the definition of almost all *circonscription* in France (Lancelot and Lancelot 1970). Except for the two largest cities in France, Paris, and Marseille, only marginal changes have been made in most *circonscription* since 1875. The fourth *circonscription* of the Isère is no exception. In 1974, it included virtually all of the same cantons and villages that it did in 1875. While the way in which *circonscriptions* were drawn initially corresponded more to the demands of political strategy than to either administrative or technical imperatives, the passage of time has diminished its artificial character. The lengthening history of political maneuvers aided as well by the partisan and personal clashes, has given voters in each *circonscription* a certain common heritage.

The fourth *circonscription* is particularly interesting because it is a marginal district.[5] Not only is victory won by the narrowest margins, but it may swing either to the right or to the left. During the Third and Fourth Republics, this *circonscription* traditionally voted for the left, but since 1958 it has swung to the right as often as to the left, frequently following national trends. Table 8.1 compares the fourth *circonscription* with metropolitan France. As may be seen, this district reflects the sentiments of the rest of the country.

After the success of the right in 1958, when an "*indépendant et paysan*" candidate won election in the fourth *circonscription*, victory went to Gaullist candidates in 1962 and 1968, and then to the Socialists in 1967 and 1973. In the 1973 Assembly elections, Jacques Gau (UGSD) managed to beat Alban Fagot (URP) in the second *tour* with only 51.70 percent of the vote. François Mitterrand obtained exactly the same percentage of the vote in the second *tour* of the presidential election on May 19, 1974.

In contrast to the volatility of the vote, the fourth *circonscription* is typified by a remarkable stability as regards political personnel. This is particularly evident with the two largest political groupings—the Gaullists and the Communists. Alban Fagot (Gaullist) has been a candidate for deputy from this *circonscription*, win or lose, since 1951. Jacques Perinetti has been the Communist candidate since 1945. Interestingly enough, Perinetti and Fagot fought together in the French underground during World War II in the nearby Vercors mountains as *maquisards*.

TABLE 8.1. The Results of the First *Tour* of the 1973 Legislative Elections in the Fourth *Circonscription* of the Isère and in Metropolitan France

	Fourth Circonscription[c]	Metropolitan France
Parti Communiste	19.4%	21.4%
UGSD[a]	23.7	20.7
PSU[b]	4.3	3.3
Other left candidates	—	1.3
Réformateurs	14.6	12.5
URP[d]	33.4	34.6
Other majority	—	3.3
Other right candidates	4.5	2.9
	100.0%	100.0%

[a] *Union de la gauche socialiste at démocratique*, including both the *Parti socialiste* and the *movement des radicaux de gauche*.

[b] *Parti socialiste unifié*.

[c] Candidates in the fourth *Circonscription* were Perinetti (PC), Gau (UGSD), Quezel (PSU), De Galbert (*Réformateurs*), Fagot (URP-UDR), Graillat (CNIP).

[d] *Union des républicains de progres*, an electoral coalition of *Union des démocrates pour la République* (UDR), *Républicains indépendants* (RI), and the *Centre démocrate et progres* (CDP).

Source: *Les Forces politiques et les élections de mars 1973*, supplément aux dossiers et documents du Monde, Le Monde, March 1973.

The Socialist party and the centrists have also tended to present the same candidates throughout this period, but somewhat less consistently. For example, the incumbent Socialist deputy, first elected in 1973, is a "*parachuté*," a very recent arrival to the region. In contrast, the candidates of the small fringe groupings (PSU; miscellaneous rightist factions), when they are represented, put up someone different almost every time.

THE STUDY

A sample of 249 respondents was selected to be interviewed for this study using standard quota-sampling techniques. Respondents were interviewed during the first two weeks of February 1974. To qualify for the interview, respondents had to be of French nationality and at least 20 years old. Every effort was made to ensure that the sample distribution reflected that of the target population, according to the census figures of 1968, in terms of sex, age, socioeconomic status and canton of residence.

Since quota sampling methods were used, there was no way to assess the sampling error. Nevertheless, the similarity of the sample with the target population may be examined by looking at the major demographic variables. Table 8.2 compares the sample with the census figures for the *circonscription*. As may be readily seen, the sample's demographic characteristics parallel those of the target *circonscription* with only a few deviations. The sex and age distributions are quite close; the patterns for occupation and size of municipality are somewhat less so. The sample underrepresents smaller towns and villages, while correspondingly overrepresenting those from towns with more than 1,000 people. Equally important, the sample underrepresents farmers (*agriculteurs*) and workers (*ouvriers*); it overrepresents businessmen (*artisans*), professionals (*cadre supérieurs*), and white-collar workers (*cadre moyens*). Finally, the sample overweights the urbanized cantons at the expense of the rural cantons. In sum, the sample may only be used as a very rough guide for the target population. Nevertheless, it should be adequate for illustrating the strategic positioning approach to campaign analysis.

Interviews were conducted by students in an advanced methodology course and lasted from 30 to 45 minutes. The highly structured questionnaire used here focused primarily on the preferences for political parties and political leaders. Political preferences were assessed by two different types of questions: first, respondents were asked to rank-order sets of parties and leaders. Next, they were presented with selected hypothetical elections, parliamentary and presidential, past and future, and asked to indicate for whom they would vote in each situation. The hypothetical elections served as a check on the validity of the ranking questions.

The ranking task was identical to that used in the U.S. studies described earlier, except for the inclusion of political parties. There were two ranking questions: one for the 8 political parties and the other for the 24 political leaders and eighteen "hypothetical candidates." Each item to be ranked was presented on a 3 × 5 card and the respondent was asked to arrange the cards so that, from top down, the stack reflected the order of his preferences for the parties or leaders. The parties were CDP, CNIP, PC, PS, PSU, *réformateurs*, RI, and UDR. The political leaders were Chaban-Delmas, Debré, Dubedout, Duclos, Fagot, Faure, de Galbert, Gau, Giscard d'Estaing, Graillat, Krivine, Lecanuet, Marchais, Mendès France, Messmer, Mitterrand, Mollet, Nicoud, Perinetti, Pompidou, Quézel, Rocard, Servan Schreiber, and Tixier Vignancourt. Table 8.3 identifies these leaders more fully.

Eighteen hypothetical candidates were included with the set of names of political leaders to be ranked, giving a total of 42 items to be ranked in this task. As in earlier studies, the hypothetical candidates were fashioned from political positions and postures that appealed to important sectors of the electorate, and represented strategic options for candidates. Hypotheses about why political leaders and parties appealed to the electorate were tested by observing where in the spatial model the hypothetical candidates positioned. Table 8.4 presents the hypothetical candidates.

TABLE 8.2. Comparison of the Sample and the Fourth *Circonscription* of the Isère

Demographic Variables		Sample (N = 249)	Fourth Circonscription
Sex	Male	47.4	48.2
	Female	52.6	51.8
Age	20–34	33.5	31.4
	35–49	30.2	30.0
	50–64	18.5	20.8
	65 +	17.7	17.7
Occupation			
Agriculteurs		8.8	11.3
Artisans, patrons de l'industrie et du commerce		9.6	9.0
Cadre supérieurs et professions liberales		4.4	3.6
Cadre moyen, employés		17.3	12.7
Ouvriers		34.5	37.0
Divers		0.8	1.3
Inactifs		24.0	25.1
Municipality size			
Less than 1,000		17.7	21.3
1,000 to 2,000		12.9	11.2
More than 2,000		69.5	67.5
Canton			
Grenoble Nord Rural		17.3	16.4
Pont-en-Royans		2.8	5.4
Rives		19.3	17.8
Saint Marcellin		16.9	18.0
Tullins		6.8	7.8
Vinay		3.6	7.0
Voiron		33.3	28.0

Source: Mauser and Freyssinet (1976).

In addition to questions concerning political preferences, respondents were asked about the intensity of their interest in politics and about their perceptions of the major political groupings. Respondents were asked to indicate which one of the groupings would be best suited to act in various ways.[6] These perceptions provided an important check of our interpretations of voters' preferences, since these data were derived separately from the preference rankings.

TABLE 8.3. The Political Leaders Included in This Study

	Left	Center	Majority
National Leaders	Duclos (PCF) Krivine (PSU) Marchais (PCF) Mendès France (PSU) Mitterrand (PS) Mollet (PS) Rocard (PSU)	Lecanuet (réf) Servan Schreiber (réf)	Chaban Delmas (UDR) Debre (UDR) Faure (UDR) Giscard (RI) Messmer (UDR) Pompidou (UDR) Tixier (CNIP)
Local Leaders	Dubedout (PSU) Gau (PS) Perinetti (PCF) Quezel Ambunaz (PSU)	de Galbert (réf)	Fagot (UDR) Graillat (CNIP) Nicoud (CNIP)

STRATEGIC ANALYSIS

This section analyzes political preferences and assesses the strategic options facing political parties in the fourth *circonscription*. First, spatial models are developed to describe the patterns of competition among the most important political leaders and parties. With this technique, the major political cleavages are immediately apparent.

In order to understand why the parties and leaders position where they do in the spatial model, hypothetical candidates were inserted to see if they position in the structure where hypothesized. Next, strategic options are assessed for the major candidates in the selected *circonscription*. Hypothetical candidates, voicing selected slogans and claims, are used to ferret out the attractiveness of positions and postures that appear promising for selected parties. This analysis serves to illustrate the strategic uses of the methodology.

Image and Ideology

This section takes up the question of how preferences for French political parties and leaders are structured. It is important to understand the patterns of voters' preferences, since these patterns shape the nature of political competition. If we can accurately map voters' perceptions and preferences, we will be able to understand, as well as predict, short-term shifts in political preferences.

The principal assumptions of the approach taken in this book to the analysis of political competition has been already outlined in Chapter 4. The most crucial assumption is that political candidates or parties seen to be

TABLE 8.4. Hypothetical Candidates Included in the Interview

25. A man like de Gaulle.
26. A person who would keep in touch with his constituents concerning local decisions.
27. A person who would like to limit the number of foreign workers in France.
28. A person who would like to limit the power of the Parisian technocrats.
29. A person who would fight for industrial democracy.
30. A person who would defend the workers.
31. A person who desires a true regional program in France.
32. A person who favors reform while maintaining political stability.
33. An independent person who is above political parties.
34. A person who favors a united Europe.
35. A person who can stand up to the oil crisis.
36. A person who is honest and above the present scandals.
37. A person who could defend the environment.
38. A person who could defend the small businessman.
39. A person who would fight for our independence from the U.S.A.
40. A person who would fight for consumers.
41. A person who could keep the French economy growing.
42. A person who could avoid unemployment problems in France.

similar to each other will appeal to the same segment of the electorate and will compete with each other more than will candidates or parties seen to be less similar to each other. As has been done in previous chapters, multidimensional scaling (MDS) techniques are used here to construct spatial models of voters' preferences for political parties and leaders. Because of the large number of political parties and movements in French politics, it is interesting to examine the political parties and leaders separately first and then, later, pool parties and leaders together to look at the full structure.

As before, the intercorrelation of voters' preferences for political parties and leaders yields a suitable index (called a "preference correlation") of the extent to which pairs of political parties or leaders are supported by the same voters. Such an index may be interpreted in the following way: a positive correlation between two parties indicates that voters who prefer one of these parties prefer the other more strongly than do most voters; while a negative correlation indicates that voters who prefer one party reject the other more strongly than do most voters.

Table 8.5 shows the correlations among the political parties so that its underlying structure may be seen. The primary cleavage is clearly between *gauche unie* and the other parties. This is evident in the fact that all positive correlations are between members of the same bloc and that almost all negative correlations are between members of different blocs. The opposition to the left is more dispersed than is the tightly knit left. This opposition is

TABLE 8.5. Interparty Correlations

	UDR	RI	CDP	Réf	PS	PSU	PC
CNIP	120	114	091	−075	−347	−303	−283
UDR		452	284	027	−589	−653	−542
RI			177	108	−551	−531	−548
CDP				083	−459	−396	−472
Réf					−304	−239	−414
PS						512	415
PSU							415

Note: Entries are Spearman correlation coefficients calculated between parties from respondents' preference rankings. The decimal points have been removed for simplicity. Correlations larger than .127 are significantly different from zero at the .05 level.

Source: Mauser and Freyssinet (1976).

centered around a nucleus of three parties: UDR, RI, and CDP, which together make up the URP (the government coalition at the time of the survey). There are two satellites loosely connected to this bloc (CNIP and *réformateurs*). The negative correlation between the CNIP and the *réformateurs* (the only example in the matrix of a negative correlation between members of the same bloc) suggests that, despite their membership in this bloc, these two parties are quite different from one another. In contrast, the left is smaller and more compact. All three parties are strongly correlated. Note however the ambiguous position of the PSU. The PSU is a little closer to the PS than is the PC, but at the same time it is farther away from the UDR than either of the two other parties on the left. This is inconsistent with a simple left-right, one-dimensional structure.

Figure 8.1 presents a two-dimensional mapping of the patterns of competition among eight political parties.[7] The same blocs are seen here as in the direct analysis of the preference correlations. The most important cleavage is between the parties of the left and all other parties. There is no ambiguity about which parties are in which bloc, as a large gulf separates these two groupings. The horizontal dimension in the figure, which spans these two blocs, may be interpreted as the classic left-right political axis. The discontinuity of this dimension suggests that it may not be possible for political leaders to position themselves between the blocs. This hypothesis is put to the test in the next section, which analyzes the political leaders.

Inspection of the figure also reveals the internal structure of the two blocs. As already seen in the correlations, the right is more dispersed than the left. Part of the explanation for this is simply that there are more parties on the right than on the left. But also the dispersion reflects the impact of the recent signing of the *programme commun* by the major parties of the left. This suggests these blocs are defined by support of, or opposition to, the *programme commun*.

FIGURE 8.1. Map of Competition Patterns for French Political Parties. Two-Dimensional TORSCA-9B Solution for Preference Correlations (8 Stimuli, Stress = 0.050, N = 242).

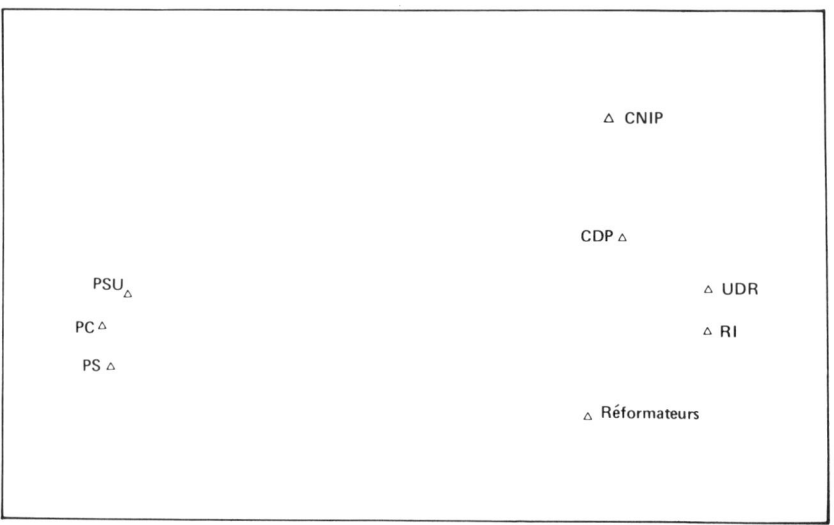

Source: Mauser and Freyssinet (1976).

Interestingly, the parties within each of these blocs are more clearly differentiated along the vertical dimension than the horizontal dimension. The left-right dimension serves as only a first rough sort of the parties into two blocs and only the second dimension permits a fine-grained comparison within blocs. On the right, for example, the CNIP is not much farther to the right than are the *réformateurs*, while they lie on the opposite ends of the vertical axis. This also holds true for the left, where the three parties are spread out vertically more than horizontally. The introduction of the second dimension explains the negative correlation between the CNIP and the *réformateurs*. The relative proximity of the RI to the *réformateurs* anticipates the later alliance of these two parties under Giscard d'Estaing.

To compare images of leaders with those of the political parties, a MDS model was constructed by intercorrelating voters' preferences for the 25 leaders and the 8 political parties.[8] Figure 8.2 presents the two-dimensional mapping of voters' preferences for both leaders and political parties. Note first that the inclusion of the leaders does not disrupt the original structure. The parties' positioning has not changed, even though 25 new items—the political leaders—have been added to the model. Note also that political leaders position close to their own party. However, there are a few striking incongruities. For example, de Gaulle is placed in the model closer to the RI than to the principal Gaullist party, the UDR, and Servan Schreiber is found closer to the CDP than the group he led, the *réformateurs*. These placements

FIGURE 8.2. Map of Competition Patterns for French Political Leaders and Parties. Two-Dimensional TORSCA-9B Solution for Preference Correlations (33 Stimuli, Stress = 0.113, N = 240).

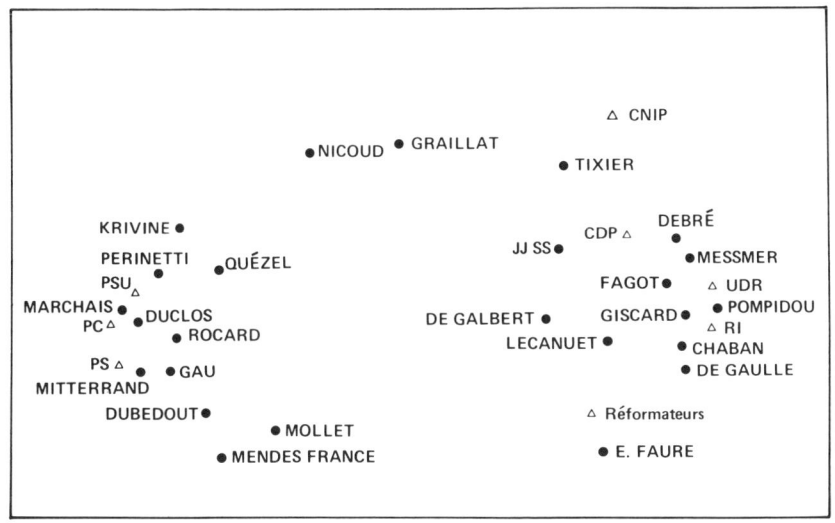

Source: Mauser (1979), Mauser and Freyssinet (1976).

do *not* agree with the correlations but rather reflect the limitations of the MDS procedure. See Table 8.6.

The same two blocs are easily seen in this model, as in the previous one. The center is again strikingly unoccupied. (Only Nicoud and Graillat are exceptions.) These results are consistent with the intense polarization of French politics. Apparently it is virtually impossible for any political leader to position himself between the two blocs that dominate French politics, since voters seem to recognize only two blocs. The unique position of Nicoud and Graillat appears to be due to the marginal roles played in the political system by these two men. Graillat is not very well known by the voters, and Nicoud, as the leader of CID/UNATI, appeals to extremists of both the right and the left.

Let's turn now to the question of interpreting the underlying structure. The first problem is that of the nature of the vertical axis. On the right, the vertical dimension, which extends from the CNIP and Tixier Vignancourt to Edgar Faure and the *réformateurs*, might be interpreted as a spectrum ranging from the traditional right (above) to the technocratic center (below). On the left this dimension shows a somewhat different face: the cleavage between Krivine and the PSU, on the one hand, and Mitterrand, Mendès France, Mollet, and the PS on the other could be seen as the opposition of

TABLE 8.6. Correlations between Principal Leaders and Political Parties

	UDR	RI	Réf	PS	PCF
Chaban-Delmas	40	45	20	−37	−43
Giscard d'Estaing	37	51	21	−36	−48
de Gaulle	47	27	04	−29	−32
Pompidou	63	44	16	−44	−52
Lecanuet	17	23	44	−28	−39
JJ SS	14	09	39	−23	−27
Mendès France	−33	−25	−07	30	21
Mitterrand	−51	−40	−15	61	43
Rocard	−46	−33	−22	35	33
Marchais	−47	−55	−34	44	74
Fagot	44	37	13	−43	−39
Gau	−38	−32	−28	46	36
de Galbert	12	13	22	−22	−21

Note: Entries are Spearman correlation coefficients without decimal points. All correlations larger than .127 are significantly different from zero at .05 level.

the supporters of revolution with the supporters of reform. Continuing still further with this analysis, a synthesis might be suggested of these interpretations by arguing that Krivine, the PSU, Tixier Vignancourt, and the CNIP share roughly the same view of the political system, while Mitterrand, Mendès France, Mollet, and Edgar Faure share another; that is to say, the vertical dimension would be interpreted as reflecting a basic acceptance or rejection of this principles of the existing political system. However, such an analysis is somewhat artificial because of the extreme heterogeneity of the political parties and leaders involved.

While there are many ways in which this structure might be viewed (as a circle or spheroid, for example), I tend to favor an interpretation in which the explanatory dimensions span the structure obliquely rather than perpendicularly, as in the earlier discussion. From this perspective, Krivine and the PSU are at the pole of a dimension running diagonally from Edgar Faure and the *réformateurs*, while Mitterrand, Mendès France, and the PS lie across from the CNIP and Tixier Vignancourt. Both of these dimensions are closely related to the left-right axis: the classic left (Mendès France) sits opposite the classic right (the CNIP) and the young, revolutionary left (Krivine) is contrasted with the new right (the *réformateurs*). This alternative interpretation of the electorate's view of the political world has the advantage of mirroring the actual political conflicts that have occurred in contemporary French society.

Such an interpretation emphasizes the importance of the left-right axis in that this cleavage is seen as capable of subsuming many other types of political conflict. The vertical dimension may then be interpreted as reflecting the historical order in which these conflicts have surfaced in French politics. This implies that new conflicts that emerge in the body politic, even when originally unrelated to the left-right cleavage, are progressively brought into alignment with the major axis of French political conflict—the left-right axis. The mechanism through which this transformation is realized involves the centralized nature of the French political system, which tends to nationalize even local conflicts. Also important is the cleavage of the political elites along left-right lines.

The *réformateurs*' position is an intriguing one. At the time of the study, they were a relatively new movement in French politics, and were seen as opposing the *majorité* as well as the left. Some voters therefore saw them as centrist. Other voters saw the young revolutionary left as the opposite to the *réformateurs* while placing both the *majorité* and classic left between these two extremes. Apparently, the French voters agree that the left-right opposition is the primary cleavage, but they do not agree about its precise nature.

The hypothetical candidates may be scaled in addition to the political leaders and parties in an effort to understand which features govern positioning of leaders in the spatial model. Each hypothetical candidate is presented to the respondents, not as a real person but as a type of person about whom all they know is a short verbal description: for example, "an independent person who is above political parties" (# 33). Eighteen hypothetical candidates were fashioned in order to test various strategic opportunities and to explore hypotheses about which features governed positioning in the model. By correlating respondents' preferences for hypothetical candidates with their preferences for the political parties and leaders, it was possible to build an MDS model of all 50 items together: 8 political parties, 24 political leaders, and 18 hypothetical candidates. See Figure 8.3.

The hypothetical candidates position, by and large, where hypothesized. (See Figure 8.3 and Table 8.7.) All five hypothetical candidates fashioned from the left's slogans (#s 28, 29, 30, 39, and 42) position on the left. Six out of the seven hypothetical candidates designed to capture the *réformateurs* promises (#s 26, 31, 32, 34, 36, 37, and 40) position in the center of the figure close to the leaders of the *réformateurs*. The one failure (# 40) is informative. Consumer protection is seen to be a goal of the far right rather than of the *réformateurs*, as had been hypothesized. This may be due to the provocative wording of the description rather than the fundamental claim itself. The two hypothetical candidates designed to appeal to the far right (#27 and 38) perform precisely as expected.

The worst performance was turned in by the hypothetical candidates designed to capture the appeal of the *majorité*. Two out of the three fail to position close to the *majorité*, but settle closer to the center. Only # 33 positioned where predicted. Close inspection of the correlation matrix shows why. Both of the errant hypothetical candidates (#s 35 and 41) appeal to the

FIGURE 8.3. Map of Competition Patterns for French Political Positions, Leaders, and Parties. Two-Dimensional TORSCA-9B Solution for Preference Correlations (50 Stimuli, Stress = 0.210, N = 240).

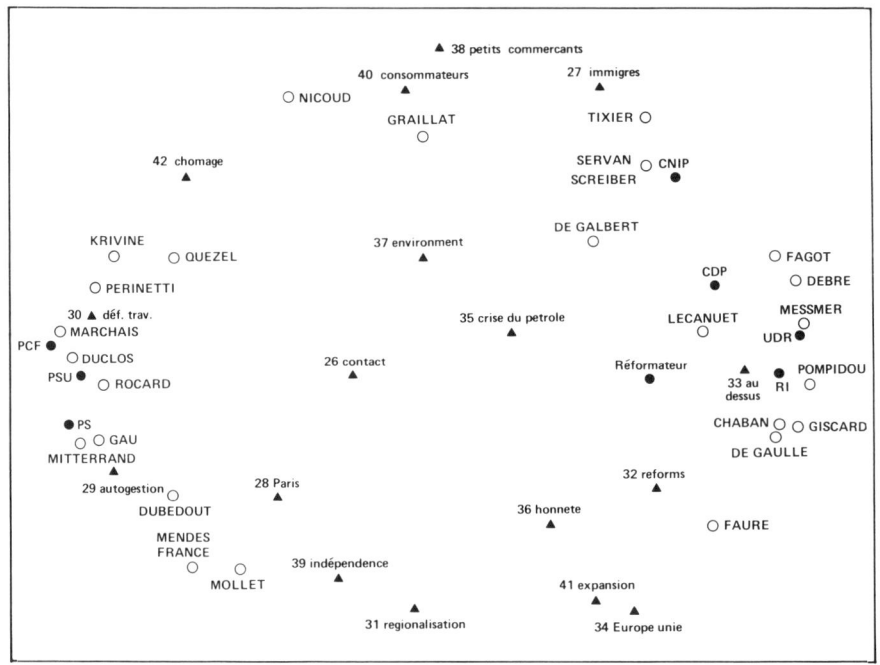

Source: Mauser (1979).

gauche as well as to the *majorité* so that they do not polarize as predicted. These hypothetical candidates end up in the center not because they are preferred by the supporters of the *réformateurs* but because they appeal to all voters and so must position equally close to both the *gauche* as to the *majorité*.

Table 8.8 summarizes these results. Fourteen out of the 17 hypothetical candidates position where hypothesized. Two of these errors fall in neighboring formations, but one (# 40) ended up at a considerable distance from where it had been predicted to position. This success supports the usefulness of hypothetical candidates in exploring spatial models.

Table 8.9 confirms the structure seen in the MDS mapping. The *majorité* is the most closely associated with the "strike force" (*force de frappe*) and with assuring political stability; it shares top billing with the Socialists on political stability, defending the interests of peasants and supporting the political development of Europe. The *gauche* is seen as capable of defending

TABLE 8.7. Correlations for Political Parties and Strategic Alternatives

	CNIP	UDR	RI	Réf	PS	PCF
26[a]	02	−16*	− 05	−10	10	11
27	06	20*	13*	03	−17*	−22*
28	06	−30*	− 07	−07	15*	12
29	−16*	−31*	− 27*	−14*	31*	25*
30	−06	−35*	− 27*	−29*	37*	38*
31	−03	−06	−002	−03	05	02
32	−00	13*	17*	07	−12	−07
33	12	18*	30*	19*	−17*	−33*
34	−03	09	19*	−02	−04	−16*
35	−07	07	08	−02	−09	−05
36	−17*	05	01	16*	−02	−15*
37	12	−10	05	−06	−05	03
38	08	10	04	−01	−12	−02
39	−04	−03	− 11	−16*	07	14*
40	09	−01	001	04	−08	−003
41	−06	08	11	005	−02	− 08
42	−04	−15*	− 19*	−06	16*	14*

Note: Entries are Spearman correlation coefficients without decimal points. All correlations larger than .127 (*) are significantly different from zero at .05 level.

[a] See Table 8.4 for complete descriptions of the strategic alternatives.

workers, consumers, and improving the status of women. Perhaps more important, the *gauche* is the only formation seen as being capable of improving the fairness of the income distribution in France and of stopping inflation. The electorate splits between the *majorité* and the *gauche* over which is more capable of defending the environment.

Political Strategy

This section illustrates the use of the strategic positioning approach in a French multiparty contest to assess strategic options. The demonstration is only illustrative, as this study was conducted after the 1973 legislative elections, so it could not have been used to develop strategy in those elections. Nevertheless, the analysis shows how the approach was used in this legislative election, since the same approach was followed in the study described in Chapter 7.

Strategic options are identified as issue-positions or postures that candidates might adopt as major planks in their electoral campaign. To assess each position or posture, hypothetical candidates, voicing each one, are presented to the respondents for their evaluation. The success of this approach depends critically on the quality of issue-positions or postures

TABLE 8.8. Predicting the Positioning of Hypothetical Candidates

Predicted Position	Observed Position[a]			
	Gauche	Réformateurs	Majorité	Far Right
Gauche	28, 29, 30, 39, 42			
Réformateurs		26, 31, 32, 34, 36, 37		40
Majorité		35, 41	33	
Far right				27, 38

[a] Determined by Euclidean distance between hypothetical candidate and political party in the two-dimensional MDS configuration.

included in the study. For best results, the researcher must have an intimate understanding of the issues and personalities involved in the contest as well as a close working relationship with his client.

To attract voters, candidates must identify the most effective positions and postures. In general, two criteria are important in selecting campaign positions: its ability to attract support to the candidate who espouses it, and the perceived compatibility of the position with the candidate's image. While it is probably obvious why political candidates would prefer to associate themselves with the most powerful positions and postures, the second criterion, that of compatibility, requires additional discussion.

There are two principal reasons why candidates should be concerned with compatibility. First, in a multiparty system, each candidate appeals to a distinct bloc of voters. Compatible positions permit a candidate to build upon this natural base, and therefore to develop his distinctive advantage. By capitalizing on his strengths, a candidate increases his chances of winning. Moreover, such a strategy increases the clarity with which a candidate can communicate to the electorate in the campaign. Most campaigners agree that campaigns have to be focused on a small number of mutually reinforcing, compatible elements in order to be effective.

The second argument hinges on maintaining a candidate's credibility. Candidates who espouse too broad a spectrum of positions, or shift their positions too readily, risk losing their credibility in the eyes of their potential supporters. A certain amount of flexibility is, of course, desirable, but beyond a certain point, flexibility risks becoming seen as mere opportunism and endangers a candidate's appeal. Due to the obvious vulnerability of candidates during an election, they must maintain greater credibility while campaigning than after being elected. Flexibility is practical only after being elected, for it is likely that passions will cool and memories fade before the next election. Moreover, the wisdom (if any) of the course of action that seemed inconsistent at the time will have had time to emerge. None of these

TABLE 8.9. Perceived Capabilities of the Political Formations

	Majorité	Réformateurs	PS	PCF	No Response	Total
(a)	11.6%	4.4%	42.2%	32.5%	9.2%	100%
(b)	32.9	8.8	32.5	8.4	17.3	100
(c)	8.0	9.2	45.4	22.1	15.3	100
(d)	18.5	12.9	24.9	6.4	37.3	100
(e)	9.6	10.4	35.3	19.7	24.9	100
(f)	14.5	6.4	25.7	19.7	33.7	100
(g)	18.1	13.7	26.1	16.9	25.3	100
(h)	63.5	2.0	5.6	3.6	25.3	100
(i)	26.5	16.5	29.7	4.0	23.3	100
(j)	9.6	6.8	39.4	19.3	24.9	100

(a) Guarantee the protection of the workers.
(b) Guarantee political stability.
(c) Permit a better distribution of incomes, for all French citizens.
(d) Protect the environment.
(e) Improve the situation of women.
(f) Stop price increases.
(g) Protect the peasants' interests.
(h) Develop an independent "strike force."
(i) Guarantee the political development of Europe.
(j) Protect consumers.

conditions is true during an election, so campaigners should be aware of the importance of being perceived as consistent consistency.

Now we are ready to evaluate the strategic options facing candidates in the fourth *circonscription*. To do so, each option, in the form of a hypothetical candidate espousing that position or posture, is compared with local candidates and with party leaders. Compatibility is assessed by correlating preference rankings of each position with those for each political leader. A positive correlation indicates that the supporters of a leader also favor that position, while a negative correlation indicates that they tend to oppose that position.[9] (See Table 8.10.)

As can be readily seen, the patterns of correlations are quite different for candidates on the left than for other candidates. This confirms, once again, the wide split between these two groups in French politics. Greater detail may also be found. The local candidates are not copies of their national leaders. For example, the pattern of support for Fagot, the local *Gaulliste* candidate, resembles that for Giscard more than that for Chaban, the national standard bearer for the *Gaullistes* at that time. In the French political system, as in the U.S. system, local candidates have considerable latitude in devising their campaigns. As discussed earlier, candidates will find it most convenient to adopt positions or postures that are already strongly correlated with them. Precisely which would depend upon the power of their draw.

TABLE 8.10. Correlations between Strategic Options and Politicians

Strategic Alternatives[a]	Draw[b]	UDR		Center		Left	
		Chaban Delmas	Fagot	Giscard d'Estaing	De Galbert	Mitterrand	Gau
42-Avoid unemployment	50%	−18[c]	−09	−19[c]	−04	18[c]	20[c]
30-Protect workers	49	−22[c]	−21[c]	−30[c]	−09	31[c]	35[c]
26-Maintain contact	46	−04	05	−01	07	−04	11
40-Protect consumers	42	−08	05	−01	11	−01	−06
41-Economic growth	42	18[c]	06	05	09	−05	−07
36-Above scandals	41	06	01	12	02	−08	−09
37-Protect environment	37	−02	−03	−06	07	−10	−17[c]

35-Stand up to oil crisis	34	06	01	01	-04	-11	-07
32-Orderly reforms	31	03	13c	10	02	-15c	-13c
33-Above political parties	30	17c	18c	25c	08	-18c	-18c
34-Support a united Europe	27	20c	00	27c	-01	-12	-06
38-Protect small business	27	-05	15c	01	03	-11	-16c
31-Regionalization	25	08	-06	05	-08	08	01
28-Limit Paris	24	-18c	-11	-12	-02	15c	08
39-Independence	24	00	-07	-01	-06	11	10
29-Industrial democracy	22	-14c	-30c	-25c	-19c	26c	28c
27-Foreign workers	18	04	14c	06	00	-08	-01

Note: The correlations are Spearman *rhos* between the rankings of each leader with the rankings of the strategic alternatives as represented by the hypothetical candidates.

[a] See Table 8.4 for full descriptions of the hypothetical candidates that embody the strategic alternatives.

[b] Draw refers to the percentage of respondents who rank each position over the three national leaders. That is, concept #42 draws 50% of the vote against Chaban, Giscard, and Mitterrand in a mock four-way contest.

[c] Correlations larger than .127 are significantly different from zero at the .05 level.

The ability of each position and posture to attract support is evaluated by determining the number of voters who prefer it *over* all major political leaders. In this contest, that meant a position or posture had to be ranked higher than Giscard, Chaban, and Mitterrand.[10] This is a stiff but fair test. Stiff, because very few positions or postures are preferred over well-known attractive national leaders. Fair, because this procedure is unbiased: each position is pitted, one at a time, against the same criterion. Compare this with another widely used procedure, that of asking respondents to rate (or pick) items out of a list of alternatives and then comparing the average or (percentage) scores of each item. Such a procedure is easily shown to be biased. To perform well in a list of alternatives, an item must not only be attractive, it must also be unique, since similar items will appeal to the same type of respondents and split their vote. If the analyst has selected positions that respondents view as being similar, as often happens when strategists are attempting to evaluate alternative formulations of a particular position, then these alternatives will split their vote and so reduce their apparent appeal. This can cause analysts to overlook potentially important strategic options.

Table 8.11 compares the "rank first" procedure with the more common "list" approach. As can be seen by comparing the orderings, the two procedures yield different results. Only two of the top five issue-positions are the same for both procedures. For the full list, there is a relatively weak correlation of 0.71, which shows that the two procedures rank the items somewhat differently.

Which are the best issues for a candidate for the *gauche* to adopt? Two issue-positions stand out on both of the criteria: # 42—"avoid unemployment" and # 30—"protect the workers." Both draw well and are strongly correlated with François Mitterrand. Two weaker positions that could also be considered since they are strongly correlated with Mitterrand, although they draw less well, are # 28—"limit Parisian power" and # 29—"industrial democracy." The eventual selection of less powerful, but highly correlated positions by the candidate would hinge upon additional criteria. With such low draws, a strategy based upon them could backfire, but conceivably some might be sleepers. No other issue in this list could be recommended since they are all negatively correlated with Mitterrand and draw poorly.

The centrists have several attractive positions from which to choose. Number 41—"maintaining the economic expansion of the country" and # 36—"being honest and keeping out of the current government scandals" draw the best but are not very strongly correlated with Giscard. For example, # 41 is correlated even more strongly with Chaban-Delmas, Giscard's principal opponent, and so would be a poor choice in the first *tour*, but may be useful as a minor theme. Number 32—"introducing orderly reforms"—draws well and is also more closely associated with Giscard than with any other major candidate. Two other positions also draw well and are very closely associated with Giscard: # 33—"being independent and above political parties" and # 34 "supporting a united Europe."

Since the centrists and the *Gaullistes* are appealing to the same voters, their problem is complicated by vote-splitting considerations. In the first *tour*

TABLE 8.11. Determination of Concept Preferences

Strategic Alternatives	Rank First[a]	List Approach[b]
42	1	3
30	2	1
26	3	8.5
40	4.5	10
41	4.5	6
36	6	2
37	7	4.5
35	8	12.5
32	9	7
33	10	4.5
34	11	12.5
38	12	16
31	13	16
28	14	8.5
39	15	16
29	16	12.5
27	17	12.5

[a] Items are ranked according to the percentage of respondents ranking positions over Chaban, Giscard, and Mitterrand as in Table 8.10.
[b] Ranked according to percentage ranking concept first over all other concepts without considering leaders.

they must differentiate themselves from each other, but in the second *tour* they have to rally the voters who supported their opponent. This is tricky but can be done. I would recommend that the centrists emphasize issue-positions #s 32 and 36, but also maintain their claims on #s 33 and 41 to keep the heat on the mainline *Gaullistes*.

The *Gaullistes* have only one position on this list that draws well and is closely associated with them; # 41—"maintaining the economic expansion of the country." Two other issues, #s 33 and 34, do well and are correlated with Chaban, but they are still more closely associated with Giscard. It is not usually wise for a candidate to orient his campaign around an issue or position that is closely associated with his opponent. Often such positions have been preempted by the first candidate so that little benefit can accrue to the second if he espouses them. It is usually preferable for a candidate to pick another position—one that he can preempt himself. Only if this is impossible would it be advisable to go head-on with another candidate on his ground.

CONCLUSIONS

This chapter illustrated the use of the strategic positioning approach to develop campaign strategy in a multiparty legislative contest in France.

Multidimensional scaling procedures were used to analyze political preferences for political leaders and parties. The MDS display aided strategic analysis by permitting a comprehensive view of the patterns of support enjoyed by each candidate in the contest. Concept evaluation procedures were used to assess the drawing power of alternative issue-positions so that candidates could select the most suitable set of issues to advocate.

The strategic positioning approach is flexible enough to be used in political contests with any number of candidates. The approach permits candidates to identify their competitive advantage, by identifying the postures and promises uniquely associated with them, and to select those that are most effective in their particular circumstances. Since the approach uses ordinal-level preference analysis, it is sensitive enough to detect vote-splitting phenomena when they occur. The typical metric approach cannot.

This approach adapts readily to the multistage electoral process, as used in France, where surviving candidates face different opponents in the second round of voting than they did in the first round. This is accomplished by simulating election outcomes from the voters' ordinal preference rankings—a simple and effective method that reflects vote-splitting when it occurs, and contrasts with typical metric procedures.

The analysis presented in this chapter was purely illustrative in that it was conducted after the 1973 legislative elections and so was not used by a legislative candidate. The strategic analysis, however, did reflect the electorate's preferences at the time of the study, and it could be used to determine strategy in that *circonscription* for elections held immediately afterward. Some support for the reasonableness of the analysis can be found in the adoption, by Giscard d'Estaing, of the positions found here to be the most suitable for the centrists—"introduce orderly reforms" and "being independent and above political parties." Moreover, the sample estimate for the results of the first round of voting for the target *circonscription* is within the limits of sampling error for samples of this size.

NOTES

1. Portions of this chapter are from "Exploring Political Space: A Study of French Voters' Preferences," by myself and Jacqueline Freyssinet-Dominjon, which appeared in *Party Identification and Beyond*, edited by I. Budge, I. Crewe, and D. Farlie (London: Wiley, 1976). Used with permission of my coauthor and publisher. This study was originally presented to the Workshop on Participation, Voting and Party Competition, at the meeting of the European Consortium for Political Research, held in Strasbourg, France, March 28—April 2, 1974, under the title "*Idéologie, image et stratégies politiques à Grenoble: une étude quasi-expérimentale dans la 4ème circonscription de l'Isère.*" A paper based on this study, comparing unidimensional and multidimensional preference models, entitled "Exploring Political Space: A Study of French Voters' Preferences," was included in Budge et al. (1976). Jacqueline Freyssinet-Dominjon (now at the *Université de Paris I, Panthéon-Sorbonne*) helped direct this study and coauthored both versions of this paper. I would like to take this opportunity to thank the students of the 2ème

cycle of the *Institut d'Etudes Politiques* for their help in conducting the study and the IEP for the financial support for the study.

2. As discussed in Chapter 7, delegates to the French National Assembly are elected from single-member constituencies (*circonscriptions*) in a manner that parallels the selection of members of the U.S. House of Representatives from congressional districts.

3. The results of this study were presented to selected political leaders during the campaign. Valéry Giscard d'Estaing, Pierre Mèndes France, and François Mitterrand were all given access to the results. After the election, a short piece appeared in *l'Express* presenting the main findings of the study.

4. The Isère is one of the 95 *départements* in continental France (*la métropole*). The *département* is an administrative region, resembling in some ways the U.S. state, but, since France does not have a federal system of government, the *département* does not have constitutional autonomy from the central government as do the U.S. states.

5. A marginal *circonscription* may be defined as one in which the margin of victory is no more than 3 percent of the vote in a two-candidate election. Such *circonscriptions* are seen as responsible for most of the fluctuations in the majority in the National Assembly (see LeGall and Riglet 1973). A similar but slightly different definition of swing districts was used in the study described in Chapter 7.

6. The text of this question was, "Considering the following political groupings (the *réformateurs*, the *majorité*, the Communists, and the Socialists), which would you judge is the best suited to. . . ."

7. The two-dimensional configuration presented in Figure 8.1 was selected because the stress (a measure of "badness-of-fit") of the one-dimensional configuration was not satisfactory and the three-dimensional configuration did not offer much more additional explanatory power than did the two-dimensional configuration. (See Chapter 4 for details for this procedure.) Splitting the sample into two arbitrary halfs and scaling the stimuli separately for each subsample yielded configurations that looked quite similar. This implies that the structure shown here is not simply random noise.

8. There are 25 leaders in this analysis, rather than the 24 mentioned earlier, because "a man like de Gaulle" is also included.

9. This follows from the fact that preference rankings are being correlated. See Chapter 4 for a full discussion of how this technique works. Chapter 6 shows the same technique in the California context.

10. National leaders were used here rather than local leaders for two reasons: they were better known than the local candidates, so that their correlational patterns were much cleaner and crisper; and they permit a glimpse into the electorate's preferences for the presidential candidates. In many local contests, it may be preferable to use local candidates rather than party leaders as the standards for comparison. In this study the results were virtually identical: all five of the best-performing alternatives against Chaban-Giscard-Mitterrand were the same against Fagot-de Galbert-Gau.

PART III:
EVALUATION

In Part III, the final section of the book, the methodology introduced in Chapter 4 will be evaluated empirically. It was assumed in Part II that the approach could be relied upon to fulfill its claims. However, the approach need not be taken entirely on faith as it may be subjected to empirical testing.

Of necessity, this section will be more technical than the preceding one, which dealt with applications of the methodology in political campaigns. Indeed, it should be of primary interest to academics rather than political campaigners. Marketing professors should be particularly interested, as this section constitutes the most systematic evaluation ever published of Stefflre's procedures for analyzing new product opportunities. Despite the technical nature of the material to be discussed, I have tried to write clearly and simply. If I have succeeded, it should be accessible to the practically oriented reader who is not a statistician, but who is simply willing to read carefully and to think logically. The reader himself will be the judge of my success.

Each of the chapters in this section takes up a distinct issue in evaluating this approach. Chapter 9 examines Stefflre's method of predicting share-of-vote for candidates. This technique is based on respondents' rank orders of 25 to 50 items at a time. Such a procedure raises eyebrows in some circles, since it is doubted that respondents can reliably rank such a large number of items. This chapter compares the ordinal procedure with alternative techniques for predicting share-of-vote and evaluates their predictive success.

Chapter 10 empirically evaluates the central premise of the belief that individuals will behave toward new things in ways that are similar to how they behave toward the familiar things that resemble the new thing. In elections, this implies that new candidates (or parties) will tend to compete with or split the vote of candidates (or parties) that voters see as similar to them. If this assertion were to be empirically supported, it would imply that, by mapping the electorate's perceptions, one could predict where any new candidate (or party) would position and from whom he would draw votes. Strategists could then evaluate alternative positionings of candidates in order to select the most useful to them.

Chapter 11 examines the stability of political perceptions and preferences. Two distinct questions are raised. First, how much agreement exists among different groups in the electorate about political perceptions and preferences? The use of an aggregate model presumes a certain amount of homogeneity across groups; without sufficient agreement, the model represents no one and its predictions are highly unreliable. The chapter looks at the extent to which subgroups, in both the French and U.S. electorates, share the same perceptions and patterns of preferences.

The second question considered in Chapter 11 is the stability of the aggregate model across time. A minimum degree of temporal stability in the model is crucial for the success of the approach. What use would it be to measure voters' perceptions or preferences, if, as soon the measures were completed, voters' perceptions or preferences drastically changed? Moreover, the degree of stability in the electorate's perceptions and preferences has immediate implications for campaign strategy. The kinds of strategies adopted depends directly upon the kinds of changes that can be introduced in the voters' perceptions and preferences. This chapter makes a tentative beginning at assessing temporal stability.

9

ESTIMATING THE SHARE-OF-VOTE

> In addition to understanding media, a candidate also must have some grasp of the research techniques that go into the production of the media he will be using in his campaign—particularly polls.
>
> Joseph Napolitan, *The Election Game*

> Politics has got so expensive that it takes lots of money to even get beat with.
>
> Will Rogers

This chapter examines a simple but powerful procedure for estimating the share-of-vote that political candidates will receive in upcoming elections and in hypothetical election scenarios. In this procedure, candidates can be identified by short verbal descriptions as well as by name, so that political campaigners may evaluate alternative positions and postures they are considering adopting. This procedure, developed by Volney Stefflre as his "rule (1)," is compared here with alternative methods of estimating share-of-vote and is empirically evaluated in selected contests in the United States and France.

The procedure described in this chapter offers political campaigners a powerful tool. It allows campaigners to estimate the share-of-vote that they would gain (or lose) if they adopted each alternative position they are considering—before they commit themselves. Moreover, this procedure indicates which types of voters would be attracted to each position and posture. Thus, candidates may select strategies that appeal to any desired target segment in the electorate.

It is important to bear in mind the limitations as well as the promise of this procedure. Since it is based on sample survey methods, this procedure simply yields a "snap shot" of the electorate at the time it is conducted. No survey can predict the future, since political preferences can be quite volatile. Between the time of the survey and the day of the election, voters' opinions about candidates or issues may change in response to unfolding world events or to the electoral campaign. Pre-election surveys are not crystal balls; they are merely estimates. Nevertheless, early polls can be quite useful in developing campaign strategy, since basic political attitudes often remain unchanged during political campaigns. Used with common sense, survey estimates can provide crucial information for the political campaigner. Despite their limitations, surveys can reveal the electorate's opinions more objectively than information from friends or lobbyists. The problem facing the political campaigner is to know how to properly use survey results.

This chapter is divided into two sections. The first presents the ordinal procedure used for estimating share-of-vote and compares this procedure with alternative approaches—traditional polling methods, a rating-scale method, and stochastic choice models. The second section examines the predictive accuracy of this procedure in selected political contests.

THE ESTIMATION PROCEDURES

A procedure has been devised that estimates the proportion of people in a target population that will choose any particular object (e.g., political candidate, party, position, or posture) over the alternatives in any set of mock elections. Estimates are obtained by simulating the aggregate share-of-vote that candidates and postures would receive from voters' indicated preferences. It is a simple but powerful approach to evaluating the drawing power of political candidates and the alternative positions and postures that they are considering (Stefflre 1961, 1968). This approach has an excellent track record in marketing. Stefflre (1979a) claims to have an average error of only 2 share points in using this approach to predict market share for new products from short verbal descriptions of product concepts. His descriptions are typically between five and seven words in length. Figure 9.1 compares his predictions with the observed market share for the 11 new products his firm has cooperated in launching.

The most important features of this approach are:

1. Estimate are derived from a representative sample of respondents.
2. Estimates are derived from respondents' ordinal preference rankings of up to about 50 objects.
3. Aggregate share of choice can be estimated for each object—in any subset—drawn from the full set of objects.
4. Alternative positions, postures, and campaign themes are evaluated by including them to be ranked in the original set of objects.

FIGURE 9.1. Predicting Market Share from New Product Concepts

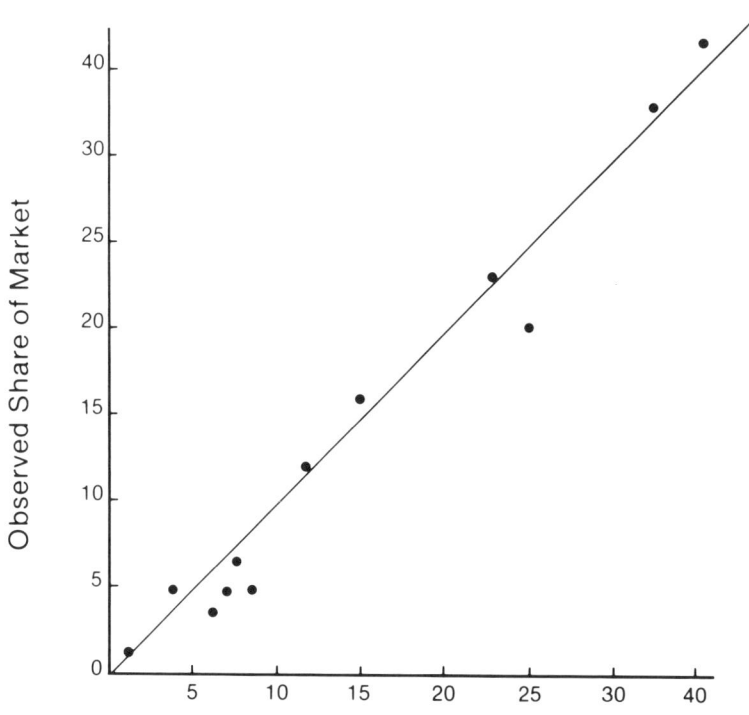

Source: Stefflre (1979a).

This estimate procedure is based on rank-order data. The rank-order method is an old established workhorse in the social sciences. However, its usefulness in estimating aggregate share-of-choice has not been very well exploited. Typically, rank-order data is used to calculate median ranks for objects, or to determine the frequency with which each object is ranked first (Guildford 1954). These analytical methods just begin to tap the usefulness of ordinal data.

If analyzed correctly, ordinal data may be used to estimate share-of-choice for objects in any subset drawn from the original collection of objects. This is rarely done. Analysts typically limit themselves to estimating share-of-choice for only the original set—ignoring the possibility of estimating subsets. As there are a very large number of subsets in any collection of objects (2^n), ordinal data offers a rich harvest. Even if we restrict our attention to *competitive* subsets (that is, those with two or more objects) there still are a large number of remaining subsets ($2^n - n - 1$).

Alternative positions and postures are evaluated by including hypothetical candidates. Each hypothetical candidate is identified by a short descriptive phrase, such as "a president who would stand up to the Russians." Estimates can be made about the drawing power, and the pattern of draw, that candidates would receive if they adopted any position or posture by assuming that people would react to a description of a candidate in the same manner as they would to a candidate that they see as matching the description. This is a powerful assumption. The extent to which descriptions of politicians and the politicians they are supposed to represent are treated in the same way by the electorate is empirically examined in Chapter 10.

In the next section, the ordinal procedure for estimating share-of-vote is described and compared with alternative estimation procedures. First, data collection methods are outlined. Next, the predictive rule is described and compared with a somewhat similar rule developed by Thurstone. The last part of this section discusses stochastic choice models, which are based on interval-level assumptions.

Data Collection Methods

Following Stefflre, data are collected by asking respondents to rank the set of politicians (or parties) in the order that they prefer them. Ranking a large number of items is not a simple matter. In order to ensure that respondents can successfully rank items presented to them, it is necessary to follow very rigorous procedures. This is particularly true if the set is larger than, say, 10 or 15 items.

The precise wording of the question is the first consideration. Respondents may be asked to rank objects according to a variety of criteria: for example, "liking," "preference," "probability of voting for them," or "admiration." In political studies, the wording can be "prefer to see elected as your (president, governor, and so on)," or, alternatively, simply "like to see elected." It is very important, whatever wording is selected, to repeat *exactly* the same wording, with *exactly* the same intonation, to *every* respondent. Otherwise, the interviewer may subtly influence the respondents' answers.

The second consideration is the ranking procedure itself. This must be carefully thought out and rigorously followed. In ranking a large number of items, it is necessary to conduct a personal interview. It is very difficult to achieve reliable rankings using mail questionnaires. In telephone interviews, if balanced lattice procedures are followed, up to eight items may be ranked accurately, but this appears to be the upper limit. Many more items may be ranked successfully in face-to-face interviews. However, the maximum here is probably around 50 items (Mauser 1972). The results discussed in this chapter are based on telephone and personal interviews, in which respondents were asked to rank lists of politicians close to these limits.

In a personal interview, a large number of items may be ranked with the help of index cards. Respondents are asked to rank items using a three-step procedure. First, they must sort the items quickly into three distinct piles according to their preferences: one pile for the items they like, one pile for the items they do not like, and a third pile for those items they feel ambivalent about—"that they neither like nor dislike."

Next, respondents are asked to sort the items within each pile according to the order of their preferences. After all three piles have been so ordered, the piles are assembled into a single pile. Respondents are then requested to look through the pile one last time to check if the final ordering reflects their preferences. Any changes they wish to make at this point are usually quite minor.

Predictive Rule

At the heart of the ordinal procedure is a simple predictive rule. The proportion of people in the sample who rank any object in a given set higher than the other objects in that set is used as an estimate of the proportion of people in the target population who would choose that same object over the other objects in that subset (Stefflre 1961).

More formally, this rule may be stated as:

$$\frac{f_{ij}}{n} \simeq \frac{F_{ij}}{N} \qquad (1)$$

where f_{ij} is the number of people who rank object i over all the other objects in subset j, and n is the total number of people in the sample. F_{ij} is the number of people in the target population who select object i when it is presented among the objects in subset j, and N is the total number of people in the target population.

This procedure is somewhat more complex and cumbersome than a standard political poll where respondents are simply asked to indicate their first choice in a mock election. However, if there are a large number of election scenarios to consider (e.g., if campaigners are unsure who will run against them), each mock election must be presented separately.[1] However, this is not necessary with rank order, since all items may be ranked simultaneously. This can be a distinct advantage, particularly if the mock elections are quite similar to each other. A large number of mock elections may be simulated using respondents' rank-order preferences for alternative candidates, positions, and postures. This permits campaigners to simulate the electorate's reaction to the introduction of new candidates or new positions into the campaign.

This rank-order procedure is similar to Thurstone's method of predicting aggregate choice that he developed for use with the successive interval scale for the situation of correlated ratings (Bock and Jones 1968; Thurstone 1945).[2] After describing a more elegant model at length, Thurstone notes its restrictive assumptions and proposes the following rule for estimating share-of-choice from rating scale data:

$$\frac{F_{ij}}{N} \simeq \frac{\sum_{t=1}^{T} \frac{(f_{ijt})}{t}}{n} \qquad (2)$$

where F_{ij}, N, and n are defined as before. But because respondents might rate more than one object in their highest rating category, it is necessary to decide how to allocate preferences in the case of ties. By assuming that tied objects will split their share of choice evenly, Thurstone could estimate the frequency with which each object i would be chosen first out of subset j by first determining the frequency that each object i would be placed in the individual's highest rating category for subset j, and then dividing by the number of objects t that are also placed in that same category. Share-of-choice estimates are calculated separately for each value of t and then summed over the full range of t observed. For example, the number of people who place object i in subset j with two other objects in their highest rating category would be divided by 3, if three objects are tied for first choice (t = 3) for these respondents. For those people who place object i in subset j alone in their highest rating category, t equals 1, so that this procedure reduces to that used with ordinal data, where ties are not permitted. With this method Thurstone successfully predicted share of servicemen's choices of food dishes out of hypothetical daily menus by using their ratings of the complete list of 40 possible dishes (Thurstone 1952).

The two estimation procedures differ primarily in their data bases. Stefflre's rule (1) is designed to be used with rank-order data while Thurstone's earlier method was conceived for rating scale data. Ties account for the second important difference. Typically, no ties are permitted in collecting rank-order data, while a large number of ties naturally occur with rating scales, since the number of objects being rated is usually greater than the number of categories on the rating scale. The loss of information due to ties probably reduces the accuracy of Thurstone's procedure. This is particularly true when there is a large number of items. However, in some circumstances, it may be preferable to use Thurstone's method, despite the problem of ties, due to the greater convenience of collecting rating-scale data compared with rank-order data.

Stochastic Choice Models

An alternative approach to estimating aggregate share-of-choice has recently attracted attention in marketing (Gensch and Recker 1979; Pessemier et al. 1971; Silk and Urban 1978). This approach is based on stochastic choice models and was originally developed, as was the ordinal approach, to evaluate new product concepts and prototypes prior to test marketing. Moreover, both stochastic and deterministic approaches rely upon consumer preferences in order to estimate share-of-choice. However, the stochastic approach assumes that individual preferences are probabilistic and can be measured at the interval level rather than at the ordinal level. In addition, the stochastic approach typically relies upon paired comparisons to collect preference data rather than rank-order as in the deterministic approach adopted here.

In the stochastic approach, individual preferences are described using a stochastic choice model. There are a variety of forms that such models can assume, depending upon the theoretical bent of the researcher and the specified type of data collected. Characteristically, however, these scaling models depend upon Luce's choice axiom.

Luce (1959) asserts that individual choice behavior is a random process and that individual choice probabilities satisfy a simple, but powerful, axiom:

$$p(x;T) = p(x;S)p(S;T), \qquad (3)$$

where $p(x;T) \neq 0, 1$ for all $x \in T$ and $S \subset T$. In words, this axiom states that the probability of choosing an object x out of an entire set T, $p(x;T)$, equals the probability of choosing x out of a subset S of T, $p(x;S)$, multiplied by the probability that the object x is in S, $p(S;T)$.

From this choice axiom, Luce derives a number of interesting consequences, two of which will now be presented. First, if S consists of two alternatives, x and y, then by the choice axiom:

$p(x;T) = p(x;R)p(R;T)$, and
$p(y;T) = p(y;R)p(R;T)$.

Dividing the first equation by the second gives:

$$\frac{p(x;T)}{p(y;T)} = \frac{p(x;R)}{p(y;R)} = \frac{p(x;y)}{p(y;x)} \qquad (4)$$

which is typically referred to as the *constant ratio rule*. This rule asserts that the probability of choosing between any two objects in a set should be unaffected by the addition (or deletion) of any other object. Luce's choice axiom can be regarded as a probabilistic version of the principle of independence of irrelevant alternatives.

Second, the probabilities of choosing objects out of any sized set can be derived from pairwise choice probabilities. Since the summation of all p(y;T) over all y $\in$ T equals 1,

$$p(x;T) = \frac{p(x;T)}{\sum_y p(y;T)} = \frac{1}{\sum_y p(y;T)/p(x;T)} = \frac{1}{\sum p(y,x)/p(x,y)} \qquad (5)$$

according to the constant ratio rule. For example, if T consists of three objects {x, y, z} then:

$$p(x;T) = \frac{1}{\frac{p(y,x)}{p(x,y)} + \frac{p(z,x)}{p(x,z)} + \frac{p(y,z)}{p(z,y)}} \qquad (6)$$

Using stochastic models of individual choice to estimate aggregate share-of-choice essentially depends upon assuming that Luce's choice axiom holds at the aggregate level. Such an assumption is quite restrictive and limits the range of situations where this approach may be successfully used. This limitation is particularly important to bear in mind in practical situations such as marketing or campaign politics.

There are two fundamental implications of Luce's choice axiom that severely limit its application at the aggregate level: the axiom implies that the homogeneity of preferences within the population and choice between objects are independent of irrelevant alternatives. These are not new criticisms of Luce's axiom. Several writers have pointed out these problems, including Luce himself, who explicitly warned against extending his model to aggregate choice behavior (Luce 1959, p. 8).[3] Unfortunately, this is a warning that few marketing or operations researchers have heeded. Each of these two criticisms now will be discussed in turn.

Homogeneity of Preferences

The use of stochastic choice models to estimate aggregate preferences depends upon individual preferences being uniform throughout a population. If subgroups exist that differ in their preferences, such as political cleavages or market segments, the model may not hold for the population even though it may hold for every individual in the population. This is demonstrated in Table 9.1, which is drawn from Luce (1959, p. 8). As can be readily seen, both individuals satisfy the axiom but the group average does not, since (.50)(.50) = .25 $\neq$ .37. This criticism is particularly acute in marketing and in politics where distinctive consumer or voter groups are quite common.[4]

TABLE 9.1. The Success of Luce's Choice Axiom at the Individual and Aggregate Levels

	p(x;T)	p(x;S)	p(S;T)
Individual A	.63	.70	.90
Individual B	.03	.10	.30
Average for the aggregate	.33	.40	.60

Note: Luce's axiom asserts that $p(x;T) = p(x;S) \, p(S;T)$.

Independence of Irrelevant Alternatives

Luce's axiom asserts that the probabilities of choosing between any two alternatives will not be affected by the addition or deletion of any other alternatives. This assumption depends upon all alternatives being seen as equally similar (or dissimilar) to each other (Luce 1977; Tversky 1972).

A few examples may illustrate the problems inherent in relying upon the assumption of the independence of irrelevant alternatives in predicting share-of-choice.[5] Consider a simple election contest with only three candidates (A, B, and C). Following Luce's axiom, paired comparisons may be used to predict share-of-choice for any size contest. Suppose that all paired comparisons split exactly 50-50, so that 50 percent of the voters prefer candidate A to candidate B, 50 percent prefer candidate B to candidate C, and 50 percent prefer candidate A to candidate C. If we assume, with Luce, the independence of irrelevant alternatives, we must then predict that all candidates will have an equal share of the vote in the elections:

Candidate	Share of Vote
A	33.3%
B	33.3
C	33.3
	100.0%

This follows immediately from Luce's axiom, since:

$$p(A; A,B,C) = \frac{1}{\frac{p(A,B)}{p(B,A)} + \frac{p(A,C)}{p(C,A)} + \frac{p(B,C)}{p(C,B)}} = \frac{1}{1+1+1} = \frac{1}{3} \qquad (7)$$

This prediction, however, does not do justice to the manifold of possibilities that might occur in such a situation. First, it is possible that similar candidates might split their vote (or that similar products would "cannibalize" each other's market share). For example, if candidates A and B were identical, the following scenario could occur, even though the three candidates split all of the paired comparisons 50-50:

Candidate	Share of Vote
A	25%
B	25
C	50
	100.0%

A somewhat different situation may be seen in polarized electorates (or in segmented markets). Two distinct groupings may exist, each of which strongly prefers their own candidate, A or C. In such a situation, candidate B might be seen by both groups as only a poor second choice to the more desirable alternatives A or C. Thus, in the paired comparisons, B would be selected by voters whenever their first choice was unavailable. That is to say, in the A-B pairing, voters who preferred C over A would choose B. Similarly for the B-C pairing, voters who preferred A over C would pick B. This implies that in the three-man contest, when both A and C were available, no one would select B:

Candidate	Share of Vote
A	50%
B	0
C	50
	100.0%

In general, the assumption of the independence of irrelevant alternatives will be violated if any two alternatives resemble each other more than either does the remaining alternatives, or if the individual preferences are too heterogeneous. Since such conditions are likely to exist in political contests, the use of models that depend upon Luce's choice axiom to predict aggregate share of choice would appear to be somewhat dubious.

Predicting Share-of-Choice

Despite their theoretical problems, stochastic choice models would still remain attractive if they could easily and accurately predict aggregate share of first choice. This does not seem to be the case. Bock and Jones (1968) reanalyzed choice data reported earlier by Thurstone (1952), using selected stochastic choice models, and found that Thurstone's simpler procedure was as good or better in predicting share-of-choice.

Thurstone's (1952) experiment consisted of predicting 254 servicemen's first choices among food dishes grouped in sets (menus) of two, three, four, and five dishes from their earlier determined preferences for 40 dishes, which had been obtained by means of a nine-interval, successive-categories rating scale. Using the predictive rule described earlier—rule (2)—Thurstone predicted quite accurately the observed share of choice. Except for a correction for ties, this procedure is quite similar to Stefflre's rule (1).

Bock and Jones (1968, pp. 248-63) discuss three stochastic choice models and compare their predictions of the share of first choice with those of Thurstone's much simpler approach. Only the four menus containing three dishes each are reanalyzed, since stochastic models become very cumbersome with more than three items, but not deterministic models. Estimates and observed proportions are based on the full sample (N = 254) for each of the predictive methods.[6] Table 9.2 compares the predictions of these models.

The three stochastic choice models compared in this study were: Bock and Jones's generalized multivariate normal model, the bivariate logistic model, and the Bradley-Terry-Luce model. Not one of the stochastic choice models could predict share of choice as well as Thurstone's much simpler procedure, which has a mean absolute deviation (MAD) of only 2.0 percent. The worst predictor was the Bradley-Terry-Luce model, with a MAD of 6.2 percent, while the best stochastic model, the multivariate model, had a MAD of 3.3 percent.[7] Particularly unsettling for proponents of stochastic models was that their predictions were much more widely dispersed than those of Thurstone's procedure. (See Table 9.2).

Recent research in marketing has supported the Bock and Jones results. Currim (1982) found that stochastic choice models based on Luce's choice axiom are not very accurate predictors of share of choice. Moreover, the stochastic models are forbiddingly complex and based on arbitrary parameters. For example, both Pessemier and colleagues (1971) and Silk and Urban (1978) use an additional parameter (β) that is determined *after* looking at the proportions of choice to be predicted. Such "predictions" depend upon the criterion to be predicted. Moreover, this parameter is completely ad hoc. There is little justification for thinking that such a parameter will continue to hold with the introduction (or deletion) of any new object to the set of objects in the marketplace. But it must do this, since the avowed goal is to evaluate new product entries in the market.

In summary, stochastic choice models do not seem to be a satisfactory alternative to either the Stefflre or the Thurstone estimation procedures for several reasons. First, they are not intrinsically accurate predictors of aggregate share of first choice. Second, only through using cumbersome ad hoc parameters can they be forced to approximate the data after the fact. Third, there are good theoretical reasons why it is inappropriate to attempt to aggregate interval level data to predict share-of-choice. Fourth, and perhaps most importantly, simpler and effective alternatives exist.

THE ELECTION STUDIES

The results of three separate studies are reported here in order to examine the power of rule (1) to estimate share-of-vote for political

TABLE 9.2. Comparison of Thurstone's Predictive Rule with Selected Stochastic Choice Models for Predicting Aggregate Share of First Choices

Menu	Foods	Observed Choices (N = 254)	Normal Model		Logistic Model		B-T-L Model[a]		Thurstone Method	
			Predicted	Deviation	Predicted	Deviation	Predicted	Deviation	Predicted	Deviation
1	Spaghetti	.427	.429	-.002	.430	-.003	.402	.025	.444	-.017
	Baked beans	.349	.351	-.002	.360	-.011	.355	-.006	.333	.016
	Salmon loaf	.224	.220	.004	.211	.013	.243	-.019	.223	.001
		1.000								
2	Blueberry pie	.337	.280	.057	.289	.048	.300	.037	.320	.017
	Chocolate cake	.400	.375	.025	.373	.027	.363	.037	.390	.010
	Pineapple	.263	.345	-.082	.338	-.075	.337	-.074	.290	-.027
		1.000								
3	Liver	.416	.381	.035	.361	.055	.360	.056	.381	.035
	Wieners	.482	.490	-.008	.496	-.014	.461	.021	.503	.021
	Sweetbreads	.102	.129	-.027	.143	-.041	.179	-.077	.116	-.014
		1.000								
4	Parsnips	.130	.191	-.061	.210	-.080	.254	-.124	.169	-.039
	Turnips	.178	.194	-.016	.210	-.032	.252	-.074	.144	.034
	Cauliflower	.692	.615	.077	.579	.113	.494	.198	.687	.005
		1.000								
Mean Absolute Deviation				.033		.043		.062		.020

[a] Predictions from Bradley-Terry-Luce Model.
Source: Bock and Jones (1968).

candidates. In order to vigorously test the predictive rule, a variety of political contests are examined. These contests differ in several ways. Some are U.S. elections, others are French. Multicandidate contests are examined as well as two-candidate contests. Finally, these contests differ in the type of political office being sought: presidential, gubernatorial, and legislative elections.

There are several questions that might be asked in evaluating share-of-vote estimates: can the winner of the election by correctly identified? what is the difference in the predicted and obtained share-of-vote for the winning candidate? and what is the percentage-point difference between estimated and obtained share-of-vote for all candidates?

While predicting the winner of an election is intuitively appealing, the strictest test of polling estimates lies in examining the percentage point spread across all candidates in the contest. It is more difficult to estimate the share-of-vote for each candidate than it is to predict who will win the contest. Moreover, only looking at the winner of an election ignores the influence of minor candidates. A technique is needed that can evaluate the impact of such candidates and issues in order to evaluate alternative campaign strategies.

The MAD is a convenient measure of the accuracy of share-of-vote estimates.[8] It indicates the extent to which the estimated share of the vote for all candidates differs from the share-of-vote actually observed. It is calculated by taking the mean of the difference (ignoring direction) between the estimated and the observed share-of-vote for each candidate in the contest.

In these studies, sample estimates of the share-of-vote using rule (1) are compared with actual election returns. Such a comparison tests more than just the validity of rule (1). Inaccurate predictions could result from either a failure to draw representative samples or from unstable political preferences. It is particularly valuable to compare rule (1) with the results of traditional polling methods, which simply present respondents with mock elections and request that they indicate their first choice. Since all of these samples were drawn at approximately the same time prior to the election, each estimation procedure faces the same difficulties in estimating share-of-vote.

It is also possible to compare estimates based on Luce's choice axiom, rule (3), with those based on rule (1), in multicandidate contests. To estimate share-of-choice using Luce's axiom in any size contest, all that is required is knowledge of the pairwise choice proportions between the candidates. Share-of-choice in these pairs is estimated from aggregate preference orders using rule (1), since not all paired comparisons were collected. After comparing estimates based on rule (1) with traditional polling methods, rule (1) will be compared with Luce's choice axiom in studies 1 and 3; it is not possible to do so in study 2 as there were no naturally occurring multi-candidate contests in the election.

Study 1

Study 1 involved a series of interviews with California registered voters drawn prior to a U.S. presidential election. In the first wave of interviews, 193 respondents ranked 50 politicians in the order that they preferred them for president of the United States. In the second wave, 1,161 respondents ranked eight politicians in their order of preference. Respondents in the first wave were interviewed in person at their homes, while the second wave was interviewed over the telephone.

The politicians included in this study were selected from the full range of well-known political figures in the United States. Twenty-five of the 50 politicians in the first sample and 3 of the 8 politicians in the second sample consisted of verbal descriptions of hypothetical candidates rather than names of actual politicians. (Sampling and interviewing procedures are described in Chapter 5.)

The first (and smaller) sample was conducted in mid-October, two weeks before election day, using quota sampling methods; 193 respondents were personally interviewed. The second, larger sample was drawn the weekend before the election in November and interviewed over the telephone. In this sample, a multistage probability sampling technique was used to draw 1,161 persons. Estimates were made using rule (1) for the proportion of the vote that each of the three candidates would receive statewide in California from both samples.

Table 9.3 compares the sample estimates based on rule (1) with the official election results and with the final estimates of two published polls.

The MAD between the proportion of the vote predicted using rule (1) and the election returns is less than 1.0 percent for the larger sample and is 1.4 percent for the smaller sample. The accuracy is even greater for the estimate of a hypothetical two-party contest between Humphrey and Nixon alone.

The estimates compare favorably with those of the public pollsters. The best estimate made by a pollster of the California vote—that of the State Poll—had a MAD of 1.5 percent, the MAD of the well-respected California Poll was 6.4 percent. To put this in perspective, Gallup has an average MAD of 2.0 percent over the nine presidential elections between 1948 and 1980 for the national vote based on the last poll taken before each election (Gallup 1980). In 1968, Gallup had a MAD of 1 percent for the estimate of the national vote (Crossley and Crossley, 1969).

The primary factors determining the accuracy of a properly conducted political poll are, of course, its sample size and its proximity to the election. The results of well-conducted polls are typically well within the confidence limits set for the sampling error expected for samples of the same size.

Table 9.4 compares sample estimates based on Luce's choice axiom with those based on rule (1) and with the official election results. As can be readily seen, Luce's axiom fails dismally to capture the patterns of competition in

TABLE 9.3. Estimating the Vote for the 1968 Presidential Contest for California Using Rule (1)

	Hubert Humphrey	Richard Nixon	George Wallace	Total	MAD[e]
Large sample estimate[a]	44.7%	47.3%	8.0%	100%	1.4%
Small sample estimate[b]	46.6	46.1	7.3	100	0.9
State poll[c]	47.2	48.3	4.5	100	1.5
California poll[c]	35.5	55.9	8.6	100	6.4
Election results[d]	45.1	48.2	6.8	100	

[a] Based on respondents' rankings of five politicians and three descriptions in the Large Scale Preference Sample (N = 1,161) drawn and interviewed November 1-4, 1968, a few days prior to the election.

[b] Based on respondents' ranking of 25 politicians and 25 descriptions in the Small Scale Preference Sample (N = 193), two weeks before the day of the election.

[c] Based on the results included in Crossley and Crossley (1969). The California Poll was published October 28, 1968, and the State Poll's estimate was published November 4, 1968. Undecided respondents were excluded from the estimate.

[d] As reported in the Statement of Vote, General Election, November 5, 1968, Office of the Secretary of State, State of California.

[e] Entries in this column are the mean absolute difference (MAD) between the proportion of vote predicted for each of the three candidates and that obtained in the election. Smaller scores indicate greater accuracy.

Source: Mauser (1972, 1979).

this election. While based on the same raw data as rule (1), which yields a close estimate, use of Luce's axiom results in a much worse estimate. The principal problem appears to be its insensitivity to vote-splitting, which is evident in the overestimate of George Wallace's vote.

Study 2

Study 2 analyzes a California gubernatorial contest; 165 respondents were selected using a multistage probability sampling technique from Los Angeles County and were asked to rank 50 politicians in the order that they preferred them for governor. Twenty-five of these politicians consisted of verbal descriptions of plausible candidates. This sample was drawn two months before the election. Estimates were made of the proportion of the vote from respondents' rankings using rule (1) and compared with the official election returns for Los Angeles County. (This study is described more fully in Chapter 6.)

Because of its small size, as well as the relatively long time before the election, it was not expected that these estimates would prove to be very

232 • POLITICAL MARKETING

TABLE 9.4. Comparing Luce's Choice Axiom and Rule (1) in the 1968 Presidential Contest in California

	Hubert Humphrey	Richard Nixon	George Wallace	Total	MAD
Rule (1)	44.7%	47.3%	8.0%	100%	1.4%
Luce's Axiom[a]	37.1	53.4	9.4	100	5.3
Election results	45.1	48.2	6.8	100	

Note: Both estimates are based on the same data: Respondents' rankings of 5 politicians and 3 descriptions in the Large Scale Preference Sample (N = 1,161) which was drawn and interviewed November 1-4, 1968, a few days prior to the election.

[a] Respondents choices in paired comparisons were estimated using respondents' rankings, and then these values were used to calculate the three-way race.

accurate. Nevertheless, a MAD of 1.7 percent was obtained (see Table 9.5). In estimating the statewide results in 1970, the California Poll's survey drawn in early October had a MAD of 5.1 percent. The estimate based on rule (1) again compares favorably with conventional polls.

Rule (1) appears to be an effective way to estimate share-of-vote for major candidates from preference orderings. The estimates in both of the California studies, which were based on rankings of up to 50 candidates, are at least as accurate as conventional polling estimates of comparable sample size and proximity to the date of the election.

Study 3

As part of a study of French political perceptions and preferences, a sample of 232 French citizens was selected from one of the *circonscriptions* (electoral districts) near Grenoble in the French Alps. This sample was drawn using mixed quota and probability sampling methods during January 1974, a few months prior to the presidential elections of 1974. (This study is described more fully in Chapter 8.)

In this interview, respondents were asked to: rank order 25 French political figures (e.g., Giscard d'Estaing and François Mitterrand) and 17 descriptions of hypothetical politicians (e.g., "a man who could institute orderly reforms in French society" and "a man like Charles de Gaulle") in the order that they preferred them; and to indicate the candidate that they would vote for in 12 mock elections. The mock elections included a variety of hypothetical contests for president, pitting the best known political leaders against each other. Respondents were also asked how they had voted in the previous legislative elections.

Mock elections permit the evaluation of estimates in a wide variety of electoral situations. By including politicians other than those in the actual election in these mock elections, it is possible to evaluate the accuracy of

TABLE 9.5. Estimating the 1970 California Gubernatorial Vote in Los Angeles County Using Rule (1)

	Jesse Unruh	Ronald Reagan	Total	MAD^c
Small sample estimate[a]	50.0%	50.0%	100%	1.7%
Election results[b]	48.3	51.7	100	

[a] Based on respondents' rankings of 25 politicians in the Small Scale Preference Sample (N = 165) drawn September 7-23, 1970, two months before the election.

[b] Los Angeles County official results, reported in the Statement of the Vote, General Election, November 3, 1970, Office of the Secretary of State, State of California.

[c] The entry in this column refers to the mean absolute difference (MAD) between the proportion of the vote predicted for each candidate and that obtained in the election. Smaller scores indicate greater accuracy.

Source: Mauser (1979).

estimates for hypothetical political candidates as well as for actual candidates. Since preferences for hypothetical candidates are probably less firmly held than are preferences for actual candidates, these mock elections provide a strong test for any predictive rule. It is particularly important to examine the accuracy of such estimates, since estimates of the performance of hypothetical candidates form the basis for evaluating the electorate's reaction to alternative positions and postures in determining campaign strategy.

In order to evaluate the estimates, respondents in the original sample were randomly assigned to one of two subsamples, and estimates of the share-of-vote that candidates would receive were calculated from respondents' preference orders in the first subsample. These estimates were then compared with results of the mock elections in the other subsample. Splitting the sample in this way yields two independent samples from the same target population. Since no respondent could be in both subsamples simultaneously, agreement between the sample results cannot be ascribed to intra-individual agreement between preferences and choice, but can only be due to the accuracy of the estimator itself.

First, let's examine rule (1). Tables 9.6 and 9.7 compare the observed share-of-vote in two of the 12 mock elections with the share-of-vote estimated from respondents' preference rankings using rule (1). As can be seen, rule (1) does an adequate job in both cases, with MADs of 7.2 and 5.1 share-points respectively.[9] These estimates are well within the error range that would be expected for samples of this size, although they are not as accurate as in the U.S. contests. This difference is most likely due to the smaller sample size in the French study, but may also be due to the greater instability of preferences for hypothetical candidates.

Rule (1) does quite well over the full set of 12 mock elections (see Figure 9.2). The MADs range from 3.9 to 20.8 share-points per contest, with a

TABLE 9.6. Estimating the Vote Using Rule (1) in the First Round of the French Legislative Elections of March 4, 1973

Candidate	Rule (1) Estimate[a]	Results of Mock Election[a]	Difference
M. Gau (UGSD-PS)	42.6%	33.7%	8.9
M. Fagot (URP-UDR)	13.0	33.7	20.7
M. Perinetti (PCF)	14.8	15.7	0.9
M. Quézel (PSU)	7.0	4.5	2.5
M. de Galbert (Réformateur/C. Rep.)	14.8	9.0	5.8
M. Graillat (CNI)	7.8	3.4	4.4
	100.0%	100.0%	7.2

[a] Estimated from even-numbered respondents' preference rankings for 42 politicians. Based on one-half of the sample drawn from the fourth *circonscription* of the Isère (N = 115).

[b] Based on odd-numbered respondents' choices among these six candidates in a mock election using the other half of the sample (N = 117).

TABLE 9.7. Estimating the Share-of-Vote in a Mock French Presidential Election Using Rule (1)

Candidate	Rule (1) Estimate[a]	Mock Election Results[b]	Difference
G. Pompidou	20.9%	35.2%	14.3
M. Rocard	12.2	9.3	2.9
J. J. Servan Schreiber	11.3	10.2	1.1
G. Marchais	18.3	11.1	7.2
F. Mitterrand	35.7	31.5	4.2
M. Tixier	1.7	2.8	1.1
	100.0%	100.0%	5.1

[a] Estimated from even-numbered respondents' preference rankings for 42 politicians. Based on one-half of the sample drawn from the fourth *circonscription* of the Isère (N = 115).

[b] Based on odd-numbered respondents' choices among these six candidates in a mock presidential election using the other half of the sample (N = 117).

mean of 10.1 across all 24 estimates. One-third of the estimates are less than 11 share-points—the error range expected for samples of this size. Interestingly enough, the estimates are more accurate for multicandidate contests than for two-candidate contests. The MADs for races among more than two candidates range from 3.9 to 8.9 share-points per contest, with a mean of 6.1 for the 8 free-for-alls, while the two-man duels ranged from 5.0 to 20.8, with a mean of 12.2 share points.

FIGURE 9.2. Predicting Share-of-Vote in Mock French Elections

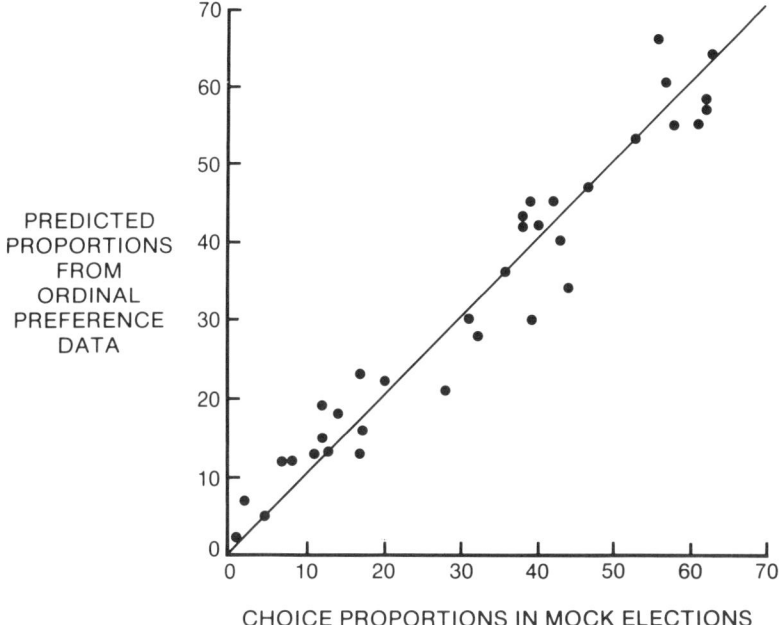

Next, Luce's choice axiom is examined. Tables 9.8 and 9.9 compare the observed share-of-vote with estimates based on Luce's choice axiom and rule (1). In every case, rule (1) predicts better than Luce's choice axiom.[10] As has been noted elsewhere, Luce's axiom tends to overestimate the share of minor candidates. Such a tendency would be particularly dangerous for campaign strategists attempting to evaluate the impact of minor candidates or new issues. Unfortunately, there does not seem to be a simple method for improving estimates based on stochastic models.[11] It would seem unwise to rely upon Luce's choice axiom in estimating share-of-choice in practical situations such as competitive elections or markets.

CONCLUSIONS

This chapter examined a simple, but powerful, procedure for estimating the share-of-vote that political candidates would receive in both real and hypothetical election scenarios. Such a procedure offers a powerful tool to political strategists, as it permits campaigners to estimate the share-of-vote that any candidate would gain (or lose) by adopting alternative positions or postures. Thus, candidates can identify effective campaign strategy and anticipate strategic moves by their opposition.

TABLE 9.8. Comparing Rule (1) and Luce's Choice Axiom in Mock French Presidential Contests: Even Estimates, Odd Contests

Observed Results in Mock Elections[a]		Rule (1)		Luce's Choice Axiom	
		Estimate[b]	Difference	Estimate[b]	Difference
G. Marchais	11.7%	19.1%	−7.4	13.5%	−1.8
F. Mitterrand	30.6	33.9	−3.3	41.7	−11.1
J. Lecanuet	17.1	11.3	5.8	13.2	3.9
V. Giscard d'Estaing	21.6	20.0	1.6	14.7	6.9
J. Chaban-Delmas	18.9	15.7	3.2	16.9	2.0
	100.0%	100.0%	4.3	100.0%	5.1
E. Faure	29.4	29.6	−0.2	29.5	−0.1
J. Lecanuet	23.5	15.7	7.8	23.9	−0.4
J. J. Servan Schreiber	15.7	21.7	−6.0	23.9	−8.2
G. Marchais	31.4	33.0	−1.6	22.7	8.7
	100.0%	100.0%	3.9	100.0%	4.4

[a] Based on the odd-numbered respondents' choices in mock presidential elections (N = 117).
[b] Based on the even-numbered respondents' preferences (N = 117).

TABLE 9.9. Comparing Rule (1) and Luce's Choice Axiom in Mock French Presidential Contests: Odd Estimates, Even Contests

Observed Mock Election Results[a]	Rule (1)		Luce's Axiom	
	Estimate[b]	Difference	Estimate[b]	Difference
G. Marchais	16.7%	14.5%	2.2	13.2%	3.5
F. Mitterrand	46.7	26.5	20.2	22.6	24.1
J. Lecanuet	9.2	15.4	6.2	21.1	11.9
V. Giscard d'Estaing	12.5	28.2	15.7	17.7	5.2
J. Chaban-Delmas	15.0	15.4	0.4	25.4	10.4
	100.0%	100.0%	8.9	100.0%	11.0
E. Faure	31.1	29.9	0.2	34.3	3.2
J. Lecanuet	17.0	27.4	10.4	26.4	9.4
J.J.Servan Schreiber	10.4	17.1	6.7	22.9	12.5
G. Marchais	41.5	25.6	15.9	16.5	25.0
	100.0%	100.0%	8.3	100.0%	12.5

[a] Based on the even-numbered respondents' choices in mock presidential elections (N = 115).
[b] Based on the odd-numbered respondents' preferences (N = 117).

The estimation procedure presented here is based on respondents' preference rankings, where items consist of either names or verbal descriptions. Special data-collection methods need to be followed to ensure valid rankings. Share-of-choice for any object in each subset is estimated using a simple predictive rule—Stefflre's rule (1). While this rule is extremely simple and powerful, few political or marketing researchers appear to know of it.

There are three criteria that are particularly important in evaluating any measurement tool, such as the estimation procedure described in this chapter: empirical validity, theoretical suitability, and practicality or usefulness.

Empirical validity is a procedure that has been shown to have a high degree of predictive accuracy. Three separate studies were analyzed to evaluate the ability of this procedure to predict aggregate share-of-choice. Predictions were made for the share-of-vote for candidates in selected U.S. and French elections. The procedure successfully estimated share-of-vote for both actual and hypothetical candidates. Predictions based on this rule were within sampling error estimates and compared favorably with predictions made by commercial pollsters. This implies that the ordinal procedure could be used to simulate a large number of election scenarios, at no loss of predictive accuracy, in lieu of presenting to respondents a burdensome series of mock elections.

Moreover, estimates based on rule (1) are consistently more accurate than those derived from sophisticated scaling models which require unrealistic assumptions, such as Luce's choice axiom, or which use *post hoc* parameters. In each of the three studies discussed in this chapter, where stochastic models were directly compared with ordinal models—either rule (1) or rule (2)—the stochastic models did poorly.

Second, the theoretical suitability of a measure involves the fit of a measure to the problem at hand as well as its fit with relevant theory or models. The ordinal predictive procedure described here fits the problem of estimating aggregate share-of-choice somewhat better than it does currently popular theory. By restricting itself to aggregating ordinal-level information (that is, whether a person prefers object A to object B) this estimation procedure contrasts sharply with alternative procedures, which are based on interval-level information (such as, individual utilities or choice probabilities). The interval-level scaling models appear to run into difficulties because they attempt to aggregate quantities that are not commensurate. A large number of writers have argued that individual utilities cannot be summed across individuals without introducing large errors. The results seen in this chapter simply add further support to this position.

Ordinal models are clearly preferable on theoretical grounds for understanding aggregate choice, and may even be more suitable in the case of individual preference as well. A variety of researchers (Debreu 1960; Green and Srinavasan 1978; Reibstein 1978; Tversky 1972; Tversky and Sattath 1979) suggest that choice is context dependent and thus inconsistent with the assumptions of most stochastic models.

Finally, with respect to practicality, the ordinal-level procedure is inexpensive, simple to understand, easy to use, and reliable. Once ordinal data has been obtained from respondents, a large number of mock elections may be easily simulated. This gives campaigners greater lattitude in strategic evaluation than is possible with traditional polls. Moreover, the computational methods are relatively simple and easy to program in contrast with the stochastic choice models. Complexity and sophistication are not necessarily advantages. It is all too easy for strategists to lose contact with their original objectives if the data analysis is too complicated. Ideally, analytical techniques should permit decision makers to have a feel for the data analysis. Divorcing the decision maker from the data easily leads to faulty decisions.

The greatest drawback of the ordinal approach is that data collection is somewhat inconvenient. It is not as easy to get respondents to rank order a large set of stimuli as to have them use rating scales or to respond to traditional polling questions. However, rank-order data is easier to collect than pair comparisons. The method of rank order poses formidable problems in either telephone interviews or mail questionnaires. Nevertheless, highly accurate rank-order data may be collected under field conditions, using both personal and telephone interviewing methods, as these studies have demonstrated.

In summary, the ordinal procedure presented in this chapter has been shown to have a high degree of predictive accuracy and to be practical to use. Its primary advantage would appear to be its simple and powerful method of estimating share-of-choice in a large number of election scenarios. Despite the simplicity and seeming obviousness of this predictive rule, it seems to be unknown in both marketing and in politics. Whatever the reasons for its obscurity, the results shown here suggest that this procedure deserves to be taken seriously as a tool for estimating share-of-choice.

NOTES

1. The number of mock elections that have to be presented to respondents increases very rapidly as the number of alternative positions and postures that need to be considered increases. For example, if a campaigner is interested in evaluating voters' perceptions of three separate postures, then three mock elections, one for each posture, must be presented to the voters for each set of opponents that he thinks he might face. If he is uncertain about who his opponents might be, the number of mock elections rapidly becomes unmanageable. Pursuing the example above, if any one of three people might run against him, there are nine possible two-candidate scenarios to consider in order to evaluate three postures (that is, three opponents by three postures). If he might have two or three opponents, then there are up to seven possible sets of opponents that he might face (three different contests with two candidates, three with three candidates, and one with all four candidates), so that, combined with the three alternative postures to consider, there are 21 mock elections to present to the respondents. Clearly, this approach is more unwieldy than asking people to rank order three postures and four politicians simultaneously in one question.

2. Thurstone's procedure for predicting share-of-choice should not be confused with the well-known unidimensional scaling approach that he developed earlier (Thurstone 1927; Torgerson 1958).

3. In an excellent review article, Luce (1977) discusses the present state of research concerning his choice axiom. He concludes that it only imperfectly describes individual preferences but that it is still useful in rational theories of individual behavior. In contrast, discussion in this chapter focuses on Luce's rule applied to aggregate behavior rather than individual behavior. All procedures described in this chapter (deterministic and stochastic) are consistent with "the independence of irrelevant alternatives" at the individual level. However, this axiom is not critical for the working of the deterministic models, while it is for the stochastic models.

4. Despite the clear inapplicability of Luce's axiom at the aggregate level, most attempts to empirically test the axiom in psychology rely upon aggregate data (Coombs, Dawes, and Tversky, 1970, p. 153). Perhaps because of this tradition, operations researchers have uncritically adopted analytical procedures incorporating Luce's rule in describing aggregate data where it is clearly inappropriate (e.g., Pessemier et al. 1971; Rao and Winter 1978; Silk and Urban 1978).

5. The following discussion is freely adapted from Stefflre's earlier discussion (1971, pp. 29-33).

6. A stricter test of the models would have been to split the sample, basing estimates and observed proportions on distinct subsamples. The use of different subsamples for the estimates and the criteria would have removed any effect of intra-individual consistency, permitting a direct test of the measures.

7. Another question to ask in comparing these models is how often each model yields the closest estimate. Thurstone's procedure again clearly beats all three other models. Out of the 36 proportions to be estimated, Thurstone's estimates are the closest 25 times, another model is closest 9 times, and there are two ties. The sign test shows that there is less than one chance out of a hundred that such a score would be observed if all models were equally good predictors.

8. An inadequate alternative approach, that is sometimes used, is to correlate the estimated and observed shares. This approach is not as strict as the MAD, regardless of the particular correlation coefficient used, since high correlations may be obtained even with fairly poor estimates.

9. The results presented here differ slightly from those included in Mauser (1979). The earlier results were based on the full sample of respondents (N = 232) rather than on separate subsamples as was done here.

10. The astute reader at this point may wonder if part of the problem of Luce's axiom is that it is based on estimates from rule (1) that already contains some error. This does not appear to be the case. Observed vote-proportions were substituted for those estimated using rule (1) wherever possible in an effort to improve upon the data base of Luce's axiom. No luck: the estimates based on observed proportions were almost always worse than those based on those simulated using rule (1). This result is probably due to the larger proportion of respondents refusing to make a choice in the mock duels. This problem crops up continually with paired comparisons.

11. A recent example illustrates the problem of using stochastic models (Silk and Urban 1978). In their approach, Silk and Urban use a multinominal logit model, which relies on Luce's rule, to estimate individual choice probabilities. Such an approach is exceptionally complex and involves assumptions about aggregate homogeneity to estimate individual parameters (β). After having developed individual choice probabilities, they simply average them across their sample to estimate market share! See Bordley and Wolff (1981) for a theoretical argument against this approach. Mauser (1980) shows that such an approach performs less well than does either of the ordinal procedures described in this chapter.

10

SIMILARITY AND COMPETITION

> Thus the special symbolic forms are not imitations but *organs* of reality, since it is solely by their agency that anything real becomes an object for intellectual apprehension, and as such is made visible to us.
>
> Ernst Cassirer, *Language and Myth*

> We cut up and organize the spread and flow of events as we do, largely because, through our mother tongue, we are parties to an agreement to do so, not because nature itself is segmented in exactly that way for all to see. Languages differ not only in how they build their sentences but also in how they break down nature to secure the elements to put in those sentences.
>
> Benjamin Lee Whorf, *Languages and Logic*

This chapter empirically examines the premise that lies at the root of spatial models that are used to analyze elections and markets: similar objects should compete more with each other than with dissimilar objects. Stefflre has put this as, "An individual will behave toward a new thing in a manner that is similar to the way he behaves toward other things he sees the new thing as being similar to" (Stefflre 1965, p. 12). This is a simple but powerful notion and it has direct application to predicting choice behavior in single-choice situations like elections or markets: new items (e.g., candidates or products) should draw most heavily from those items that they most resemble. Moreover, if the attributes (or features) can be identified that determine which items are seen to be similar, strategists can predict: where in the similarity structure any new item having specific attributes will position, and therefore how people will react to it, and what attributes a new item must have to position in a specific place in the similarity structure, in order to elicit the desired reactions.

To test this notion, independent measures are required for the perceived similarity of items, and the similarity in the behavior toward pairs of items. A set of techniques designed to do this has been developed with specific attention to single-choice situations such as markets and elections (Mauser 1972, 1979; Stefflre 1971, 1972, 1979a).

Empirical support for this hypothesis has been somewhat mixed. Stefflre (1972) reports strong correlations between perceptions and preferences across a variety of domains. While Mauser (1972, 1979) and Doehlert (1968) find similar results, a few other researchers have found only weak or insignificant correlations (Klahr 1969). The principal reason for these contrasting results appears to be that the researchers tested somewhat different hypotheses. Stefflre and Mauser compared *aggregate* patterns of perceived similarity with patterns of competition; while Doehlert and Klahr attempted to predict *individual* preference levels for items from their perceived similarity for each individual. These tests differ in two important ways: whether patterns or levels of preference are predicted from item similarity, and whether the hypothesis is tested at the aggregate or individual level.

Stefflre (1972) has argued that an item's position in a perceived similarity structure determines the pattern of preferences it elicits but not its level of preference. Pattern of preference, as used here, refers to the distribution of preferences for items in a population (that is, who likes what), while level of preference refers to how much some items are preferred over other items (individually or in the aggregate). Essentially, this argument rests on the degree of uniqueness that is assumed to exist in the determinants of preferences for an item, or using the spatial metaphor, that the "local dimensionality" may differ from "global dimensionality." The spatial model becomes much more flexible, if the dimensions that are seen to exist in various "corners" of the space—local dimensionality—may differ from those which span the entire structure—global dimensionality. This approach does not accept the spatial model literally, but rather takes it as a limited but useful heuristic in generating testable hypotheses.

Alternatively, other researchers (Coombs 1964; Carroll and Chang 1970; Downs 1957; Klahr 1969; Riker and Ordeshook 1973) place somewhat greater faith in the spatial model. The Coombsian approach assumes that a simple algorithm can be found for predicting individual "ideal points" from the spatial coordinates of items. The search for such an algorithm has occupied marketers in their attempts to apply multidimensional scaling models (e.g., TORSCA, M-D-SCAL, MDPREF). If found, an algorithm of this type might also be used as a formula for constructing new items that are highly preferred. Unfortunately, the problem does not appear to be so simple. Green (1975) continues to think such a "psychophysical transform" is worth searching for, but others have joined Stefflre in doubting that a simple mechanical algorithm exists (Myers 1979; Rothberg 1980). Recent attempts to search for successful new items have focused on conjoint measurement (e.g., Green and Srinavasan 1978; Luce and Tukey 1964) and multi-attribute models (e.g., Ryan and Bonfield 1975; Wilkie and Pessemier 1973).

The second reason that contrasting results were found is that the hypothesis was tested at different levels of analysis. Stefflre compared aggregate perceptions and preferences since he was primarily concerned with the practical implications of analyzing market phenomena. Other researchers (e.g., Green), oriented more toward technology and following the Coombsian approach, have focused on intra-individual perceptions and preferences. It is important to point out that quite a different role is implied in the two approaches for perceptual structure. Stefflre sees perception as a source of hypotheses about where new objects will position in the structure, which can then be tested in later steps, while Green and his coworkers seek mechanical algorithms. This fundamental difference in approach has led researchers in different directions in testing the same basic hypothesis. In the Coombsian model, all differences among the stimuli in the space are assumed to be due to interstimuli differences. Thus, any intrusion of intersubject differences interferes with the theoretical relationship, so that researchers have naturally gravitated toward examining individual subjects. Since Stefflre does not accept the Coombsian framework, nor is he searching for a simple mechanical algorithm linking perceptions and preferences, his approach is less concerned with the existence of individual differences. Stefflre's approach does not require as close an articulation between perception and preferences as the Coombsian framework, so this approach can tolerate the confounding of the two sources of variance.[1]

This chapter empirically examines the relationship between perceptions and preferences in the electoral contests included in this book. Support will be sought for Stefflre's hypothesis that there is a strong and reliable relationship between patterns of aggregate perception and preferences. No effort will be made to examine the validity of the Coombsian position.

Specifically, four distinct hypotheses will be tested:

1. Aggregate measures of perceived item-item similarity allow predictions of patterns of competition among those items.
2. Aggregate measures of patterns of item-item correlation allow predictions of switching patterns (patterns of draw) in single choice situations such as elections.
3. For any new item that is introduced into a specific single-choice situation, aggregate measures of item-item similarity allow prediction of patterns of differential competition and draw.
4. Knowledge of the key features of items allows predictions of the positioning of those items vis-a-vis the other items in the domain.

The relationship that is hypothesized to exist in hypotheses (1) through (3) should hold whether the new item is identified using the name of a well-known person or the description of a hypothetical candidate or political party.[2]

A COMMON UNDERLYING STRUCTURE

This section examines the first two hypotheses dealing with the interrelationships between aggregate measures of similarity, competition, and switching patterns. To test these hypotheses independent measures are required for each of these three concepts.[3] The similarity of pairs of items can be measured by aggregating respondents' judgments of perceived similarity. The extent to which two items compete with each other is determined by intercorrelating respondents' preferences for the items; switching (patterns of draw) is measured here by asking respondents for their second choice if the first choice is not available. To ensure independence, each of these measures is based on a separate sample from the same target population.

Hypothesis 1: Aggregate measures of perceived item-item Similarity allow predictions of patterns of competition. This hypothesis may be tested by intercorrelating the matrix of item-item judged similarities for a given domain with the matrix of preference correlations (indices of patterns of competition) for the same items. Stefflre (1972) reports finding correlations that range from .45 to .85, with a median of .70 for "approximately 20 different sectors of the world of objects, ranging from coffee to Peace Corps volunteers."

Two of the four political studies described in this book sampled judged similarity and competition patterns independently. Table 10.1 shows the correlations between the judged similarity matrix and the pattern of competition matrix for these two studies. Spearman *rho* correlations are calculated, in both cases, between two 25 × 25 matrices.

As can be readily seen, there is a modest but reliable correlation between similarity and competition in both domains. The correlations fall within the range found by Stefflre (1972), but are somewhat below the median. Correlations of this size indicate that there is a sizable, but not intimate, relationship between the similarity of political leaders and the extent to which they compete with each other. It would appear that the relationship is not as close as would be assumed by those following the Coombsian tradition, but it would be close enough to support the use of ad hoc hypotheses, following Stefflre, about which politicians would compete more with each other.

TABLE 10.1. Correlations between Judged Similarity of Political Leaders and Their Patterns of Competition

California (1968)	.53[a]
Los Angeles (1970)	.59

Note: Sample sizes range between 65 and 193 respondents, based on four independent, nonoverlapping samples. Twenty-five politicians were included in each of the California studies.

[a]Entries are Spearman *rho* correlations between two symmetric 25 × 25 matrices: one for judged similarity and the other for patterns of competition.

Source: Mauser (1979).

The question naturally emerges about how the relationship between similarity and competition holds for particular politicians. Well-known politicians would be expected to have a stronger than average relationship between their images and their patterns of competition. Table 10.2 shows the range of correlations observed in 1970 for each of the 25 politicians included in the study. As can be immediately seen, there is considerable variation in the extent to which the perceived similarity of a candidate correlates with his (or her) pattern of competition. It appears that lesser-known politicians, as hypothesized, enjoy lower correlations and, therefore, have greater flexibility in changing their images during a political campaign.

Hypothesis 2: Aggregate measures of patterns of item-item competition allow predictions of switching patterns (that is, patterns of draw) between the politicians in single choice situations such as elections. This hypothesis may be tested by comparing independent measures of items' patterns of competition with their switching patterns in mock elections. Patterns of competition are measured here in the same manner as before, that is, by intercorrelating respondents' preferences for the leaders (or parties). This yields an index of the extent to which leaders (or parties) appeal to the same voters. Switching patterns are determined by asking respondents to indicate their second choice for leader (or party) after they have given their first choice.

As French elections are typically contested by several political parties, this hypothesis is easily examined in the context of French politics. Table 10.3 shows the correlations between patterns of competition for each of the French political parties and the percentage of each party's supporters who chose each of the other parties as their second choice. Such percentages indicate the extent to which the supporters of each party would consider switching to each of the other parties if the party they prefer most were not available in the second round of voting.[4]

There is a significant correlation between the patterns of competition and the switching patterns for almost every party. Except for the *Parti Radical*, a small centrist party left over from the Fourth Republic, the correlations are respectable, ranging from .400 to .905. The median for all eight parties is .658, which provides modest support for the hypothesis. For the full set of parties, there is a gamma correlation of .80 between patterns of competition and switching patterns among parties.[5]

In summary, support was found for the first two hypotheses in both of the political contests where tested. While data-collection limitations restricted the extent to which the hypotheses could be systematically examined in each of the election contests, support does appear to be firm for the hypotheses in the studies where tested. For each of the domains, measures of judged similarity were strongly related to patterns of competition, and measures of patterns of competition in turn predicted switching patterns. These relationships held for the full set of politicians and parties as

TABLE 10.2. Correlations between Judged Similarity and Patterns of Competition for Individual Politicians

Politician	Preference Correlation[a]
R. Reagan	.889
M. Rafferty	.836
S. Agnew	.833
S. Yorty	.773
L. B. Johnson	.754
G. Murphy	.737
G. Brown	.704
H. Humphrey	.696
P. Brown	.654
S. Hayakawa	.630
J. Unruh	.622
J. Tunney	.613
R. Kennedy	.600
R. Nader	.563
A. Cranston	.559
E. Muskie	.514
N. Rockefeller	.505
T. Bradley	.501
B. Cosby	.479
N. Simon	.428
A. Davis	.400
E. Warren	.354
R. Carson	.317
B. Graham	.262
R. Finch	.206
Median	.560

Note: Based on the 1970 study of Los Angeles citizens' political perceptions and preferences that is described in Chapter 6. Two samples were involved: the judged similarity sample included 75 respondents, while the pattern of preference sample included held 239.

[a] Correlations are Spearman *rho* correlation coefficients calculated for each politician across the other 24 politicians in the study. All correlations are statistically significant from zero at the .05 level of confidence.

Source: Mauser (1979).

well as for individual leaders and for individual political parties. The first two hypotheses concerned perceptions of, and preferences for, items which were fairly well known to respondents. The next section examines how these relationships hold up when we turn to *descriptions* of new items.

PREDICTING PATTERNS OF DRAW

This section takes up the hypothesis that "new items" (politicians or parties) introduced into specific electoral contests will compete more with,

TABLE 10.3. Correlations between Patterns of Competition and Switching Patterns

Political Party	Preference Correlation[a]
Centre du Progrès et Démocratie Moderne	.905
Parti Communiste Français	.900
Républicains Indépendants	.789
Centre Démocrate et Progrès	.700
Parti Socialiste	.619
Parti Socialiste Unifié	.428
Union pour la Défense de la République	.400
Parti Radical	.143
Median	.658

Note: Based on 165 respondents from the Rhône-Alpes region of France interviewed in 1973 prior to the legislative elections that year. The two measures are *not* based on independent samples. See Chapter 7 for further details about sampling and interviewing methods.

[a] Entries are gamma correlations between the patterns of preference for each party and the percentage of that party's supporters which chooses each of the remaining seven parties as their second choice (that is, switching patterns).

Source: Mauser (1979).

and draw more votes from, those items that the new item is seen to resemble more. This hypothesis lies at the heart of the spatial approach to analyzing elections, and, if supported, offers campaign strategists a powerful tool for predicting how the electorate will respond to new candidates, new parties, or new strategies on the part of current candidates, and (b) deciding among alternative positions or postures that they are considering.

Specifically the hypothesis to be tested may be stated as:

Hypothesis 3: For any new item (e.g., candidate or party) introduced into a specific single-choice situation (e.g., election), aggregate measures of item-item similarity allow prediction of patterns of competition and draw from each of the current items (e.g., candidates) in the contest. To test this hypothesis, independent measures are required for similarity, competition, and draw. Independence is achieved here, as before, by basing each measure on different types of questions and on separate samples of respondents. Mock elections are simulated from preference rankings in order to examine the performance of a variety of candidates in a range of hypothetical scenarios. While there is no way to be sure that voters would actually react to these mock elections as the simulations imply, the success of the method of simulation in estimating share of vote for actual candidates in real elections permits us to have some confidence in the verisimilitude of these mock elections. For further details the reader may refer to Chapter 9, in which these simulation techniques are discussed more thoroughly.

In each electoral contest, two major candidates will be taken as a "kernel contest" and all other candidates that had been included in the interview will be considered, somewhat arbitrarily, as "new candidates" to be introduced one at a time to the kernel contest. Such a procedure permits predictions to be made about the extent to which new candidates draw votes from each of their kernel candidates on the basis of the new candidates' relative similarity with each of the kernel candidates.

An example may help clarify this procedure. Consider the 1980 presidential contest, where there were three major candidates: Ronald Reagan, Jimmy Carter, and John Anderson. Let Reagan and Carter be considered as comprising the kernel contest and Anderson be the new candidate. Now, the hypothesis asserts that we can predict both whether Anderson appeals more to Carter's or Reagan's supporters, and whether Anderson draws more votes from Carter or Reagan in the election, by determining whether Anderson is seen by the electorate as a whole as resembling Carter or Reagan more.

Moreover, the hypothesis asserts that new candidates draw votes from kernel candidates to the extent of their similarity, so that across the variety of possible new candidates, the extent to which each draw votes from the kernel candidates is directly proportional to their perceived similarity. Most importantly, this relationship is asserted to hold for *descriptions* of new objects as well as for *names* of well-known political or social leaders.

Each of the three measures will now be briefly described. First the criterion measure: *patterns of draw*. An estimate of which kernel candidate a new candidate will draw more votes from may be determined by comparing the draw ratios of the new candidate for each of the two kernal candidates. The draw ratio refers to the proportion of a candidate's supporters who would shift to the second candidate. The difference between these two draw ratios for the new candidate may be termed the differential draw.

Predictions about whom the new candidate will compete more with are determined by calculating the difference between the similarity indices of the new candidate with each of the two candidates in kernel contest. This difference is defined as the differential similarity of a new candidate. In a parallel fashion, the differential competitiveness can be estimated for each of the possible new candidates by taking the differences of the two patterns of correlation with each of the two kernel candidates.

The hypothesis can now be restated in a stronger form: new candidates will draw votes from current candidates to the extent that they are seen as similar to those candidates, or they have similar patterns of competition; also new candidates' patterns of similarity with the current candidates should predict their patterns of competition.

Table 10.4 shows the intercorrelations for the relevant measures. Firm and consistent support is found for this hypothesis. New candidates draw more votes from, and compete more with, the candidates in the kernel contest in direct proportion to their differential similarity. The correlations range from .657 to 1.000 for these three electoral contests with a median correlation

TABLE 10.4. Predicting Patterns of Competition and Draw Patterns for New Candidates in Selected Electoral Contests in France and California (Names Only)

	Similarity[a]/Competition[b]	Similarity/Draws[c]	Competition/Draws
California 1968[d]	.830[g]	.680	.825
California 1968[d]	1.000[h]	.800	.657
California 1970[e]	.874	.728	.797[i]
France 1974[f]	—[j]	—[j]	.903[i]

[a] Estimates of candidate similarities are based on respondents' judgments of the relative similarities of 25 political leaders. (Sample sizes vary from 65 in 1968 to 75 in 1970.)

[b] Estimates of competition patterns were determined by intercorrelating respondents' preference rankings for the 25 political leaders. (Sample sizes vary from 165 in 1974, through 193 in 1968, to 239 in 1970.)

[c] Draws were estimated by simulating (from respondents' preference rankings) the proportion of each kernel candidate's supporters who would shift to the new candidate if he entered the contest. (Sample size ranged from 193 to 1,161 and the number of new candidates varied from 6 to 23.)

[d] Humphrey and Nixon were considered as the two kernel candidates in the U.S. presidential contest that year. (Refer to Chapter 5 for details about the study.)

[e] Unruh and Reagan served as the two kernel candidates in the 1970 California gubernatorial contest. (See Chapter 6 for details.)

[f] Giscard d'Estaing and Mitterrand served as the kernel candidates in this study of the 1974 French presidential elections. (See Chapter 8 for details.) In addition to the 24 names, 18 descriptions were included in this study.

[g] All entries in this table are Spearman *rho* correlation coefficients calculated between independent samples (except where indicated). High positive correlations indicate that new candidates tend to draw votes from (substitute for) the kernel candidate that they are judged to be more similar to (or that they substitute more for). All correlations involve 23 pairs of candidates except where indicated.

[h] In 1968, two samples of respondents were drawn independently to be interviewed about their political preferences. The Small Scale Preference sample (N = 193) and the Large Scale Preference Sample (N = 1,161). This row of the table shows the correlations between various indices and the Large Scale Preference Sample, involving only 6 new candidates rather than the 23 included in the Small Scale Preference Sample.

[i] As only one preference sample was drawn in this study, this correlation is not based on independent samples.

[j] No independent sample was drawn in this study to determine judged similarity of candidates.

of .813. For well-known political candidates at least, aggregate measures of perceived similarity would appear able to predict patterns of competition for new entrants into political contests.

Will the hypothesis hold for description of new political candidates? In each of these three studies, a number of descriptions of plausible but hypothetical candidates were included for respondents to rank according to their preferences. These descriptions consisted of seven to ten words identifying issue stands, leadership postures, or campaign slogans that would be plausible for some candidates in the election to espouse. If the hypothesis holds for names of candidates, it should also hold for descriptions of hypothetical candidates. Table 10.5 shows the correlations between the differential patterns of competition of the candidate description with their differential draws in each of these three studies.

As can be easily seen, there is a strong correlation between competition pattern and the pattern of draws for candidate descriptions. The strength of this relationship compares favorably with that for the candidates themselves.

KEY FEATURES AND POSITIONING

For strategists to turn the close relationship between similarity and competition into a practical tool, it is necessary to be able to discover what attributes (or features) of the items are important in determining how people categorize them and how people react to them. If we can determine these key features, then we can predict where new items will position, and identify which attributes are necessary for an item to position in any specific place in the similarity structure.

This section examines the fourth hypothesis that knowledge of the key features of items allows predictions of their positioning of those items vis-a-vis the other items in the domain. It was possible in three of the four studies

TABLE 10.5. Predicting Patterns of Draw for Descriptions of New Candidates in U.S. and French Electoral Contests

	Competition/Draws[a]
California (1968)	.910[b]
California (1970)	.781
France (1974)	.779

[a]The competition pattern of a candidate for each of the kernel candidates is determined by correlating their preference rankings. Draws are estimated by simulating the proportion of each kernel candidate's supporters that would shift to a new candidate if he were to enter the contest.

[b]All entries are Spearman *rho* correlations and are based on the Small Scale Preference Sample (N ≃ 200) for approximately 20 candidate descriptions. None of these correlations is based on independent samples.

to test the predictions about where items would position on the basis of their key features.[6] In each of these studies, descriptions of plausible but hypothetical candidates were developed after preliminary analysis identified the features that determined the positioning of items in the structure. Two of these preliminary analyses were based on voters' judged similarities, while the third consisted of informal discussions with knowledgeable informants— French political scientists.

To test these hypotheses, candidate descriptions were submitted to an independent sample of respondents to be ranked in terms of their political preferences. The preference rankings were then intercorrelated to obtain an index of the patterns of competition. This index may be interpreted as indicating the extent to which politicians, descriptions, and/or political parties are preferred by the same voters. Items that cluster together are preferred by the same voters. Table 10.6 shows the types of items included in each of these three studies.

California 1968

Five clusters of politicians were identified in the judged-similarity structure. Descriptions of hypothetical candidates were concocted using features thought to be determinant and predictions made about which cluster the descriptions would position in. Table 10.7 compares predicted with observed positioning.

As may be seen, 18 out of the 25 descriptions position in that cluster where predicted. All but one of the "errors" position in adjacent clusters. One description positioned on the extreme right while it had been predicted to position on the far left: "a man who is willing to stand up for his beliefs regardless of the consequences." This error probably reflects my own personal biases.

California 1970

In this study, descriptions were devised primarily to explore the limits of each candidate's appeal. No effort was made to identify clusters any more

TABLE 10.6. Types and Numbers of Items Included in Each Study

Study	Type	Numbers
California (1968)	Candidate names	25
	Descriptions	25
California (1970)	Candidate names	25
	Descriptions	25
France (1974)	Political parties	8
	Candidate names	24
	Descriptions	18

TABLE 10.7. Predicted and Observed Positioning of Candidate Descriptions (California 1968)

Predicted Cluster[b]	Observed Cluster[a]				
	Nixon/Wallace	Ike	LBJ	JFK	Carmichael/Spock
Nixon/Wallace	8	1			
Eisenhower	1	2			
LBJ			1	2	
JFK				3	2
Carmichael/Spock	1				4

[a] Observed positions were identified in the three-dimensional configuration of the Pattern of Competition Data.
[b] Descriptions were designed to position in one of the five clusters that voters perceived as existing—using Judged Similarity Data.

precisely than a simple dichotomy based on which of the two candidate's supporters did the description appeal to (see Table 10.8). As before, 18 out of the 25 descriptions were correctly predicted, while 7 were found to be associated with neither candidate. These results should not be too surprising as one of the goals of the study was to find out new issues that had not yet been preempted by either candidate. No description varied widely from initial predictions.

France 1974

In this study, it was hypothesized that the politicians would position closest to (i.e., correlated most highly with) their own political party than to any other and that the descriptions would position closest to that party judged by French political scientists to be the most similar to that type of candidate. While the partisan affiliation of each politician was relatively easy to identify, it was somewhat more difficult to determine the most appropriate political party for each description. In order to accomplish this, three political scientists at the University of Grenoble (all French citizens) were asked to classify each description. Some of the descriptions were judged as not uniquely appropriate for any single party but were seen as consistent with the rhetoric of a group of parties, while other descriptions elicited a variety of opinions as to which party they most resembled. Despite these problems, a single political party was selected as being most appropriate for each description in order to make the predictions.

Table 10.9 compares predicted with observed positions for French politicians and descriptions. As can be seen from this table, all but 6 of the 42 politicians and descriptions positioned where predicted. All six items that did

TABLE 10.8. Predicted and Observed Positioning of Descriptions (California 1970)

	Observed Cluster[b]		
Predicted[a]	Unruh	Reagan	Neither
Unruh	10		5
Reagan		8	2

[a] Descriptions were designed to appeal to the supporters of one or the other of the two main candidates based on voters' perceptions of them.
[b] Observed positions of descriptions in spatial model based on preference correlations (that is, pattern of competition data).

not position correctly were descriptions. Nevertheless, all but one of these descriptions positioned close to parties associated with the predicted party.

One description was way off: "a President who would fight to protect consumers." Instead of positioning close to the *réformateurs*, who were the only French party who explicitly championed the rights of consumers as such, the description was closely associated with the CNIP, a right-wing extremist group. It is not entirely clear why this was the case. Perhaps the French electorate equates the interests of consumers with those of small shopkeepers. If so, then this positioning is consistent with the CNIP's strong support for shopkeepers. Alternatively, the electorate may have been responding more to the tone of the item than to its literal content. The strident militant tone of the item may have caused voters to view it as extremist, so that it may have been relegated to the extreme right even without the electorate seeing it as closely associated with any particular political group.

CONCLUSIONS

Solid support was found in the studies examined here for the assertion that there is a strong and reliable relationship between aggregate patterns of perceived similarity and patterns of competition. Four distinct hypotheses were tested and support found for each:

1. Aggregate measures of perceived item-item similarity allow predictions of patterns of competition among those items.
2. Aggregate measures of patterns of item-item correlation (competition) allow predictions of switching patterns (patterns of draw) in single choice situations such as elections.
3. For any new item that may be introduced into a specific single-choice situation, aggregate measures of item-item similarity allow prediction of patterns of differential competition and draw.

TABLE 10.9. Predicting Positioning of French Politicians and Descriptions from Party Affiliation (France 1974)

Predicted	Observed								
	Leftist	PSU	PCF	PS	Réf	CDP	UDR	RI	CNIP
Leftist	1								
PSU	1	1	1	1					
PCF			4						
PS				7					
Réf					8				1
CDP						1			
UDR					2		8		
RI								1	
CNIP									5

Note: Predictions are based on the simple rule that politicians and descriptions would position closest to their party (or group) than to any other. Observed positions are those found in TORSCA two-dimensional solutions of all 50 stimuli (stress = .210) for the pattern of competition data for all respondents in the 1974 French sample (N = 240).

Source: Mauser (1979).

4. Knowledge of the key features of items allows predictions of the positioning of those items vis-a-vis the other items in the domain.

These relationships were hypothesized to hold for both names of politicians and verbal descriptions of hypothetical candidates.

The first hypothesis was tested by intercorrelating matrices of judged similarity of political leaders with their aggregate patterns of competition. A modest but reliable correlation was found that indicated a sizable, but not intimate relationship existed. Such a finding supports Stefflre's approach of using ad hoc hypotheses. Importantly, the strength of this relationship was found to vary tremendously for individual political figures depending, evidently, on their level of public awareness.

The second hypotheses also was supported. Switching patterns across the full range of French political parties are significantly related to the patterns of competition among them. Interestingly, the strength of this relationship varies across the political spectrum: it is considerably weaker for centrist political parties than for more extremist parties.

The third hypothesis focused on predicting patterns of draw in selected political contests. Strong consistent support was found for each of variations of this hypothesis tested: new candidates drew votes from current candidates to the extent that they were judged similar to them, or to the extent that they had matching patterns of competition. The hypothesis was found to hold for names and verbal descriptions in both the United States and in France.

In accordance with the fourth hypothesis, the bulk of the descriptions positioned precisely as they were predicted, although roughly 25 percent of the descriptions were not so well behaved. Nevertheless, in general, the errors in positioning were not extensive, as descriptions tended to position in the general neighborhood of where they were designed to go. A few descriptions were surprisingly way off. However, it usually seemed obvious, after the fact, why the predictions had erred. Efforts here were limited to quite broad-gauge predictions from features having high *a priori* importance. An error rate of 25 percent indicates that finer-grained predictions would be still more difficult to make. For practical purposes, strategists would be well-advised to recognize the importance of trial and error in identifying key features. Rather than searching for a simple mechanical algorithm, an approach is needed that emphasizes the generating and testing of alternative hypotheses about what features determine perceptions and preferences.

NOTES

1. The extent to which perceptions are homogeneous has been the subject of a longstanding debate in marketing. Stefflre has long argued for the existence of homogeneity of perceptions, even with heterogeneity of preferences, while others have been more impressed by the heterogeneity of perception in the same population. This issue is taken up in the next chapter.

2. This chapter is partially based on work published earlier (Mauser 1972, 1979). Because of space limitations in these earlier papers, it was not possible to fully explore these hypotheses. This chapter pulls together this earlier material and treats it comprehensibly for the first time.

3. These measures are described in detail in Chapter 4 and will only be touched on very briefly here.

4. As the reader may recall, French elections involve two rounds of voting. In the first round, which is typically contested by several parties, an absolute majority (more than 50 percent) of the vote cast is needed to win the election. If no party wins a clear majority a second round is held a short time afterward in which only a plurality, the largest obtained percentage, is required to win. Not all parties contest both rounds, since some are eliminated for not drawing sufficient support, while others withdraw voluntarily to throw their support to other parties after interparty negotiations. For further details, see Chapter 7.

5. The correlation for the full set of parties involves 56 pairs—the full 8×8 matrix minus the main diagonal, while the correlations for individual parties includes only seven pairs—one row in the 8×8 party matrix.

6. The exception was the 1973 study of the French legislative elections held that year, for which I did not have direct access to the data.

11
STABILITY OF PERCEPTIONS AND PREFERENCES

> The fact of the matter is that the real world is to a large extent unconsciously built up on the language habits of the group. . . . We see and hear and otherwise experience very largely as we do because the language habits of our community predispose certain choices of interpretation.
>
> Edward Sapir, *Language, Culture and Personality*

> Man lives with his objects chiefly—in fact, since his feeling and acting depends on his perceptions, one may say exclusively—as language presents them to him. By the same process whereby he spins language out of his own being, he ensnares himself in it; and each language draws a magic circle round the people to which it belongs, a circle from which there is no escape by stepping out of it into another.
>
> W. von Humboldt, *Einleitung zum Kawi-Werk*

The electoral analyses presented in this book rely upon aggregate models of political perceptions and preferences, and it has been assumed that such models can adequately represent a target population. But how can we know if the target population is homogeneous enough to be represented by a single model? Perhaps the population contains subgroups, so distinct that each must be modeled separately? Moreover, even if the target population is relatively homogeneous, political perceptions or preferences may change so rapidly and frequently that any model would be out-of-date by the time it was built. If aggregate models are to serve any practical purpose, they must meet at least minimum standards of stability across both time and people.

This chapter examines the stability of the aggregate models of political perceptions and preferences that were presented in this book. Both French and

U.S. data will be analyzed. The question of the homogeneity of the target population is addressed first, followed by the question of temporal stability.

HOMOGENEITY

Models of aggregate phenomena, as any statistics, are most useful if the target population is homogeneous. A mean, for example, does not adequately describe a data set if the data are too heterogeneous or are multimodal (that is, if there is more than one "hump" in the plot of the distribution). Homogeneity is even more important if there are qualitative differences in a population. For example, what is the "average" sex, given that some people are male and some are female? If the population is very heterogeneous, it may not be sensible to assume that one model will describe the entire group.

On the other hand, there is always some diversity among elements in any naturally occurring data set—even one that is unimodal and compact. The use of summary statistics, whether simple ones such as averages, or more complex kinds such as multidimensional scaling models, necessarily involves a simplification and loss of some potentially important information. Such a loss is inherent in any attempt to generalize. It would be unnecessarily complex to develop separate models for every individual, or even groups of individuals, if they were not required. How can researchers decide when there is "enough" homogeneity in a data set to support an aggregate model?

Some help may be found by considering the notion of culture as developed in anthropology. Culture is seen as including "symbolically learned patterns of behavior" that a specific group of people share in common (Fried 1968, p. 1). Anthropologists, however, point out that people who share the same culture, the same country, the same language, or the same life experiences, also tend to share the same basic assumptions (perceptions) about the world that they live in (Cassirer 1946; Hall 1959; Spradley and McCurdy 1975). Within any given culture, it may be difficult to recognize such basic similarities because they are taken for granted. They are too ubiquitous. Individual and subgroup differences may be much more salient to a local observer, but may, ultimately, be less important than they first appear due to the underlying communalities that cut across the subgroup within that culture. For example, blacks and whites in the United States share more basic political and social beliefs than is generally realized. Their similarities are immediately apparent when Americans, black or white, are compared with European or African nationals.

There is substantial empirical support for the assertion that a high degree of homogeneity exists within a population about basic beliefs and perceptions, even though preferences may differ considerably. Osgood and his associates found that the same small number of semantic factors recur as the most important in a wide variety of judgmental situations across extremely diverse groups of people (Osgood and Suci 1955; Osgood et al. 1957; Snider and Osgood 1969). Abelson (1955) and Messick (1956, 1961) found a surprisingly high degree of agreement in the perceptions (similarity judgments) and attitude structures (Thurstone scales) of respondents from selected groups.

Some recent work in marketing assumes that all individuals in a group share the same basic perceptual structure and then searches for individual differences in the *weightings* of the axes in the common group space (Green and Rao 1972; Green and Wind 1973). This approach relies upon the INDSCAL model developed by Carroll and Chang (1970).

Stefflre asserts that there is a considerable amount of homogeneity of perceptions in a population, or in his words, "about what is similar to what," even though considerable diversity exists about "what is good" (1968, p. 256). A similar point has been made about political beliefs by Converse (1964) who argues that notions of "what goes with what" are widely shared in mass publics, while explanations about *why* such a relationship existed would be "incoherent or irrelevant" for the majority of people. Despite the sweeping nature of these claims there have been surprisingly few attempts to empirically evaluate these assertions, either in political science or in marketing.

The studies of California and French politics discussed earlier provide an opportunity to examine the homogeneity of political perceptions and preferences. Table 11.1 summarizes the samples drawn in these studies that were used in this effort. To test homogeneity, separate models were constructed for independent subsamples, drawn from these samples, and then intercorrelated. In each case, the models being compared are the aggregate perception (or preference) measures themselves, not the spatial models that rely on these measures. This was done in order to keep the structures to be compared close to the collected data and as unprocessed as possible.

First, consider the homogeneity to be found in the political perceptions of the electorate. Table 11.2 shows the intercorrelations between aggregate judged similarity structures constructed for both arbitrary and partisan subsamples.[1] As can be seen, there are substantial correlations for both arbitrary and partisan samples—ranging from .5 to .7—in both years. The lowest correlations involve independents, which may be due to the small number of respondents in this sample. While the correlation between arbitrarily defined subsamples is larger than that between partisan subgroups, this difference is not very large. This implies that Americans, regardless of partisan loyalties, tend to share the same perceptions of their political leaders, for the most part, and provides strong support for a common aggregate model.

In contrast with the judged similarity structures, there is somewhat less homogeneity in the aggregate patterns of competition. While the correlations between arbitrary subsamples remain substantial—ranging from .5 to .8—

TABLE 11.1. Samples Included in the California and French Studies

	Samples	Target Population	Sample Size	Measure	Stimuli	Date Interviewed
Pilot study (1967)	Combination	Orange County	59	Judged similarity Competition patterns Draws	25 politicians	July 1967
U.S. presidential election (1968)	Judged Similarity	California	65	Judged similarity	25 politicians	June/Sept. 1968
	Small Scale Preference	California	193	Competition patterns Draws	25 politicians 25 descriptions	October 1968
	Large Scale Preference	California	1,161	Competition patterns Draws	5 politicians 3 descriptions	November 1-4, 1968
California gubernatorial election (1970)	Judged Similarity	Los Angeles County	75	Judged similarity	25 politicians	August 1970
	Small Scale Preference	Los Angeles County	165	Competition patterns Draws	25 politicians 25 descriptions	Sept. 1970
French legislative elections (1974)	Small Scale Preference	Fourth Circonscription of Isère (France)	240	Competition patterns Draws	8 parties 24 politicians 18 descriptions	January 1974

Source: Mauser (1979).

TABLE 11.2. Stability of Aggregate Similarity Judgments (California)

Stimuli	Arbitrary[a]	Partisan[b]		
	Odd/Even	D/R	D/I	R/I
1968 Politicians	.707[c]	.648	.640	.552
1970 Politicians	[d]	.630	[d]	[d]

[a] Aggregate matrices were determined by calculating indices of Judged Similarity for both "odd" and "even" groupings of respondents. "Odd" and "even" groupings found by arbitrarily numbering all respondents.

[b] Aggregate matrices were determined by calculating indices of Judged Similarity for Democratic, Republican, and Independent respondents.

[c] All entries are Spearman correlations between aggregate 25 × 25 matrices.

[d] Not calculated.

Source: Mauser (1979).

the correlations between partisan groups are much smaller (see Table 11.3). Interestingly, there is a high level of agreement across groups for the descriptions of hypothetical candidates, while there is much less agreement for the names of politicians. The correlation of .419 found in Table 11.3 indicates that Democrats and Republicans share, to some extent, notions about which leaders compete with each other, but that there is an area of considerable disagreement that cannot be overlooked. In contrast with the judged similarity structures, where the Democrat/Republican correlation was .64, which could explain 40 percent of the common variance, there is very little overlap in patterns of competition, as the correlation between aggregate Democratic and Republican preference structures can account for only 18 percent of the common variance.

A few other comments remain to be made about Table 11.3. First, the correlations involving independent respondents are much lower than those between Democrats and Republicans—usually ranging from .022 to .678. This may be due to the small numbers of independent respondents and the consequently highly variable structures. Second, the strikingly low correlations for the combined names and descriptions data set contrast with the higher correlations for the data sets involving either names or verbal descriptions of politicians. It is not clear why this is the case.

The French data provide additional support for the inferences about the stability of patterns of competition seen in the California data. As in the U.S. data, the correlations between arbitrary groups are much higher than the partisan correlations. The only exception is the correlation for descriptions, which is surprisingly low.[2] The differences among the three principal segments of the French electorate appear to be about the same magnitude as those between Democrats and Republicans in the United States.

TABLE 11.3. Stability of Aggregate Patterns of Competition (California)

Stimuli	Arbitrary[a]	Partisan[b]		
	Odd/Even	D/R	D/I	R/I
1968 Names of politicians	.894[c]	.419	.024	−.022
1968 Descriptions	.868	.716	.678	.657
1968 Names and descriptions	.494	.328	.298	.276
1970 Names of politicians	.749	[d]	[d]	[d]

[a] Aggregate matrices were computed by intercorrelating preference rankings of stimuli for both odd and even groupings of respondents. Odd and even groupings were found by arbitrarily numbering all respondents.

[b] Aggregate matrices were computed by intercorrelating preference rankings of stimuli for Democratic, Republican, and Independent respondents separately.

[c] All entries are Spearman *rho* correlations between aggregate n × n matrices. There were 25 names and 25 descriptions included, so that all but one of the matrices were 25 × 25. The sole exception, Names and Descriptions, was 50 × 50.

[d] Not calculated.

Source: Mauser (1972, 1979).

Intergroup correlations support the construction of aggregate models in California and in France, for both perceptions and preferences. This can be seen in Tables 11.2 to 11.4. All intergroup correlations between arbitrary groupings are significantly different from zero, and, with few exceptions, account for a large proportion of the variance. Moreover, the correlations between the major partisan groupings, Democratic and Republican in the United States and the left and the majority in France, are quite sizable.

To further explore the question of subgroups in the U.S. electorate, the respondents in one of the studies were scaled (rather than the stimuli) in a manner analogous to inverse factor analysis (Harman 1976). Preference data was selected for analysis, rather than perception data, because of its lower intergroup correlations.[3] The two-dimensional configuration is shown in Figure 11.1. Visual inspection of this figure shows that Democrats and Republicans may be partitioned into two separate clusters. However, voters in these two groups overlap to some extent, which accounts for the modest correlation between their competition structures. This analysis suggests that, under some conditions, Democrats and Republicans may need to be modeled separately.

Interestingly enough, Democrats and Republicans, when modeled separately, demonstrate quite similar configurations. The same clusters of candidates are observed, and the same dimensions span both models. This is particularly true for the descriptions of hypothetical candidates. However, these configurations are much less polarized. Despite the relatively modest intercorrelation, it does not appear necessary to develop separate models for Democrats and Republicans.

FIGURE 11.1. Two-Dimensional MD-SCAL Solution for Inverse Voter Preference Correlations (45 Stimuli; Stress = .132).

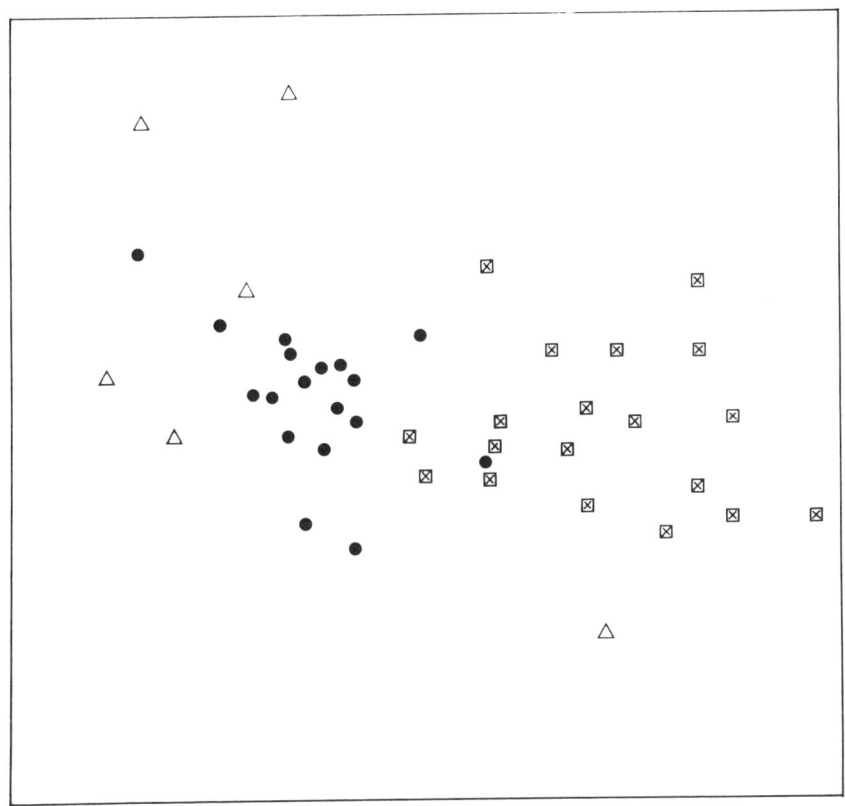

Note: Solid circles are Democratic respondents, crossed squares are Republican respondents, and open triangles are Independent respondents.
Source: Mauser (1972).

In summary, there appears to be somewhat more homogeneity in political perceptions than there is in patterns of competition. While partisanship appears to have little influence on the framework that voters use in judging the political similarity of politicians, partisanship is a strong determinant of the nature of the competition structure. There is approximately the same level of interpartisan agreement in the United States and in France, despite the considerable differences between the two political systems. These results are quite consistent with the use of aggregate models to represent both political perceptions and preferences.

TEMPORAL STABILITY

To be useful, models of political perceptions and preferences need to be stable across time. If there were no temporal stability, there would be little use for formulating aggregate models. Without a minimum level of temporal stability yesterday's model might not hold the following day. Temporal stability is also important for strategy. How permanent are voters' memories of past political claims and promises? How much freedom do candidates actually have to maneuver? The greater the structural stability, the lower the likelihood that candidates could reposition themselves in the structure. Lower degrees of stability implies that candidates could radically change their images from one election to another.

Despite the importance of temporal stability, both theoretically and practically, few investigators have concerned themselves with this question because of the difficulty of conducting longitudinal studies. Almost all survey studies are simply snapshots, that is, limited to only one point in time. Such studies are necessarily mute about the kinds of changes that might be observed if the survey were to be repeated across time.[4]

In the 1968 California study it was possible to look at the evolution of the electorate's political perception across the 15 months preceding the fall 1968 election. Independent waves of interviews were conducted at three separate times prior to these elections: in summer 1967, summer 1968, and fall 1968.[5] By comparing the results of these studies, it was possible to track the stability of perceptions during the period of campaigning. Unfortunately, a number of politicians rose to prominence during the campaign who had been unknown a year earlier. Since these names had not been included in the first interview in summer 1967, it was necessary to conduct two separate interviews in summer 1968: one, using the old list, and another using the new list. While this permitted comparisons across time as well as incorporating the new figures, the number of politicians included on both lists was reduced, limiting comparisons between lists, so that it was not possible to compare changes across the full span of time. Nevertheless, comparisons remain possible across two time periods and these are shown in Table 11.4.

Despite the small sample size, relatively strong correlations are found across both of the two time periods investigated.[6] The correlations are only slightly diminished when Democratic and Republican voters are examined separately. These correlations probably underestimate the degree of stability that exists in the aggregate judged similarity structure. Visual inspection of the scaling configurations shows that the same basic clusters reappear in each, although the positions of a few candidates vary widely. Interesting enough, much of the change across time appears to be taking place within clusters. Unfortunately, the size of these samples make it impossible to determine how much of this variation is due to sampling fluctuations and how much is due to actual changes in the electorate's perceptions of the political leaders. More work needs to be done on this question.

TABLE 11.4. Stability of Aggregate Patterns of Competition (France)

Stimuli	Arbitrary[a]	Partisan[b]		
	Odd/Even	L/M	L/C	M/C
Names of politicians	.888[c]	.526	.533	.527
Descriptions	.419	.459	.324	.262
Names and descriptions	.732	.472	.397	.396

[a] Respondents were divided into odd and even groupings by arbitrarily numbering all respondents. Aggregate matrices were then calculated for each grouping by intercorrelating respondents' preference rankings using Spearman *rho* correlations.

[b] Respondents were divided into three types of partisan groupings: left, center, and majority, according to their first choice for presidential candidate. Respondents selecting either PS, PC, or PSU politicians were classified as left, those respondents choosing UDR or CNIP candidates were classified as majority, and those choosing *réformateur*, RI, or CDP were classified as center. Aggregate matrices were then calculated for each grouping by intercorrelating respondents' preference rankings.

[c] Entries are Spearman *rho* correlations between aggregate correlation matrices. Matrices were 25 × 25 for names, 17 × 17 for descriptions, and 42 × 42 for combined names and descriptions.

The degree of change appears to be about the same across the 12 months preceding the presidential nominating conventions, as in the three months that followed. If change is independent of the length of time between samples, the change taking place may be random. If so, the correlation between the full 15 months would also be expected to be about the same as those across the two intervening time periods. Unfortunately, this cannot be verified since the lists used in the two comparisons differed to too great an extent. However, the stability of the cluster structure, found in all four configurations, suggests that random fluctuations, within clusters, account for most of the changes.

CONCLUSIONS

This chapter examined the stability, across both time and people, of the aggregate models relied upon in this book to map the political perceptions and preferences of the electorate. Questions of stability of this sort are very important to political campaigners. First, a minimum degree of stability must exist for campaigners to use the information provided to formulate campaign strategy. If the electorate is so diverse, or changes its perceptions or preferences drastically from moment to moment, aggregate models of any kind are useless. Second, a candidate's freedom of maneuverability is directly related to the stability of the electorate's political perceptions and preferences. The greater the stability, the less maneuverability available to a

TABLE 11.5. Temporal Stability of Aggregate Similarity Judgments

Time Period	All Respondents	Democrats Only	Republicans Only
Twelve months[b]	.693[a]	.531	.591
Three months[c]	.712	.557	.555

Note: It was not possible to compare the results across the full 15 months due to the use of different lists of politicians in the two pairs of samples.

[a] All entries are Spearman correlations between 25 × 25 matrices of Judged Similarities of politicians for the specified groupings of respondents.

[b] Two independent samples of California registered voters were drawn: the first (N = 59) in summer 1967, and the second (N = 30) in June 1968.

[c] Two independent samples of California registered voters were drawn immediately before and after the Democratic and Republican national conventions: the first (N = 36) in June 1968 and the second (N = 29) in September 1968.

Source: Mauser (1979) and Mauser and Stefflre (1974).

candidate in adapting to changing conditions, or to differing opinions across the electorate.

A modest, but reliable, degree of homogeneity was found for both political perception and for patterns of competition. Partisan groups were found to have sufficient homogeneity to justify the use of aggregate models. Despite their differences in opinion, partisan groups, in both France and the United States, were found to share the same basic framework for evaluating their political options. Intergroup agreement was particularly strong for political perception, but less so when patterns of competition were considered. This is not to deny that partisan differences do exist, but simply to insist upon the recognition of certain interpartisan similarities in political perception and preferences.

This chapter also examined the temporal stability of political perceptions and found a modest degree of stability across the pre-election period. Interestingly enough, the degree of change did not seem to be related to the passage of time. The same correlations were found between aggregate structures regardless of the number of months that separated them. Moreover, basic cluster structure remained the same across the 15-month period studied.

If the degree of stability observed in this election is close to what would be observed in other elections, certain inferences may be drawn about which kinds of strategies might be effective.[7] First, well-known political candidates do not appear to have much opportunity to fundamentally alter their image. Once politicians become well known, their images become relatively fixed for the bulk of the electorate. Second, there remains some latitude in which to maneuver, but politicians need to consider the inertia of the electorate's beliefs and the limits of the power of advertising to effect changes in their images.

The following strategies appear to be the most effective given the relatively high level of stability of the electorate's perceptions:

1. Stress the importance of those features that are most attractive to the target electorate.
2. Avoid, or state as euphemistically as possible, the features that are deemed to be undesirable.
3. Coordinate all information and advertising to reinforce the most important features of the candidate.
4. If possible, attempt to move the candidate along those dimensions that can place him in an advantageous position.

NOTES

1. Only California samples are included here because separate judged similarity samples were not drawn in France.

2. Despite careful checking and recalculation, this correlation remained stubbornly low. No errors could be found that accounted for this anomaly.

3. See Mauser (1972) for further details concerning this analysis.

4. A striking exception to this state of affairs is the work by Nie, Verba, and Petrocik (1976).

5. These samples were drawn using crude quota sampling methods. All respondents were registered California voters. In 1967, respondents were drawn exclusively from Orange County, in southern California, while in 1968 respondents were interviewed across the entire state. See Mauser (1969, 1970) for further details concerning sampling methods and interviewing procedures.

6. A similarly strong relationship was also found in the French data. A strong correlation was found between the 1973 and 1974 patterns of competition data sets despite the differing target populations.

7. Some support for the generality of these results may be found in Leduc's (1976) study of the images of British political parties in the general electorate. He found a correlation of 0.95 between the 1966 and 1970 labor party structure.

12

A CONCLUDING NOTE

That all my striving I unloose is the whole purpose of the pact.
Goethe *Faust*

There are three ways for a politician to ruin his career: chasing women, gambling, and trusting experts. The first is the most pleasant, the second the quickest, but trusting experts is the surest.
Georges Pompidou

The purpose of this final chapter is to review the arguments of the preceding pages, summarize the empirical findings, and assess the impact on electoral politics of the increasing use of sophisticated marketing research technology such as the strategic positioning procedure. I argue that use of the strategic positioning procedure will clarify the nature of the electoral politics rather than to reform or corrupt the process. This procedure has been shown to help political candidates identify strategic opportunities in electoral campaigns and to position themselves to take advantage of those opportunities. How it is to be used depends upon the motives of the political campaigner who employs it. However, the increasing complexity of modern political campaigns, and the attendant increase in sophistication of campaigning technology, requires that political campaigners learn how to manage large and complex campaign organizations. Political campaigning is becoming a big business.

REVIEW

This book presented a procedure for strategically positioning political candidates in electoral contests by aiding campaigners to identify and exploit the opportunities available to them. The approach relies upon empirically generated spatial models to display candidates' images. In addition to political candidates, the spatial model can simultaneously include political parties, candidates' stands on issues, or postures of a variety of sorts. The spatial models are derived from voters' political perceptions and preferences using multidimensional scaling techniques.

The strategic positioning procedure is designed to map the competitive terrain of political campaigns. Detailed information of this sort permits candidates

- to identify their own image as seen by the electorate.
- to identify the images of their competitors (real or potential) in the same spatial model.
- to simulate the impact of new candidates entering the contest.
- to simulate the effects of any candidate adopting a new position or posture on the patterns of competition in the contest.

The strategic positioning procedure is one example of what marketing has to offer political campaigners. Due to the strong parallels between electoral campaigning and the marketing of commercial products, this book has argued that marketing offers a variety of valuable concepts and techniques that can help political candidates gain and hold political office. As a science, marketing offers a pragmatic and realistic framework for analyzing the problems that face campaigners in attempting to mount electoral campaigns. Political campaigners and commercial marketers face common problems, for example, assessing collective needs and wants, strategically analyzing competitive situations, and effectively communicating to mass audiences.

Marketing offers a professional approach to analyzing and managing political campaigns. In the past 20 years, marketers have developed a body of knowledge and technical expertise directly related to the analysis and persuasion of large groups of people. Marketers routinely use sophisticated techniques for surveying the public and identifying opportunities for new products or problems with the current product line. Moreover, marketers have developed powerful tools for designing offerings to fit the needs they identify, as well as methods of communicating the advantages of the new products. Much of this expertise is readily applicable to political campaigning.

The strategic positioning procedure has been derived from a procedure originally used to identify opportunities for new products in commercial markets (Stefflre 1968, 1972, 1979). It has been used to position new products in a wide variety of markets (e.g., scotch whiskey, several brands of coffee, candy bars, snacks, breakfast cereals, and pharmaceutical drugs) in several countries (e.g., the United States, Brazil, France, Germany, and Great Britain). The Stefflre procedure is one of several designed in the past 20 years

Concluding Note • 271

to assist management to discover and to screen concepts of new products. These procedures were reviewed in Chapter 3.

Stefflre was one of the first researchers to develop a multidimensional analytical procedure, based on consumer input, expressly to generate and evaluate new product concepts. His approach is based on work that he had done earlier in psycholinguistics on the relationship between language and behavior (Stefflre 1965; Stefflre et al. 1971). Stefflre describes his approach as resting on three interlocking assumptions about human behavior.

1. An individual will behave similarly toward things that seem similar to him.
2. If a new item is introduced into an individual's culture, the individual will behave toward it in a manner similar to the way he behaves toward familiar items that he sees as similar to the new item.
3. The close relationship between psychological similarity and patterns of behavior holds across individuals and across cultures despite the wide variation between individuals and cultures as to which objects are seen as similar and in how the objects or situations are behaved toward (Stefflre 1972, pp. 213-14).

These are quite simple ideas, but they have powerful implications about human behavior. In developing new products, these assumptions imply that products compete with each other to the extent that consumers see them as being similar to each other, so that the patterns of competition for any new product can be predicted from its pattern of perceived similarity with the other products in the market. Practically speaking, this means that marketers can design products to compete with their competitors' products, rather than with their own, simply by analyzing the perceived similarity of products. Moreover, Stefflre argues that consumers' verbal reactions to descriptions of new products can be used to predict how the market would respond to an actual product that was seen as matching the description, were it to be produced and introduced in the market.

The assertion that individuals behave similarly toward things that they see as being similar is, of course, tautological unless behavior and perceptions are measured independently. This means developing measures for perceived similarity of products/brand and for competitiveness. Specifically, the following hypotheses follow from Stefflre's general assumptions:

1. Objects will compete with each other to the extent that they are judged to be similar to each other.
2. New objects will compete with old objects to the extent that the descriptions of the new objects are seen to resemble the old objects.
3. The close relationship between the perceived similarity of objects and their patterns of competition or substitution will hold across individuals and across cultures despite the great diversity that exists with respect to what is seen as similar to what and which objects compete more with which other objects.

Stefflre's approach is directly applicable to campaign politics, where it is termed the strategic positioning procedure. Chapter 4 shows how multidimensional scaling techniques are used to construct empirical models of the electorate's perceptions and preferences. The perceptual model is based on voters' judged similarity of political candidates (or parties), while the preference model uses intercorrelated preferences to estimate patterns of competition among candidates (or parties). First, campaign strategists inspect the perceptual model searching for hypotheses about which features determine positioning in the model and, therefore, govern voter preferences. These hypotheses are then tested against the preference data by concocting descriptions of hypothetical new candidates (or parties), by combining these features, and seeing where they position in the preference model—based on a second sample of respondents.

The strategic positioning procedure is designed to empirically screen a large number of hypotheses—between 20 and 30 per sample. This permits a wide range of campaign strategies to be evaluated and frees campaigners from having to focus prematurely on a limited set of options. The increased breadth of alternatives considered by campaigners improves their chances of discovering unanticipated but viable strategies. All too often strategists overlook powerful strategies because they have restricted their search prematurely to only a few variations of a single basic strategy.

The strategic positioning procedure is applicable in any electoral system, in any democratic country in the world—as long as the votes are fairly counted. It is not limited to any particular type of electoral system (e.g., presidential or parliamentary), any type of voting procedure (e.g., plurality, majority, or proportional representation), or any type of party system (e.g., two-party or multiparty). To support this claim, a variety of political campaigns were analyzed in this book using this procedure.

Four separate cases were presented. The campaigns include: two-party and multiparty contests; presidential, gubernatorial, and parliamentary elections; French and U.S. political systems; and campaigns that elicited a high degree of voter interest as well as those that were less interesting. In each case, the procedure demonstrated that it could provide a readily understandable map of the patterns of competition that underlay the political contests. Such maps permit a more comprehensive understanding of the campaign, so that campaigners can position themselves to their best advantage. The strategic positioning procedure identified potentially promising alternative strategies and screened alternative ways to position the candidate in order that he might be able to select the most effective one.

The first case was the 1968 presidential campaign in California. In Chapter 5, the strategic positioning approach was used to analyze the patterns of vote-splitting in this multicandidate contest for both real and hypothetical "third candidates." It was found that, by and large, third candidates drew votes from the major candidate (either Democratic or Republican) to the extent that they were judged to resemble them. The hypothesis held for verbal descriptions of hypothetical candidates as well as for names of contemporary political leaders. Most important, the patterns of vote-splitting at the time of election were generally predictable from aggregate perceptions early in the campaign—over a year before the election.

The second case, presented in Chapter 6, was the 1970 campaign for governor of California. In this campaign, the strategic positioning approach was used to identify strategic options for the Democratic candidate for governor. A number of issue-positions and postures that the candidate was considering were empirically evaluated in order to identify those that met the candidate's criteria: to be highly popular and to appeal simultaneously to the segment of the electorate that had been supporting him to date. The campaign staff had strongly doubted such positions or postures existed, but the strategic positioning procedure identified several positions that met the criteria. Since the electorate's preferences were found to be multidimensional, rather than unidimensional, the candidate was not required to choose between either pragmatically adopting popular positions or inviting defeat by remaining "pure."

The next two cases, described in Chapters 7 and 8, involved the 1973 French parliamentary elections. The first showed how the strategic positioning approach was adopted by one of the major political parties to identify a national campaign strategy for their candidates throughout France. A number of legislative constituencies were targeted for analysis by the client. In almost all of these constituencies, issue-positions and postures were identified that met the client's criteria; in a few, where the faction's candidate had little chance of winning, we recommended that the faction cut their losses by minimizing support for those candidates.

The last case focused upon a single French constituency in the 1973 parliamentary elections and illustrated how the strategic positioning approach could be used to identify issue-positions and postures for the major political factions in that contest. Even though this study was conducted a year after the one reported in the previous chapter, the same clusters of political leaders and parties reappeared in the spatial model and were associated with the same campaign themes as before. Interestingly enough, two postures emerged as particularly promising for the centrists, "introducing orderly reforms" and "remaining independent and above the political parties," which presaged Giscard d'Estaing's use of them in the presidential contest that spring.

The third section of the book empirically examined methodological and theoretical issues in the use of the strategic positioning procedure. First, Stefflre's rule (1), an ordinal technique employed for predicting share-of-vote, was compared in Chapter 9 with alternative techniques and its predictive success evaluated. In rule (1), respondents are asked to rank order up to 50 items, including both actual and hypothetical political candidates.

Hypothetical candidates consist of verbal descriptions stating positions and postures that candidates could take or have taken. The share-of-vote for candidates in a variety of scenarios is then estimated from the rankings. This technique offers a powerful tool to political strategists, since it permits campaigners to estimate the share-of-vote any candidate could gain (or lose) by adopting alternative positions or postures.

Stefflre's rule (1) was shown to be able to predict successfully the share-of-vote for both actual and hypothetical candidates. Predictions were within sampling-error estimates and compared favorably with predictions made by commercial pollsters. The ordinal technique was also compared with predictions based on various stochastic methods; in every case the stochastic model did worse than rule (1).

The greatest drawback to the use of Stefflre's rule (1) is the difficulty of data-collection. It is somewhat more awkward to get respondents to rank order a large set of items than it is to have them use rating scales or to respond to traditional polling questions. On the other hand, rank order is easier to use than are the data-collection procedures typically required by stochastic models.

The central premise of the strategic positioning approach is that individuals will behave toward new things in ways that are similar to how they behave toward the familiar things that resemble the new thing. This hypothesis was evaluated in Chapter 10 by first intercorrelating aggregate measures of the perceived similarity of items with aggregate measures of patterns of competition. Each of these measures, described originally in Chapter 4, consists of matrices of estimates of candidate-candidate relationships. Moderate support was found for this hypothesis: independent studies found aggregate correlations ranging from .5 to .6. The hypothesis that it should be possible to predict the extent to which minor candidates could draw votes from each of the major candidates in any electoral contest was strongly supported. A series of independent studies found correlations ranging from .65 to 1.0 for names of well-known candidates, and from .77 to .91 for verbal descriptions of hypothetical candidates. Interestingly enough, the correlation between the perceived similarity of a candidate and his pattern of competition depended upon the extent to which the electorate was familiar with him. Well-known personages had high correlations, while lesser-known names enjoyed lower correlations. The hypothesis that verbal descriptions of new objects position where predicted in the spatial model was also supported: the bulk (over 70 percent) of the verbal descriptions positioned where predicted in all of the studies.

Chapter 11 examined another set of hypotheses concerning the homogeneity of political perceptions and preferences. For spatial models to adequately represent the electorate, the target population must be sufficiently homogeneous. Intercorrelations between partisan and arbitrary subgroups provided modest, but not strong, support for the homogeneity hypothesis. In both France and the United States, partisan groups were found to share the same basic orientations, but differed in important ways from each other. Greater agreement was found in political perceptions than in patterns of preferences.

The final hypothesis tested was that of temporal stability. In one of the California studies, a series of independent samples was drawn to assess the extent to which perceptions of political leaders remained stable throughout the pre-election period. This was the only study in the book that directly bore on this hypothesis, since none of the others included repeated samples of the same type. Strong, reliable correlations were found between political perceptions at every time period compared. Moreover, these correlations were as strong as any of those found between subgroups at the same point in time. These results suggested that political perceptions were relatively stable for approximately a year preceding an election. This is not to say that there was no change in the electorate's perceptions of political leaders; that is demonstrably not the case. It is only to assert that the electorate's basic framework for comprehending political events remained the same. Inspection of the spatial models derived from these samples showed the same basic clusters of leaders throughout this time period. Almost all of the variation across time could be accounted for by movement within clusters, although a few individuals did jump between clusters in response to major political events.

EVALUATION

This section assesses the implications for electoral politics of the increasing use of advanced technology, such as the strategic positioning procedure. Only the most immediate political consequences are examined due to the difficulties of predicting second-order effects in a complex society.[1] The discussion focuses on the use of only one kind of technology, that of marketing research technology, and does not include any discussion of the technology of persuasion, whether advertising, propaganda, or psychoanalysis. That will be left for other books. Two separate but interrelated issues are taken up here: the implications of the use of sophisticated marketing research technology for the relationships between candidates and the electorate, and the implications for the relationships between candidates and their advisors.

Discussion of the first issue is very brief and limited to two main points. First, I observe that political surveys provide the feedback necessary in campaigns for effective communications. Next, I argue that the increasing use of marketing research technology in political campaigns will act primarily to clarify politics, rather than to reform or to corrupt it, since such research technology is, in principle, identical to other survey research methods. The second issue touched on here, that of the effect of marketing research technology on the relationships between candidates and their advisors, is treated in a similarly brief manner. The most important difficulties that face candidates in managing survey specialists are outlined and the impact of marketing research technology is assessed.

The first issue to be looked at here is the implication of the use of sophisticated marketing research technology, such as the strategic positioning procedure, for the relationships between political candidates and the electorate. This procedure, as any survey research tool, is designed to aid political actors understand the electorate by providing detailed information about the voters' perceptions and preferences. Political candidates require accurate information in order to develop strategy in competitive elections as well as to communicate effectively. Since elections are necessarily competitive in a democracy, candidates who hope to be elected are required to think strategically. Therefore, it is natural and legitimate for candidates, in order to campaign effectively, to search out those analytical tools, such as the strategic positioning procedure, that yield the most accurate information about the electorate.

Effective communication in any situation requires immediate and pertinent feedback. In education, politics, and normal conversation, a speaker needs to recognize what his listeners know and what they do not know, in order to decide how to present what he wants to say. Similarly, all speakers, political or otherwise, must know what concerns motivate their listeners if they wish to ensure that what they say will be listened to. In normal everyday conversations all of us are continually engaged in eliciting feedback from our listeners to guide our future words. In conversation, this is so natural we hardly recognize it. However, it is not so effortless in political campaigning. Candidates must actively search for feedback from the electorate in order to communicate effectively. Political surveys, as well as other forms of monitoring the public, provide this vital feedback. However, it is possible to be overconcerned about feedback. Too great a preoccupation about how an audience will react can inhibit or distort what a speaker says. This is as true for political candidates on the campaign trail as it is for all of us in everyday conversations. But, such a possibility does not negate the value of feedback.

The strategic positioning procedure, in providing information about the electorate, acts primarily to clarify the situation rather than to corrupt or reform it. The procedure is designed to aid political strategists achieve their goals, not to restrict or to shape those goals in any way. As such, its use reflects, and perhaps intensifies, the *a priori* motives of political actors. Basically, it does not change them. All political candidates must decide what they wish to do on the basis of the information they receive.

If candidates cynically wish to find appealing promises to make to an unsuspecting electorate, the strategic positioning approach will help them identify such promises. If candidates are afraid to take bold stands on important issues facing the nation and are merely seeking popular positions to avoid displeasing any portion of the electorate, the strategic positioning procedure will help them to do just that.

But not all politicians are weak or cynical. There are many brave and honest people holding, or running for, political office. Indeed, without such people, no democratic system could long function regardless of the reforms introduced to protect the public. If candidates desire to educate the electorate, and to provide forthright leadership, the strategic positioning procedure will help them do that just as readily as to mislead voters. Education, as well as demagoguery, depends on an accurate assessment of the audience's perceptions and preferences.

The strategic positioning procedure, by improving a candidate's ability to identify and to react to opportunities in political campaigns, permits candidates to be more courageous and to speak out more forcefully on the issues that concern them. All too frequently, due to lack of good information, political candidates must choose among strategies that are not very personally appealing. Without detailed knowledge of the electorate's perceptions and preferences, political candidates can overlook potential opportunities and compromise too quickly, limiting their strategic planning to easily recognized alternatives. With better strategic information, political candidates will have a greater opportunity to identify opportunities that match their personal criteria, and, thus, they can avoid being forced to support less desirable alternatives. At the very least, improved knowledge of strategic opportunities permits candidates to avoid stupid blunders.

An example of the improved insights possible with this technique was seen in the campaign for governor of California, described in Chapter 6. Here, the strategic positioning procedure identified specific opportunities that had been overlooked by the campaign staff. Due to lack of adequate information, the staff had ruled out of consideration, as idealistic and naive, the issue-positions that were most preferred by the candidate. The use of the strategic positioning procedure increased the range of options open to the candidate and allowed him to find ways to support the positions closer to his personal ideals than he had thought possible.

The responsibility for campaigning decisions remains with the political candidate, not on the information he receives or on his advisors. Only he can decide what to do on the basis of his information. Nevertheless, candidates often rely on advisors to explain political polls and even to outline their alternatives to them, since typically they have little or no real understanding of survey methods. Thus, survey researchers are invited to share responsibility for the campaigning decisions with the candidate's other advisors. This leads naturally to the second issue that will be discussed here—that of the way sophisticated marketing research technology influences the relationship between a candidate and his advisors.

For a number of years now, political candidates have been engaging survey researchers, but the alliance between candidate and these specialists has been, and still is, a rather uncomfortable relationship. The tension primarily arises from the specialized nature of political surveys and the difficulties of effectively managing specialists. Survey research is a complex endeavor, requiring expert knowledge of probabilistic sampling methods, questionnaire formulation, and data analysis. Unfortunately, few political candidates have enough experience with survey research to be able to assess the quality of the advice they receive. The introduction of still more sophisticated technology promises to exacerbate some of the existing tensions, even while it acts to resolve others.

The difficulties that face candidates in effectively managing survey specialists lead to certain types of problems. The most important of these will be briefly outlined here and speculations made about the effect of the introduction of still more sophisticated technology, such as the strategic positioning procedure.[2] First, by not being familiar with the limitations of political surveys, candidates may expect greater precision than is technically possible. This can lead to candidates being misled by glib promises by an overeager salesman. Since research firms, as all private firms, are under pressure to make a profit, candidates must know what they are buying if they wish to get the most for their money. Good salesmen may not be good researchers. At the very least, a candidate, or someone on his staff, must understand the rudiments of survey sampling, for example, the importance of probabilistic sampling, what size of sample is required, and how to ask unbiased questions. Introducing more sophisticated analytical techniques will further exacerbate the problem of evaluating the limits of political surveys. Candidates may forget the importance of the "basics," such as sample size, in their excitement over "sexy" computer-generated displays, such as spatial models. No analytical technique can compensate for poor data collection methods.

Second, if candidates cannot judge the quality of surveys, they may be led to rely on cost considerations alone in selecting a survey. All too frequently, low-cost surveys are of such poor quality that they are worse than none at all. Surveys conducted "on-the-cheap," by inexperienced volunteers, for example, can easily be riddled with gross errors in sampling or in question formulation. If so, the survey may not be representative of the target population, or the questions asked may be so biased or naive that the results are worthless. In research, as in other areas of life, one gets only what one pays for. As before, the introduction of sophisticated analytical techniques may lead candidates to forget the importance of sampling, or even to frighten candidates away from survey research altogether by its forbidding complexity. On the other hand, the new analytical techniques are "friendlier" than earlier techniques, in that they are designed to be easier for nontechnicians to understand. The spatial model is an example of a friendly technique, since it is such a natural way for candidates to view politics. Thus, the new techniques may prove so attractive that candidates will be encouraged to use them.

Third, candidates may place too much credence in transitory or noisy data by not fully understanding the limits of survey estimates. Campaigning decisions cannot be said to be dictated by the data but instead depend upon how the data are interpreted and the nature of a candidate's objectives. For example, candidates need not drop out of the race if they score badly in early "trial heats," where they are pitted against their opposition early in a campaign, since sample surveys are only rough estimates of inherently variable phenomena, not predictors of the future. Responsible researchers must apprise their clients of the limitations of their surveys. Depending on the situation, it may be possible for a candidate to dramatically improve his standing with adroit campaigning. A challenger may not be very well known so that the electorate may not have had a good chance to assess him. An incumbent may have had to make unpopular decisions, which may ultimately cause the electorate to rally around him, once the people have had the chance to hear his explanations. This may be true even if his decisions remain unpopular. The clues for determining campaign strategy may be found in survey results, but often they are not obvious. It is a difficult and delicate task to shape campaign strategy from surveys. The identification of effective strategy requires a good working relationship between a candidate and his advisors.

The introduction of sophisticated analytical techniques, such as the strategic positioning procedure, promises to improve this situation, since the spatial model is such a natural way to view competitive electoral politics that political candidates can rapidly learn how to analyze complex relationships. The spatial metaphor is pervasive in political discussions so that the use of spatial models could provide a common analytical language for both candidates and researchers, which should facilitate a fruitful working relationship and thus improve the chances of developing a campaign strategy that is firmly grounded in the candidate's objectives as well as a reliable reading of public opinion.

In conclusion, the introduction of increasingly sophisticated techniques into electoral campaigning is not expected to drastically transform the relationship between candidate and his advisors, or even between candidate and citizen, but will act to clarify, and perhaps intensify, the nature of the existing relationship. The increasing size of most electorates due to the pressures of population growth, coupled with competitive pressures to use even more sophisticated marketing techniques, has transformed and will continue to transform political campaigning into a big business. Candidates for political office will increasingly be required to learn how to manage complex organizations, including a variety of specialists, in attempting to mount a political campaign. To do this, successful candidates do not need to become experts in each of the required specialities but they do need to learn how to manage specialists.

NOTES

1. The prediction of second-order consequences is difficult, as can be seen in these examples. Few observers in the early part of this century predicted how the introduction of the automobile was to transform American society. In hindsight, such institutions as freeways, suburbs, commuting long distances to work, and even—according to some observers—the liberalization of sexual mores, stem, at least in part, from the ready availability of the automobile. A second example is the birth control pill. When "the pill" was introduced, the inventors reportedly saw only the immediate benefits to women of the regulation of their menstrual cycles, but not the contraceptive implications, nor, of course, the social implications of having effectively placed women in control of birth control decisions. I must confess to a similar ignorance about the future impact of introducing improved technology, such as the strategic positioning procedure, into political campaigning. Nevertheless, some guesses may be hazarded, particularly concerning the immediate implications of the use of the strategic positioning procedure, since marketing research technology has been filtering into politics for some time.

2. For further discussion of the problems involved with using traditional polls in politics, see Gallup (1972), Key (1961), Roll and Cantril (1980), or Sabato (1981).

BIBLIOGRAPHY

Aaker, David, A., and John G. Myers. *Advertising Management.* Englewood Cliffs, N.J.: Prentice-Hall, 1975.

Abelson, Robert P. "A Technique and a Model for Multidimensional Attitude Scaling," *Public Opinion Quarterly* 18 (winter 1955); 405–18.

Agranoff, Robert. *The Management of Election Campaigns.* Boston: Holbrook, 1976.

Ahtola, Olli. "The Vector Model of Preferences: An Alternative to the Fishbein Model," *Journal of Marketing Research* 12 (February 1975); 52–59.

Albers, Sonke, and Klaus Brockhoff. "A Procedure for New Product Positioning in an Attribute Space," *European Journal of Operational Research* (1977); 230–38.

Alderson, Wroe. "The Analytical Framework for Marketing," in Delbert Duncan, ed., *Proceedings: Conference of Marketing Teachers From Far Western States.* Berkeley: University of California, 1958, pp. 15–28.

Alexander, Ernest R. "The Design of Alternatives in Organizational Contexts: A Pilot Study." *Administrative Science Quarterly* (September 1979); 382–404.

American Marketing Association, Committee on Terms. *Marketing Definitions: A Glossary of Marketing Terms.* Chicago: American Marketing Association, 1960.

Amstutz, A. E. *Computer Simulation of Competitive Market Response.* Cambridge, Mass.: MIT Press, 1967.

Arrow, Kenneth J. *Social Choice and Individual Values.* 2nd ed. New York: Wiley, 1963 (original pub. 1951).

Asher, Herbert. *Presidential Elections and American Politics.* Rev. ed. Homewood, Ill.: Dorsey Press, 1980.

Baker, Norman, and James Freeland. "Recent Advances in R&D Benefit Measurement and Project Selection Methods." *Management Science* 21 (June 1975); 1164–75.

Barral, P. *Le départment de l'Iserè sous la troisième république.* Paris: Colin, 1962.

Bauer, R. A. "The Obstinate Audience: The Influence Process From the Point of View of Social Communication." *American Psychologist* 19 (July 1964); 319–28.

Baus, Herbert M., and William B. Ross. *Politics Battle Plan.* New York: Macmillan, 1968.

Beals, R., Krantz, D. H., and Tversky, A. "Foundations of Multidimensional Scaling," *Psychological Review* 75 (March 1968); 127–42.

Bell, Charles G., and Charles M. Price. *California Government Today: Politics of Reform.* Homewood, Ill.: Dorsey, 1980.

Benham, T. W. "Polling for a Presidential Candidate: Some Observations on the 1964 Campaign." *Public Opinion Quarterly* 29 (Summer 1965); 185–99.

Beniger, James R. "Avoiding Interpersonal Comparison of Preference Intensity: A Rank-Distance Approach to Attitude Scaling." *Political Marketing* 6 (August 1979); 247–74.

Bennett, W. Lance. "The Growth of Knowledge in Mass Relief Studies: An Epistemological Critique." *American Journal of Political Science* 21 (August 1977); 465–500.
Benson, Purnell H. "Analysis of Irregular Two Dimensional Distributions of Consumer Buying Choice." *Journal of Marketing Research* 3 (August 1966); 278–88.
Berelson, Bernard R., Paul F. Lazarsfeld, and William N. McPhee. *Voting*. Chicago: University of Chicago Press. 1954
Berlin, Brent, and Paul Kay. *Basic Color Terms: Their Universality and Evolution*. Berkeley: University of California Press, 1969.
Black, M., and D. Metzger. "Ethnographic Description and the Study of the Law," in L. Nader, ed. *The Ethnography and the Law. American Anthropologist Special Issue* 67 (December 1965); 141–65.
Blumenthal, Sidney. *The Permanent Campaign Inside the World of Elite Political Operatives*. Boston: Beacon Press, 1980.
Blumler, Jay G., and Denis McQuail. *Television in Politics, Its Uses and Influence*. Chicago: University of Chicago Press, 1969.
Bock, R. Darrell, and Lyle V. Jones. *The Measurement and Prediction of Judgment and Choice*. San Francisco: Holden-Day, 1968.
Booz, Allen and Hamilton, Inc. "A Program for New Product Evolution," in *Management of New Products*. New York, 1968, pp. 7–12.
de Borda, Jean-Charles. "Mémoire sur les Elections au Scrutin." *Mémoires de l'Académie Royale des Sciences*, (1781), pp. 657–65. Translated and commented upon by A. De Grazia, "Mathematical Derivation of an Election System." *Isis* 44 (June 1953); 42–51.
Bordley, R. F., and R. W. Wolff. "On the Aggregation of Individual Probability Estimates." *Management Science* 27 (August 1981); 959–64.
Brams, Steven J. *Presidential Election Game*. New Haven, Conn.: Yale University Press, 1978.
Brown, M. P., R. N. Cardozo, S. M. Cunningham, W. J. Salman, and R. G. M. Sultan. "Maxwell House Division, A Market Structure and Segmentation Project," in *Problems in Marketing*. 4th ed. New York: McGraw Hill, 1968, pp. 439–66. (Harvard Business School Case M266).
Brown, Roger. *Words and Things*. New York: Free Press, 1958.
Brown, Steven R. "Consistency and Persistence of Ideology: Some Experimental Results." *Public Opinion Quarterly* 34 (Spring 1970); 60–68.
Bruner, Jerome S., Jacqueline J. Goodnow, and George A. Austin. *A Study of Thinking*. New York: Wiley, 1956.
———, and Renato Tagiuri. "The Perception of People," in G. Lindzey, ed. *Handbook of Social Psychology*. Cambridge, Mass.: Addison-Wesley, 1954.
Buchanan, James M., and Gordon Tullock. *The Calculus of Consent*. Ann Arbor: University of Michigan Press, 1965.
Budge, I., I. Crewe, and D. Farlie, eds. *Party Identification and Beyond*. London: Wiley, 1976.
Campbell, Angus, Philip E. Converse, Warren E. Miller, and Donald E. Stokes. *Elections and the Political Order*. New York: Wiley, 1966.
———, *The American Voter*. New York: Wiley, 1960.
———, *The Voter Decides*. Evanston, Ill.: Row, Peterson, 1954.

Campbell, D. T., and J. C. Stanley. *Experimental and Quasi-Experimental Designs for Research*. Chicago: Rand McNally, 1963.

Capon, Noel, and Gary Mauser. "A Review of Nonprofit Marketing Texts." *Journal of Marketing* 46 (Summer 1982); 125-29.

Carman, James M. "On the Universality of Marketing." *Journal of Contemporary Business* 2 (Autumn 1973); 14.

Carroll, J. D., and J. J. Chang. "Analysis of Individual Differences in Multidimensional Scaling Via an N-Way Generalization of Eckart-Young Decomposition." *Psychometrika* 35 (September 1970); 283-319.

Cassirer, Ernst. *Language and Myth*. Translated by S. K. Langer. New York: Harper, 1946.

Chaffee, Steven H. *Political Communication, Issues and Strategies for Research*. Sage Annual Reviews of Communication Research, Vol. IV, Beverly Hills, Calif.: Sage, 1975.

Chamberlin, E. H. *The Theory of Monopolistic Competition*. Cambridge, Mass.: Harvard University Press, 1962.

Charnes, A., W. W. Cooper, J. K. Devoe, and D. B. Learner. "DEMON: A Management Model for Marketing New Products." *California Management Review* 11 (Fall 1968); 31-46.

The Conference Board. *Evaluating New Product Proposals*. New York: The Conference Board, 1973.

Congressional Quarterly. *Elections '80*, Washington, D.C.: C.Q. Press, 1980.

Converse, Philip E. "The Problem of Party Distances in Models of Voting Change," in M. Kent Jennings and L. Harmon Zeigler, eds. *The Electoral Process*. Englewood Cliffs, N.J.: Prentice-Hall, 1966, pp. 175-207.

―――. "The Nature of Belief Systems in Mass Publics," in David E. Apter, ed. *Ideology and Discontent*. New York: Free Press, 1964, pp. 206-61.

―――, A. R. Clausen, and Warren E. Miller, "Electoral Myth and Reality: The 1964 Election." *American Political Science Review* 59 (June 1965); 321-36.

―――, Warren E. Miller, Jerrold G. Rusk, and Arthur C. Wolfe. "Continuity and Change in American Politics: Parties and Issues in the 1968 Election." *American Political Science Review* 63 (December 1969); 1083-1105.

Coombs, C.H. *A Theory of Data*, New York: Wiley, 1964.

Coombs, C.I., R.I. Dawes, and D. Tversky. *Mathematical Psychology, An Elementary Introduction*. Englewood Cliffs, N.J.: Prentice-Hall, 1970.

Crossley, A., and H. Crossley. "Polling in 1968," *Public Opinion Quarterly* 33 (Spring 1969); 1-16.

Crouse, Timothy. *The Boys on the Bus*. New York: Ballantine, 1973.

Currim, Imran S. "Predictive Testing of Consumer Choice Models Not Subject to Independence of Irrelevant Alternatives." *Journal of Marketing Research* 19 (May 1982); 208-22.

Cutright, Phillips. "Measuring the Impact of Local Party Activity on the General Election Vote." *Public Opinion Quarterly* 27 (Fall 1963): 372-86.

Davis, Otto A., and Melvin Hinich. "A Mathematical Model of Policy Formation in a Democratic Society," in J. Bernd, ed. *Mathematical Applications in Political Science*, Vol. II. Dallas: Southern Methodist Press, 1966.

Day, George S. *Buyer Attitudes and Brand Choice Behavior*. New York: The Free Press, 1970.

_____, Allan D. Shocker, and R.K. Srivastava. "Customer-Oriented Approaches to Identifying Product-Markets." *Journal of Marketing* 43 (Fall 1979); 1–19.

Debreu, G. "A Review of Individual Choice Behavior: A Theoretical Analysis." *American Economic Review* 50 (December 1960); 186–88.

Deese, James. *The Structure of Association in Language and Thought.* Baltimore, Md.: James Hopkins Press, 1965.

Degerman, R.L. "The Geometric Representation of Some Simple Structures," in R. Shepard, A.K. Romney, and S.B. Nerlove, eds. *Multidimensional Scaling: Theory and Applications in the Behavioral Sciences,* Vol. 1. New York: Seminar Press, 1972, pp. 194–212.

Dennis, Jack, ed. *Socialization to Politics.* New York: Wiley, 1973.

Doehlert, D.H. "Similarity and Preference Mapping: A Color Example," in R.L. King, ed. *Marketing and the New Science of Planning.* Chicago: American Marketing Association, 1968, pp. 250–57.

Donnelly, James H. Jr., and John M. Ivancevich. "A Methodology for Identifying Innovator Characteristics of New Brand Purchasers." *Journal of Marketing Research* 9 (August 1974); 331–34.

Doob, L.W. *Public Opinion and Propaganda.* New York: Holt, 1948.

Downs, Anthony. *An Economic Theory of Democracy.* New York: Harper & Row, 1957.

Dunn, S.W., and A.M. Barban. *Advertising: Its Role in Modern Marketing.* 4th ed. Hinsdale, Ill.: Dryden, 1978.

Easton, David, and Jack Dennis. *Children in the Political System.* New York: McGraw-Hill, 1969.

Edelman, Murray. *Politics as Symbolic Action.* Chicago: Markham, 1971.

_____. *The Symbolic Uses of Politics.* Urbana: University of Illinois Press, 1964.

Ehrmann, Henry W. *Politics in France.* 3rd ed. Boston: Little, Brown, 1976.

Ekman, G. "Dimensions of Color Vision." *Journal of Psychology* 38 (July 1954); 467–74.

Eldersveld, Samuel J. "Experimental Propaganda Techniques and Voting Behavior." *American Political Science Review* 50 (March 1956); 154–65.

Ellul, Jacques. *Propagandes.* Paris: Colin, 1962.

Engel, J.F., D.T. Kollat, and R.D. Blackwell. *Consumer Behavior.* Hinsdale, Ill.: Dryden Press, 1968, 1978.

Erikson, Robert S., and N.R. Luttbeg. *American Public Opinion: Its Origins, Content, and Impact,* New York: Wiley, 1973.

Farquarson, R. *Theory of Voting.* New Haven, Conn.: Yale University Press, 1969.

Feldman, Shel, ed. *Cognitive Consistency.* New York: Academic Press, 1966.

Festinger, Leon. *A Theory of Cognitive Dissonance.* Evanston, Ill.: Row, Peterson, 1957.

Field, Mervin D. *The California Poll* no. 691 (October 30, 1970).

Fiorina, Morris P. *Retrospective Voting in American National Elections.* New Haven, Conn.: Yale University Press, 1981.

_____. "Formal Models in Political Science." *American Journal of Political Science* 19 (February 1975); 133–59.

Fishbein, Martin. *Readings in Attitude Theory and Measurement.* New York: Wiley, 1967.

———. "A Consideration of Beliefs, Attitudes, and Their Relationships," in I.D. Steiner and M. Fishbein, eds. *Current Studies in Social Psychology*. New York: Holt, Rinehart and Winston, 1965, pp. 107–20.

———. "An Investigation of the Relationship Between Beliefs About an Object and the Attitude Toward That Object." *Human Relations*. 16 (August 1963); 233–40.

———, and Icek Ajzen. *Belief, Attitude, Intention and Behavior: An Introduction to Theory and Research*. Reading, Mass.: Addison-Wesley, 1975.

Fishel, Jeff, ed. *Parties and Elections in an Anti-Party Age*. Bloomington; Indiana University Press, 1978.

Frake, C.O. "Ethnographic Study of Cognitive Systems," in T. Gladwin and W.C. Sturtevant, eds. *Anthropology and Behavior*. Washington, D.C.: Anthropological Society of Washington, 1962.

Frank, R.E., W.F. Massy, and Y. Wind. *Market Segmentation*. Englewood Cliffs, N.J.: Prentice-Hall, 1972.

Fried, M.H. *Readings in Anthropology*. 2nd ed. *Cultural Anthropology*, Vol. II. New York: Crowell, 1968.

Gallup, George. *The Gallup Opinion Index*, Report No. 34 (April 1968); No. 35 (May 1968); No. 37 (July 1968); No. 38 (August 1968); No. 39 (September 1968); No. 163 (February 1979); No. 183 (December 1980). Princeton, N.J.: American Institute of Public Opinion.

———. *The Sophisticated Poll-Watcher's Guide*. Princeton, N.J.: Opinion Press, 1972.

Gensch, Dennis H., and Wilfred W. Recker. "The Multinomial, Multiattribute Logit Choice Model." *Journal of Marketing Research* 16 (February 1979); 124–32.

Goffman, Ervings. *Strategic Interaction*. Oxford: Basil Blackwell, 1970.

———. *The Presentation of Self in Everyday Life*. New York: Doubleday, 1959.

Goldwin, Robert A., ed. *Political Parties in the Eighties*. Washington, D.C.: American Enterprise Institute, 1980.

Goodenough, W.H. *Explorations in Cultural Anthropology*. New York: McGraw Hill, 1964.

Gosnell, H.F. *Getting Out the Vote: An Expt. in the Stimulation of Voting* . Chicago: University of Chicago Press, 1927.

Graber, Doris A. *Mass Media and American Politics*. Washington, D.C.: Congressional Quarterly Press, 1980.

Grayson, C.J., Jr. "Management Science and Business Practice." *Harvard Business Review* 51 (July-August 1973); 41–48.

Green, P. "Marketing Applications of MDS: Assessment and Outlook." *Journal of Marketing* 39 (January 1975); 24–31.

———, and F. Carmone. *MDS and Related Techniques*. Boston: Allyn and Bacon, 1970.

———, and V.R. Rao. *Applied Multidimensional Scaling*. New York: Holt, Rinehart and Winston, 1972.

———, and V.R. Rao. "Multidimensional Scaling and Individual Differences," *Journal of Marketing Research* 8 (February 1971); 71–77.

———, and V. Srinavasan. "Conjoint Analysis in Consumer Research: Issues and Outlook." *Journal of Consumer Research* 5 (September 1978); 103–23.

———, and D.S. Tull. *Research for Marketing Decisions*. Englewood Cliffs, N.J.: Prentice-Hall, 1970, 1975, 1978.

———, and Y. Wind. *Multiattribute Decisions in Marketing*. Hinsdale, Ill.: Dryden Press, 1973.

Greenfield, Jeff. *Playing to Win: An Insider's Guide to Politics*. New York: Simon and Schuster, 1980.

Guilford, J.P. *Psychometric Methods*. 2nd ed. New York: McGraw Hill, 1954.

Guttman, L. "A New Approach to Factor Analysis: The Radex," in P.F. Lazardsfeld, ed. *Mathematical Thinking in the Social Sciences*. Glencoe, Ill.: Free Press, 1954, pp. 258–348.

Hall, E.T. *The Silent Language*. New York: Doubleday, 1959.

Harding, Joe. "Anthropology and Architectural Planning." *Practicing Anthropology* (Summer 1979): pp. 3–4, 23–25.

———, and D. Clement. "Features Affecting Acceptability of Fertility Regulating Methods in Korea." Paper presented at the American Anthropological Association meetings, Mexico City, November 1974.

Hare, T. *The Election of Representatives*. London: Longmans Green, 1859.

Harman, H.H. *Modern Factor Analysis*. 3rd ed. Chicago: University of Chicago Press, 1976.

Harris, Lou. "Nixon Leads, Wallace Gains." *Los Angeles Times*. Part II, September 13, 1968, p. 8.

———. "Union Members for Wallace." *Los Angeles Times*. Part II, August 24, 1968, p. 6.

Harvey, J.H., W.F. Ickes, and R.F. Kidd. *New Directions in Attitude Research*. Vols. I and II. New York: Wiley, 1976.

Hauser, J.R., and F.S. Koppelman. "Alternative Perceptual Mapping Techniques: Relative Accuracy and Usefulness." *Journal of Marketing Research* 16 (November 1979); pp. 495–506.

———, and Glen L. Urban. 'A Normative Methodology for Modelling Consumer Response to Innovation." *Operations Research* 25 (July–August 1977); 579–619.

Hershey, Marjorie Randon. *The Making of Campaign Strategy*. London and Lexington, Mass.: D.C. Heath (Lexington Books), 1974.

Hiebert, R.E., R.F. Jones, J. Lorenz, and E.A. Lotito, eds. *The Political Image Merchants: Strategies for the Seventies*. Washington, D.C.: Acropolis Books, 1975.

Hinich, Melvin J. "Some Evidence on Non-voting Models in the Spatial Theory of Electoral Competition." *Public Choice* 33, no. 2 (1978); 83–102.

Hotelling, Harold. "Stability in Competition." *Economic Journal* 39 (March 1929); 41–57.

Hovland, C.I., I.L. Janis, and H.H. Kelley. *Communication and Persuasion*. New Haven, Conn.: Yale University Press, 1953.

———, and M. Rosenberg, eds. *Attitude Organization and Change*. New Haven, Conn.: Yale University Press, 1960.

Howard, John A. *Consumer Behavior: Application of Theory*. New York: McGraw Hill, 1977.

———, and Jagdish N. Sheth. *The Theory of Buyer Behavior.* New York: Wiley, 1969.
Huber, Joel, and M.B. Holbrook. "Using Attribute Ratings for Product Positioning: Some Distinctions Among Compositional Approaches." *Journal of Marketing Research* 16 (November 1979); 507–16.
Hyman, Herbert H. *Political Socialization.* New York: The Free Press, 1959.
Jakobson, Roman, and M. Halle. *Fundamentals of Language.* The Hague: Mouton, 1956.
Jay, Anthony. *Management and Machiavelli.* New York: Holt, Rinehart and Winston, 1967.
Jewell, Malcolm E., and David M. Olson. *American State Political Parties and Elections.* Rev. ed. Homewood, Ill.: Dorsey, 1982.
Johnson, Samuel C., and Conrad Jones. "How to Organize for New Products." *Harvard Business Review* 35 (May-June 1957); 49–62.
Johnson, Steven. "Hierarchical Clustering Schemes." *Psychometrika* 32 (September 1967): 241–54.
Jones, B.D. "Some Considerations in the Use of Nonmetric Multidimensional Scaling." *Political Methodology* 1 (fall 1974); 1–30.
Katz, Daniel, and Samuel J. Elverseveld. "The Impact of Local Party Activity upon the Electorate." *Public Opinion Quarterly* 25 (Spring 1961) 1–24.
Katz, Elihu, and Paul F. Lazarsfeld. *Personal Influence.* New York: The Free Press, 1955.
Kelley, Stanley, Jr. *Political Campaigning.* Washington, D.C.: Brookings Institution, 1960.
———. *Professional Public Relations and Political Power.* Baltimore, Md.: Johns Hopkins Press, 1956.
———, Richard E. Ayres, and William G. Bowen. "Registration and Voting: Putting First Things First." *American Political Science Review* 61 (June 1967); 359–79.
Kessel, John. *Presidential Campaign Politics.* Homewood, Ill.: Dorsey, 1980.
Key, V.O., Jr. *The Responsible Electorate.* Cambridge, Mass.: Harvard University Press, 1966.
———. *Politics, Parties and Pressure Groups.* 5th ed. New York: Crowell, 1964.
———. *Public Opinion and American Democracy.* New York: Knopf, 1961.
King, William R. *Quantitative Analysis for Marketing Management.* New York: McGraw Hill, 1967.
Kingdon, John W. *Candidates for Office*: Beliefs and Strategies, New York: Random House, 1966.
Kish, L. *Survey Sampling.* New York: Wiley, 1965.
Klahr, D. "A Monte Carlo Investigation of the Statistical Significance of Kruskal's Nonmetric Scaling Procedure." *Psychometrika* 34 (September 1969); 319–30.
Klapper, Joseph T. *The Effects of Mass Communication.* Glencoe, Ill.: The Free Press, 1960.
Kline, F. Gerald, and Philip J. Tichenor, eds. *Current Perspectives in Mass Communications Research.* Sage Annual Reviews of Communication Research, Vol. I. London: Sage Publications, 1972.
Kotler, Philip. *Marketing for Nonprofit Organization.* Englewood Cliffs, N.J.: Prentice-Hall, 1975 and 1982.

———. "A Generic Concept of Marketing." *Journal of Marketing* 36 (April 1972); 46–54.

———, and Sidney J. Levy. "Broadening the Concept of Marketing." *Journal of Marketing* 33 (January 1969); 10–15.

Kover, Arthur J. "Careers and Noncommunication: The Case of Academic and Applied Marketing Research." *Journal of Marketing Research* (November 1976); 339–44.

Kramer, Gerald. "A Decision Theoretic Analysis of a Problem in Political Campaigning," in J. L. Bernd, ed. *Mathematical Applications in Political Science*. Vol. 2, Dallas: Southern Methodist University Press, 1966, pp. 137–60.

Kraus, Sidney, and Dennis Davis, eds. *The Effects of Mass Communication on Political Behavior*. University Park: Pennsylvania State University Press, 1976.

Kruskal, J.B. "Multidimensional Scaling by Optimizing Goodness of Fit to a Nonmetric Hypothesis." *Psychometrika* 29 (March 1964); 1–27 (a).

———. "Nonmetric Multidimensional Scaling: A Numerical Method." *Psychometrika* (June 1964); 115–29 (b).

Kuehn, Alfred A., and Ralph L. Day. "Strategy of Product Quality." *Harvard Business Review* 40 (November-December 1962): 100–10.

Ladd, Everett C., Jr. *Where Have All the Voters Gone?* New York: Norton, 1977.

Lakeman, E., and J.D. Lambert. *Voting in Democracies: A Study of Majority and Proportional Election Systems*. London: Faber and Faber, 1955.

Lamb, Karl A., and Paul A. Smith. *Campaign Decision-Making*. Belmont, Calif.: Wadsworth, 1968.

Lancaster, Kelvin. *Consumer Demand: A New Approach*. New York: Columbia University Press, 1971.

———. "A New Approach to Consumer Theory." *Journal of Political Economy* 74 (April 1966); 132–57.

Lancelot, Marie-Thérèse, and Alain Lancelot. *Atlas des circonscriptions électorales en France depuis 1875*. Paris: Colin, 1970.

Lang, Kurt, and Gladys Lang. *Politics and Television*. Chicago: Quadrangle, 1970.

Lantz, D., and V. Stefflre. "Language and Cognition Revisited." *Journal of Abnormal and Social Psychology* 69 (November 1964); 472–81.

Lazarsfeld, Paul F., Bernard R. Berelson, and Hazel Gaudet. *The People's Choice*. New York: Duell, Sloan and Pierce, 1944.

Leary, Mary Ellen. *Phantom Politics, Campaigning in California*. Washington, D.C.: Public Affairs Press, 1977.

Leduc, Lawrence. "Semantic Differential Measures of British Party Images." *British Journal of Political Science* 6 (January 1976); 115–23.

LeGall, G., and M. Riglet. "Les circonscriptions marginales aux élections législatives de 1967 et 1968." *Revue Française de Science Politique* 21 (February 1973); 86–109.

Lehmann, Donald R. "Evaluating Marketing Strategy in a Multiple Brand Market." *Journal of Business Administration* 3 (fall 1971); 15–26.

Lengle, J.I., and B.E. Shafer, eds. *Presidential Politics*. New York: St. Martin's Press, 1980.

Leuthold, David A. *Electioneering in a Democracy, Campaigns for Congress*. New York: Wiley, 1968.

Levelt, W.J.M., J.P. Van de Geer, and R. Plomp. "Triadic Comparisons of Musical Intervals." *British Journal of Mathematical and Statistical Psychology* 19 (November 1966); 163–79.
Levin, Murray B. *Kennedy Campaigning*. Boston: Beacon Press, 1966.
_____, *The Compleat Politician*. New York: Bobbs Merrill, 1962.
Little, John. "Models and Managers: The Concept of a Decision Calculus." *Management Science* 16 (April 1970); B-466–85.
Luce, R.D. "The Choice Axiom After Twenty Years." *Journal of Mathematical Psychology* 15 (June 1977); 215–33.
_____, *Individual Choice Behavior*. New York: Wiley, 1959.
_____, and Howard Raiffa. *Games and Decisions: Introduction and Critical Survey*. New York: Wiley, 1957.
_____, and J. Tukey. "Simultaneous Conjoint Measurement: A New Type of Fundamental Measurement." *Journal of Mathematical Psychology* 1 (February 1964); 1–27.
Lucey, John A., and Richard A. Shweder. "Whorf and His Critics: Linguistic and Nonlinguistic Influences in Color." *American Anthropologist* 81 (September 1979); 581–615.
Luck, David. "Broadening the Concept of Marketing—Too Far." *Journal of Marketing* 33 (July 1969); 54.
McCarthy, E. J. *Basic Marketing*. Homewood, Ill.: Richard D. Irwin, 1960.
McClure, Robert D., and Thomas E. Patterson. "Television News and Voter Behavior in the 1972 Presidential Election." Paper presented at the 1973 annual meeting of the American Political Science Association, September 4–8, New Orleans, Louisiana.
McCombs, Maxwell E. "Mass Communication in Political Campaigns: Information, Gratification, and Persuasion." in F. Gerald Kline and Philip J. Tichnor, eds. *Current Perspectives in Mass Communications Research*, Beverly Hills: Sage, 1972, pp. 169–94.
McDonald, Morgan B. Jr. "Estimating Market Potential," in *Appraising the Market for New Industrial Products*. SBP No. 123. New York: The Conference Board, 1967, pp. 38–62.
McGinniss, Joe. *The Selling of the President, 1968*. New York: Trident Press, 1969.
McGuire, William J. "The Nature of Attitudes and Attitude Change," in G. Lindzey and E. Aronson, eds. *Handbook of Social Psychology*, 2nd ed. Vol. 3. Reading, Mass.: Addison-Wesley, 1969, pp. 136–314.
Machiavelli, Niccolo. *The Prince and the Discourses*. New York: The Modern Library, 1950.
Marcus, George E., David Tabb, and John L. Sullivan. "The Application of Individual Differences Scaling to the Measurement of Political Ideologies." *American Journal of Political Science* 18 (May 1974); 405–20.
Marshall, Thomas. *Presidential Nominations in a Reform Age*. New York: Praeger, 1981.
Mauser, Gary. "Positioning Political Candidates—An Application of Concept Evaluation Techniques." *Journal of the Market Research Society* 22 (July 1980); 181–91.

———. "A Technology for Marketing Political Candidates," in Allan D. Shocker, ed. *Analytical Approaches to Product and Marketing Planning*. Cambridge, Mass.: Marketing Science Institute, 1979.

———. "A Structural Approach to Predicting Patterns of Electoral Substitution," in A.K. Romney, R.N. Shepard, and S.B. Nerlove, eds. *Multidimensional Scaling: Theory and Applications in the Behavioral Sciences*, Vol. 2, New York: Seminar Press, 1972, pp. 245–87.

———. "A Structural Approach to Predicting Patterns of Electoral Substitution: A Study of the 1968 Presidential Contest in California." Doctoral dissertation, University of California at Irvine, 1970.

———. "Predicting Patterns of Competition in Multiple Candidate Elections." *Proceedings, 77th Annual Convention*, American Psychological Association, 1969, pp. 435–36.

———, and Jacqueline Freyssinet. "Exploring Political Space: A Study of French Voters' Preferences," in I. Budge, I. Crewe, and D. Farlie, eds. *Party Identification and Beyond*. Wiley, 1976, pp. 203–24.

———, and Volney J. Stefflre. "Similitude et Substitution dans une Election." *Revue Francaise du Marketing* 50 (spring 1974); 19–38.

Mazmanian, Daniel A. *Third Parties in Presidential Elections*. Washington, D.C.: The Brookings Institution, 1974.

Messick, S.J. "The Perceived Structure of Political Relationships." *Sociometry* (September 1961); 270–78.

———. "The Perception of Social Attitudes" *Journal of Abnormal and Social Psychology* 52 (January 1956); 57–66.

Metzger, D., and G. Williams. "A Formal Ethnographic Analysis of Tenehapa Ladino Weddings." *American Anthropologist* 65 (October 1963); 1076–1101.

Miller, Arthur H., and Warren E. Miller. "Issues, Candidates and Partisan Divisions in the 1972 U.S. Elections." *British Journal of Political Science* (September 1976); 393–434.

Miller, George A. "The Magical Number Seven, Plus or Minus Two." *Psychological Review* 63 (March 1956); 81–97.

Minsky, M. "A Framework for Representing Knowledge," in Patrick H. Winston, ed. *The Psychology of Computer Vision*. New York: McGraw Hill, 1975.

Le Monde, Les forces politiques et les élections de mars 1973. Supplement to "Dossiers et Documents du Monde." Paris: Le Monde, March 1973.

Montgomery, D.B., and G.L. Urban. *Application of Management Science in Marketing*. Englewood Cliffs, N.J.: Prentice-Hall, 1969.

Myers, James H. "Positioning Maps—Where Are We?" *Proceedings of Division 23 Program 87th Annual Convention of the American Psychological Association*, New York City, September 1–5, 1979.

———. "Benefit Structure Analysis: A New Tool for Product Planning." *Journal of Marketing* 40 (October 1976); 23–32.

———, and Allan D. Shocker. "The Nature of Product Attributes." Working paper, Claremont Graduate School, January 1980.

———, and Edward Tauber. *Market Structure Analysis*. Chicago: American Marketing Association, 1977.

Nanson, E.J. "Methods of Election." Transaction and Proceedings of the Royal Society of Victoria, Vol. XIX, 1883, pp. 197–200 (original series).

Napolitan, Joseph. "Media Costs and Effects in Political Campaigns," *The Annals of the American Academy of Political and Social Science* 427 (September 1976); 114–24.

―――. *The Election Game and How to Win It.* New York: Doubleday, 1972.

Nie, Norman H., Sidney Verba, and John R. Petrocik. *The Changing American Voter.* Cambridge, Mass.: Harvard University Press, 1976.

Nimmo, Dan. *The Political Persuaders, The Techniques of Modern Election Campaigns.* Englewood Cliffs, N.J.: Prentice-Hall, 1970.

Nygren, Thomas E., and Lawrence E. Jones. "Individual Differences in Perceptions and Preferences for Political Candidates." *Journal of Experimental Social Psychology* 13 (March 1977); 182–97.

O'Keefe, Garrett J. "Political Campaigns and Mass Communications Research," in Steven H. Chaffee, ed. *Political Communication: Issues and Strategies for Research.* Sage Annual Reviews of Communications Research, Vol. IV. Beverly Hills, Calif.: Sage Publications, 1975.

Ordeshook, Peter C. "The Spatial Theory of Elections: A Review and a Critique," in Ian Budge, Ivor Crewe, and Dennis Farlie, eds. *Party Identification and Beyond.* London: Wiley, 1976, pp. 285–314.

Osgood, C.E., and T.A. Sebeok. *Psycholinguistics: A Theory and Research Problems.* Bloomington: Indiana University Press, 1965.

―――, and G.J. Suci. "Factor Analysis of Meaning." *Journal of Experimental Psychology* 50 (November 1955); 325–38.

―――. G.J. Suci, and P.H. Tannenbaum. *The Measurement of Meaning.* Urbana: University of Illinois Press, 1957.

Page, Benjamin I. "Elections and Social Choice: The State of the Evidence." *American Journal of Political Science* 21 (August 1977); 639–68.

―――. "The Theory of Political Ambiguity." *American Political Science Review* 70 (September 1976): 742–52.

―――, and Richard A. Brody. "Policy Voting and the Electoral Process: The Vietnam War Issue." *American Political Science Review* 66 (September 1972); 979–95.

Patterson, Thomas. *The Mass Media Election.* New York: Praeger, 1980.

―――, and Robert D. McClure. *The Unseeing Eye: The Myth of Television Power in National Elections.* New York. G.P. Putnam's Sons, 1976.

―――, and Robert D. McClure. "Political Advertising: Voter Reaction." Paper presented at the annual meeting of the American Association for Public Opinion Research, Ashville, North Carolina, May 17-20, 1973.

Pessemier, Edgar A. *Product Management, Strategy and Organization.* New York: Wiley, 1977.

―――. "Market Structure Analysis of New Product and Market Opportunities." *Journal of Contemporary Business* 4 (spring 1975): 35–65.

―――, Philip Burger, Richard Teach, and Douglas Tigert. "Using Laboratory Brand Preference Scales to Predict Consumer Brand Preferences." *Management Science* 17 (February 1971); B-371–B-385.

Plott, Charles R. "Axiomatic Social Choice Theory: An Overview and Interpretation." *American Journal of Political Science* 20 (August 1976); 511–96.

Pomper, Gerald, R.K. Baker, K.A. Frankovic, C.E. Jacob, W.C. McWilliams, and H.A. Plotkin. *The Election of 1980.* Chatham, N.J.: Chatham House, 1981.

Pool, Ithiel de S., Robert P. Abelson, and Samuel Popkin. *Candidates, Issues and Strategies: A Computer Simulation of the 1960 and 1964 Presidential Elections.* Cambridge, Mass.: MIT Press, 1964.

Rabinowitz, G.A. "An Introduction to Nonmetric Multidimensional Scaling." *American Journal of Political Science* 19 (May 1975); 343–90.

Rados, David L. *Marketing for Nonprofit Organizations,* Boston, Mass.: Auburn House, 1981.

Rae, Douglas W. *The Political Consequences of Electoral Laws.* New Haven, Conn.: Yale University Press, 1971.

Ranney, Austin. "Changing the Rules of the Presidential Nominating Game: Party Reform in America," in James D. Barber, ed. *Choosing the President,* Englewood Cliffs, N.J.: Prentice-Hall, 1974.

Rao, V.R., and Ralph Katz. "Alternative Multidimensional Scaling Methods for Large Stimulus Sets." *Journal of Marketing Research* 8 (November 1970); 488–94.

_____, and F. Winter. "An Application of the Multivariate Probit Model to Market Segmentation and Product Design." *Journal of Marketing Research* 15 (August 1978); 361–68.

Ray, M.L., A.G. Sawyer, M.L. Rothschild, R.M. Heeler, E.C. Strong, and J.B. Reed. "Marketing Communication and Hierarchy of Effects," in P. Clarke, ed. *New Models for Mass Communications Research.* Sage Annual Reviews of Communications Research, Vol. II Beverly Hills, Calif.: Sage Publications, 1973.

Reibstein, David J. "The Prediction of Individual Probabilities of Brand Choice." *Journal of Consumer Research* 5 (December 1978); 163–68.

Riker, William H. *The Theory of Political Coalitions.* New Haven, Conn.: Yale University Press, 1962.

_____, and Peter C. Ordeshook. "A Theory of the Calculus of Voting." *American Political Science Review* 62 (March 1968); 25–42.

_____, and Peter C. Ordeshook. *An Introduction to Positive Political Theory.* Englewood Cliffs, N.J.: Prentice-Hall, 1973.

Riordon, William L. *Plunkitt of Tammany Hall,* New York: Dutton, 1963 (original pub. 1905).

Robertson, Thomas S. *Innovative Behavior and Communication.* New York: Holt, Rinehart and Winston, 1971.

_____, and James H. Myers. "Personality Correlates of Opinion Leadership and Innovative Buying Behavior." *Journal of Marketing Research* 6 (May 1969); 164–68.

Rogers, Everett. *Diffusion of Innovations.* Glencoe, Ill.: The Free Press, 1965 and 1971.

_____, and F. Floyd Shoemaker. *Communication in Innovations.* New York: The Free Press, 1971.

Rokeach, Milton. *Beliefs, Attitudes and Values.* San Francisco: Jossey-Bass, 1968.

Roll, Charles W., Jr., and Albert H. Cantril. *Polls, Their Use and Misuse in Politics.* 2nd ed. New York: Basic Books, 1980.

Romney, A.K., R. Shepard, and S.B. Nerlove. *Multidimensional Scaling, Vol. II/Applications*. New York: Seminar Press, 1972.

Rose, Richard. *Influencing Voters*. London: Faber and Faber, 1967.

Rosenberg, M. *The Logic of Survey Analysis*. New York: Basic Books, 1968.

Rossi, P.H. "Trends in Voting Behavior Research: 1933–1963," in E.C. Dreyer and W.A. Rosenbaum, eds. *Political Opinion and Electoral Behavior*. Belmont, Calif.: Wadsworth, 1966, pp. 67–78.

Rothberg, Robert R. "Strategic Considerations in the Design and Use of New Product Screening Models." Paper presented at the AMA Theory Conference, Phoenix, Arizona, February 1980.

───, ed. *Corporate Strategy and Product Innovation*. New York: The Free Press, 1976 and 1981.

Rothschild, Michael L. "Political Advertising: A Neglected Policy Issue in Marketing." *Journal of Marketing Research* 15 (February 1978); 58–71.

───. "On the Use of Multiple Methods and Multiple Situations in Political Communications Research," in Steven H. Chaffee, ed. *Political Communications: Issues and Strategies for Research*. Sage Annual Reviews of Communications Research, Vol. IV. Beverly Hills, Calif.: Sage Publications, 1975.

Ryan, Michael J., and Edward H. Bonfield. "The Fishbein Extended Model and Consumer Behavior." *Journal of Consumer Research* 2 (September 1975); 118–36.

Ryans, Adrian B. "Estimating Customer Preferences for a New Durable Brand in an Established Product Class." *Journal of Marketing Research* (November 1974); 431–43.

Sabato, L.J. *The Rise of Political Consultants*. New York: Basic Books, 1981.

Sartori, G. *Parties and Party Structures*. Cambridge, Mass.: Cambridge University Press, 1976.

Scammon, Richard M., and Ben J. Wattenberg. *The Real Majority*. New York: Coward, McCann and Geoghegan, 1970.

Schiffman, Susan S. *Introduction to Multidimensional Scaling Theory, Methods and Applications*. New York: Academic Press, 1981.

Schram, Martin. *Running for President: The Carter Campaign*, New York: Pocket Books, 1976; Stein and Day, 1976.

Schumpeter, Joseph A. *Capitalism, Socialism and Democracy*. New York: Harper and Brothers, 1950.

Sears, David O. "Political Behavior," in G. Lindzey and E. Aronson, eds. *Handbook of Social Psychology, Vol. 5*. 2nd ed. Reading, Mass.: Addison-Wesley, 1969, pp. 315–458.

Shadegg, Stephen. *The New How to Win an Election*. New York: Taplinger, 1972.

───, *How to Win an Election: The Art of Political Victory*. New York: Taplinger, 1964.

Shepard, Roger N. "Representation of Structure in Similarity Data: Problems and Prospects." *Psychometrika* 39 (December 1974); 373–421.

───. "Circularity in Judgments of Relative Pitch." *Journal of the Acoustical Society of America* 36 (December 1964); 2346–53.

───. "The Analysis of Proximities: Multidimensional Scaling With an Unknown Distance Function, Part One." *Psychometrika* 27 (June 1962); 125–139 (a).

———, "The Analysis of Proximities: Multidimensional Scaling With an Unknown Distance Function, Part Two." *Psychometrika* (September 1962); 219–246 (b).

———, A.K. Romney, and S.B. Nerlove. *Multidimensional Scaling, Vol. I/Theory.* New York: Seminar Press, 1972.

Shepsle, Kenneth A. "The Strategy of Ambiguity: Uncertainty and Electoral Competition." *American Political Science Review* 66 (June 1972): 555–65.

Sherif, Carolyn, Muzafer Sherif, and Roger E. Nebergall. *Attitude and Attitude Change: The Social Judgement-Involvement Approach.* Philadelphia: Saunders, 1965.

Sherif, Muzafer, and C.I. Hovland. *Social Judgement: Assimilation and Contrast Effects in Communication and Attitude Change.* New Haven, Conn.: Yale University Press, 1961.

Shocker, Allan, ed. *Analytic Approaches to Product and Marketing Planning,* Report No. 79–104. Cambridge, Mass.: Marketing Science Institute, April 1979.

———, Dennis Gensch, and Leonard S. Simon. "Toward the Improvement of New Product Search and Screening," in P.R. McDonald, ed. *1969 Fall Conference Proceedings of the American Marketing Association,* Chicago, 1969, pp. 168–75.

———, and V. Srinivasan. "Multiattribute Approaches for Product Concept Evaluation and Generation: A Critical Review." *Journal of Marketing Research* 16 (May 1979); 159–80.

———, and V. Srinivasan. "A Consumer-Based Methodology for the Identification of New Product Ideas." *Management Science* 20 (February 1974); 921–37.

Silk, Alvin J. "Preference and Perception Measures in New Product Development: An Exposition and Review," *Industrial Management Review* 7 (fall 1969); 21–37.

———, and Glen L. Urban. "Pre-Test-Market Evaluation of New Packaged Goods: A Model and Measurement Methodology." *Journal of Marketing Research* 15 (May 1978); 171–91.

Smithies, Arthur. "Optimum Location in Spatial Competition." *Journal of Political Economy* 49 (June 1941); 423–29.

Snider, J.G., and C.E. Osgood. *Semantic Differential Technique.* Chicago: Aldine, 1969.

Spence, Ian. "A Monte Carlo Evaluation of Three Nonmetric Multidimensional Scaling Algorithms." *Psychometrika* 37 (December 1972); 461–86.

———, and John C. Ogilvie. "A Table of Expected Stress Values for Random Rankings in Nonmetric Multidimensional Scaling." *Multivariate Behavioral Research* 8 (October 1973); 511–17.

Sperling, G., Jr. "Wallace Inroads Grow." *The Christian Science Monitor,* July 12, 1968, p. 1.

Spradley, J.P., and D.W. McCurdy. *Anthropology—The Cultural Perspective.* New York: Wiley, 1975.

Stefflre, Volney J. Personal communication, 1982.

———, "New Products: Organizational and Technical Problems and Opportunities," in A. Shocker, ed. *Analytic Approaches to Product and Marketing Planning.* Cambridge, Mass.: Marketing Science Institute, 1979 (a).

———, "Multidimensional Scaling as a Model for Human Information Processing." *Proceedings of the 1978 Marketing Educators Meeting*. Chicago, Ill.: AMA, 1979 (b).

———. "Some Applications of Multidimensional Scaling to Social Science Problems," in A.K. Romney, R.N. Shepard, and S.B. Nerlove, eds. *Multidimensional Scaling: Theory and Applications in the Behavioral Sciences*, Vol. 2. New York: Seminar Press, 1972, pp. 211–48.

———. *New Products and New Enterprises: A Report of an Experiment in Applied Social Science*. University of California, Irvine, March 1971.

———. "Market Structure Studies: New Products for Old Markets and New Markets (Foreign) for Old Products," in F.M. Bass, C.N. King, and E.A. Pessemier, eds. *Application of the Sciences in Marketing*. New York: Wiley, 1968, pp. 251–68.

———. "Simulation of People's Behavior Toward New Objects and Events." *The American Behavioral Scientist* 8 (May 1965); 12–15.

———. "Similarity, Substitutability and the Prediction of Choice: I, The Single Choice Situation." Unpublished manuscript, Harvard University, 1961.

———, P. Reich, and M. McClaran. "Some Eliciting and Computational Procedures for Descriptive Semantics," in P. Kay, ed. *Explorations in Mathematical Anthropology*. Cambridge, Mass.: MIT Press, 1971, pp. 79–116.

———, Victor C. Vales, and Linda Morley. "Language and Cognition in Yucatan: A Cross-Cultural Replication." *Journal of Personality and Social Psychology* 4 (July 1966); 112–15.

Steinberg, Arnold. *Political Campaign Management, A Systems Approach*. Lexington, Mass.: Heath and Company, 1976 (a).

———. *The Political Campaign Handbook*. Lexington, Mass.: Heath and Company, 1976 (b).

Stenson, H. and Knoll, R. "Goodness of Fit for Random Rankings in Kruskal's Nonmetric Scaling Procedure." *Psychological Bulletin* 71 (February 1969); 122–26.

Stokes, Donald E. "Spatial Models of Party Competition." *American Political Science Review* 57 (June 1963); 368–77.

Tagiuri, Renato. "Person Perception," in Gardner Lindzey and Elliot Aronson, eds. *The Handbook of Social Psychology*, Vol. 3. 2nd Ed. Reading, Mass.: Addison-Wesley, 1969, pp. 395–449.

———, and Luigi Petrollo, eds. *Person Perception and Interpersonal Behavior*. Stanford, Calif.: Stanford University Press, 1958.

Thompson, Hunter S. *Fear and Loathing on the Campaign Trail 1972*. San Francisco: Straight Arrow, 1973.

Thurstone, L.L. "The Prediction of Choice." *Psychometrika* 10 (December 1945); 237–53. Reprinted in Thurstone, L.L., *The Measurement of Values*. Chicago: University of Chicago Press, 1959, Chapter 13.

———. "An Experiment in the Prediction of Choice." *Proceedings of the Fourth Research Conference*, 1952, American Meat Institute, pp. 58–66. Reprinted in Thurstone, L.L., *The Measurement of Values*. Chicago: University of Chicago Press, 1959, Chapter 14.

———, "A Law of Comparative Judgement." *Psychological Review* 34 (June 1927); pp. 273–86.

Torgerson, W. *Theory and Methods of Scaling*. New York: Wiley, 1958.
Tulving, E., and W. Donaldson, eds. *The Organization of Memory*. New York: Academic Press, 1972.
Tversky, Amos. "Features of Similarity." *Psychological Review* 84 (July 1977); 327–52.
―――. "Elimination by Aspects: A Theory of Choice," *Psychological Review* 79 (July 1972); 281–99.
―――, and D. Kahnemann. "The Framing of Decisions and Psychology of Choice." *Science* 211 (January 1981); 453–58.
―――, and Shmuel Sattath. "Preference Trees." *Psychological Review* 86 (November 1979); 542–73.
Tyler, Stephen A., ed. *Cognitive Anthropology*. New York: Holt, Rinehart and Winston, 1969.
Urban, Glen L. "PERCEPTOR: A Model for Product Positioning." *Management Science* 21 (April 1975); 858–71.
―――. "SPRINTER Mod. III: A Model for the Analysis of New Frequently Purchased Consumer Products." *Operations Research* 18 (September-October 1970); 805–53.
―――, and John R. Hauser. *Design and Marketing of New Products*. Englewood Cliffs, N.J.: Prentice-Hall, 1980.
Viguerie, Richard A. "Direct Mail: Campaigning's Sleeping Giant," in Ray E. Hiebert, Robert F. Jones, John Lorenz, and Ernest A. Lotito. *The Political Image Merchants: Strategies for the Seventies*. Washington, D.C.: Acropolis Books, 1975.
von Hippel, Eric. "Successful Industrial Products From Consumer Ideas." *Journal of Marketing* 42 (January 1978); 39–49.
The Wall Street Journal. "They Also Run: Splinter Parties, All With a Cause, Could Sway National Voting Results." August 27, 1964, p. 24.
Walters, Dan. "Political Dirty Tricks." *California Journal* 12 (May 1981); 160–62.
Wayne, Stephen J. *The Road to the White House*. New York: St. Martin's Press, 1980.
Weisberg, W.F., and H.F. Rusk. "Dimensions of Candidate Evaluation." *American Political Science Review* 64 (December 1970); 1167–185.
Weiss, Walter. "Effects of the Mass Media of Communication," in G. Lindzey and E. Aronson, eds. *The Handbook of Social Psychology*, Vol. 5. 2nd ed. Reading, Mass.: Addison-Wesley, 1969.
White, Theodore H. *The Making of the President, 1960*. New York: Atheneum, 1961 (also 1964, 1968, 1972).
Wilkie, William L., and Edgar A. Pessemier. "Issues in Marketing's Use of Multi-Attribute Attitude Models." *Journal of Marketing Research* 10 (November 1973); 428–41.
Wind, Yoram. "A New Procedure for Concept Evaluation." *Journal of Marketing* 37 (October 1973); 2–11.
Witcover, Jules. *Marathon, The Pursuit of the Presidency 1972–1976*. New York: New American Library, 1977.
Wittgenstein, L. *Philosophical Investigations*. 3rd ed. Translated by G.E.M. Anscombe. New York: Macmillan, 1966.

Wyer, Jr., Robert, and Donald Carlston. *Social Cognition, Inference and Attribution.* New York: Halsted, 1979.

Young, F.W., and W. Torgerson. "A FORTRAN IV Program for Shepard-Kruskal Multidimensional Scaling Analysis." *Behavioral Science* 12 (November 1967); 498.

Zufryden, Fred S. "ZIPMAP—A Zero-One Integer Programming Model for Market Segmentation and Product Positioning." Working paper, Los Angeles: Graduate School of Business Administration, University of Southern California, 1976.

INDEX

Aaker, D. A., 82
Abelson, R. P., 90, 117, 259
academic perspective, 21, 29
  behavioralism, 31-36
  communications approach, 31, 36-39
  positive approach, 31, 40-48
ad hoc guidelines, 96
aggregate preference structure, 44-45
  blocs of voters, 45
  consistent meaning, 45
  continuous dimensions, 45
Agranoff, R., 49
Ahtola, O., 63
Ajzen, 57, 63
Albers, S., 80
Alderson, W., 4
Alexander, E. R., 73, 82
American Marketing Association, 4
Amstutz, A. E., 61
Arrow, K. J., 48
Asher, H., 140

Baker, N., 62
Barban, A. M., 23, 103
Barral, P., 191
Bauer, R. A., 37
Baus, H. M., 49
Beals, R., 104
behavioralism
  social–psychological approach, 34-36
  sociological approach, 31-34
Bell, C. G., 52, 164
Benham, T. W., 37
Beniger, J. R., 104
Bennett, W. L., 35
Benson, P. H., 65
Berelson, B. R., 32, 33, 36, 37, 93, 148
Berlin, B., 99
Black, M., 89, 99, 121
Blackwell, R. D., 63

Blumenthal, S., 19, 51
Blumler, J. G., 16, 37, 39
Bock, R. D., 222, 226-27
Bonfield, E. H., 63, 243
Booz, Allen and Hamilton, Inc., 58, 59, 60
de Borda, J., 111
Bordley, R. F., 240
Brams, S. J., 40, 54
Brockhoff, K., 80
Brody, R. A., 35
Brown, M. P., 18, 64, 66, 82, 102
Brown, R., 54
Brown, S. R., 35
Bruner, J. S., 54, 91, 99, 155
Buchanan, J. M., 41
Budge, I., 35, 47, 210
Bureau of Applied Social Research, 32, 35

campaign
  French legislative, 167-69, 175-86, 189-210, 232-35, 252-54, 261-63
  gubernatorial, 143-64, 232, 251-52, 273, 277
  management, 11-14
  organization, 16-17
  presidential, 17, 32, 39, 110, 112-39, 157, 230-31, 246-51, 259-67, 272
campaign analysis
  academic approach, 21, 53
  pragmatic approach, 21, 30-31
campaign strategies, 14-18
  evaluating, 88, 92-93
campaigning mix, 14
Campbell, A., 31, 34, 43, 44, 99, 155
Campbell, D. T., 32
candidate
  compatibility, 204-05
  14-15

candidates
  hypothetical, 91, 99, 118, 126, 153, 157, 193-95, 201-02, 219-20, 232-35, 274
  third party, 112-14
Capon, N., 5
Carlston, D., 54, 91
Carman, J. M., 5
Carmone, F., 82, 83, 91, 97, 103
Carroll, J. D., 80, 91, 242, 259
Cassirer, E., 167, 241, 258
Chaffee, S. H., 33, 34, 35, 37
Chamberlin, E. H., 6
Chang, J. J., 80, 91, 242, 259
Charnes, A., 61
civil rights movement, 52
Clement, D., 67
communication channels, 10-11
communications
  approach, 31, 36-39
  hypodermic model of, 37
  medium of, 50-53
  mix, 10, 15-16
  program, 15-16
competition
  identifying, 86-87, 89-90
  patterns of, 88, 91-92, 101-02, 127-31, 178, 197-98, 272, 274
  similarity and, 131-33, 241-54
  spatial models of party, 41-48
competitive advantage, 12
compositional approach, 75-76
Conference Board, 62
constant ratio rule, 223-24
consumer
  behavior, 63-65
  response, 61
continuous dimensions, 45
Converse, P. E., 24, 41, 44, 45, 90, 104, 110, 116, 188, 259
Coombs, C. H., 100, 240, 242
Coombs, C. I., 240
Crewe, I., 210
cross-validation, 96-97
Crossley, A., 230
Crossley, H., 230
Crouse, T., 46, 49

Currim, I. S., 227
Cutright, P., 37

Davis, D., 37
Davis, O. A., 42
Dawes, R. I., 240
Day, G. S., 63, 82
Day, R. L., 65
Debreu, G., 238
decompositional approach, 75-76
Deese, J., 54
De Gaulle, C., 57
Degerman, R. L., 45, 97, 140
Dennis, J., 54
differential
  advantage, 6, 7
  competitiveness, 248
  draw, 248, 250
  similarity, 248-50
dimensionality, 95-96
Donaldson, W., 99
Doehlert, D. H., 242
Donnelly, J. H., Jr., 63
Doob, L. W., 54
Downs, A., 7, 24, 41, 42, 46, 93, 109, 242
draw
  patterns of, 246-50
  ratio, 248
Dunn, S. W., 23, 24, 103

Easton, D., 54
Edelman, M., 44, 54
Ehrmann, H. W., 187
Ekman, G., 140
Eldersveld, S. J., 37, 39
electioneering
  medium of communications, 50-53
  professionalism, 49-53
electoral politics
  channels of communication, 6, 10-11
  citizen's role, 6, 8-9
  competitive situation, 6-8
Ellul, J., 54
Engel, J. F., 63, 64
Erikson, R. S., 44

Farquarson, R., 111
Farlie, D., 210

Faust, G., 267
Fauvet, J., 167
Feldman, S., 63
Field, M. D., 164
Fiorina, M. P., 40, 42, 47, 55
Fishbein, M., 54, 63
Frake, C. O., 121
Frank, R. E., 82
Freeland, J., 62
french politics
　electoral system, 169-71
　legislative constituency, 189-210, 232-35, 273
　legislative elections, 175-86, 245-46, 252-55, 261-62, 273
　political parties, 171-74
　strategic positioning, 167-69, 175-86, 203-10
frequency, 16
Freyssinet, J., 45, 46, 210, 211
Fried, M. H., 258
full information, 44
fund raising, 17

Gallup, G., 44
Gensch, D. H., 83, 223
gimmicks, 3
Goffman, E., 54
Goldwin, R. A., 140
Goodenough, W. H., 99
Gosnell, H. F., 37
Graber, D. A., 37
Grayson, C. J., Jr., 62-63
Green, P., 63, 73, 75, 82, 83, 91, 97, 98, 103, 157, 238, 243, 259
Greenfield, J., 49, 103
gubernatorial campaign, 143-64, 231-32, 251-52, 273, 277
Guildford, J. P., 219
Guttman, L., 140

Hall, E. T., 258
Halle, M., 99
Harding, J., 67
Hare, T., 111
Harman, H. H., 262
Harvey, J. H., 54
Hauser, J. R., 18, 61, 64, 73, 75, 81, 83
Hershey, M. R., 49

heuristics, 11
Hiebert, R. E., 146
Hinich, M. J., 42, 45
Holbrook, M. B., 76, 102
homogeneity, 258-62
Hotelling, H., 41, 46
Hovland, C. I., 37, 54, 140
Howard, J. A., 63, 104
Huber, J., 102
Hyman, H. H., 54
hypothetical candidates, 9J, 99, 118, 126-27, 153, 157, 193-95, 201-02, 220, 232-35, 274

Ickes, W. F., 54
ideal point model, 76
index of political predisposition, 32
indifference, 42
individual preferences
　full information, 44
　instrumentality, 43
　modeling, 73-81
　public policy, 43-44
　rank-order, 43-44
Institute for Social Research, 34-35, 36
instrumentality, 43
issue-positions, 144
　French, 183-96, 204-10
　gubernatorial, 152-55, 158-64
Ivancevich, J. M., 63

Janis, I. L., 54
Jakobson, R., 99
Jay, A., 82
Jensen, D., 83
Jewell, M. E., 139
Johnson, H., 145
Johnson, S., 119
Johnson, S. C., 61, 119
Jones, B. D., 103
Jones, C., 61
Jones, L. E., 46
Jones, L. V., 222, 226-27
judged similarity
　interview, 117-18, 120-21, 126, 134-35, 176-77
　measure, 100-01, 272
　sample, 117-18, 259-61

technique, 150-51
verbatims, 128-30

Kahnemann, D., 140
Katz, D., 37
Katz, E., 37
Katz, R., 100
Kay, P., 99
Kelley, H. H., 54
Kelley, S. Jr., 24, 103
Kessel, J., 41, 48
Key, V. O., Jr., 35-36, 109, 114
Kidd, R. F., 54
King, W. R., 61
Kingdon, J. W., 49
Kish, L., 118
Klahr, D., 96, 242
Klapper, J. T., 33, 35, 37
Kline, F. G., 37
Knoll, R., 96, 140
Kollat, D. T., 63
Koppelman, F. S., 75, 76
Kotler, P., 4-5, 23, 24, 103
Kover, A. J., 64
Kramer, G., 41
Krantz, D. H., 104
Kraus, S., 37
Kruskal, J. B., 83, 94, 96, 140
Kuehn, A. A., 65

Ladd, E. C., Jr., 140
Lakeman, E., 111
Lambert, J. D., 111
Lamb, K. A., 24, 49
Lancaster, K., 54
Lancelot, A., 191
Lancelot, M., 191
Lang, G., 37
Lang, K., 37
Lanz, D., 66
Lazarsfeld, P. F., 31-33, 36-37, 39, 93, 148
Leary, M. E., 52, 146
Leduc, L., 267
LeGall, G., 187, 211
Lehmann, D. R., 81
Lengle, J. I., 140

Lerner, M., 29, 49
Leuthold, D. A., 49, 103
Levelt, W. J. M., 140
Levin, M. B., 24
Levy, S. J., 4
limited effects model, 33
Lincoln, A., 1
Little, J., 62
Luce, R. D., 54, 223-25, 227, 229, 231, 235, 238, 240, 243
Lucey, J. A., 54, 65
Luck, D., 5
Luttbeg, N. R., 44

McCarthy, E. J., 4
McClure, R. D., 16, 37, 38, 44
McCombs, M. E., 37
McCurdy, D. W., 258
McDonald, M. B., Jr., 61
McGinniss, J., 44
McQuail, D., 16, 37, 39
Machiavelli, N., 1, 17
Machiavellianism, 2, 3
management science, 61-63
mapping
  patterns of competition, 88, 91-92
  procedures, 94-99
  voters' perception, 86-87, 90-91
Marcus, G. E., 35
marketing
  campaign strategy and, 1-5
  definition of, 3-5
  electoral politics and, 5-11
  mix, 4, 14
  political, 52-53
marketing approach
  to political campaigning, 11-20
Marshall, T., 140
mass media, 15, 37-39, 50-53
Massy, W. F., 82
Mauser, G., 5, 41, 44, 45-46, 48, 65, 90, 100, 104, 118, 119, 134, 139, 140, 221, 240, 242, 255, 267
Mazmanian, D. A., 139
mean absolute difference, 229-35
media scheduling, 10
medium of communications, 50-53
Messick, S. J., 90, 100, 117, 188, 259

Metzger, D., 89, 99, 121
Miller, A. H., 114
Miller, G. A., 99, 155
Miller, W. E., 114
Minsky, M., 99
Monte Carlo simulation, 96
Montgomery, D. B., 61, 63, 83
movements
  civil rights, 52
  protest and reform, 51-52
multidimensional scaling
  determining dimensionality, 95-96
  interpreting configuration, 97-99
  model, 198-202
  procedures, 94-95
  proximity measures, 100-02
  solution evaluation, 96-97
  techniques, 94, 119-27, 150-52, 154-58
Myers, J. G., 83
Myers, J. H., 63, 98, 103, 157, 242

Nanson, E. J., 111
Napolitan, J., 16, 24, 49, 103, 217
Nebergall, R. E., 54, 63
new products
  consumer behavior and, 63-65
  definition of, 58-59
  development, 57-59
  planning, 59-61
  strategic positioning, 21, 65-82
Nie, N. H., 35, 36, 38, 43, 44, 46, 109, 155, 267
Nimmo, D., 103
normative models, 61-63
Nygren, T. E., 46

O'Keefe, G. J., 39
Ogilvie, J. C., 96, 140
Olson, D. M., 139
Ordeshook, P. E., 7, 24, 40, 42, 44, 47, 48, 97, 242
Osgood, C. E., 54, 75, 90, 100, 117, 188, 259

Page, B. I., 24, 35, 41, 42-43, 47, 48, 54
party competition
  spatial models of, 41-48
party machine, 50

Patterson, T. E., 16, 37, 38, 44, 99
perception
  aggregate, 259-67, 272
  data, 176-77
  measures, 100-01
  political, 118-27, 150-52
  sample, 117-18
personal contact, 50
Pessemier, E. A., 63, 75, 80, 223, 227, 240, 243
Petrocik, J. R., 267
Petrullo, L., 54
Plott, C. R., 48
political campaigning
  academic perspective, 31-48
  framework for strategy, 11-18
  pragmatic framework, 48-53
  strategic positioning, 18-20, 21
political marketing, 52-53
Pompidou, G., 267
Pool, I., 49
Popkin, S., 49
positive approach, 31, 40-48
pragmatic
  approach, 21, 29-31, 147-48
  framework, 48-54
preference
  aggregate, 223-27, 259-67
  correlation, 196-97, 205-10, 272
  data, 176-77
  measures, 100-02
  political, 152-58
  ranking, 218-22, 251-53
  sample, 117-18
presidential campaigns, 16-17, 32, 39, 110, 112-39, 157, 230-31, 246-51, 259-67, 273
professional organizer, 50-51
protest movements, 51-52
public policy, 43-44
purist approach, 148-49

Rabinowitz, G. A., 96, 104
Rados, D. L., 5
Rae, D. W., 111
Raiffa, H., 54
rank-order preferences, 43-44
Ranney, A., 140

Rao, V. R., 73, 83, 100, 240, 259
Ray, M. L., 23, 37, 39
reach, 16
Recker, W. W., 223
reform movements, 51-52
Reibstein, D. J., 238
Riglet, M., 187, 211
Riker, W. H., 7, 21, 40, 41, 42, 44, 48, 97, 242
Riordan, W. L., 29, 50
Robertson, T. S., 63
Rogers, E., 54, 63
Rogers, W., 217
Rokeach, M., 54, 63
Romney, A. K., 104
Rose, R., 37
Rosenberg, M., 54, 132
Ross, W. B., 49
Rossi, P. H., 33
Rothberg, R. R., 61, 62, 72, 242
Rothschild, M. L., 23, 37, 38, 39
Rusk, H. F., 24, 41, 45, 46, 48, 97, 104
Ryan, A. B., 63
Ryan, M. J., 243

Sapir, E., 257
Sartori, G., 140
Sattath, S., 65, 238
scaling
   multidimensional, 94-102, 118-28, 151-52, 154-58
Scammon, R. M., 93, 110
Schiffman, S. S., 104
Schram, M., 49
Schumpeter, J. A., 6
Schlesinger, A., 109
Sears, D. O., 33, 35
Sears, J., 51
Sebeok, T. A., 54
Shadegg, S., 24, 49, 51, 103, 143
Shafer, B. E., 140
share of choice
   stochastic approach, 223-27
   Thurstone's method, 222-23, 226-27
share-of-vote
   data collection methods, 220-21
   election studies, 227-39
   estimation procedure, 217-20

predictive rule, 221-22
stochastic choice models, 223-27
Shepard, R. N., 83, 104, 140
Shepsle, K. A., 48
Sherif, C., 37, 54, 63
Sherif, M., 54, 63, 140
Sheth, J. N., 63, 104
Shocker, A. D., 18, 61, 62, 64, 72, 73-74, 81, 83, 98
Shweder, R. A., 54, 65
Shoemaker, 54, 63
Silk, A. J., 63, 64, 73, 83, 102, 104, 223, 227, 240
similarity
   competition and, 131-33, 241-54
   judged, 100-01, 117-18, 134, 176-77, 259-61
Simon, L. S., 83
Smith, P. A., 24, 49
Smithies, A., 41
Snider, J. G., 90, 188, 259
social-psychological approach, 34-36
sociological approach, 31-34
Southern Christian Leadership Conference, 52
spatial models, 21, 31, 41-43, 54, 57-58, 65-66
   aggregate preference structure, 44-45
   common frame of reference, 46
   critique, 47-48, 53-54
   image and ideology, 195-203
   individual preferences, 43-44
   political perceptions, 150-52
   political preferences, 150-58
   stability of political preferences, 46
Spence, I., 96, 140
Sperling, G., Jr., 116
Spradley, J. P., 258
Srinavasan, V., 73, 74, 81, 83, 98, 238, 243
Stanley, J. C., 32
Stefflre, V. J., 18-20, 21, 46, 58, 60-61, 64-65, 66-82, 85, 90-91, 99, 102, 104, 118, 139, 140, 155, 168, 187, 217, 218, 220, 221, 222, 226, 227, 238, 240, 241-44, 254, 255, 259, 271-72, 273, 274

Stefflre's analytical procedure, 21, 66-85, 270-72
Steinberg, A., 17, 24, 103
Stenson, H., 96, 140
stochastic choice models
  approach, 223-24
  homogeneity of preferences, 224
  independence of irrelevant alternatives, 225-26
Stokes, D. E., 42, 43, 45, 46, 47
strategic positioning, 21ff
  approach, 65-82
  evaluation, 275-79
  framework for, 86-103
  french legislative elections, 167-69, 175-86, 245-46, 252-54, 261-63, 273
  french legislative constituency, 189-210, 232-35, 273
  gubernatorial campaign, 143-64, 231-32, 251-52, 273, 277
  presidential campaign, 104-39, 230-31, 247-51, 259-67, 272-73
  procedure for, 18-20, 276-77
  review, 269-75
strategy
  determination, 12
  implementation, 14-18
stress-dimensionality, 96-97
Suci, G. J., 90, 100, 117, 259
Sullivan, J. L., 35
Sun Yat-sen, 1
swing vote, 148-49

Tabb, D., 35
Tagiuri, R., 54, 91
Tannenbaum, P. H., 90, 100, 117, 259
Tauber, E., 83
temporal stability, 264-67
third party candidates, 112-14
Thompson, H. T., 49
Thurstone, L. L., 220, 222-23, 227, 240, 259
Tichenor, P. J., 37

Torgerson, W., 83, 150, 240
Tukey, J., 243
Tull, D. S., 82
Tullock, G., 41
Tulving, E., 99
Tversky, A., 140, 225, 238, 240
Tyler, S. A., 89, 121, 155

Urban, G. L., 18, 61, 63, 64, 73, 81, 83, 104, 223, 227, 240
uses and gratification approach, 37

vector model, 76
Verba, 267
Viguerie, R. A., 17, 52
von Hippel, E., 62
von Humboldt, W., 257
vote-splitting, 109-12
  predicting patterns of, 133-39
voters' perceptions, 86-87, 90-91
voting
  drive, 17-18
  patterns, 32-33

Walters, D., 139
Wattenberg, B. J., 93, 110
Wayne, S. J., 140
Weisberg, W. F., 24, 41, 45, 46, 48, 97, 104
Weiss, W., 37
White, T. H., 46, 49
Whorf, B. L., 241
Wilkie, W. L., 63, 243
Williams, G., 121
Wind, Y., 18, 63, 259
Winter, F., 240
Wolff, R. W., 240
Wyer, R., Jr., 54, 91

Young, F. W., 150

Zufryden, F. S., 80

ABOUT THE AUTHOR

GARY A. MAUSER is Associate Professor of Business Administration at Simon Fraser University in Burnaby, British Columbia, Canada. He consults regularly for public and private firms as well as for political candidates. During 1979 and 1980 he was Visiting Professor, *Faculté des sciences de l'administration, Université Laval* in Quebec City, Quebec. He is active in several professional associations, including the American Marketing Association, the Association for Consumer Research, the Administrative Sciences Association of Canada, and has twice been elected President of the Canadian Association for Applied Social Research.

Dr. Mauser has published widely in marketing and political science. His articles and reviews have appeared in the *Journal of Marketing, The Journal of Marketing Research, The Journal of the Marketing Research Society, Public Choice, Revue Française du Marketing, Journal of Business Administration, the Canadian Marketer*, and the *Journal of the Academy of Marketing Science*.

Dr. Mauser received his Ph.D. from the University of California at Irvine, and his B.A. from the University of California at Berkeley. He has previously taught at the Université des Sciences Sociales de Grenoble (France) and Loyola University in New Orleans, Louisiana.